EXCELLENCIES
of CHRIST:

An Exploration into the Endless Fascination of the God-Man

by Allen Hood
Forerunner School of Ministry

Julia Palermo

Forerunner BOOKS Ⓕ
Kansas City, Missouri

Excellencies of Christ
By Allen Hood
Forerunner School of Ministry
International House of Prayer

Published by Forerunner Books
International House of Prayer
3535 East Red Bridge Road
Kansas City, Missouri 64137
(816) 763-0200 Ext. 675
forerunnerbooks@ihop.org
www.IHOP.org

Unless otherwise noted, all Scripture quotations are from the New King James Version of the Bible. Copyright © 1988 by Broadman and Holman Publishers, Nashville, Tennessee. Used by permission.

Scripture quotations marked KJV are from the King James Version of the Bible.

Scripture quotations marked NIV are from the Holy Bible, New International Version. Copyright © 1973, 1978, 1984, International Bible Society. Used by permission.

Cover design by Tom Morse-Brown
Interior design by Dale Jimmo

Printed in the United States of America

TABLE OF CONTENTS

Introduction

I. BEHOLDING THE GLORY OF CHRIST IS THE FULFILLMENT ALL GODLY DESIRES

Father, I desire that they also whom You gave Me may be with Me where I am, that they may behold My glory which You have given Me; for You loved Me before the foundation of the world. O righteous Father! The world has not known You, but I have known You; and these have known that You sent Me. And I have declared to them Your name, and will declare it, that the love with which You loved Me may be in them, and I in them. (John 17:24–26)

A. I find my heart longing today, lonely, hungry for something authentic. Something is awakening in the depths, stirred in this season by an unknown hand, an unseen Helper. My heart can barely stand the thought of another unique teaching or keen insight from another anointed vessel. I am aching only for Jesus, wanting Him and Him alone, undone by the piercing depths of His heart, His life, and His love.

B. We are creatures of desire and longing. At this very moment, you have unfulfilled yearnings that you want to fulfill. You are willing to go to great lengths and pay great prices for some of your desires. This is because we are creatures made in the image of a God of desire. He needs nothing, but He intensely yearns for certain things. In fact, history is the story of God's desires unfolding in the affairs of men and women. The close of natural human history is a divine crescendo of both godly and ungodly desires.

C. If we are to make sense of our lives and the world around us, we must first come to grips with God's desires. Psalm 115:3 declares that "our God is in heaven; He does whatever He pleases." The desires of God are shaping all of human history and will prevail over every competing desire. Evil at the end of the age will not force God's hand. Humanity's failed solutions to our own ecological, financial, and societal problems will not force the arm of the Lord. One thing and one thing alone is moving this world and its systems towards the climax of history. It's the longing in God the Father to give His Son a Bride, and the request of the Son that she would be His and His alone.

D. John 17 takes place just prior to His rejection, scourging, and crucifixion. After Jesus passed the bread and the cup and shared encouraging words with His disciples, He offered up His high priestly prayer. In v. 1–5, He connected with the desires of His Father. He had done all that His Father requested. Then, in v. 6–19, He prayed for His disciples. He proclaimed that their faith is authentic and that He had kept them safe. He ended His prayer for the disciples by interceding for their protection from the evil one and for their sanctification in truth.

E. Finally, Jesus envisioned the unfolding of the future. He was viewing all those who would come to believe in Him through the apostles' witness. He was looking at you. He was looking at me. Suddenly, the Son entered into a new place of prayer. In verse 24, an explosion happened in the heart of Jesus. I call this the thunder of Jesus' heart cry. He erupted with the groan of intercession: "Father, I desire…" In this moment of passion, the Son explodes with His last request to His Father. This is the height of yearning love.

F. "Father, if I go to the cross, then this is what I want. I want a companion, Father. I want a remnant from the human race to be with me where I am. I want them to see My glory, and I want them to fall madly in love with Me. Father, this is My sole longing, and this is what I am willing to die for." Can you hear the request of Jesus? The Cross was not drudgery for Him. The Cross was necessary for Him to receive the greatest yearning of His heart—you.

G. These last words in prayer before His betrayal in the Garden of Gethsemane reveal the motivation of His heart in ministry. Jesus told the Father that He had declared the Father's name and would continue to declare it in order that human beings would love Him the way that the Father loves Him. He pointedly asked that the love which His Father has for Him would be in all believers. Jesus is looking for more than servants. The Son of God desires to have companions who voluntarily love Him with their whole hearts, just as the Father loves Him with His whole heart.

H.   Jesus did the unthinkable. He asked the Father to give the redeemed of the human race the highest possible pleasure—to behold the unparalleled splendor of God in Jesus and to feel the same love that the Father has for His Son. God's intentions are not to simply give us the right set of Gospel facts in order for us to pass the test to get into Heaven. He has something far more magnificent. He wants to share the most glorious thing He has—Himself in the person of His Son, in all of His glory and all of His love.

I.   In this brief study I have but one desire: that Jesus' prayer to His Father would be answered in you. I pray that your gaze would be lifted higher than your current struggle to please God by enduring your quiet time. I pray that you would be encountered by God in Christ Jesus and that your eyes would be enlightened unto wholehearted love.

II.   ALL THINGS SUMMED UP IN CHRIST

*Having made known to us the mystery of His will, according to His good pleasure which He purposed in Himself, that in the dispensation of the fullness of the times **He might gather together in one all things in Christ, both which are in heaven and which are on earth**—in Him. (Ephesians 1:9–10, emphasis added)*

A.   Paul tells us that it was God's good pleasure in the dispensation of the fullness of the times to gather together in one all things in Heaven and on Earth in Christ. The Bible opens with the heavenly, supernatural presence of God in harmony with the earthly, natural realm. God walked with Adam in the cool of the day. Communion and cooperation took place between these two realms. The supernatural activity of God pervaded the natural order, and God called it "very good." God's purposes and personality are fully expressed in the joining of the earthly and heavenly realms.

B.   Shortly after creation, humanity's sin caused the withdrawal of the heavenly, supernatural realm from the natural, earthly one. Adam was driven from Eden and cherubim were put on guard over the tree of life. Where is the tree of life now? Revelation 22:2 tells us that it waits in the New Jerusalem. Its leaves will be for the healing of the nations. The heavenly realm has withdrawn until the ultimate day of redemption. On that day, the new heaven and new earth will be brought forth with the New Jerusalem, joining both realms together in perfect harmony. God will make His tabernacle with men, and the throne of God and the Lamb shall be there. What was God's answer to the great schism? Christ!

C.   Christ brought with Him the Kingdom of God. He was the One who reestablished the government of God in the affairs of men. The blueprint of God was restored. God now dwells with man in Christ, and in Christ all things are brought together in Heaven and on Earth.

D.   God's answer to the great divorce of human history between Himself and man is Christ. Through Him all things were created, and through Him all things are redeemed and brought together in love. Jesus is our starting point and He is our culmination. All things are summed up in Him. In ages past, God spoke to the human race through the prophets, but now the Father has spoken to us in His Son. Christ is the beginning and ending point of the human race.

     "I am the Alpha and the Omega, the Beginning and the End, the First and the Last." (Revelation 22:13)

     God, who at various times and in various ways spoke in time past to the fathers by the prophets, has in these last days spoken to us by His Son, whom He has appointed heir of all things, through whom also He made the worlds; who being the brightness of His glory and the express image of His person, and upholding all things by the word of His power, when He had by Himself purged our sins, sat down at the right hand of the Majesty on high, having become so much better than the angels, as He has by inheritance obtained a more excellent name than they. (Hebrews 1:1–4)

III.   THE WISDOM OF STUDYING CHRISTOLOGY

A.   The Church is presently consumed with many things other than Jesus, yet this is about to change. His glory will no longer be concealed, for God is arranging a scenario at the end of the age that will clearly demonstrate the glory of His Son over every opposing passion.

B.   God's strategy is to highlight His Son and to cause us to fall in love with Him at the end of the age. The enemy's strategy is to defame God's Son and remove His uniqueness and splendor so that the Church doesn't walk in the fullness of love, being left open to the lawlessness of this age. Having our hearts gripped with Christ Jesus saves us from the perversion and sin which dominate the present age. Because of this, the enemy assaults the subject matter of Jesus—His pre-existence, divinity, resurrection, salvation through His name alone, second coming, millennial reign, and judgment seat.

C.   Jesus is the crucial subject at the end of the age. We must comprehend from the Scriptures who He is and what He has accomplished. Without the correct knowledge and understanding of Jesus, the pressures at the end of the age will be unbearable. Isaiah 33:6 tells us that, at the end of the age, wisdom and knowledge will be our stability.

Wisdom and knowledge will be the stability of your times, and the strength of salvation; the fear of the LORD is His treasure. (Isaiah 33:6)

IV.   MESSENGERS OF DARKNESS

A.   The Bible also clearly describes an hour coming of unparalleled deception. Messengers of darkness will arise to deceive many. As the end approaches, Lucifer ("light bringer," "morning star") will fight for the right to have human hearts under his sway. 1 John 5:19 tells us that the whole world lies under the sway of the wicked one, and the New Testament makes clear that he is the "ruler of this world" and the "god of this age" (John 12:31, 14:30, 16:11; 2 Corinthians 4:4; Ephesians 6:12).

B.   Satan ("adversary") is a being filled with personal hatred, wickedness, and animosity toward God. He will not relinquish his position and power easily, for the loss of this battle means he will be condemned to the bottomless pit and the lake of fire forever. As a main part of his strategy to resist the coming Kingdom of God, he will produce messengers who will work to deceive the human race concerning the things of God and His Son.

V.   MATTHEW 24:1–5—TAKE HEED THAT NO ONE DECEIVES YOU

Then Jesus went out and departed from the temple, and His disciples came up to show Him the buildings of the temple. And Jesus said to them, "Do you not see all these things? Assuredly, I say to you, not one stone shall be left here upon another, that shall not be thrown down." Now as He sat on the Mount of Olives, the disciples came to Him privately, saying, "Tell us, when will these things be? And what will be the sign of Your coming, and of the end of the age?" **And Jesus answered and said to them: "Take heed that no one deceives you. For many will come in My name, saying, 'I am the Christ,' and will deceive many."'** *(Matthew 24:1-5, emphasis added)*

A.   The week began with Jesus' cleansing of the Temple; healings, signs and wonders; preaching of the Word; and the people's attempt to make Jesus their king. Yet, by Tuesday, Jesus gave His last public sermon to the religious leaders of the day with a seething reproach. The leaders were unable to recognize that their Messiah of Psalm 110 was before them. Finally, Jesus announced that they had missed their hour of visitation and that they would not see Him again until they say, "Blessed is He who comes in the name of the LORD" (Matthew 23:39). The leaders rejected Jesus and plotted to kill Him. Solomon's Temple had lost the Ark of God's might during the Babylonian exile, and now in Herod's Temple the nation of Israel rejected the manifest glory of God in the person of His Son. The dialogue in this passage began out of the disciples' admiration for the Temple, but Jesus was not admiring the buildings. He was thinking of the impending judgment and the consequences of Israel's rejection of the Messiah. He was saddened over the city, which is ordained to be the resting place of His eternal rule, but now had been left desolate.

B.   The mood was sober. Messiah's first coming was typified by Israel's hardness of heart and slowness to believe what the prophets had written. It ended with Israel's rejection and killing of Jesus. What will precede the Messiah's second coming? Jesus' first words set the context. "Take heed that no one deceives you. For many will come in My name, saying, 'I am the Christ,' and will deceive many" (Matthew 24:5). In the context of war, natural disasters, persecution, and lawlessness, false prophets and false messiahs will come forth to deceive many. Deception will typify the next coming. Jesus charged His disciples, "Take heed. Do not take this lightly. Understand the strategy of the evil one. In the midst of great calamity, Satan will raise up messengers of darkness who will distribute lies concerning Me. Because of lawlessness, the people's hearts will be exceptionally cold and receptive to deception. Take heed, for this deception will come with dark messengers doing great signs and wonders to deceive, if possible, even the elect. The magnitude of this wave of deception is unlike anything you have ever seen. Know this; I have warned you. Take heed!"

*And then many will be offended, will betray one another, and will hate one another. **Then many false prophets will rise up and deceive many.** And because lawlessness will abound, the love of many will grow cold. (Matthew 24:10–12, emphasis added)*

Then if anyone says to you, "Look, here is the Christ!" or "There!" do not believe it. For false christs and false prophets will rise and show great signs and wonders to deceive, if possible, even the elect. See, I have told you beforehand. (Matthew 24:23–25)

C.   Three times Jesus emphatically warned the disciples of the coming deception and identified the subject matter of the discussion—the person of Christ. Who is Israel's true Messiah? It must be noted that Jesus gives this discourse on the very mount upon which He will return. Jesus fully understood Zechariah 14:1–5. He fully recognized that His next coming to Jerusalem will be in a time of great desolation when the nations are ravaging Israel (Jerusalem in particular). AD 70 will be a foreshadowing of this event, but the events before Jesus' return will be larger and greater than Jerusalem's destruction by Titus of Rome. All the nations, led by a ruler who will be filled with Satan, will attack and ravage Jerusalem. The very city that rejected her true Messiah offering her peace will accept a false messiah empowered by Satan. This covenant with death set up by the Antichrist will lead to Israel's and Jerusalem's destruction. Yet, the city which rejected Jesus will one day be delivered by Him. First, however, the city must kill her true King before receiving her false one.

D.   All things are leading to this end, the climax of the ages when Jesus returns as all the prophets have foretold in the Scriptures. As it nears, we must heed the words of Jesus. Deception is coming, and we must be watchful in all things.

VI.   THE APOSTOLIC CHARGE—CONTEND FOR THE FAITH

A.   The apostolic era of the Church

1.   Corinth

But I fear, lest somehow, as the serpent deceived Eve by his craftiness, so your minds may be corrupted from the simplicity that is in Christ. (2 Corinthians 11:3)

2.   Galatia

But even if we, or an angel from heaven, preach any other gospel to you than what we have preached to you, let him be accursed. As we have said before, so now I say again, if anyone preaches any other gospel to you than what you have received, let him be accursed. (Galatians 1:8–9)

O foolish Galatians! Who has bewitched you that you should not obey the truth, before whose eyes Jesus Christ was clearly portrayed among you as crucified? (Galatians 3:1)

3. Colossae

For I want you to know what a great conflict I have for you and those in Laodicea, and for as many as have not seen my face in the flesh, that their hearts may be encouraged, being knit together in love, and attaining to all riches of the full assurance of understanding, to the knowledge of the mystery of God, both of the Father and of Christ, in whom are hidden all the treasures of wisdom and knowledge. Now this I say lest anyone should deceive you with persuasive words. (Colossians 2:1–4)

As you therefore have received Christ Jesus the Lord, so walk in Him, rooted and built up in Him and established in the faith, as you have been taught, abounding in it with thanksgiving. (Colossians 2:6–7)

4. Thessalonica

2 Thessalonians 2:1–12. Paul opens his exhortation concerning the end of the age with "Let no one deceive you by any means" (verse 3).

5. Ephesus and the Churches of Asia Minor

Now the Spirit expressly says that in latter times some will depart from the faith, giving heed to deceiving spirits and doctrines of demons, speaking lies in hypocrisy, having their own conscience seared with a hot iron. (1 Timothy 4:1–2)

Now as Jannes and Jambres resisted Moses, so do these also resist the truth: men of corrupt minds, disapproved concerning the faith. (2 Timothy 3:8)

But evil men and impostors will grow worse and worse, deceiving and being deceived. But you must continue in the things which you have learned and been assured of, knowing from whom you have learned them, and that from childhood you have known the Holy Scriptures, which are able to make you wise for salvation through faith which is in Christ Jesus. All Scripture is given by inspiration of God, and is profitable for doctrine, for reproof, for correction, for instruction in righteousness, that the man of God may be complete, thoroughly equipped for every good work. I charge you therefore before God and the Lord Jesus Christ, who will judge the living and the dead at His appearing and His kingdom: Preach the word! Be ready in season and out of season. Convince, rebuke, exhort, with all longsuffering and teaching. For the time will come when they will not endure sound doctrine, but according to their own desires, because they have itching ears, they will heap up for themselves teachers; and they will turn their ears away from the truth, and be turned aside to fables. (2 Timothy 3:13–4:4, emphasis added)

6. Petrine Letters

But there were also false prophets among the people, even as there will be false teachers among you, who will secretly bring in destructive heresies, even denying the Lord who bought them, and bring on themselves swift destruction. And many will follow their destructive ways, because of whom the way of truth will be blasphemed. By covetousness they will exploit you with deceptive words; for a long time their judgment has not been idle, and their destruction does not slumber. (2 Peter 2:1–3, emphasis added)

Beloved, I now write to you this second epistle (in both of which I stir up your pure minds by way of reminder), that you may be mindful of the words which were spoken before by the holy prophets, and of the commandment of us, the apostles of the Lord and Savior, knowing this first: that scoffers will come in the last days, walking according to their own lusts, and saying, "Where is the promise of His coming? For since the fathers fell asleep, all things continue as they were from the beginning of creation." (2 Peter 3:1–4, emphasis added)

You therefore, beloved, since you know this beforehand, beware lest you also fall from your own steadfastness, being led away with the error of the wicked. (2 Peter 3:17)

7.   Johannine Letters

1 John 2:18–26

*Little children, **it is the last hour; and as you have heard that the Antichrist is coming, even now many antichrists have come, by which we know that it is the last hour.** (1 John 2:18, emphasis added)*

***Who is a liar but he who denies that Jesus is the Christ? He is antichrist who denies the Father and the Son.** (1 John 2:22, emphasis added)*

These things I have written to you concerning those who try to deceive you. But the anointing which you have received from Him abides in you, and you do not need that anyone teach you; but as the same anointing teaches you concerning all things, and is true, and is not a lie, and just as it has taught you, you will abide in Him. (1 John 2:26–27)

*For **many deceivers have gone out into the world who do not confess Jesus Christ as coming in the flesh. This is a deceiver and an antichrist.** Look to yourselves, that we do not lose those things we worked for, but that we may receive a full reward. **Whoever transgresses and does not abide in the doctrine of Christ does not have God. He who abides in the doctrine of Christ has both the Father and the Son.** (2 John 1:7–9, emphasis added)*

8.   Jude

*Beloved, while I was very diligent to write to you concerning our common salvation, I found it necessary to write to you **exhorting you to contend earnestly for the faith which was once for all delivered to the saints.** For certain men have crept in unnoticed, who long ago were marked out for this condemnation, ungodly men, who turn the grace of our God into lewdness and deny the only Lord God and our Lord Jesus Christ. (Jude 3–4, emphasis added)*

But you, beloved, remember the words which were spoken before by the apostles of our Lord Jesus Christ: how they told you that there would be mockers in the last time who would walk according to their own ungodly lusts. (Jude 17–18)

9.   Revelation

     Revelation 2–3: Jesus addresses the seven churches of Asia Minor and identifies deception as a key element in producing false apostles, Nicolaitans, the doctrine of Balaam, the immoral deception of the false prophetess Jezebel, and the blasphemies of the synagogue of Satan.

     And he was given a mouth speaking great things and blasphemies, and he was given authority to continue for forty-two months. Then he opened his mouth in blasphemy against God, to blaspheme His name, His tabernacle, and those who dwell in heaven. It was granted to him to make war with the saints and to overcome them. And authority was given him over every tribe, tongue, and nation. All who dwell on the earth will worship him, whose names have not been written in the Book of Life of the Lamb slain from the foundation of the world. (Revelation 13:5–8)

     Then I saw another beast coming up out of the earth, and he had two horns like a lamb and spoke like a dragon. And he exercises all the authority of the first beast in his presence, and causes the earth and those who dwell in it to worship the first beast, whose deadly wound was healed. He performs great signs, so that he even makes fire come down from heaven on the earth in the sight of men. And he deceives those who dwell on the earth by those signs which he was granted to do in the sight of the beast, telling those who dwell on the earth to make an image to the beast who was wounded by the sword and lived. (Revelation 13:11–14)

     Then the second angel poured out his bowl on the sea, and it became blood as of a dead man; and every living creature in the sea died. (Revelation 16:3)

     Revelation 17–18: Harlot Babylon

B.   The seeds of deception—wrong beliefs sown in the Church

1.   **Universalism**: Hell is an earthly and present reality. It is not an eternal punishment for those who reject certain truth claims. In addition, Satan is an antiquated concept. The devil and hell have long since vanished from among the educated masses.

2. **The denial of original sin**: Humanity is a blank slate ("tabula rosa"—David Hume) and can be conditioned toward good or evil. Thus, socialization, not atonement, is the answer to humanity's problems.

3. **The "Bono Syndrome"**[1]: Jesus is one way among many ways, and all religions serve the same God. All religious claims are the same and come from the same source of humanity's desire for meaning, hope, and the establishment of good. Today, the religious dogmatism must end with all the religions coming together around the subject matter of the poor.

4. **Secular morality is a great good**: the Gospel is no longer about faith in God and one's need for redemption; it's about humanism. The Church is a social organization called to relieve some of the unfortunate ills of society.

5. **Grace as licentiousness**: a false doctrine of grace is presented, providing an excuse to continue in sin. Grace is wrongly mistaken for God's mercy and is wrongly perceived as being available in spite of our sin. In contrast, true grace divinely enables us to overcome the temptation to sin after we have received His mercy.

C. We must focus ourselves on the major truths of the faith—the incarnation, life, death, resurrection, ascension and second coming of the Lord. Paul prayed that the churches in Colossae and Laodicea would attain "to all riches of the full assurance of understanding, to the knowledge of the mystery of God, both of the Father and of Christ, in whom are hidden all the treasures of wisdom and knowledge" (Colossians 2:2–3). The subject matter of Christ is what causes our hearts to love God and encourages us in the hour of trial. The Book of Revelation is a book sent by God to strengthen the Church and prepare her for persecution and suffering. The revelation given to the Church for strength is the revelation of Jesus Christ. In fact, this revelation of God not only strengthens us for persecution, it is the endless subject matter of worship for angels and humans.

---

1 Bono is the lead singer of the rock band U2 and was named TIME Magazine's Person of the Year for his humanitarian work in Africa and his efforts to cancel Third World debt. He spoke at the National Day of Prayer breakfast in Washington, D.C. in 2006, advocating an equality of all religions as the way to God because of every religion's concern for the poor. The transcript of this speech can be found at: http://www.data.org/archives/000774.php.

D.   Presently, the three monotheistic religions represented in Jerusalem each believe different things about Jesus, about how He relates to Jerusalem, and about His role at the end of the age.

1.   Islam: Muslims believe that the Dome of the Rock is the very site where the prophet Muhammad ascended to Heaven. Inscriptions around the octagonal structure on the outside and on the inside deny the Incarnation and Resurrection of Jesus, as well as the Trinity.

Inscriptions on the outside of the Dome of the Rock declare that God has no begotten son, thus denying that Jesus is the Son of God:

S: In the name of God the Merciful, the Compassionate. There is no god but God alone, without partner. Say: He is God, One, God, the Everlasting, who has not begotten and has not been begotten. He is without equal. [Qur'an 112] Muhammad is God's messenger, may God bless him.[2]

Inscriptions on the inside walls deny Jesus as the Son of God, His resurrection, and the Trinity:

*S: In the name of God the Merciful, the Compassionate. There is no god but God alone, **without partner**. To Him belongs dominion and to Him belongs praise. He gives life and He makes to die; He is powerful over all things. [conflation of Qur'an 64:1 and 57:2] Muhammad is God's servant and His messenger.*

---

2   "Anti-Christ Monument in Jerusalem." <http://www.angelfire.com/journal2/dome_images/>.

SE: *God and His angels send blessings on the Prophet. 0 you who believe, send blessings on him and salute him with all respect. [Qur'an 33:56] May God bless him and grant him peace and mercy. 0 people of the book, do not go beyond the bounds in your religion,*

E: *nor say anything but the truth about God. The Messiah Jesus son of Mary, was only God's messenger, His word that He committed to Mary, and a spirit proceeding from Him. So believe in God and His messengers. Do not say 'three'. Refrain,*

NE: *it is better for you. For God is one god. Glory be to Him—* ***that He should have a son!*** *To Him belongs all that is in the heavens and in the earth. God suffices for a guardian [Qur'an 4:171]. The Messiah will not disdain to be*

N: *God's servant; nor will the angels who are stationed near to Him. Whoever disdains to serve him and waxes proud, He will muster them to Him, all of them. [Qur'an 4:172]* 0 ***God, bless your messenger and servant, Jesus.***

NW: *son of Mary. Peace be upon him the day he was born, the day he dies, and the day he is raised up alive. That is Jesus son of Mary, in word of truth, about which they are doubting. It is not for God to take a son. Glory be to Him.*[3]

2. Judaism denies that Jesus is the Jewish Messiah.

Some have argued that it is not so much what Judaism affirms that is important, but what it denies. A central tenet of rabbinic Judaism is a denial that Jesus is the Messiah, much less, that He is God. Since the historicity of Jesus is difficult to deny, Judaism has embraced Him only as He is divested of deity and of His role as Messiah. When Jewish scholars speak of reclaiming the Jewishness of Jesus, they most often refer to the Jewish learning and concepts which Jesus expressed, but admit no authority or originality to Him. He was simply a humble Jewish reformer and teacher. Such a teacher only needs to be "reclaimed" as an obscure footnote in Jewish history. A Jesus that does not need to be rejected, however, does not need to be reclaimed.[4]

---

3 "Anti-Christ Monument in Jerusalem." <http://www.angelfire.com/journal2/dome_images/>. Emphasis added.

4 "Judaism." *Apologetics: A Reasoned Defense of Christianity.* 2005. North American Mission Board. <http://www.4truth.net/site/apps/nl/content3.asp?c=hiKXLbPNLrF&b=784517&ct=932111>

VII. RAISING UP WITNESSES—A COMING APOSTOLIC MOVEMENT

A.   What is God's answer to the deception of the enemy? Messengers! Apostolic preachers who proclaim Christ and all of His glories. Presently, the Holy Spirit is restoring the fascination and love for Jesus through the revelation of all His excellencies. This revelation will produce the greatest messengers in church history. These messengers will help usher in revival in the Church and restore the first commandment to first place in the hearts of believers. The Holy Spirit is preparing such vessels to make Jesus known and to be burning and shining lamps during the world's darkest hour.

B.   The Excellencies of Christ

    1.   His Pre-Existence

    2.   His Incarnation

    3.   His Solidarity

    4.   His Humility and Meekness

    5.   His Sovereign Power

    6.   His Tenderness and Kindness

    7.   His Joy

    8.   His Holiness

    9.   His Cross

    10.   His Resurrection

    11.   His Ascension

    12.   His Session and Leadership

    13.   His Judgments

14. His Second Coming

15. His Millennial Reign and Eternal Kingdom

C. The Spirit is raising up messengers who will search the Scriptures to gain an understanding of Christ and His Kingdom. He is still taking people on the road to Emmaus, revealing to them how the Christ had to suffer before He entered into His glory. As we wait in the place of prayer and meditate upon the Word of God, the Spirit will lead us through the Law, the Psalms, and the Prophets, showing us God's eternal purpose in Christ Jesus.

D. The Spirit is also orchestrating a world-wide prayer and fasting movement to contend for the outpouring of the Holy Spirit.

1. God will establish houses of prayer that will be committed to worship, meditation, diligent study, and prayer for the breakthrough of God in cities all over the earth.

2. God is raising up people who believe that the methodology set forth in Joel 2 is the route back to God's manifest presence in the Church.

   "Now, therefore," says the LORD, "Turn to Me with all your heart, with fasting, with weeping, and with mourning." So rend your heart, and not your garments; return to the LORD your God, for He is gracious and merciful, slow to anger, and of great kindness; and He relents from doing harm. Who knows if He will turn and relent, and leave a blessing behind Him—a grain offering and a drink offering for the LORD your God? Blow the trumpet in Zion, consecrate a fast, call a sacred assembly; gather the people, sanctify the congregation, assemble the elders, gather the children and nursing babes; let the bridegroom go out from his chamber, and the bride from her dressing room. Let the priests, who minister to the LORD, weep between the porch and the altar; let them say, "Spare Your people, O LORD, and do not give Your heritage to reproach, that the nations should rule over them. Why should they say among the peoples, 'Where is their God?'" (Joel 2:12–17)

VIII. THE LAST GREAT WITNESS—ACTS 2:17 AND REVELATION 10–12

Behold, I send the Promise of My Father upon you; but tarry in the city of Jerusalem until you are endued with power from on high. (Luke 24:49)

But you shall receive power when the Holy Spirit has come upon you; and you shall be witnesses to Me in Jerusalem, and in all Judea and Samaria, and to the end of the earth. (Acts 1:8)

But Peter, standing up with the eleven, raised his voice and said to them, "Men of Judea and all who dwell in Jerusalem, let this be known to you, and heed my words. For these are not drunk, as you suppose, since it is only the third hour of the day. But this is what was spoken by the prophet Joel: **'And it shall come to pass in the last days, says God, that I will pour out of My Spirit on all flesh; your sons and your daughters shall prophesy, your young men shall see visions, your old men shall dream dreams.** *And on My menservants and on My maidservants I will pour out My Spirit in those days; and they shall prophesy. I will show wonders in heaven above and signs in the earth beneath: blood and fire and vapor of smoke. The sun shall be turned into darkness, and the moon into blood, before the coming of the great and awesome day of the* LORD. *And it shall come to pass that whoever calls on the name of the* LORD *shall be saved.'"* (Acts 2:14–21, emphasis added)

And with many other words he testified and exhorted them, saying, "Be saved from this perverse generation." Then those who gladly received his word were baptized; and that day about three thousand souls were added to them. And they continued steadfastly in the apostles' doctrine and fellowship, in the breaking of bread, and in prayers. Then fear came upon every soul, and many wonders and signs were done through the apostles. Now all who believed were together, and had all things in common, and sold their possessions and goods, and divided them among all, as anyone had need. So continuing daily with one accord in the temple, and breaking bread from house to house, they ate their food with gladness and simplicity of heart, praising God and having favor with all the people. And the Lord added to the church daily those who were being saved. (Acts 2:40–47)

A. At Pentecost, the Apostles were attempting the impossible. They were going back to the city that had, just days earlier, rejected and crucified Jesus, the most powerful Man who had ever walked the earth. Picture this in your mind. When Jesus said, "Tarry in Jerusalem," the apostles were not thinking, "Oh, that makes sense." The apostles were wondering, "What in the world is He saying?! Jerusalem? We had more effectiveness in Capernaum! He first told us to meet in Galilee. Can't we start in Galilee? Why Jerusalem?! Jerusalem is where they kill the prophets!"

B.   Jesus was the greatest messenger, healer, evangelist, prophet, deliverer, exorcist, and teacher in history. Yet the inhabitants of Jerusalem killed Him. Why did the disciples have to start in Jerusalem? Wouldn't God want the disciples to start somewhere else? If Jerusalem had refused and killed the master, certainly His servants would not fare any better. You might hear the Lord say in response, "I precisely chose Jerusalem in order to display My great power. At the very beginning of the propagation of the gospel, I want to demonstrate what true unction is. I want to show the difference between human words speaking forth ideas and Holy Spirit power that takes weak words and penetrates the hardest of hearts."

C.   Before the Second Coming of Jesus, God is going to release a great witness to His Son by the outpouring of the Holy Spirit. This outpouring will culminate in the greatest apostolic preaching ever seen and heard. Hearts will be torn asunder as signs and wonders testify to the truth of the Gospel of Jesus Christ. Jesus will be restored to preeminence within the Church, and the earth will shake before the demonstrations of power which will accompany the witness.

D.   The Book of Acts revisited:

   1.   Prophetic preaching and singing with power

   2.   Signs and wonders

   3.   Faithful unto death

E.   Revelation 10–12 describes end-time messengers who will prophesy concerning Christ in the darkest hour of human history.

So I went to the angel and said to him, "Give me the little book." And he said to me, "Take and eat it; and it will make your stomach bitter, but it will be as sweet as honey in your mouth." Then I took the little book out of the angel's hand and ate it, and it was as sweet as honey in my mouth. But when I had eaten it, my stomach became bitter. And he said to me, "You must prophesy again about many peoples, nations, tongues, and kings." (Revelation 10:9–11, emphasis added)

"And I will give power to my two witnesses, and they will prophesy one thousand two hundred and sixty days, clothed in sackcloth." These are the two olive trees and the two lampstands standing before the God of the earth. And if anyone wants to harm them, fire proceeds from their mouth and devours their enemies. And if anyone wants to harm them, he must be killed in this manner. These have power to shut heaven, so that no rain falls in the days of their prophecy; and they have power over waters to turn them to blood, and to strike the earth with all plagues, as often as they desire. (Revelation 11:3–6)

Then I heard a loud voice saying in heaven, "Now salvation, and strength, and the kingdom of our God, and the power of His Christ have come, for the accuser of our brethren, who accused them before our God day and night, has been cast down. And they overcame him by the blood of the Lamb and by the word of their testimony, and they did not love their lives to the death." (Revelation 12:10–11)

F. In this context of the Day of the Lord, preachers will come forth and warn the Earth of the impending return of the Lord Jesus and of His awesome judgments, which will precede and attend His coming.

Blow the trumpet in Zion, and sound an alarm in My holy mountain! *Let all the inhabitants of the land tremble; for the day of the* Lord *is coming, for it is at hand: a day of darkness and gloominess, a day of clouds and thick darkness, like the morning clouds spread over the mountains. A people come, great and strong, the like of whom has never been; nor will there ever be any such after them, even for many successive generations. (Joel 2:1–2, emphasis added)*

Blow the trumpet in Zion, consecrate a fast, call a sacred assembly; gather the people, sanctify the congregation, assemble the elders, gather the children and nursing babes; let the bridegroom go out from his chamber, and the bride from her dressing room. Let the priests, who minister to the Lord, *weep between the porch and the altar; let them say, "Spare Your people, O* Lord, *and do not give Your heritage to reproach, that the nations should rule over them. Why should they say among the peoples, 'Where is their God?'" (Joel 2:15–17)*

G. Jesus has prayed to His Father, asking for a Companion who will love Him and be faithful to Him. Will you answer the invitation? Word has it that He is longing for you to come closer, to see His glory, and to fall in love with Him. Perhaps He is calling you to prepare for a coming hour when you will be a bright light in the midst of great darkness. Perhaps He has saved this high calling for you.

Session One: Beholding Christ in the Beauty of Holiness

I.   **THE HOLY — "THE MYSTERIUM TREMENDUM"**

    A.   All cultures and all religions contain the idea of the mysterious, the holy. At the core of religious belief and practice is the mysterious, supernaturally threatening presence. In the soul of humanity is the indelible knowledge that something out there is so awesome, so powerful, and so beautiful that it is terrifying to think on and hazardous to behold. Deep within the framework of humanity is a dread, a terrifying sense that something out there is worthy of our worship and can either help us or hurt us in our frail condition.

    B.   *The feeling for mystery, even for the Great Mystery, is basic in human nature and indispensable to religious faith, but it is not enough. Because of it men may whisper, "That awful thing," but they do not cry, "Mine Holy One!" In the Hebrew and Christian Scriptures God carries forward His self-revelation and gives it personality and moral content. This awful Presence is shown to be not a Thing but a moral Being with all the warm qualities of genuine personality. More than this, He is the absolute quintessence of moral excellence, infinitely perfect in righteousness, purity, rectitude, and incomprehensible holiness. And in all this He is uncreated, self-sufficient and beyond the power of human thought to conceive or human speech to utter.*[1]

II. **THE KNOWLEDGE OF THE HOLY**

    A.   We know God because He chooses to reveal Himself. He is the Holy One who loves to disclose Himself. He is the Mystery made known. The Scriptures testify that while the other nations worship that which they do not know, we worship the One True God who has made Himself known.

            Jesus said to her, "Woman, believe Me, the hour is coming when you will neither on this mountain, nor in Jerusalem, worship the Father. You worship what you do not know; we know what we worship, for salvation is of the Jews." (John 4:21–22)

---

1   Tozer, A.W. *The Knowledge of the Holy* (San Francisco: HarperSanFrancisco, 1961), p. 105.

B.   "The glorious gospel of the blessed God" (1 Timothy 1:11): God is the blessed, happy God. God loves Himself. He infinitely enjoys Himself as the most lovely, beautiful, righteous, kind, pure Being that exists. God is eternally happy; He is the consummation of all perfection. "In Your presence is fullness of joy; at Your right hand are pleasures forevermore" (Psalm 16:11). The radiance of all His attributes, working in perfect harmony, perfect purity, perfect potency, and perfect gladness, is His holiness. He is beyond all things. No one can compare with the God who lacks nothing and who overflows with all of His excellencies.

C.   God is the God of pleasure who loves to share Himself, who loves to delight the senses of the ones formed in His image. He is the glorious, delightful God who constructs reality around revelation, around the unfolding of beauty and light and love; the God who loves to manifest and display the illustrious, incandescent essence of the divine, all for fascination. **He is pleasure immeasurable and delight consummate. The highest honor and joy He could give us is to base our relationship around the subject matter of Himself.** He is the overflowing God.

1.   The only reason you exist is pleasure. It's the only reason you were made. You have no other function than enjoying and being enjoyed by God. None. Not one. Why do you exist? Does God need your help? Have you ever seen the angels around His throne? He doesn't need you to do anything for Him. You're the one creature made to mine the depths of the living God. Everything for you has been built around the revelation of God, Him letting you know something about Himself.

2.   He is the God who loves to manifest Himself, to unfold beauty. Everything in reality is constructed around God revealing Himself. Have you ever asked yourself why He manifests Himself the way He does? Why those weird voices, strange creatures, light, colors, and smells described in Revelation 4, Ezekiel 1, and other passages? Why does God do that? One reason: your pleasure.

D.   *Shall I call holiness an attribute? Is it not rather the glorious combination of all his attributes into one perfect whole? As all his attributes proceed from the absolute, so all again converge and meet in holiness. As from the insufferable white light of the Absolute they all seem to diverge and separate into prismatic hues, so they all seem again to converge and meet and combine in the dazzling white radiance of his holiness. This, therefore, is rather the intense whiteness, purity, clearness, the infinite luster and splendor of his perfect nature—like a gem without flaw, without stain, and without color. All of his attributes are glorious, but in this we have a combination of all into a still more glorious whole. It is for this reason that it is so frequently in Scripture associated with the Divine beauty. The poetic nature of the psalmist is exalted to ecstasy in contemplation of the beauty of holiness, the beauty of the Lord. Beauty is a combination of elements according to the laws of harmony; the more beautiful the parts or elements, and the more perfect the harmonious combination, the higher the beauty. How high and glorious, therefore, must be the beauty of this attribute which is the perfect combination of all his infinite perfections!*

YOU SEE, THEN, WHY THIS ATTRIBUTE IS AWFUL TO US. IN THE IDEAL MAN ALL THE FACULTIES AND POWERS, MENTAL, MORAL, AND BODILY, WORK TOGETHER IN PERFECT HARMONY, MAKING SWEET MUSIC—THE IMAGE OF GOD IS CLEAR AND PURE IN THE HUMAN HEART. BUT, ALAS! HOW FAR ARE WE FROM THE IDEAL! IN THE ACTUAL MAN THE PURITY IS STAINED, THE BEAUTY IS DEFACED, THE HARMONY IS CHANGED INTO JARRING DISCORD, LIKE SWEET BELLS JANGLED OUT OF TUNE. HOW IT CAME SO, WE ARE NOT NOW INQUIRING. WE ALL FEEL THAT IT IS SO. THEREFORE IS THIS ATTRIBUTE SO AWFUL TO US. IT IS THE AWFULNESS OF ABSOLUTE PURITY IN THE PRESENCE OF IMPURITY; IT IS THE AWFULNESS OF PERFECT BEAUTY IN THE PRESENCE OF DEFORMITY; IT IS THE AWFULNESS OF HONOR IN THE PRESENCE OF DISHONOR AND SHAME; IN ONE WORD, IT IS THE AWFULNESS OF HOLINESS IN THE PRESENCE OF SINFULNESS. HOW, THEN, SHALL WE APPROACH HIM BEFORE WHOM ANGELS BOW AND ARCHANGELS VEIL THEIR FACES— HIM IN WHOSE SIGHT THE WHITE RADIANCE OF HEAVEN ITSELF IS STAINED WITH IMPURITY?[2]

III.   THE FORMING OF HUMANITY

And the LORD God formed man of the dust of the ground, and breathed into his nostrils the breath of life; and man became a living being. (Genesis 2:7)

---

2   Spurgeon, Charles. *The Treasury of David* (Chicago: Moody, 1978), p. 234.

A.   Genesis 1:1–2:3 is focused on the brooding presence of the Spirit and the power of God to speak forth all that is, setting the broad context. In chapter one, the main character is introduced—the all-powerful, lovely Creator God. Chapter two focuses on the darling of creation, the focus of the main character's affections. In fact, St. John of the Cross called all of creation trinkets of love given for the delight of God's most prized creation.[3] The curtains are drawn back, and chapter two announces the intricacies of the Image Bearers.

B.   The formation of man did not come through a simple creative word, such as one that created the heavens. The very hand of the Word Himself worked this masterpiece, and His very breath ushered in a living soul. The breath and life-force of God fashioned and formed the heart of man, and God left His indelible mark upon Adam, His holy breath filling a treasured soul.

C.   Proverbs 8 and Psalm 139

The LORD possessed me at the beginning of His way, before His works of old. I have been established from everlasting, from the beginning, before there was ever an earth. When there were no depths I was brought forth, when there were no fountains abounding with water. Before the mountains were settled, before the hills, I was brought forth; while as yet He had not made the earth or the fields, or the primal dust of the world. When He prepared the heavens, I was there, when He drew a circle on the face of the deep, when He established the clouds above, when He strengthened the fountains of the deep, when He assigned to the sea its limit, so that the waters would not transgress His command, when He marked out the foundations of the earth, then **I was beside Him as a master craftsman; and I was daily His delight, rejoicing always before Him, rejoicing in His inhabited world, and my delight was with the sons of men**. *(Proverbs 8:22–31, emphasis added)*

---

3   Dubay, Thomas. *Fire Within* (San Francisco: Ignatius Press, 1989), p. 49-51.

*For **You formed my inward parts; You covered me in my mother's womb. I will praise You, for I am fearfully and wonderfully made; marvelous are Your works, and that my soul knows very well.** My frame was not hidden from You, when I was made in secret, and skillfully wrought in the lowest parts of the earth. Your eyes saw my substance, being yet unformed. And in Your book they all were written, the days fashioned for me, when as yet there were none of them. How precious also are Your thoughts to (concerning) me, O God! How great is the sum of them! If I should count them, they would be more in number than the sand; when I awake, I am still with You. (Psalm 139:13–18, emphasis added, parenthetical comment added)*

D.   The connecting point of Heaven and Earth is humanity. The place where God chose for Heaven and Earth to come together is humanity, made in His image and filled with His Spirit. In humanity, God's nature is reflected and God's government is implemented for the rest of the earth. Creation witnesses the character and power of God through humanity, and in humanity God receives the highest praises and glory from the created order.

IV.   THE GARDEN OF DELIGHT

The LORD God planted a garden eastward in Eden, and there He put the man whom He had formed. And out of the ground the LORD God made every tree grow that is pleasant to the sight and good for food. The tree of life was also in the midst of the garden, and the tree of the knowledge of good and evil. (Genesis 2:8–9)

A.   God spoke forth plants and trees, but here God personally planted a garden, and this garden was for the delight of a living soul. With wondrous intent, God placed man in this garden. Out of all the places on the globe, God chose a garden as the place where He would meet with man. This is the place of encounter, where even the trees will be pleasing to the eye and good for food.

B.   The garden became the place of pleasure, encounter and delight, where hearts are refreshed and love is exchanged in the cool of the shade. Kings and rulers of the earth will follow suit and compete over the beauty and complexity of their gardens for ages to come. A garden was the place where Xerxes longed to display the beauty of Vashti. It was the place where Queen Esther threw banquets for her lover and king. Jesus prayed in a garden before the hour of His crucifixion, was buried in a garden, and rose again in a garden.

C. The head river that fed all the land's tributaries flowed from this garden. Out of Eden came forth bountiful treasures, fragrant aromas, and beautiful jewels. The place of encounter feeds all other delights. Eden is the fountain, the qualifying standard of all other pleasures.

V. ADAM'S OCCUPATION: TO TEND THE PLACE OF ENCOUNTER

Then the LORD God took the man and put him in the garden of Eden to tend and keep it. And the LORD God commanded the man, saying, "Of every tree of the garden you may freely eat; but of the tree of the knowledge of good and evil you shall not eat, for in the day that you eat of it you shall surely die." (Genesis 2:15–17)

A. Man's primary task was to tend the place of pleasure. Delight was humanity's main occupation. He was to nurture the place of encounter, to feed the place of passion, to weed its beds, and to aid its seasons of beauty.

B. In the garden, freedom was given and the joy of obedience was offered. The cultivation of delight would be a voluntary enterprise. Freedom of will was accompanied by safe boundaries for the enjoyment of beauty. That was why the Lord said, "You shall not eat of the tree of the knowledge of good and evil." Humans were not made for rulership based upon their independent observations and understandings of the environment in which they lived. We were made for encounter and rulership flowing from intimate communion with the living God, the Ruler of all things.

1. *Then the LORD spoke to Moses, saying: "Speak to the children of Israel, that they bring Me an offering. From everyone who gives it willingly with his heart you shall take My offering." (Exodus 25:1–2)*

2. *Furthermore King David said to all the assembly: "My son Solomon, whom alone God has chosen, is young and inexperienced; and the work is great, because the temple is not for man but for the LORD God. **Now for the house of my God I have prepared with all my might:** gold for things to be made of gold, silver for things of silver, bronze for things of bronze, iron for things of iron, wood for things of wood, onyx stones, stones to be set, glistening stones of various colors, all kinds of precious stones, and marble slabs in abundance. **Moreover, because I have set my affection on the house of my God, I have given to the house of my God, over and above all that I have prepared for the holy house, my own special treasure of gold***

*and silver: three thousand talents of gold, of the gold of Ophir, and seven thousand talents of refined silver, to overlay the walls of the houses; the gold for things of gold and the silver for things of silver, and for all kinds of work to be done by the hands of craftsmen. **Who then is willing to consecrate himself this day to the Lord?" Then the leaders of the fathers' houses, leaders of the tribes of Israel, the captains of thousands and of hundreds, with the officers over the king's work, offered willingly.** They gave for the work of the house of God five thousand talents and ten thousand darics of gold, ten thousand talents of silver, eighteen thousand talents of bronze, and one hundred thousand talents of iron. And whoever had precious stones gave them to the treasury of the house of the Lord, into the hand of Jehiel the Gershonite. **Then the people rejoiced, for they had offered willingly, because with a loyal heart they had offered willingly to the Lord; and King David also rejoiced greatly.** (1 Chronicles 29:1–9, emphasis added)*

C.   The foundational work of man is to nurture the place of encounter with His Maker. The means of this nurture will not come through the depth of man's knowledge, but the cultivation of inner beauty through encounter with life—with the living God. God desired that Adam's source of dominion would be communion with God, not insight based upon human wisdom. As the Image Bearer of God, Adam's life was wrapped up in God's. Humanity cannot function outside of communion with the Creator. Knowledge of principles and rules can never sustain the life of humanity. Knowledge outside of communion with God always leads to independence and self-exertion, for man was made for God to reflect God. The two trees in Eden were placed there to present a choice: what would be the source of humanity's exercise of authority?

D.   God has forever connected government and intimacy. Our dominion is forever linked with our dependency upon God through intimacy and asking. Governmental decisions are never made outside the context of intimacy, love, and fascination. This is why God's government is ruled through intercession. God loves to be asked, He loves to hear, and He loves to thrill us through the answers. God designs the creatures made in His image with the governmental delight of communing and asking Him for things. This is life—to forever lean upon our Bridegroom God and ask Him for decisions on the earth. Intercession is, at the base level, what it means to be human and made in the image of the living God. Government is never simply making decisions with a given set of facts. That approach is from the Tree of the Knowledge of Good and Evil. Government should always be indelibly marked with leaning on Him, communing, and asking. Government is more than enforcing divine order. It is filled with intimacy, light, and love. It is the fascinated interplay of human asking and divine answering unto worship, wonder, and whispers of love.

VI.   THE CULTIVATION OF LONGING

And the Lord God said, "It is not good that man should be alone; I will make him a helper comparable to him." Out of the ground the Lord God formed every beast of the field and every bird of the air, and brought them to Adam to see what he would call them. And whatever Adam called each living creature, that was its name. So Adam gave names to all cattle, to the birds of the air, and to every beast of the field. But for Adam there was not found a helper comparable to him. (Genesis 2:18–20)

A.   From the beginning, God defined reality for man in this garden. God desired a companion for Adam. This was not an alternative plan to a debunked system. This was the clarifying of reality for man and was the prophetic foreshadowing of the nature of things for the second Adam to come. Just as God desired to create humanity in His image and join us unto Himself in the person of His Son, so God desired that the first Adam be joined to a companion.

B.   God used loneliness to cultivate something in the heart of Adam. God created longing in his heart and made Adam endure a rigorous process of recognizing his lacking. Loneliness became the birthplace for longing and desire. Aloneness presupposes desire and longing. Without the longing for something else, loneliness is impossible. While Adam bore the weight of naming all that was created, his heart began to notice that something was missing and also that something was being kindled in him. Desire for a companion was growing. God was setting forth the ultimate object lesson for Adam to understand something of himself. He was a creature of desire and intimacy, made in the image of His Creator. God stamped His own longing for communion on the very nature on human beings.

C.   This was the design of God: to create longing and passion in the heart of humanity. We are designed to feel the longing of love, the relentless pursuit of the heart for another person like no other creature. Humanity would share in the experience of God with longing love.

D.   No suitable helper is found. God used the naming of the animals for much more than a display of Adam's authority. He used the naming of the animals to help Adam discover the God-given attributes of love and desire. Can you imagine the pain of Adam as he named them, two of each kind, all the while recognizing his lack of a companion and discovering the power of a new emotion? Desire was reaching its climax, but wait— a wedding is coming.

VII.   THE PROPHETIC DECREE OF DESIRE

And the LORD God caused a deep sleep to fall on Adam, and he slept; and He took one of his ribs, and closed up the flesh in its place. Then the rib which the LORD God had taken from man He made into a woman, and He brought her to the man. (Genesis 2:21–22)

A.   The foreshadowing of the Cross: the Bride of both the first and second Adam will come forth through the suffering love of the Groom. The wise God sets forth the story of His Son and His Bride from the very first. Adam longed for a companion. In his longing, the heavenly Father satisfied his heart. He put him to sleep, and from Adam's broken side God fashioned a beautiful spouse for His beautiful son and brought her to Adam. It is the story of the ages. The wedding of the ages is established from the very beginning in the DNA of humanity.

B.   This is a divine betrothal planned in the heart of God. It will take a supernatural intervention of God to pull off this wedding. The Son yearns for a companion. The Father puts Him to sleep and forms her from the Son's wounded side. The Spirit brings the beautiful Spouse to the Son with great joy.

VIII.   THE CONSUMMATION OF LOVE—LONGING SATISFIED

And Adam said: "This is now bone of my bones and flesh of my flesh; she shall be called Woman, because she was taken out of Man." Therefore a man shall leave his father and mother and be joined to his wife, and they shall become one flesh. (Genesis 2:23–24)

A.   The climax of joy. The consummation of love. Desire reaches its fulfillment and becomes the basis for human interaction, foreshadowing a glorious day to come. From the initial union of Adam and Eve, God gives us a glimpse into His own heart, where the wedding of the next age has been planned between His Son and a Bride chosen from the remnant of humanity.

B.   *And I heard, as it were, the voice of a great multitude, as the sound of many waters and as the sound of mighty thunderings, saying, "Alleluia! For the Lord God Omnipotent reigns! Let us be glad and rejoice and give Him glory, for the marriage of the Lamb has come, and His wife has made herself ready." And to her it was granted to be arrayed in fine linen, clean and bright, for the fine linen is the righteous acts of the saints. Then he said to me, "Write: 'Blessed are those who are called to the marriage supper of the Lamb!'" And he said to me, "These are the true sayings of God." And I fell at his feet to worship him. But he said to me, "See that you do not do that! I am your fellow servant, and of your brethren who have the testimony of Jesus. Worship God! For the testimony of Jesus is the spirit of prophecy." (Revelation 19:6–10)*

IX.   THE FALL AND THE COMING SEED

A.   Genesis 3 reveals to us the tragic moment when humanity entered the rebellion of Satan. Somewhere between Genesis 1:31, when God saw that all things were good, and Genesis 3, a conflict began in Heaven. Tradition holds that Satan, a powerful and high-ranking angel, became proud of his angelic grandeur and exalted himself to be like God. He sought the worship of God's created order and secured the following of a third of Heaven's angels.

You were the seal of perfection, full of wisdom and perfect in beauty. You were in Eden, the garden of God; every precious stone was your covering: the sardius, topaz, and diamond, beryl, onyx, and jasper, sapphire, turquoise, and emerald with gold. The workmanship of your timbrels and pipes was prepared for you on the day you were created. You were the anointed cherub who covers; I established you; you were on the holy mountain of God; you walked back and forth in the midst of fiery stones. You were perfect in your ways from the day you were created, till iniquity was found in you. By the abundance of your trading you became filled with violence within, and you sinned; therefore I cast you as a profane thing out of the mountain of God; and I destroyed you, O covering cherub, from the midst of the fiery stones. Your heart was lifted up because of your beauty; you corrupted your wisdom for the sake of your splendor; I cast you to the ground, I laid you before kings, that they might gaze at you. (Ezekiel 28:12–17)

How you are fallen from heaven, O Lucifer, son of the morning! How you are cut down to the ground, you who weakened the nations! For you have said in your heart: "I will ascend into heaven, I will exalt my throne above the stars of God; I will also sit on the mount of the congregation on the farthest sides of the north; I will ascend above the heights of the clouds, I will be like the Most High." Yet you shall be brought down to Sheol, to the lowest depths of the Pit. (Isaiah 14:12–15)

B.   The rebellion expanded to Earth as Satan established his kingdom in the natural realm by seducing God's most prized creature. Adam and Eve's decision was over much more than what fruit to eat. It was over whom humanity should listen to and follow. Humanity joined the resistance against God's plan, and the consequences of this rebellion have changed the entire landscape of the created order. The effects have been disastrous and deadly.

        1.   Humanity, in following Satan, fell from God's Kingdom. Through the Fall, lordship over the earth transferred over to Satan. The kingdom of darkness had a stronghold, and the kingdoms of the world would come under the sway of the evil one.

                Again, the devil took Him up on an exceedingly high mountain, and showed Him all the kingdoms of the world and their glory. And he said to Him, "All these things I will give You if You will fall down and worship me." (Matthew 4:8–9, emphasis added)

*We know that we are of God, and **the whole world lies under the sway of the wicked one.** (1 John 5:19, emphasis added)*

2. Physical, spiritual, and eternal death entered into the human experience. We were spiritually separated from God and physically condemned to die.

    *But of the tree of the knowledge of good and evil you shall not eat, for **in the day that you eat of it you shall surely die.** (Genesis 2:17, emphasis added)*

    ***For the wages of sin is death,** but the gift of God is eternal life in Christ Jesus our Lord. (Romans 6:23, emphasis added)*

    *For since **by man came death**, by Man also came the resurrection of the dead. For as **in Adam all die,** even so in Christ all shall be made alive. (1 Corinthians 15:21–22, emphasis added)*

    *And as **it is appointed for men to die once, but after this the judgment.** (Hebrews 9:27, emphasis added)*

    *And I saw the dead, small and great, standing before God, and books were opened. And another book was opened, which is the Book of Life. And the dead were judged according to their works, by the things which were written in the books. The sea gave up the dead who were in it, and Death and Hades delivered up the dead who were in them. And **they were judged, each one according to his works. Then Death and Hades were cast into the lake of fire.** This is the second death. And anyone not found written in the Book of Life was cast into the lake of fire. (Revelation 20:12–15, emphasis added)*

3. The guilt of sin and God's just punishment of sin entered into the human experience.

    ***For the wrath of God is revealed from heaven against all ungodliness and unrighteousness of men, who suppress the truth in unrighteousness.** (Romans 1:18, emphasis added)*

    ***But in accordance with your hardness and your impenitent heart you are treasuring up for yourself wrath in the day of wrath and revelation of the righteous judgment of God, who "will render to each one according to his deeds."** (Romans 2:5–6, emphasis added)*

4.   Creation would experience the groan of the effects of sin.

*For the earnest expectation of the creation eagerly waits for the revealing of the sons of God. For the **creation was subjected to futility,** not willingly, but because of Him who subjected it in hope; because the creation itself also will be delivered from the bondage of corruption into the glorious liberty of the children of God. (Romans 8:19–21, emphasis added)*

5.   Humanity would not only experience separation from God, but the effect of sin would cause social separation and injustice.

But if we walk in the light as He is in the light, we have fellowship with one another, and the blood of Jesus Christ His Son cleanses us from all sin. (1 John 1:7)

C.   The promise of the coming seed: after the Fall, God prophesied of a coming King who would make all things right by crushing the powers of darkness. The unfolding of all revelation will concern the coming of this Anointed One who will destroy the works of darkness, make all things new, and bless all the families of the earth. The Bible is the record of how God would bring forth the Promised One.

And I will put enmity between you and the woman, and between your seed and her Seed; He shall bruise your head, and you shall bruise His heel. (Genesis 3:15)

X.   THE DISPLAY OF WONDER—A HOLY GOD DRAWS NEAR

The Hebrew word for "holy" is "qadowsh" or "qadosh," meaning brightness or separatedness. "Brightness suggests the unapproachable God; separatedness is the positive quality which distinguishes or defines God."[4] The radiant, bright God illumined in the complexity and perfection of all His attributes unveils Himself to the objects of His affections. God draws near.

---

4   Motyer, J. Alec. *The Prophecy of Isaiah* (Downers Grove, IL: InterVarsity, 1993), p. 77.

God's holiness relates to His glory. It relates to the inapproachable light surrounding Him in His theophanies. God clothes Himself in light. He is wrapped with the luster of all His attributes as they work in perfect harmony and perfect potency. In Scripture, we read about God manifesting in light, in thunder, in lightning, in clouds and whirlwinds, and in fire. The Bible declares how His voice can split cedars and shake deserts. His eyes are like a flame of fire that melts mountains. From His presence proceed rumblings, voices, lightnings, and thunders. Clouds, fire, and darkness surrounded Him as He led Israel through the wilderness, and blinding light surrounded Jesus on the road to Damascus. God's nature manifests in terrifyingly beautiful ways.

All Old Testament worship, including the priestly and prophetic ministries, was birthed out of confrontation with the Holy. When God unveiled Himself to the children of Israel, He revealed Himself as Holy. He displayed the luster and beauty of all His attributes in order to fascinate the heart and produce the response of worship. It is the encounter with the beautiful, terrifying God that produces worship, ushers in faithfulness, and writes the covenant on the hearts of men and women.

A. The relationship in the Garden of Eden: Humanity was made in God's image, bearing the glory of the Holy God. Humanity was created to reflect divine glory from the place of encounter with God. Adam would walk with God in the cool of the day and then reflect God's glory to the rest of creation. **God made us for dominion that flows out of fascinating encounter. Even now, He is looking for more than a mental assent to a doctrine. He is looking for provocation unto worship. He wants worship.** Worship is the heart saying, "Oh, my God." It is the heart being rent and undone on a thousand levels, saying, "I love you," while trembling at the same time. God has always wanted it this way. He set it up this way in the garden and He hasn't changed.

B. Abraham: God called Abram out of the land of his father and then appeared to him at the terebinth tree of Moreh. The glory of the Lord appeared to Abram and he built an altar. Worship was his response to encountering the beauty of the Holy. The seed would come from Abraham through the tribe of Judah.

    *Then **the Lord appeared to Abram** and said, "To your descendants I will give this land." And there he built an altar to the Lord, who had appeared to him. (Genesis 12:7, emphasis added)*

Then Melchizedek king of Salem brought out bread and wine; he was the priest of God Most High. And he blessed him and said: "Blessed be Abram of God Most High, possessor of heaven and earth; and blessed be God Most High, who has delivered your enemies into your hand." And he gave him a tithe of all. (Genesis 14:18–20)

Now when the sun was going down, a deep sleep fell upon Abram; and behold, horror and great darkness fell upon him. Then He said to Abram: "Know certainly that your descendants will be strangers in a land that is not theirs, and will serve them, and they will afflict them four hundred years. And also the nation whom they serve I will judge; afterward they shall come out with great possessions. Now as for you, you shall go to your fathers in peace; you shall be buried at a good old age. But in the fourth generation they shall return here, for the iniquity of the Amorites is not yet complete." And it came to pass, when the sun went down and it was dark, that behold, there appeared a smoking oven and a burning torch that passed between those pieces. On the same day the LORD made a covenant with Abram, saying: "To your descendants I have given this land, from the river of Egypt to the great river, the River Euphrates." (Genesis 15:12–18)

*When Abram was ninety-nine years old, **the Lord appeared to Abram** and said to him, "I am Almighty God; walk before Me and be blameless. And I will make My covenant between Me and you, and will multiply you exceedingly." Then Abram fell on his face, and God talked with him, saying: "As for Me, behold, My covenant is with you, and you shall be a father of many nations. No longer shall your name be called Abram, but your name shall be Abraham; for I have made you a father of many nations. I will make you exceedingly fruitful; and I will make nations of you, and kings shall come from you. And I will establish My covenant between Me and you and your descendants after you in their generations, for an everlasting covenant, to be God to you and your descendants after you." (Genesis 17:1–7, emphasis added)*

*And he said, "Brethren and fathers, listen: **The God of glory appeared to our father Abraham when he was in Mesopotamia,** before he dwelt in Haran, and said to him, 'Get out of your country and from your relatives, and come to a land that I will show you.'" (Acts 7:2–3, emphasis added)*

Then the Angel of the LORD called to Abraham a second time out of heaven, and said: "By Myself I have sworn, says the LORD, because you have done this thing, and have not withheld your son, your only son—blessing I will bless you, and multiplying I will multiply your descendants as the stars of the heaven and as the sand which is on the seashore; and your descendants shall possess the gate of their enemies. In your seed all the nations of the earth shall be blessed, because you have obeyed My voice." (Genesis 22:15–18)

The scepter shall not depart from Judah, nor a lawgiver from between his feet, until Shiloh comes; and to Him shall be the obedience of the people. (Genesis 49:10)

C.   Moses: God appeared to Moses in the burning bush and told Moses that he was standing on holy ground. This is the first time the word "holy" appears in Scripture.

And the Angel of the LORD appeared to him in a flame of fire from the midst of a bush. So he looked, and behold, the bush was burning with fire, but the bush was not consumed. Then Moses said, "I will now turn aside and see this great sight, why the bush does not burn." So when the LORD saw that he turned aside to look, God called to him from the midst of the bush and said, "Moses, Moses!" And he said, "Here I am." Then He said, "Do not draw near this place. Take your sandals off your feet, for the place where you stand is holy ground." (Exodus 3:2–5)

1.   God was manifesting Himself in the fire of His glory. The fascinating God was revealing the intrigue, the light of His presence. From this day forward, God begins to establish a nation through the display of His splendor. After God demonstrated the perfection of His judgments, the depth of His power and the immensity of His pleasure towards His people, Moses broke out in song and exclaimed that there was no God like the Lord who was glorious in holiness.

Who is like You, O LORD, among the gods? Who is like You, glorious in holiness, fearful in praises, doing wonders? (Exodus 15:11)

2.   Look what the burning, shining God from the burning bush has done. He has given us the timeless message that He alone is holy. He alone is God. God was displaying the vastness of His excellencies in order to demonstrate that He was not one god among many gods. He alone is God. He alone is Holy. God then gave Moses a clear picture for the world and to the nation of Israel of how to relate to this beautifully terrifying, holy God. Just as God is set apart from any other thing, any other god, so Israel would be set apart as God's special treasure, as a holy nation, as a kingdom of priests. They would display the beauty of God's character to the nations.

    a.   Exodus 19–20

    b.   Exodus 24–25

       And let them make Me a sanctuary, that I may dwell among them. (Exodus 25:8)

3.   Within Israel, God would set apart a holy people, the priesthood and the Levites. They were and are holy to the Lord. The Lord would set up various rules and various places to display different facets of His nature and to display the difference between that which is common and that which is holy. God would set apart holy garments for the priests. They would wear the garments of beauty and glory. This foreshadowed the coming day when the Holy God would cloak Himself in flesh; when Jesus, the Great High Priest, would put on flesh, and flesh would be adorned with deity.

    a.   Exodus 33

    b.   *For I proclaim the name of the LORD: ascribe greatness to our God. He is the Rock, His work is perfect; for all His ways are justice, a God of truth and without injustice; righteous and upright is He. (Deuteronomy 32:3–4)*

4.   In Moses' final address to the children of Israel, he declared the coming of another Prophet:

The Lord your God will raise up for you a Prophet like me from your midst, from your brethren. Him you shall hear, according to all you desired of the Lord your God in Horeb in the day of the assembly, saying, "Let me not hear again the voice of the Lord my God, nor let me see this great fire anymore, lest I die." And the Lord said to me: "What they have spoken is good. I will raise up for them a Prophet like you from among their brethren, and will put My words in His mouth, and He shall speak to them all that I command Him. And it shall be that whoever will not hear My words, which He speaks in My name, I will require it of him." (Deuteronomy 18:15–19)

D. Joshua: through the Captain of the Lord's armies, God reaffirmed to Joshua that He was leading the conquest. The Holy One was heading this campaign and Joshua was on holy ground. At the end of his days, Joshua reminded the people of the Holy God and exhorted them to "choose for yourselves this day whom you shall serve" (Joshua 24:15). This was no trite decision. This was life or death, for the terrifyingly beautiful God would tolerate no other lovers.

1. *And it came to pass, when Joshua was by Jericho, that he lifted his eyes and looked, and behold, a Man stood opposite him with His sword drawn in His hand. And Joshua went to Him and said to Him, "Are You for us or for our adversaries?" So He said, "No, but as Commander of the army of the LORD I have now come." And Joshua fell on his face to the earth and worshiped, and said to Him, "What does my Lord say to His servant?" Then the Commander of the LORD's army said to Joshua, "Take your sandal off your foot, for the place where you stand is holy." And Joshua did so. (Joshua 5:13–15)*

2. *So the people answered and said: "Far be it from us that we should forsake the LORD to serve other gods; for the LORD our God is He who brought us and our fathers up out of the land of Egypt, from the house of bondage, who did those great signs in our sight, and preserved us in all the way that we went and among all the people through whom we passed. And the LORD drove out from before us all the people, including the Amorites who dwelt in the land. We also will serve the LORD, for He is our God." But Joshua said to the people, "You cannot serve the LORD, for He is a holy God. He is a jealous God; He will not forgive your transgressions nor your sins. If you forsake the LORD and serve foreign gods, then He will turn and do you harm and consume you, after He has done you good." (Joshua 24:16–20)*

E. Hannah's prayer: God answered the prayer of barren Hannah and raised up a prophet to bring His revelation to the people. God left the witness of His Presence in the midst of the people, using the prophet Samuel to declare His Word and demonstrate His power.

And Hannah prayed and said: "My heart rejoices in the LORD; my horn is exalted in the LORD. I smile at my enemies, because I rejoice in Your salvation. No one is holy like the LORD, for there is none besides You, nor is there any rock like our God." (1 Samuel 2:1–2)

So Samuel grew, and the LORD was with him and let none of his words fall to the ground. And all Israel from Dan to Beersheba knew that Samuel had been established as a prophet of the LORD. Then the LORD appeared again in Shiloh. For the LORD revealed Himself to Samuel in Shiloh by the word of the LORD. And the word of Samuel came to all Israel. Now Israel went out to battle against the Philistines, and encamped beside Ebenezer; and the Philistines encamped in Aphek. (1 Samuel 3:19–4:1)

XI. WORSHIPING THE BEAUTY OF HOLINESS—SINGING TO THE GLORY

David inaugurated a new season of revelation. David encountered the Holy, and God gave David plans for a new tabernacle. The holiness of God was not to be forever separated by veils. The tabernacle of David made known that Yahweh desired to be in the presence of His people, to be looked upon and worshipped night and day in song.

A.   The formation of the tabernacle of David: the establishment of David's tabernacle was unfathomable to the Israelites. God strictly prohibited everyone from entering the Holy of Holies and looking upon the Ark of the Covenant, for above the mercy seat His glory would appear. In fact, the high priest was allowed to enter the most holy chamber only once a year, and only after he had atoned for his personal and household sins. Upon entering the Holy of Holies, the high priest would have to create a smoky barrier of incense to protect himself from the glory of the Lord over the mercy seat as he atoned for the sins of the people.

You shall put the mercy seat on top of the ark, and in the ark you shall put the Testimony that I will give you. And there I will meet with you, and I will speak with you from above the mercy seat, from between the two cherubim which are on the ark of the Testimony, about everything which I will give you in commandment to the children of Israel. (Exodus 25:21–22, emphasis added)

And the Lord said to Moses: **"Tell Aaron your brother not to come at just any time into the Holy Place inside the veil, before the mercy seat which is on the ark, lest he die; for I will appear in the cloud above the mercy seat** *... Then he shall take a censer full of burning coals of fire from the altar before the Lord, with his hands full of sweet incense beaten fine, and bring it inside the veil. And* **he shall put the incense on the fire before the Lord, that the cloud of incense may cover the mercy seat that is on the Testimony, lest he die."** *(Leviticus 16:2,12–13, emphasis added)*

"Consider now, for the Lord has chosen you to build a house for the sanctuary; be strong, and do it." Then David gave his son Solomon the plans for the vestibule, its houses, its treasuries, its upper chambers, its inner chambers, and the place of the mercy seat; and the plans for all that he had by the Spirit, of the courts of the house of the Lord, of all the chambers all around, of the treasuries of the house of God, and of the treasuries for the dedicated things; also for the division of the priests and the Levites, for all the work of the service of the house of the Lord, and for all the articles of service in the house of the Lord *... "All this," said David, "the Lord made me understand in writing, by His hand upon me, all the works of these plans." (1 Chronicles 28:10–13,19, emphasis added)*

For the LORD is great and greatly to be praised; **He is also to be feared above all gods.** *For all the gods of the peoples are idols, but the LORD made the heavens.* **Honor and majesty are before Him; Strength and gladness are in His place.** *Give to the LORD, O families of the peoples, give to the LORD glory and strength. Give to the LORD the glory due His name; bring an offering, and come before Him.* **Oh, worship the LORD in the beauty of holiness! Tremble before Him, all the earth.** *The world also is firmly established, it shall not be moved. (1 Chronicles 16:25–30, emphasis added)*

B.   The Psalms of the Beautiful and the Majestic

1.   *Yet I have set My King on My holy hill of Zion. I will declare the decree: the LORD has said to Me, "You are My Son, today I have begotten You. Ask of Me, and I will give You the nations for Your inheritance, and the ends of the earth for Your possession." (Psalm 2:6–8)*

2.   *The LORD is in His holy temple, the LORD's throne is in heaven; His eyes behold, His eyelids test the sons of men. (Psalm 11:4)*

3.   *But You are holy, enthroned in the praises of Israel. Our fathers trusted in You; they trusted, and You delivered them. (Psalm 22:3–4)*

4.   *Give unto the LORD the glory due to His name; worship the LORD in the beauty of holiness. The voice of the LORD is over the waters; the God of glory thunders; the LORD is over many waters. (Psalm 29:2–3)*

5.   *God reigns over the nations; God sits on His holy throne. (Psalm 47:8)*

6.   *God has spoken in His holiness: "I will rejoice; I will divide Shechem and measure out the Valley of Succoth." (Psalm 60:6)*

7.   *The floods have lifted up, O LORD, the floods have lifted up their voice; the floods lift up their waves. The LORD on high is mightier than the noise of many waters, than the mighty waves of the sea. Your testimonies are very sure; holiness adorns Your house, O LORD, forever. (Psalm 93:3–5)*

8.   *Oh, worship the* Lord *in the beauty of holiness! Tremble before Him, all the earth. (Psalm 96:9)*

9.   *Clouds and darkness surround Him; righteousness and justice are the foundation of His throne. A fire goes before Him, and burns up His enemies round about. His lightnings light the world; the earth sees and trembles. The mountains melt like wax at the presence of the* Lord, *at the presence of the Lord of the whole earth. The heavens declare His righteousness, and all the peoples see His glory … Rejoice in the* Lord, *you righteous, and give thanks at the remembrance of His holy name. (Psalm 97:2–6,12)*

10.   *Oh, sing to the* Lord *a new song! For He has done marvelous things; His right hand and His holy arm have gained Him the victory. The* Lord *has made known His salvation; His righteousness He has revealed in the sight of the nations. (Psalm 98:1–2)*

11.   *The* Lord *reigns; let the peoples tremble! He dwells between the cherubim; let the earth be moved! The* Lord *is great in Zion, and He is high above all the peoples. Let them praise Your great and awesome name—He is holy. (Psalm 99:1–3)*

12.   *Glory in His holy name; let the hearts of those rejoice who seek the* Lord*! (Psalm 105:3)*

13.   Announcement of the Messiah's Reign (Matthew 22:44; Acts 2:34–35)

      The Lord *said to my Lord, "Sit at My right hand, till I make Your enemies Your footstool." The* Lord *shall send the rod of Your strength out of Zion. Rule in the midst of Your enemies! (Psalm 110:1–2)*

14.   *He has sent redemption to His people; He has commanded His covenant forever: Holy and awesome is His name. (Psalm 111:9)*

15.   *I will meditate on the glorious splendor of Your majesty, and on Your wondrous works. Men shall speak of the might of Your awesome acts, and I will declare Your greatness. (Psalm 145:5–6)*

XII. ISAIAH—THE PROPHET OF THE BEAUTY OF THE LORD

A.   Isaiah is the prophet of the beauty of the Lord. He gives more insight into the Messiah's nature, identity, and mission (in this age and the next) than any other Old Testament prophet. "The expectation of Messiah is so strong in Isaiah, that Jerome to *Paulinus* calls his book not a prophecy, but the *gospel:* 'He is not so much a prophet as an evangelist.'" [5] I would dare say that no other biblical work compares with the Book of Isaiah's glorious picture of the restoration of Israel and the Messiah's millennial reign. Unlike any other prophet, Isaiah saw the Lord Jesus in His exalted majesty, His shameless humility, and His anointed kingship. He saw that Jesus' role is to end wickedness and fulfill the Father's purpose for all of creation—the bringing together in Christ of all things both in heaven and on the earth (Ephesians 1:9–10). Jesus comes to us in Isaiah with many faces.

B.   Isaiah 2:1–4: God gave Isaiah a glimpse of Jerusalem's final restoration and destiny under the theocratic rule of the Lord. God will use Israel in a royal and priestly function to release His glory to the rest of the nations. Under God's rule, the Law of the Lord for every arena of life will go forth from Zion. The nations will stream into Jerusalem to understand His ways and receive His wise counsel in all facets of life. Jesus is only hinted at here. Isaiah 4, 9, and 11 fill in the blanks, letting us know that Yahweh's rule is carried forth through the Branch of the Lord, who is both a human and the Mighty God. This Messianic King, who is God in the flesh, will lead a literal world-wide government from Jerusalem. His government will instruct the nations in every sphere of life and judge the course of nations. Righteousness and peace will be taught through the word of the Lord and enforced through His swift justice.

C.   Isaiah 4:2–6: the Branch in all His glory is the One orchestrating all things. It is His Day, and He is doing everything for Israel's good. He will cleanse the nation, including the daughters of Zion. Isaiah prophesied that the Branch will cleanse, save, establish, protect, and prosper Israel. Like Moses did in the Exodus, the Branch will free the remnant and lead Israel's religious and governmental expression in a new season of redemptive history. The cloud by day and fire by night that were present in the Exodus will be a bridal canopy over the nation. The Branch will be seen as beautiful, glorious, excellent, and appealing by the remnant and those in Jerusalem who have survived the Antichrist's persecution. Jesus' person and work will be admired as He saves and establishes a world-wide government from Zion.

---

5   Jamieson, R., Fausset, A. R., & Brown, D. "Isaiah." *A Commentary, Critical and Explanatory, on the Old and New Testaments*. Oak Harbor, WA: Logos Research Systems, Inc., 1997.

1. "In that day the Branch of the LORD shall be beautiful and glorious; and the fruit of the earth shall be excellent and appealing for those of Israel who have escaped" (Isaiah 4:2). This is the four-fold splendor of the God-Man: He is beautiful, glorious, excellent, and appealing. Isaiah listed four characteristics of Jesus that are experienced and enjoyed by the survivors in Jerusalem. These characteristics display both the intrinsic and extrinsic qualities of the God-Man. He will literally be the boast of all Jerusalem.

2. He will externally manifest all the intrinsic glory of His Father when He returns. Light will literally adorn Him.

   Then they will see the Son of Man coming in a cloud with power and great glory. *(Luke 21:27, emphasis added)*

   For the Son of Man will come in the glory of His Father with His angels, and then He will reward each according to his works. *(Matthew 16:27, emphasis added)*

   The city had no need of the sun or of the moon to shine in it, for the glory of God illuminated it. ***The Lamb is its light.*** *(Revelation 21:23, emphasis added)*

   Then the moon will be disgraced and the sun ashamed; for the LORD of hosts will reign on Mount Zion and in Jerusalem and before His elders, gloriously. *(Isaiah 24:23, emphasis added)*

3. The extrinsic features of His rule will be the boast of the whole earth. He will govern with such wisdom and kindness that peace and righteousness will burst forth in all the earth. The brilliance of His leadership and the weight of His authority will be displayed as He rules the nations from Zion. On that day, the survivors will honor and love Him.

D. Isaiah's commission: Isaiah 6:1–3 and John 12:41

In the year that King Uzziah died, I saw the LORD sitting on a throne, high and lifted up, and the train of His robe filled the temple. Above it stood seraphim; each one had six wings: with two he covered his face, with two he covered his feet, and with two he flew. And one cried to another and said: "Holy, holy, holy is the LORD of hosts; the whole earth is full of His glory!" (Isaiah 6:1–3)

These things Isaiah said when he saw His glory and spoke of Him. (John 12:41)

1. In the year King Uzziah died, Isaiah was invited into the Holy. It was the day of commissioning into the office of a prophet. It was the day that Isaiah was swept up into God. It was the day beauty left His mark upon Isaiah.

2. Isaiah saw the King in all of His glory. Isaiah told of the throne, the height of His glory, and the vastness of His robe's train, but the brilliance of the King Himself was beyond his words. The description of the King escaped him. This is the loftiest of all subjects—God Himself. How do you describe eternal greatness and glory, unending majesty, self-replenishing beauty and grandeur? How do you speak of the primal, raw, uncreated, original Deity? Isaiah could mention the expanse of the glory filling the heavenly Temple, but he could not yet utter the holiest words of all. As of yet, he could not speak of the King Himself. He was beholding Someone so beautiful and terrifying that he could only describe the surroundings. Words failed him. He simply did not have the capacity to speak these holy words.

3. The Seraphim: literally, "burning ones." Isaiah's eyes were drawn above the heavenly throne to the seraphim, the burning ones who are filled with revelation. They are consecrated by revelation for the purpose of giving witness. They give the heavenly, governmental witness of the King on His throne to the rest of creation.

4. After seeing the King, the Lord of Hosts, Isaiah realized that his witness and the witness of his nation were not consistent with the Holy One. Whatever was spoken in the past did not produce reverence or the weight of holiness. That witness did not invoke the majestic Presence. It shook nothing. It provoked nothing.

5.　　He saw the beautiful, and he realized that the paltry, famished theological prayers, songs, and sermons of his day, which were laced with pride, accusation, and unbelief, had not given the Holy One the witness due His name. Isaiah cried out, "Woe is me!" He was saying, "I am destroyed. I am dead, consumed by Someone greater than I ever imagined." He cried out for cleanness of speech. He would not accuse. **He would not speak less of God than what God truly is, and he would not speak more of man than what man truly is in his sinfulness.**

6.　　A Burning One took a coal from the altar and touched Isaiah's lips. His sin was atoned for. He was not destroyed. Divine love kept him alive.

7.　　Isaiah saw the Holy. He glimpsed the King in His glorious majesty and heard the unfallen, uncompromised testimony of Heaven. He saw the depths of humanity's iniquity, their absolute inability to see God in His greatness, in His transcendent beauty. Finally, he discovered the kindness of the King—the gap between humanity and God is closed through atonement. Isaiah was now prepared for intercession. Now he was ready to go, and not a second before.

E.　　Isaiah 9:6–7, 11:1–16: Immanuel will come to both Ephraim and Judah. A land which has suffered great distress from the Lord will receive the greatest promise of all. A Child from the House of David will come forth and establish the theocratic kingdom from Jerusalem. He will be both David's ancestor and Almighty God, the root and the offspring of David. Immanuel will shatter the yoke of the oppressor, deliver Jerusalem, gather the remnant, judge the nations, and rule the earth with righteousness and justice forever. Peace will be restored in creation and among the nations as the "earth shall be full of the knowledge of the Lord as the waters cover the sea" (Isaiah 11:9). He will be called Wonderful Counselor, Almighty God, Everlasting Father, and Prince of Peace. He will be anointed with the seven-fold Spirit of God to redeem Israel and rule over the nations. All the earth will rejoice and the children of Israel will proclaim, "Behold, God is my salvation, I will trust and not be afraid; 'For Yᴀʜ, the Lᴏʀᴅ, is my strength and song; He also has become my salvation'" (Isaiah 12:2).

F.   Isaiah 24:21–23: "In that day"—the appointed Day, referring to the climax of this age and the transition into the next. It is the appointed day for giving account. The wicked shall be punished and the righteous shall be rewarded with the Lord's very presence in Jerusalem. The Lord of Hosts will reign on Mount Zion. He shall punish both the spiritual powers of darkness and the earthly powers of darkness. The Lord of Hosts, as the Davidic King, will be present in Jerusalem, ruling gloriously before His elders. This is physical and actual. No longer is God's presence manifested only in the glory resting over the mercy seat. It is the Lord as the Davidic King, Immanuel, who will rule from His throne on Zion. This reign will be glorious. The canopy of light and glory will serve as a covering over all of Israel. Isaiah 4:2–6 is established.

G.   Isaiah 28:5: Jesus is seen as the crown and diadem for the people.

In that day the LORD of hosts will be for a crown of glory and a diadem of beauty to the remnant of His people. (Isaiah 28:5)

H.   Isaiah 32:1–4: As the King, Jesus will reign in righteousness and bring Israel into the knowledge of God.

I.   Isaiah 40:5: God is jealous to unfold and unveil His glory before all the nations of the earth. He is going to display His glory in the coming of His Son. Forerunners (end-time messengers) will declare the knowledge of God and His intention to glorify His Son. Jesus, who is the demonstration of the beauty of holiness and the consummation of all perfection, will demonstrate His Father's glory when He returns to Planet Earth. God will put on the ultimate light show at the end of the age with the coming of His Son, and all flesh will see it together. See Joel 2:30–31; Matthew 16:27, 24:29–31; 1 Thessalonians 4:16–17; 2 Thessalonians 1:7–10; Jude 14; Revelation 1:7, 6:12, 19:11–16.

J. Isaiah 42:1–13: Jesus is the Servant of the Lord. He is the Lord's Chosen One in whom His soul delights. He will have the Lord's very Spirit upon Him, and through gentleness He will bring forth justice and righteousness for the whole world. The Servant will not use His strength in inappropriate ways. He will not snuff out the weak and oppressed; rather, by the Spirit of the Lord, He will use His strength to help the weak and oppressed of the earth. He will not rule through political maneuvering and coercive power. He will come as a servant. Walking in the way of meekness, He will receive the promise of Psalm 37:11. His mission is broad and determined: to bring justice to the ends of the earth. He will not fail nor be discouraged till it is accomplished. The gentle, meek Servant shall ultimately manifest Himself to the nations of the earth as a conquering King. The Conquering Servant will end His season of restraint and set the nations free from their blindness, darkness, and oppression caused by worshipping idols.

K. Isaiah has seen the King in all of His glory, but he has no frame of reference for what is coming next. At the core of God's heart is a meek ruler. Yes, He shatters the enemy and breaks the bow and the spear. Yes, He will usher in the greatest reign of glory on the earth. Yet the enemy lurks within the court, and the adversary is much closer than national boundaries. The people of the covenant are against Him! Will righteousness and justice Himself oppose the promise God made to Israel? The Gentile king Cyrus may deliver Israel from Babylon (Isaiah 41–48), but who will deliver Israel from Israel? Who will save Judah from Judah? How can the Lord, the King of righteousness, fulfill the promise He made to a rebellious people who do not receive correction? His Son is the answer. Isaiah shouted from the rooftops that another world ruler is coming; through this Servant, the God of all power and glory would provide atonement (Isaiah 49–57). The King destined for glory will first become a servant and bear the iniquities of many (52:13–53:12).

L. Isaiah 49:1–13: Jesus is the Servant of rulers who is called to His purpose from the womb. His ministry is at first despised and abhorred. His ministry will appear to be in vain, but the Father promises to give Him as a covenant to Israel and to the nations. He will restore the earth.

M. Isaiah 52:13–53:12: Jesus is beautifully seen as the tender shoot who grows up among the people, only to become the Man of sorrows who makes atonement for sin through His death. He will bear the reproach of the nation and die for the sin of humanity. Yet the Father will raise Him to life and exalt His name above every name. Jesus, as the Lamb, will justify many and be exalted to the highest place.

N.   What Israel, as the servant of the Lord, could not fulfill for the nations, God Himself will execute (Isaiah 58–66). From Judah's lowly state, a Servant will come forth. From an unexpected vantage point—the lowliest of places—a Ruler will serve the hearts of men and women. Though despised and rejected, the One who could not keep Himself alive will not only restore the fortunes of Zion, but will open the gate of salvation to all the nations of the earth. The meek one will remove transgression from Jacob and make a way for foreigners to enter into the House of the Lord. Israel is getting prepared for a grand purpose. A King is coming, and Israel will walk in unprecedented glory, but first Israel must learn what it means to be a servant. A Servant King is coming and will save Israel from transgression, open a way for the Gentiles to know God, and usher in all that the prophets have spoken.

O.   Isaiah 59:16–21: Jesus, as the arm of the Lord, is coming to Zion again. This time He is coming not as the Servant to atone for sin, but as the Anointed Conqueror. He will serve by delivering Israel from her blindness and by glorifying her in order to bring redemption to the nations.

P.   Isaiah 61:1–9: Jesus is portrayed as the Anointed One who redeems Israel from her devastation. Healing, deliverance, salvation, righteousness and praise will be the result of His millennial ministry.

Q.   Isaiah 63:1–6: As the Anointed Conqueror, Jesus is revealed in His glory and terrifying power as He rids the earth of iniquity in the battle of Armageddon. In the last days, we will see the fury of the Bridegroom as He removes the power of Satan from the planet. The Lion of the tribe of Judah will triumph over all the works of darkness. This is the premeditated and predetermined plan of God. The fury of the Bridegroom is not an outburst of rage from a weak-willed Man. **This is a calculated strike against the kingdom of darkness. God's passion and power will explode against darkness with His full control and His wise administration of perfect justice.** God has prophesied about this event for six thousand years; the Bible pictures Him as a Lion ready to pounce upon His prey. Jesus alone has the resolve and the courage to do what is necessary to completely remove evil from the human experience. He is mighty to establish His government of love and goodness on Earth once and for all. His actions are the consummation of Calvary, not contradictory to Calvary. He will finish what He began on Calvary.

R. The many faces of Jesus in Isaiah: the Branch of the Lord; Adonai; the Exalted King; the Holy, Holy, Holy; the Lord of Hosts; Immanuel; a Stumbling Stone; a Rock of Offense; Wonderful Counselor; Almighty God; Everlasting Father; Prince of Peace; Root of Jesse; a Banner to the Nations; Gatherer of the Remnant/Outcasts; Holy One of Israel; Righteous One; Crown of Glory; a Diadem of Beauty; a Stone; the King Reigning in Righteousness; the King in His Beauty; Judge; Lawgiver; Savior; Glory of the Lord; Excellency of our God; Shepherd; Redeemer; Servant; God's Elect One; Yahweh; Warrior; Light to the Gentiles; Despised by Man; Mighty One of Jacob; Arm of the Lord; Tender Plant; Man of Sorrows; Smitten by God; God's Righteous Servant; Maker; Husband; High and Lofty One; Zealous Warrior; Everlasting Light; Anointed One; the Speaker of Righteousness; the Trampler of the Nations; Angel of God's Presence; the Glory of Israel and the Glory of the Nations.

XIII. THE LOSS OF THE KNOWLEDGE OF GOD

A. How far we have fallen from the garden. We have lost communion. We have lost the place of encounter. We have lost the ability to tend the place of encounter. We have lost the ability to rightly perceive God and reflect His glory.

B. As God continued to unveil Himself to the nation of Israel, even they could not remember their encounters. They could not remember the knowledge of the glory of God, and they could not maintain the witness of His glory to the earth. God's contention with humanity has always revolved around the knowledge of who He is and the response of worship that should be—but often is not—commensurate with the beauty revealed to His people.

> *But Jeshurun grew fat and kicked; you grew fat, you grew thick, you are obese!* ***Then he forsook God who made him****, and scornfully esteemed the Rock of his salvation. They provoked Him to jealousy with foreign gods; with abominations they provoked Him to anger. They sacrificed to demons, not to God, to gods they did not know, to new gods, new arrivals that your fathers did not fear. Of the Rock who begot you, you are unmindful, and have forgotten the God who fathered you. And when the* LORD *saw it, He spurned them, because of the provocation of His sons and His daughters. (Deuteronomy 32:15–19, emphasis added)*

*So the children of Israel did evil in the sight of the LORD. **They forgot the LORD their God**, and served the Baals and Asherahs. (Judges 3:7, emphasis added)*

*And when **they forgot the LORD their God,** He sold them into the hand of Sisera, commander of the army of Hazor, into the hand of the Philistines, and into the hand of the king of Moab; and they fought against them. (1 Samuel 12:9, emphasis added)*

*And **forgot His works And His wonders** that He had shown them. (Psalm 78:11, emphasis added)*

***They forgot God their Savior**, who had done great things in Egypt. (Psalm 106:21, emphasis added)*

*"I will punish her for the days of the Baals to which she burned incense. She decked herself with her earrings and jewelry, and went after her lovers; b**ut Me she forgot**," says the LORD. (Hosea 2:13, emphasis added)*

***My people are destroyed for lack of knowledge**. Because you have rejected knowledge, I also will reject you from being priest for Me; because you have forgotten the law of your God, I also will forget your children. (Hosea 4:6, emphasis added)*

***For Israel has forgotten his Maker**, and has built temples; Judah also has multiplied fortified cities; but I will send fire upon his cities, and it shall devour his palaces. (Hosea 8:14, emphasis added)*

*When they had pasture, they were filled; they were filled and their heart was exalted; therefore **they forgot Me.** (Hosea 13:6, emphasis added)*

*And **no one considers in his heart, nor is there knowledge nor understanding** to say, "I have burned half of it in the fire, yes, I have also baked bread on its coals; I have roasted meat and eaten it; and shall I make the rest of it an abomination? Shall I fall down before a block of wood?" (Isaiah 44:19, emphasis added)*

*Can a virgin forget her ornaments, or a bride her attire? **Yet My people have forgotten Me days without number.** (Jeremiah 2:32, emphasis added)*

*A voice was heard on the desolate heights, weeping and supplications of the children of Israel. For **they have perverted their way; they have forgotten the LORD their God**. (Jeremiah 3:21, emphasis added)*

Everyone is dull-hearted, without knowledge; every metalsmith is put to shame by an image; for his molded image is falsehood, and there is no breath in them. (Jeremiah 10:14, emphasis added)

*"This is your lot, the portion of your measures from Me," says the Lord, "Because **you have forgotten Me and trusted in falsehood.**" (Jeremiah 13:25, emphasis added)*

*Because **My people have forgotten Me**, they have burned incense to worthless idols. And they have caused themselves to stumble in their ways, from the ancient paths, to walk in pathways and not on a highway. (Jeremiah 18:15, emphasis added)*

***My people have been lost sheep.** Their shepherds have led them astray; they have turned them away on the mountains. They have gone from mountain to hill; **they have forgotten their resting place**. (Jeremiah 50:6, emphasis added)*

*"In you they take bribes to shed blood; you take usury and increase; you have made profit from your neighbors by extortion, and **have forgotten Me**," says the Lord God. (Ezekiel 22:12, emphasis added)*

*Therefore thus says the Lord God: **"Because you have forgotten Me and cast Me behind your back, therefore you shall bear the penalty of your lewdness and your harlotry."** (Ezekiel 23:35, emphasis added)*

XIV. PROPHETIC HOPE

A. The prophets began to prophesy of a time when the knowledge of God would be restored to the nation of Israel, even affecting the Gentile nations and all of created order. They foretold that God would establish a new covenant, which would entail the forgiveness of sins and the knowledge of God placed within the hearts of men forever.

B. This new covenant would be established by a descendant of David, an anointed one who would sit on the throne of his father David in Jerusalem, establishing a world-wide government of peace between the nations. Through this Davidic ruler, the priestly and kingly ministries would function together to reestablish the government of God throughout the whole earth, bringing the nations into the worship of Yahweh and restoring creation through the knowledge of God.

The word that Isaiah the son of Amoz saw concerning Judah and Jerusalem. Now it shall come to pass in the latter days **that the mountain of the LORD's house shall be established on the top of the mountains, and shall be exalted above the hills; and all nations shall flow to it. Many people shall come and say, "Come, and let us go up to the mountain of the LORD, to the house of the God of Jacob; He will teach us His ways, and we shall walk in His paths."** *For out of Zion shall go forth the law, and the word of the LORD from Jerusalem. (Isaiah 2:1–3, emphasis added)*

For unto **us a Child is born, unto us a Son is given; and the government will be upon His shoulder. And His name will be called Wonderful, Counselor, Mighty God, Everlasting Father, Prince of Peace. Of the increase of His government and peace there will be no end, upon the throne of David and over His kingdom, to order it and establish it with judgment and justice from that time forward, even forever.** *The zeal of the Lord of hosts will perform this. (Isaiah 9:6–7, emphasis added)*

There shall come forth a Rod from the stem of Jesse, and a Branch shall grow out of his roots. The Spirit of the LORD shall rest upon Him, the Spirit of wisdom and understanding, the Spirit of counsel and might, the Spirit of knowledge and of the fear of the LORD. *His delight is in the fear of the LORD, and He shall not judge by the sight of His eyes, nor decide by the hearing of His ears. (Isaiah 11:1–3, emphasis added)*

They shall not hurt nor destroy in all My holy mountain, **for the earth shall be full of the knowledge of the LORD as the waters cover the sea. And in that day there shall be a Root of Jesse, who shall stand as a banner to the people; for the Gentiles shall seek Him, and His resting place shall be glorious.** *(Isaiah 11:9–10, emphasis added)*

Behold, a king will reign in righteousness, *and princes will rule with justice. A man will be as a hiding place from the wind, and a cover from the tempest, as rivers of water in a dry place, as the shadow of a great rock in a weary land. The eyes of those who see will not be dim, and the ears of those who hear will listen.* **Also the heart of the rash will understand knowledge, and the tongue of the stammerers will be ready to speak plainly.** *(Isaiah 32:1–4, emphasis added)*

He shall see the labor of His soul, and be satisfied. **By His knowledge My righteous Servant shall justify many, for He shall bear their iniquities.** *(Isaiah 53:11, emphasis added)*

*"The Redeemer will come to Zion, and to those who turn from transgression in Jacob," says the L*ORD. *"As for Me," says the L*ORD, *"this is My covenant with them: My Spirit who is upon you, and My words which I have put in your mouth, shall not depart from your mouth, nor from the mouth of your descendants, nor from the mouth of your descendants' descendants," says the L*ORD, *"from this time and forevermore."* (Isaiah 59:20–21, emphasis added)

Now it shall come to pass in the latter days **that the mountain of the L**ORD'**s house shall be established on the top of the mountains, and shall be exalted above the hills; and peoples shall flow to it. Many nations shall come and say, "Come, and let us go up to the mountain of the L**ORD, **to the house of the God of Jacob; He will teach us His ways, and we shall walk in His paths." For out of Zion the law shall go forth, and the word of the L**ORD **from Jerusalem.** *(Micah 4:1–2, emphasis added)*

Now gather yourself in troops, O daughter of troops; He has laid siege against us; they will strike the judge of Israel with a rod on the cheek. **"But you, Bethlehem Ephrathah, though you are little among the thousands of Judah, yet out of you shall come forth to Me the One to be Ruler in Israel, whose goings forth are from of old, from everlasting."** *Therefore He shall give them up, until the time that she who is in labor has given birth; then the remnant of His brethren shall return to the children of Israel.* **And He shall stand and feed His flock in the strength of the L**ORD, **in the majesty of the name of the L**ORD **His God; and they shall abide, for now He shall be great to the ends of the earth; and this One shall be peace.** *When the Assyrian comes into our land, and when he treads in our palaces, then we will raise against him seven shepherds and eight princely men.* (Micah 5:1–5, emphasis added)

And I will give you shepherds according to My heart, who will feed you with knowledge and understanding. *(Jeremiah 3:15, emphasis added)*

*Behold, the days are coming, says the L*ORD*, when **I will make a new covenant with the house of Israel and with the house of Judah***—not according to the covenant that I made with their fathers in the day that I took them by the hand to lead them out of the land of Egypt, My covenant which they broke, though I was a husband to them, says the L*ORD*. **But this is the covenant that I will make with the house of Israel after those days, says the L*ORD*: I will put My law in their minds, and write it on their hearts; and I will be their God, and they shall be My people. No more shall every man teach his neighbor, and every man his brother, saying, "Know the L*ORD*," for they all shall know Me, from the least of them to the greatest of them, says the L*ORD*. For I will forgive their iniquity, and their sin I will remember no more.** (Jeremiah 31:31–34, emphasis added)*

*F**or the earth will be filled with the knowledge of the glory of the L*ORD*, as the waters cover the sea.** (Habakkuk 2:14, emphasis added)*

XV. A VOICE CRYING IN THE WILDERNESS—"PREPARE YE THE WAY OF THE LORD"

A. God prophesied through Amos that a day was coming when God would send a famine of His Word to the land of Israel. Thus, for over four hundred years prior to the coming of John the Baptist, no prophets prophesied. For the vast majority of these years, Israel was ruled by foreign powers with no Davidic king in place, no ark with the Shekinah glory resting over the mercy seat in the rebuilt Temple, and no prophet speaking God's word and direction to the people.

*"Behold, the days are coming," says the Lord G*OD*, "that I will send a famine on the land, not a famine of bread, nor a thirst for water, but of hearing the words of the L*ORD*. They shall wander from sea to sea, and from north to east; they shall run to and fro, seeking the word of the L*ORD*, but shall not find it."* (Amos 8:11–12)

B. In this context of silence—of foreign domination, priestly perversion, and a non-Davidic king named Herod on Rome's puppet throne—the word of the Lord came to John in the wilderness. John called the nation of Israel to repent of its sins as preparation for the coming Davidic King foretold by the prophets, the One who would redeem Israel from her sins and establish the kingdom of God on earth.

*Blessed is the Lord God of Israel, for He has visited and redeemed His people, and has **raised up a horn of salvation for us in the house of His servant David, as He spoke by the mouth of His holy prophets, who have been since the world began, that we should be saved from our enemies and from the hand of all who hate us, to perform the mercy promised to our fathers and to remember His holy covenant, the oath which He swore to our father Abraham: to grant us that we, being delivered from the hand of our enemies, might serve Him without fear, in holiness and righteousness before Him all the days of our life. And you, child, will be called the prophet of the Highest; for you will go before the face of the Lord to prepare His ways, to give knowledge of salvation to His people by the remission of their sins,** through the tender mercy of our God, with which the Dayspring from on high has visited us; to give light to those who sit in darkness and the shadow of death, to guide our feet into the way of peace. (Luke 1:68–79, emphasis added)*

*Now in the fifteenth year of the reign of Tiberius Caesar, Pontius Pilate being governor of Judea, Herod being tetrarch of Galilee, his brother Philip tetrarch of Iturea and the region of Trachonitis, and Lysanias tetrarch of Abilene, while Annas and Caiaphas were high priests, **the word of God came to John the son of Zacharias in the wilderness.** And he went into all the region around the Jordan, **preaching a baptism of repentance for the remission of sins, as it is written in the book of the words of Isaiah the prophet, saying: "The voice of one crying in the wilderness: 'Prepare the way of the Lord; make His paths straight.*** Every valley shall be filled and every mountain and hill brought low; the crooked places shall be made straight and the rough ways smooth; and all flesh shall see the salvation of God.'" (Luke 3:1–6, emphasis added)*

There was a man sent from God, whose name was John. This man came for a witness, to bear witness of the Light, that all through him might believe. He was not that Light, but was sent to bear witness of that Light. *(John 1:6–8, emphasis added)*

And the Word became flesh and dwelt among us, and we beheld His glory, the glory as of the only begotten of the Father, full of grace and truth. **John bore witness of Him and cried out, saying, "This was He of whom I said, 'He who comes after me is preferred before me, for He was before me.'"** *And of His fullness we have all received, and grace for grace. For the law was given through Moses, but grace and truth came through Jesus Christ. No one has seen God at any time. The only begotten Son, who is in the bosom of the Father, He has declared Him. (John 1:14–18, emphasis added)*

John answered them, saying, "I baptize with water, but there stands One among you whom you do not know. It is He who, coming after me, is preferred before me, whose sandal strap I am not worthy to loose." These things were done in Bethabara beyond the Jordan, where John was baptizing. The next day John saw Jesus coming toward him, and said, "Behold! The Lamb of God who takes away the sin of the world! This is He of whom I said, 'After me comes a Man who is preferred before me, for He was before me.' I did not know Him; but that He should be revealed to Israel, therefore I came baptizing with water." And John bore witness, saying, "I saw the Spirit descending from heaven like a dove, and He remained upon Him. I did not know Him, but He who sent me to baptize with water said to me, 'Upon whom you see the Spirit descending, and remaining on Him, this is He who baptizes with the Holy Spirit.' And I have seen and testified that this is the Son of God. **Again, the next day, John stood with two of his disciples. And looking at Jesus as He walked, he said, "Behold the Lamb of God!"** *The two disciples heard him speak, and they followed Jesus. (John 1:26–37, emphasis added)*

XVI. GOD REVEALS HIMSELF FULLY IN THE PERSON OF JESUS

A. *As long as God has been God (eternally) He has been conscious of Himself; and the image that He has of Himself is so perfect and so complete and so full as to be the living, personal reproduction (or begetting) of Himself. And this living personal image or radiance or form of God is God, namely God the Son. . . . God's delight in the Son is delight in Himself. The original, the primal, the deepest, the foundational joy of God is the joy He has in His own perfections as He sees them reflected in the glory of His Son. Paul speaks of "the glory of God in the face of Christ" (2 Cor. 4:6). From all eternity God had beheld the panorama of His own perfections in the face His Son. All that He is He sees reflected fully and perfectly in the countenance of His Son. And in this He rejoices with infinite joy.*[6]

---

6 Piper, John. *The Pleasures of God* (Sisters, OR: Multnomah, 2002), p. 38.

B. In the fullness of time, at the wisest point in history, God overflowed and fully revealed the delight of delights, His Son. God prepared Planet Earth and formed Israel for the unveiling of unparalleled splendor and unimaginable brightness. The Word became flesh and made His dwelling in us. The eternal Son became Jesus of Nazareth. What the Father had always so enjoyed, now men and women could enjoy, too. The object of the Father's gaze had now become the object of humanity's. "And the Word became flesh and dwelt among us, and we beheld His glory, the glory as of the only begotten of the Father, full of grace and truth" (John 1:14).

C. God's revelation to and interaction with all of creation is expressed in the person of His Son. **God will go to piercing depths to clarify Himself. Revelation took on flesh and subjected Himself to man's rejection and God's wrath. His depths must be seen! His excellencies must be displayed! They are the content of pleasures evermore, joy unspeakable.** They exemplify the vast, immense desire of God to be seen, to be looked upon, to be the object of our gaze and pleasure.

D. God, in His infinite wisdom, manifested the very radiance of His glory and the express image of Himself in Jesus. He sent His Son to be born of a virgin; to display the love and power of the Father; to be crucified, dead and buried; to descend to the depths of hell; to rise from the dead; to ascend into Heaven; to rule at the right hand of the Majesty; and to be admired and loved for all eternity by those redeemed with His own blood.

XVII. BEHOLDING CHRIST'S EXCELLENCIES AS THE WAY OF TRANSFORMATION

A. Jesus testified that He was the full revelation of the Father and the redeemer of humanity. In one Man, God summed up all things. He manifested His fullness in bodily form. He reestablished His full revelation to humanity and reestablished humanity's ability to receive and reflect the revelation of Him. God did something unprecedented, something which would make kings shut their mouths. He became focused in bodily form. From this point onward, God's depths were to be seen in the person of Jesus Christ. And through this heavenly and Davidic King, God released the knowledge of Himself throughout the whole earth.

B.   Beholding the knowledge of God in Christ Jesus is both the foundation of salvation and the way of transformation. We enter into saving faith when the revelation of Christ—who He is and what He has done—strikes our hearts, causing us to believe His testimony. We also continue in sanctifying grace as His revelation strikes our hearts, conforms our wills, renews our minds, and subdues our members for righteousness (the beholding/becoming principle).

And the Word became flesh and dwelt among us, and we beheld His glory, the glory as of the only begotten of the Father, full of grace and truth. (John 1:14, emphasis added)

You search the Scriptures, for in them you think you have eternal life; and these are they which testify of Me. (John 5:39, emphasis added)

"If you had known Me, you would have known My Father also; and from now on you know Him and have seen Him." Philip said to Him, "Lord, show us the Father, and it is sufficient for us." Jesus said to him, "Have I been with you so long, and yet you have not known Me, Philip? He who has seen Me has seen the Father; so how can you say, 'Show us the Father'? Do you not believe that I am in the Father, and the Father in Me? The words that I speak to you I do not speak on My own authority; but the Father who dwells in Me does the works. Believe Me that I am in the Father and the Father in Me, or else believe Me for the sake of the works themselves." (John 14:7–11, emphasis added)

And this is eternal life, that they may know You, the only true God, and Jesus Christ whom You have sent. (John 17:3, emphasis added)

*Father, I desire that they also whom You gave Me may be with Me where I am, **that they may behold My glory which You have given Me;** for You loved Me before the foundation of the world. (John 17:24, emphasis added)*

In that hour Jesus rejoiced in the Spirit and said, "I thank You, Father, Lord of heaven and earth, that You have hidden these things from the wise and prudent and revealed them to babes. Even so, Father, for so it seemed good in Your sight. All things have been delivered to Me by My Father, and no one knows who the Son is except the Father, and who the Father is except the Son, and the one to whom the Son wills to reveal Him." Then He turned to His disciples and said privately, **"Blessed are the eyes which see the things you see; for I tell you that many prophets and kings have desired to see what you see, and have not seen it, and to hear what you hear, and have not heard it."** *(Luke 10:21–24, emphasis added)*

But we all, with unveiled face, beholding as in a mirror the glory of the Lord, are being transformed into the same image from glory to glory, just as by the Spirit of the Lord. *(2 Corinthians 3:18, emphasis added)*

That the God of our Lord Jesus Christ, the Father of glory, **may give to you the spirit of wisdom and revelation in the knowledge of Him**. *(Ephesians 1:17, emphasis added)*

O foolish Galatians! Who has bewitched you that you should not obey the truth, **before whose eyes Jesus Christ was clearly portrayed among you as crucified?** *(Galatians 3:1, emphasis added)*

But what things were gain to me, these I have counted loss for Christ. **Yet indeed I also count all things loss for the excellence of the knowledge of Christ Jesus my Lord,** *for whom I have suffered the loss of all things, and count them as rubbish, that I may gain Christ and be found in Him, not having my own righteousness, which is from the law, but that which is through faith in Christ, the righteousness which is from God by faith; that I may know Him and the power of His resurrection, and the fellowship of His sufferings, being conformed to His death. (Philippians 3:7–10, emphasis added)*

Colossians—Paul was combating two errors: wrong ideas about (1) who the person of Jesus is and (2) the process of transformation. He addressed these two realities back to back precisely because they are intricately connected in the heart of God. By beholding the glory of the Christ Jesus, we are transformed into His likeness.

*If then you were raised with Christ, **seek those things which are above, where Christ is, sitting at the right hand of God. Set your mind on things above, not on things on the earth.** For you died, and your life is hidden with Christ in God. When Christ who is our life appears, then you also will appear with Him in glory. (Colossians 3:1–4, emphasis added)*

Hebrews 1–2:9

***God, who at various times and in various ways spoke in time past to the fathers by the prophets, has in these last days spoken to us by His Son,** whom He has appointed heir of all things, through whom also He made the worlds. (Hebrews 1:1–2, emphasis added)*

*"You have made him a little lower than the angels; You have crowned him with glory and honor, and set him over the works of Your hands. You have put all things in subjection under his feet." For in that He put all in subjection under him, He left nothing that is not put under him. **But now we do not yet see all things put under him. But we see Jesus,** who was made a little lower than the angels, for the suffering of death crowned with glory and honor, that He, by the grace of God, might taste death for everyone. (Hebrews 2:7–9, emphasis added)*

*Therefore we also, since we are surrounded by so great a cloud of witnesses, **let us lay aside every weight, and the sin which so easily ensnares us, and let us run with endurance the race that is set before us, looking unto Jesus, the author and finisher of our faith,** who for the joy that was set before Him endured the cross, despising the shame, and has sat down at the right hand of the throne of God. (Hebrews 12:1–2, emphasis added)*

***Behold what manner of love the Father has bestowed on us, that we should be called children of God!** Therefore the world does not know us, because it did not know Him. Beloved, now we are children of God; **and it has not yet been revealed what we shall be, but we know that when He is revealed, we shall be like Him, for we shall see Him as He is. And everyone who has this hope in Him purifies himself, just as He is pure.** (1 John 3:1–3, emphasis added)*

C.   The wisdom of beholding! The grand design of the eye! The eyes are the gateways of fascination. The affections of the heart follow the locked gaze of the eyes. The God of pleasure designed us to delight in that which we behold. Jesus said in Matthew 6:22–23, "The lamp of the body is the eye. If therefore your eye is good, your whole body will be full of light. But if your eye is bad, your whole body will be full of darkness. If therefore the light that is in you is darkness, how great is that darkness!" Simply put, whatever you focus your gaze on is what you become. Don't commit your gaze to anything less than the nobility of Jesus. This is why Jesus called us to consider the gravity of our lust of the eyes and the lust of the flesh in Matthew 5:29: "If your right eye causes you to sin, pluck it out and cast it from you; for it is more profitable for you that one of your members perish, than for your whole body to be cast into hell."

*For the Father loves the Son, and shows Him all things that He Himself does; and **He will show Him greater works than these, that you may marvel.** (John 5:20, emphasis added)*

D.   The beholding/becoming principle: the first step into holy, violent love is to fix the adoring gaze of the heart on the person of Jesus. It takes fierce determination to believe that we can commune with the Almighty, for the many enemies of the soul try to subvert this process of God revealing God to the human heart. We can live our lives doing religious services and exercises, yet never gazing, never adoring the object of worship. We were made for encounter, for experiencing the presence and depths of God. Even fragments of revelation are enough to transform and thrill the human heart. Dim glimpses of God are enough to fascinate the heart, transform the mind, and apprehend the will to gaze on glory.

Now the Lord is the Spirit; and where the Spirit of the Lord is, there is liberty. But we all, with unveiled face, beholding as in a mirror the glory of the Lord, are being transformed into the same image from glory to glory, just as by the Spirit of the Lord. (2 Corinthians 3:17–18)

E.   The highest pleasure of the human race is for God to reveal Himself to us. This is more pleasurable, intoxicating, wondrous, and terrifying than any other thing in the universe. We were made to experience His depths, to search the vast ocean of the Deity, to mine the treasures that all of creation longs to look into.

1.　Old Testament Scriptures demonstrate that God loves to fascinate the eyes: the garden; the calling of Abraham (Genesis 12, Acts 7:2); the burning bush (Exodus 3); the exodus (Exodus 5–15); Mount Sinai (Exodus 19, Exodus 24, Exodus 33–34); Balaam (Numbers 24:15); crossing the Jordan (Joshua 3); the whole concept of the Ark and the Tabernacle; David's Tabernacle; the angel appearing to David and the fire from Heaven (1 Chronicles 21); fire and glory at the dedication of Solomon's Temple (2 Chronicles 5–7); Mount Carmel (1 Kings 18); prophetic dreams and visions (Numbers 12); and God's encounters with Jacob, Joseph, Solomon, Isaiah, Jeremiah, Ezekiel, Daniel, Zechariah, etc. (This does not even include all of the times Jesus displayed Himself to Israel as the Angel of the Lord).

2.　Jesus: baptism of Jesus; calling of Nathanael; healings and miracles; feeding the 5,000; calming the Sea of Galilee, walking on water, and Peter walking on water; the Mount of Transfiguration; Resurrection appearances; the translation of Philip; Stephen's open vision; Saul/Paul; the Apostle John; and the Second Coming. All of His excellencies were set before the Apostles.

And they were all amazed, and they glorified God and were filled with fear, saying, **"We have seen strange things today!"** *(Luke 5:26, emphasis added)*

But He said to them, "Where is your faith?" **And they were afraid, and marveled, saying to one another, "Who can this be? For He commands even the winds and water, and they obey Him!"** *(Luke 8:25, emphasis added)*

F.　At the end of the age, God's strategy will be to unfold the splendor of His Son in such a way that lovesickness, wholeheartedness, and exploits of faith are produced in His people.

In that day **the Branch of the Lᴏʀᴅ shall be beautiful and glorious;** *and the fruit of the earth shall be excellent and appealing for those of Israel who have escaped. (Isaiah 4:2, emphasis added)*

They shall not hurt nor destroy in all My holy mountain, for the earth shall be full of the knowledge of the LORD *as the waters cover the sea. "And in that day there shall be* **a Root of Jesse, who shall stand as a banner to the people; for the Gentiles shall seek Him, and His resting place shall be glorious.***" (Isaiah 11:9–10, emphasis added)*

In that day the LORD *of hosts will be for* **a crown of glory and a diadem of beauty to the remnant of His people***. (Isaiah 28:5, emphasis added)*

Your eyes will see the King in His beauty*; they will see the land that is very far off. (Isaiah 33:17, emphasis added)*

Therefore if they say to you, "Look, He is in the desert!" do not go out; or "Look, He is in the inner rooms!" do not believe it. **For as the lightning comes from the east and flashes to the west, so also will the coming of the Son of Man be.** *For wherever the carcass is, there the eagles will be gathered together.* **Immediately after the tribulation of those days the sun will be darkened, and the moon will not give its light; the stars will fall from heaven, and the powers of the heavens will be shaken. Then the sign of the Son of Man will appear in heaven, and then all the tribes of the earth will mourn, and they will see the Son of Man coming on the clouds of heaven with power and great glory. And He will send His angels with a great sound of a trumpet, and they will gather together His elect from the four winds, from one end of heaven to the other.** *(Matthew 24:26–31, emphasis added)*

Behold, He is coming with clouds, and every eye will see Him, even they who pierced Him. And all the tribes of the earth will mourn because of Him. Even so, Amen. (Revelation 1:7)

XVIII. HEAVEN'S WITNESS—REVELATION 4 AND 5

A.   Have you ever wondered what Heaven thinks of God? Our thoughts are so cluttered, so random, so fractured that we fail to maintain a consistent mental and emotional posture towards our Maker. Oh, for the day when our minds, wills and emotions will engage the Almighty with perfect clarity, when with perfect aptitude, resolve, and affection we will look upon the One who formed us in our mother's womb! Yet, right now, what is the perfect witness of Heaven? When unfallen creatures gaze upon God, what is their response? Revelation 4 describes a door opening in Heaven. Going through that door, the beloved Apostle John found himself eavesdropping on the worship of the four living creatures around (seraphim) God's throne. They have one purpose: to gaze on God and give witness to what they see. They have eyes within and without that open and close as they plummet and mine the depths of their Maker. They peer into God's depths and give ceaseless testimony to the rest of created order about what He is like. What do they find? What do they discover?

B.   Searching God's endless being, they unanimously proclaim three times over that He is Holy. God is not only all-powerful; He is dazzling in His beauty, beyond comprehension. They shout to the rest of creation through the simplest phrase, "Holy, Holy, Holy," that there is none like God. His beauty requires their constant witness: "Your Maker is lovely and beyond anything you could ever imagine. He is infinitely more dazzling and powerful than anything in the universe. His attributes operate in true perfection. There is no flaw in Him. He has perfect symmetry, perfect harmony. He is the Lord God Almighty. He is Holy, Holy, Holy!"

C.   The governmental leaders of Heaven are described as being overcome by their own witness. They are trembling with fascination before the brilliant potency of God's being. They must fall down. They must join in. We too must hear the pure witness of Heaven. We must fall down. We must join in. For it is in this place of worship we find pleasures untold and beauty unrestrained.

XIX. SOMETHING GREATER THAN SERAPHIM—THE SPIRIT WHO SEARCHES

A. The Road to Emmaus: The resurrected Jesus took two disciples on a guided tour of the Scriptures in regard to the sufferings of the Messiah and His following glory. During the encounter, their hearts burned within them. Reading this story, many times I have wished that I could have eavesdropped on their conversation. The truth is that I can. God has sent us His Spirit who will take all that is known of Jesus and give that knowledge to us. The Spirit searches the deep things of God and freely makes them known to us.

Then He said to them, "O foolish ones, and slow of heart to believe in all that the prophets have spoken! Ought not the Christ to have suffered these things and to enter into His glory?" And beginning at Moses and all the Prophets, He expounded to them in all the Scriptures the things concerning Himself. (Luke 24:25–27)

And they said to one another, "Did not our heart burn within us while He talked with us on the road, and while He opened the Scriptures to us?" (Luke 24:32)

God, who at various times and in various ways spoke in time past to the fathers by the prophets, has in these last days spoken to us by His Son, whom He has appointed heir of all things, through whom also He made the worlds; who being the brightness of His glory and the express image of His person, and upholding all things by the word of His power, when He had by Himself purged our sins, sat down at the right hand of the Majesty on high, having become so much better than the angels, as He has by inheritance obtained a more excellent name than they. (Hebrews 1:1–4)

*But as it is written: "Eye has not seen, nor ear heard, nor have entered into the heart of man the things which God has prepared for those who love Him." **But God has revealed them to us through His Spirit. For the Spirit searches all things, yes, the deep things of God.** For what man knows the things of a man except the spirit of the man which is in him? Even so no one knows the things of God except the Spirit of God. Now we have received, not the spirit of the world, but the Spirit who is from God, that we might know the things that have been freely given to us by God. (1 Corinthians 2:9–12, emphasis added)*

But the Helper, the Holy Spirit, whom the Father will send in My name, He will teach you all things, and bring to your remembrance all things that I said to you. (John 14:26)

However, when He, the Spirit of truth, has come, He will guide you into all truth; for He will not speak on His own authority, but whatever He hears He will speak; and He will tell you things to come. He will glorify Me, for He will take of what is Mine and declare it to you. All things that the Father has are Mine. Therefore I said that He will take of Mine and declare it to you. (John 16:13–15)

B.   Revelation 19:12 tells us that Jesus even has a name that we do not yet know: "His eyes were like a flame of fire, and on His head were many crowns. He had a name written that no one knew except Himself."

XX.   PROCESS OF BEHOLDING BY FAITH

It is by beholding the glory of Christ by faith that we are spiritually edified and built up in this world, for as we behold His glory, the life and power of faith grow stronger. It is by faith that we grow to love Christ. So if we desire strong faith and powerful love, which give us rest, peace and satisfaction, we must seek them by diligently beholding the glory of Christ by faith. In this duty I desire to live and to die. On Christ's glory I would fix all my thoughts and desires, and the more I see of the glory of Christ, the more the painted beauties of this world will wither in my eyes and I will be more and more crucified to this world. It will become to me like something dead and putrid, impossible for me to enjoy.[7]

A.   Let us get it fixed in our minds that this glory of Christ in His divine-human person, is the best, the most noble and beneficial truth that we can think about or set our hearts on.[8]

---

7 Owen, John. *The Glory of Christ* (Carlisle, PA, Banner of Truth Trust, 1994), p. 7.

8 Points A-E are taken from Owen, John. *The Glory of Christ* (Carlisle, PA, Banner of Truth Trust, 1994), pp. 30-36.

The true way to improve and ennoble our souls is, by fixing our love on the divine perfections, that we may have them always before us, and derive an impression of them on ourselves, and 'beholding with open face, as in a glass, the glory of the Lord, we may be changed into the same image, from glory to glory'. He who, with a generous and holy ambition, hath raised his eyes toward that uncreated beauty and goodness, and fixed his affection there, is quite of another spirit, of a more excellent and heroic temper than the rest of the world, and cannot but infinitely disdain all mean and unworthy things; will not entertain any low or base thoughts which might disparage his high and noble pretensions.[9]

B.   Let us diligently study the Bible and the revelations of the glory of Christ revealed there, staying within safe confines—2 Corinthians 12:4 and Revelation 10:4. We must study:

   1.   Direct descriptions of His glorious Person and Incarnation.

   2.   Prophecies, promises and clear instructions concerning Him, all leading our thoughts to behold His glory.

   3.   Sacred institutions of divine worship. Types and shadows representing His Person, office or work.

   4.   Psalms, hymns and poetry

C.   Having come to the light of the knowledge of the glory of Christ from Scripture or by preaching of the Gospel, let us regard it as our duty to meditate frequently on His glory.

D.   Let your thoughts of Christ be many, increasing more and more each day.

E.   Let all our thoughts concerning Christ and His glory be accompanied with admiration, adoration and thanksgiving.

F.   Ask to behold Him in dreams, visions and visitations. Ask God to reveal Christ to you in all the many facets of divine communication. Dedicate your sleep to the Lord, asking Him to reveal His person and His ways through dreams.

---

9   Henry Scougal, *The Life of God in the Soul of Man* (Great Britain: Christian Focus Publications, reprinted in 2001), p. 69.

G.   Say "breath" prayers throughout the day, unceasingly praying to the Lord in all of the day's menial affairs.

H.   As you behold Him, worship Him with psalms, hymns and spiritual songs. Sing and pray with your mind and with your spirit. Paul tells us that when we pray and sing with our mind, we gain understanding; when we pray and sing with our spirit, we speak mysteries unto God and edify ourselves.

> *For he who speaks in a tongue does not speak to men but to God, for no one understands him; however, **in the spirit he speaks mysteries**. But he who prophesies speaks edification and exhortation and comfort to men. **He who speaks in a tongue edifies himself,** but he who prophesies edifies the church. (1 Corinthians 14:2–4, emphasis added)*

> *What is the conclusion then? I will pray with the spirit, and I will also pray with the understanding. **I will sing with the spirit, and I will also sing with the understanding.** Otherwise, if you bless with the spirit, how will he who occupies the place of the uninformed say "Amen" at your giving of thanks, since he does not understand what you say? For you indeed give thanks well, but the other is not edified. **I thank my God I speak with tongues more than you all.** (1 Corinthians 14:15–18, emphasis added)*

> *And do not be drunk with wine, in which is dissipation; but **be filled with the Spirit, speaking to one another in psalms and hymns and spiritual songs, singing and making melody in your heart to the Lord,** giving thanks always for all things to God the Father in the name of our Lord Jesus Christ. (Ephesians 5:18–20, emphasis added)*

> ***Let the word of Christ dwell in you richly in all wisdom, teaching and admonishing one another in psalms and hymns and spiritual songs, singing with grace in your hearts to the Lord.** (Colossians 3:16, emphasis added)*

> *But you, beloved, **building yourselves up on your most holy faith, praying in the Holy Spirit,** keep yourselves in the love of God, looking for the mercy of our Lord Jesus Christ unto eternal life. (Jude 20–21, emphasis added)*

Session Two: The Pre-Existence of Christ Jesus

I. THE FOUNDATION: THE TRINITY—ONE GOD IN THREE PERSONS

A. "Without the premise of pre-existence, there can be no talk of the incarnation."[1] The Incarnation necessitates that the Son previously existed. He is the only begotten, sent from the Father. His origin is from everlasting to everlasting. Jesus is the eternal God with us. As Jesus taught, He has a special relationship with the Father. To see Him is to see the Father. To hear Him is to hear the Father. To encounter Him is to encounter the Father. He tells Philip that He and the Father are One. He shocked the crowds by claiming greater authority than Abraham, and did so by asserting that He existed before Abraham existed as God Himself. "Before Abraham was, I am" (John 8:58). In the troubling hour before the Cross, He went further still and strengthened Himself in love with the memories of His eternal relationship with the Father. He reflected on the prior glory He had with the Father before the world began. He meditated on the love that the Father had for Him before the foundation of the world (John 17).

B. After the Resurrection, Jesus was worshipped and exalted as both Lord and Christ. He received the worship only given to Yahweh. Hear Thomas as he slipped his hand into the side of Jesus: "My Lord and my God!" (John 20:28). As He ascended into the heavens, they fell and worshiped Him. The minds of the five hundred Jews who saw the risen Jesus were then in a theological quandary: "He receives worship and does not stop them. How can 'the Lord thy God' be One God, yet exist now forever as the God-Man?"

---

1 Oden, Thomas. *The Word of Life, Systematic Theology: Volume Two* (1st HarperCollins paperback ed. San Francisco, CA: HarperSanFrancisco, 1992), p. 66.

C.   The *Shema* meets Immanuel: in the wake of the Resurrection, the revelation of God is made clear—God is One God in Three Persons, equal in substance. Thus, Jesus declared in Matthew 28:18–19, "All authority has been given to Me in heaven and on earth. Go therefore and make disciples of all the nations, baptizing them in the name of the Father and of the Son and of the Holy Spirit." And Paul blesses the church of Corinth in 2 Corinthians 13 by saying, "The grace of the Lord Jesus Christ, and the love of God, and the communion of the Holy Spirit be with you all." But Paul also affirmed the Oneness of God in 1 Corinthians 8.

The Shema: Hear, O Israel: The Lord our God, the Lord is one! You shall love the Lord your God with all your heart, with all your soul, and with all your strength. (Deuteronomy 6:4–5)

Therefore the Lord Himself will give you a sign: Behold, the virgin shall conceive and bear a Son, and shall call His name Immanuel. (Isaiah 7:14)

The grace of the Lord Jesus Christ, and the love of God, and the communion of the Holy Spirit be with you all. Amen. (2 Corinthians 13:14)

*Therefore concerning the eating of things offered to idols, we know that an idol is nothing in the world, and that **there is no other God but one**. For even if there are so-called gods, whether in heaven or on earth (as there are many gods and many lords), yet for us **there is one God**, the Father, of whom are all things, and we for Him; and one Lord Jesus Christ, through whom are all things, and through whom we live. (1 Corinthians 8:4–6, emphasis added)*

D.   Thus, the Trinity is one of the great mysteries of the faith. The doctrine of the Trinity holds that God is One in Three distinct Persons: Father, Son, and Holy Spirit. The three Persons share one nature. Norman Geisler describes it this way: "The three Whos (persons) each share the same What (essence). So God is a unity of essence with a plurality of persons. Each person is different, yet they share a common nature … God is one in his substance. The unity is in his essence (what God is), and the plurality is in God's persons (how he relates within himself). This plurality of relationships is both internal and external. Within the Trinity each member relates to the others in certain ways. These are somewhat analogous to human relationships."[2]

---

2 Geisler, Norman. "The Trinity-Part Two." *Ankerberg Theological Research Institute–The John Ankerberg Show*. Dec. 2000. <http://www.johnankerberg.org/Articles/theological-dictionary/TD0100W2.htm>

E.   St. Augustine illustrated the Trinity by emphasizing the relational dynamic of God in Three Persons. God is love. Love involves three aspects: a lover, a beloved, and the spirit of love between them. The Father is likened to the Lover. The Son is the One loved. The Spirit is the love between both the Father and the Son.

All those Catholic expounders of the divine Scriptures, both Old and New, whom I have been able to read, who have written before me concerning the Trinity, Who is God, have purposed to teach, according to the Scriptures, this doctrine, that the Father, and the Son, and the Holy Spirit intimate a divine unity of one and the same substance in an indivisible equality; and therefore that they are not three Gods, but one God: although the Father hath begotten the Son, and so He who is the Father is not the Son; and the Son is begotten by the Father, and so He who is the Son is not the Father; and the Holy Spirit is neither the Father nor the Son, but only the Spirit of the Father and of the Son, Himself also co-equal with the Father and the Son, and pertaining to the unity of the Trinity.[3]

F.   Jonathan Edwards, as quoted by John Piper, attempted to describe the great mystery of the Trinity. He conceded, "I am far from pretending to explain the Trinity so as to render it no longer a mystery. I think it to be the highest and deepest of all Divine mysteries still."

If a man could have an absolutely perfect idea of all that passed in his mind, all the series of ideas and exercises in every respect perfect as to order, degree, circumstance and for any particular space of time past, suppose the last hour, he would really to all intents and purpose be over again what he was that last hour. And if it were possible for a man by reflection perfectly to contemplate all that is in his own mind in an hour, as it is and at the same time that it is there in its first and direct existence; if a man, that is, had a perfect reflex or contemplative idea of every thought at the same moment or moments that that thought was and of every exercise at and during the same time that that exercise was, and so through a whole hour, a man would really be two during that time, he would be indeed double, he would be twice at once. The idea he has of himself would be himself again...

---

3   Schaff, Philip. "NPNF1-03: On the Holy Trinity; Doctrinal Treatises; Moral Treatises." New York: The Christian Literature Publishing Co., 1890. July 13, 2005. *Christian Classics Ethereal Library.* <http://www.ccel.org/ccel/schaff/npnf103.html>

Therefore as God with perfect clearness, fullness and strength, understands Himself, views His own essence (in which there is no distinction of substance and act but which is wholly substance and wholly act), that idea which God hath of Himself is absolutely Himself. This representation of the Divine nature and essence is the Divine nature and essence again: so that by God's thinking of the Deity must certainly be generated. Hereby there is another person begotten, there is another Infinite Eternal Almighty and most holy and the same God, the very same Divine nature…

The Godhead being thus begotten by God's loving an idea of Himself and shewing forth in a distinct subsistence or person in that idea, there proceeds a most pure act, and an infinitely holy and sacred energy arises between the Father and Son in mutually loving and delighting in each other, for their love and joy is mutual, (Prov. 8: 30) "I was daily His delight rejoicing always before Him." This is the eternal and most perfect and essential act of the Divine nature, wherein the Godhead acts to an infinite degree and in the most perfect manner possible. The Deity becomes all act, the Divine essence itself flows out and is as it were breathed forth in love and joy. So that the Godhead therein stands forth in yet another manner of subsistence, and there proceeds the third Person in the Trinity, the Holy Spirit, viz., the Deity in act, for there is no other act but the act of the will…

And this I suppose to be that blessed Trinity that we read of in the Holy Scriptures. The Father is the Deity subsisting in the prime, un-originated and most absolute manner, or the Deity in its direct existence. The Son is the Deity generated by God's understanding, or having an idea of Himself and subsisting in that idea. The Holy Ghost is the Deity subsisting in act, or the Divine essence flowing out and breathed forth in God's Infinite love to and delight in Himself. And I believe the whole Divine essence does truly and distinctly subsist both in the Divine idea and Divine love, and that each of them are properly distinct Persons.[4]

II. OLD TESTAMENT THEOPHANIES AND PROPHECIES

A. Angel of Yahweh

---

4 Piper, John. *The Pleasures of God,* (Sisters, OR: Multnomah, 2000), pp. 42-45.

1. *The Angel of the* L*ORD* *said to her, "Return to your mistress, and submit yourself under her hand." Then the Angel of the* L*ORD* *said to her, "I will multiply your descendants exceedingly, so that they shall not be counted for multitude." And the Angel of the* L*ORD* *said to her: "Behold, you are with child, and you shall bear a son. You shall call his name Ishmael, because the* L*ORD* *has heard your affliction." (Genesis 16:9–11)*

2. *And God heard the voice of the lad. Then the angel of God called to Hagar out of heaven, and said to her, "What ails you, Hagar? Fear not, for God has heard the voice of the lad where he is." (Genesis 21:17)*

3. *But the Angel of the* L*ORD* *called to him from heaven and said, "Abraham, Abraham!" So he said, "Here I am." And He said, "Do not lay your hand on the lad, or do anything to him; for now I know that you fear God, since you have not withheld your son, your only son, from Me." Then Abraham lifted his eyes and looked, and there behind him was a ram caught in a thicket by its horns. So Abraham went and took the ram, and offered it up for a burnt offering instead of his son. And Abraham called the name of the place, The- L*ORD*-Will-Provide; as it is said to this day, "In the Mount of the* L*ORD* *it shall be provided." Then the Angel of the* L*ORD* *called to Abraham a second time out of heaven, (Genesis 22:11–15)*

4. *Then the Angel of God spoke to me in a dream, saying, "Jacob." And I said, "Here I am." (Genesis 31:11)*

5. *Then Jacob was left alone; and a Man wrestled with him until the breaking of day. (Genesis 32:24)*

6. *And he blessed Joseph, and said: "God, before whom my fathers Abraham and Isaac walked, the God who has fed me all my life long to this day." (Genesis 48:15)*

7. *And the Angel of the* L*ORD* *appeared to him in a flame of fire from the midst of a bush. So he looked, and behold, the bush was burning with fire, but the bush was not consumed. (Exodus 3:2)*

8. Numbers 22:22–35

9. Joshua 5:13–6:2

10. *Then the Angel of the L*ORD *came up from Gilgal to Bochim, and said: "I led you up from Egypt and brought you to the land of which I swore to your fathers; and I said, 'I will never break My covenant with you. And you shall make no covenant with the inhabitants of this land; you shall tear down their altars.' But you have not obeyed My voice. Why have you done this? Therefore I also said, 'I will not drive them out before you; but they shall be thorns in your side, and their gods shall be a snare to you.'" So it was, when the Angel of the L*ORD *spoke these words to all the children of Israel, that the people lifted up their voices and wept. (Judges 2:1–4)*

11. *Now the Angel of the L*ORD *came and sat under the terebinth tree which was in Ophrah, which belonged to Joash the Abiezrite, while his son Gideon threshed wheat in the winepress, in order to hide it from the Midianites. And the Angel of the L*ORD *appeared to him, and said to him, "The L*ORD *is with you, you mighty man of valor!" Gideon said to Him, "O my lord, if the L*ORD *is with us, why then has all this happened to us? And where are all His miracles which our fathers told us about, saying, 'Did not the L*ORD *bring us up from Egypt?' But now the L*ORD *has forsaken us and delivered us into the hands of the Midianites." Then the L*ORD *turned to him and said, "Go in this might of yours, and you shall save Israel from the hand of the Midianites. Have I not sent you?" (Judges 6:11–14)*

12. Judges 13:3–22

13. *Then the Angel of the L*ORD *answered and said, "O L*ORD *of hosts, how long will You not have mercy on Jerusalem and on the cities of Judah, against which You were angry these seventy years?" And the L*ORD *answered the angel who talked to me, with good and comforting words. (Zechariah 1:12–13)*

14. *Then he showed me Joshua the high priest standing before the Angel of the L*ORD, *and Satan standing at his right hand to oppose him. (Zechariah 3:1)*

15. *In that day the L*ORD *will defend the inhabitants of Jerusalem; the one who is feeble among them in that day shall be like David, and the house of David shall be like God, like the Angel of the L*ORD *before them. (Zechariah 12:8)*

B.   Major Prophets

1. Isaiah

> **In that day the Branch of the LORD shall be beautiful and glorious; and the fruit of the earth shall be excellent and appealing** *for those of Israel who have escaped. And it shall come to pass that he who is left in Zion and remains in Jerusalem will be called holy—everyone who is recorded among the living in Jerusalem. When the Lord has washed away the filth of the daughters of Zion, and purged the blood of Jerusalem from her midst, by the spirit of judgment and by the spirit of burning, then the LORD will create above every dwelling place of Mount Zion, and above her assemblies, a cloud and smoke by day and the shining of a flaming fire by night. For over all the glory there will be a covering. And there will be a tabernacle for shade in the daytime from the heat, for a place of refuge, and for a shelter from storm and rain. (Isaiah 4:2-6, emphasis added)*

> *In the year that King Uzziah died,* **I saw the LORD sitting on a throne, high and lifted up, and the train of His robe filled the temple.** *Above it stood seraphim; each one had six wings: with two he covered his face, with two he covered his feet, and with two he flew. And one cried to another and said: "Holy, holy, holy is the LORD of hosts; the whole earth is full of His glory!" And the posts of the door were shaken by the voice of him who cried out, and the house was filled with smoke. So I said: "Woe is me, for I am undone! Because I am a man of unclean lips, and I dwell in the midst of a people of unclean lips; for my eyes have seen the King, the LORD of hosts." (Isaiah 6:1–5, emphasis added)*

> **These things Isaiah said when he saw His glory and spoke of Him.** *(John 12:41, emphasis added)*

> **Therefore the LORD Himself will give you a sign: Behold, the virgin shall conceive and bear a Son, and shall call His name Immanuel.** *(Isaiah 7:14, emphasis added)*

> **For unto us a Child is born, unto us a Son is given; and the government will be upon His shoulder. And His name will be called Wonderful, Counselor, Mighty God, Everlasting Father, Prince of Peace.** *(Isaiah 9:6, emphasis added)*

> There shall come forth a **Rod from the stem of Jesse, and a Branch shall grow out of his roots** … *and in that day* **there shall be a Root of Jesse**, *who shall stand as a banner to the people; for the Gentiles shall seek Him, and His resting place shall be glorious. (Isaiah 11:1,10, emphasis added)*

2. *And above the firmament over their heads was the likeness of a throne, in appearance like a sapphire stone; on the likeness of the throne was a likeness with the appearance of a man high above it. Also from the appearance of His waist and upward I saw, as it were, the color of amber with the appearance of fire all around within it; and from the appearance of His waist and downward I saw, as it were, the appearance of fire with brightness all around. Like the appearance of a rainbow in a cloud on a rainy day, so was the appearance of the brightness all around it. This was the appearance of the likeness of the glory of the Lord. So when I saw it, I fell on my face, and I heard a voice of One speaking. (Ezekiel 1:26–28)*

C.   Minor Prophets

1. *I was watching in the night visions, and behold, One like the Son of Man, coming with the clouds of heaven! He came to the Ancient of Days, and they brought Him near before Him. Then to Him was given dominion and glory and a kingdom, that all peoples, nations, and languages should serve Him. His dominion is an everlasting dominion, which shall not pass away, And His kingdom the one which shall not be destroyed. (Daniel 7:13–14)*

2. *Now gather yourself in troops, O daughter of troops; He has laid siege against us; they will strike the judge of Israel with a rod on the cheek. "But you, Bethlehem Ephrathah, though you are little among the thousands of Judah, yet out of you shall come forth to Me the One to be Ruler in Israel, whose goings forth are from of old, from everlasting." Therefore He shall give them up, until the time that she who is in labor has given birth; then the remnant of His brethren shall return to the children of Israel. And He shall stand and feed His flock in the strength of the Lord, in the majesty of the name of the Lord His God; and they shall abide, for now He shall be great to the ends of the earth; and this One shall be peace. When the Assyrian comes into our land, and when he treads in our palaces, then we will raise against him seven shepherds and eight princely men. (Micah 5:1–5)*

III. THE WITNESS OF JOHN THE BAPTIST

A. As early as John the Baptist, Jesus' pre-existence was proclaimed.

John bore witness of Him and cried out, saying, "This was He of whom I said, 'He who comes after me is preferred before me, for He was before me.'" And of His fullness we have all received, and grace for grace. For the law was given through Moses, but grace and truth came through Jesus Christ. (John 1:15–17)

John answered them, saying, "I baptize with water, but there stands One among you whom you do not know." (John 1:26)

B. John's first public sermon concerning Jesus presented a highly developed Christology. He declared both the birth and pre-existence of Jesus.

The next day John saw Jesus coming toward him, and said, "Behold! **The Lamb of God** *who takes away the sin of the world! This is He of whom I said,* **'After me comes a Man who is preferred before me, for He was before me.'** *I did not know Him; but that He should be revealed to Israel, therefore I came baptizing with water." And John bore witness, saying, "I saw the Spirit descending from heaven like a dove, and He remained upon Him. I did not know Him, but He who sent me to baptize with water said to me, 'Upon whom you see the Spirit descending, and remaining on Him, this is* **He who baptizes with the Holy Spirit.' And I have seen and testified that this is the Son of God."** *(John 1:29–34, emphasis added)*

C. John once again addressed the identity of Jesus when a dispute arose among his disciples concerning how the crowds were turning to Jesus' disciples for water baptism.

*John answered and said, "A man can receive nothing unless it has been given to him from heaven. You yourselves bear me witness, that I said, 'I am not the Christ,' but, 'I have been sent before Him.' He who has the bride is the bridegroom; but the friend of the bridegroom, who stands and hears him, rejoices greatly because of the bridegroom's voice. Therefore this joy of mine is fulfilled. He must increase, but I must decrease. **He who comes from above is above all; he who is of the earth is earthly and speaks of the earth. He who comes from heaven is above all.** And what He has seen and heard, that He testifies; and no one receives His testimony. He who has received His testimony has certified that God is true. For He whom God has sent speaks the words of God, for God does not give the Spirit by measure. **The Father loves the Son, and has given all things into His hand. He who believes in the Son has everlasting life; and he who does not believe the Son shall not see life, but the wrath of God abides on him."** (John 3:27–36, emphasis added)*

IV.   WISDOM/WORD TRADITION

A.   Wisdom in the Old Testament is personified and seen as the creative agent used by God in creation. God's Word goes forth as wisdom personified. Proverbs 8:22–30 gives us the best Old Testament example of wisdom personified and gives us a clear picture of the pre-incarnate Christ.

1.   Proverbs 8:22–31

   a.   Proverbs 8:22–26: the personification and eternity of wisdom.

   b.   Proverbs 8:27–29: Wisdom's presence during creation.

   c.   Proverbs 8:28–31

      (1) Wisdom, as the instrument of creation, is portrayed as the craftsman at the Father's side. Wisdom is the object of the Father's highest affections and highest pleasures. The Father delighted to create through the Son and for the Son.

      (2) Wisdom/the Son is always rejoicing, always delighting in His Father.

(3) Wisdom rejoices in humanity.

2. John 1:1–18/Genesis 1

In the beginning was the Word, and the Word was with God, and the Word was God. He was in the beginning with God. All things were made through Him, and without Him nothing was made that was made. In Him was life, and the life was the light of men. (John 1:1–4, emphasis added)

a. Hebraic Source of Logos: the source of New Testament usage of "Logos" is found in the Hebraic concept of "Dabar Yahweh." "Dabar Yahweh," the "Word of God," is that which made the world and which inspired the prophets. It is viewed as the creative force of the Deity. The Word of God creates. It goes forth, accomplishing its purpose (Isaiah 55).

b. In the Gospel of John, Christ is seen as separate from God, at the same time fully being God. Jesus, as the Logos, is the very instrument of creation.

B. Pauline Texts: in Paul's letters, Christ is seen as the wisdom of God and the mediator of all creation. As E. J. Schnabel wrote, "The preexistent Christ is the mediator of creation and the incarnated Christ is the mediator of salvation."[5]

But to those who are called, both Jews and Greeks, Christ the power of God and the wisdom of God. (1 Corinthians 1:24, emphasis added)

But of Him you are in Christ Jesus, who became for us wisdom from God—and righteousness and sanctification and redemption. (1 Corinthians 1:30, emphasis added)

But we speak the wisdom of God in a mystery, the hidden wisdom which God ordained before the ages for our glory. (1 Corinthians 2:7)

---

5 Schnabel, E. J. "Wisdom." *Dictionary of Paul and His Letters* (Downers Grove, IL: InterVarsity, 1993), p. 970.

For the wisdom of this world is foolishness with God. For it is written, "He catches the wise in their own craftiness"; and again, "The Lord knows the thoughts of the wise, that they are futile." Therefore let no one boast in men. For all things are yours: whether Paul or Apollos or Cephas, or the world or life or death, or things present or things to come—all are yours. And you are Christ's, and Christ is God's. (1 Corinthians 3:19–23)

Yet for us there is one God, the Father, of whom are all things, and we for Him; and **one Lord Jesus Christ, through whom are all things, and through whom we live.** *(1 Corinthians 8:6, emphasis added)*

He is the image of the invisible God, the firstborn over all creation. **For by Him all things were created that are in heaven and that are on earth, visible and invisible, whether thrones or dominions or principalities or powers. All things were created through Him and for Him. And He is before all things, and in Him all things consist.** *And He is the head of the body, the church, who is the beginning, the firstborn from the dead, that in all things He may have the preeminence. (Colossians 1:15–18, emphasis added)*

God, who at various times and in various ways spoke in time past to the fathers by the prophets, has in these last days spoken to us by His Son, whom He has appointed heir of all things, through whom also He made the worlds; who being the brightness of His glory and the express image of His person, and **upholding all things by the word of His power,** *when He had by Himself purged our sins, sat down at the right hand of the Majesty on high. (Hebrews 1:1–3, emphasis added)*

C. Book of Revelation: The Father and Jesus share the same title of Alpha and Omega.

"I am the Alpha and the Omega, the Beginning and the End," *says the Lord, "who is and who was and who is to come, the Almighty." (Revelation 1:8, emphasis added)*

"I am the Alpha and the Omega, the First and the Last," *and, "What you see, write in a book and send it to the seven churches which are in Asia: to Ephesus, to Smyrna, to Pergamos, to Thyatira, to Sardis, to Philadelphia, and to Laodicea." (Revelation 1:11, emphasis added)*

V.   PRE-PAULINE ORAL

A.   Early after the Resurrection, believers in Christ—most likely Jewish believers who wanted to simulate early synagogue worship—began to fashion hymns and liturgical creeds to be used in their worship settings. Hymns and fragments of liturgy are found throughout the Pauline corpus and declare both the person and work of Jesus Christ.

B.   Pliny the Younger, the governor of Pontus and Bithynia from AD 110–113, wrote a letter to the Roman Emperor Trajan, inquiring about the process by which one should judge Christians in regard to their refusal to worship the Roman gods. In his letter, he refers to their singing of songs to Christ.

*They asserted, however, that the sum and substance of their fault or error had been that they were **accustomed to meet on a fixed day before dawn and sing responsively a hymn to Christ as to a god**, and to bind themselves by oath, not to some crime, but not to commit fraud, theft, or adultery, not falsify their trust, nor to refuse to return a trust when called upon to do so.[6]*

C.   Commenting on the Christological aspect of the hymns, Ralph P. Martin wrote, "The New Testament teaching on the person of Christ is contained in its hymns … The Christian's Lord is depicted in a cosmological role in the double sense of that adjective. First, his pre-existence and pretemporal activity in creation are made the frontispiece of the hymns, and from the divine order in which he eternally exists, he 'comes down' as the incarnate one in an epiphany. Second, at the conclusion of his earthly life he takes his place in God's presence by receiving the universal homage and acclamation of the cosmic spirit powers, which confess his lordship and so are forced to abandon their title of control over human destiny."[7]

---

6   Pliny the Younger. "Pliny to the Emperor Trajan." *Letters 10.96-97.* <http://ccat.sas.upenn.edu/jod/texts/pliny.html.>

7   Martin, Ralph P. "Hymns, Hymn Fragments, Songs, Spiritual Songs." *Dictionary of Paul and His Letters*, (Downers Grove, IL: InterVarsity, 1993), p. 422.

*Let this mind be in you which was also in Christ Jesus, **who, being in the form of God**, did not consider it robbery to be equal with God, but made Himself of no reputation, **taking the form of a bondservant, and coming in the likeness of men.** And being found in appearance as a man, He humbled Himself and became obedient to the point of death, even the death of the cross. Therefore God also has highly exalted Him and given Him the name which is above every name, that at the name of Jesus every knee should bow, of those in heaven, and of those on earth, and of those under the earth, and that every tongue should confess that Jesus Christ is Lord, to the glory of God the Father. (Philippians 2:5–11, emphasis added)*

*He is the image of the invisible God, the firstborn over all creation. **For by Him all things were created that are in heaven and that are on earth, visible and invisible, whether thrones or dominions or principalities or powers. All things were created through Him and for Him. And He is before all things, and in Him all things consist.** And He is the head of the body, the church, who is the beginning, the firstborn from the dead, that in all things He may have the preeminence. (Colossians 1:15–18, emphasis added)*

*And without controversy great is the mystery of godliness: **God was manifested in the flesh**, justified in the Spirit, seen by angels, preached among the Gentiles, believed on in the world, received up in glory. (1 Timothy 3:16, emphasis added)*

*The first man was of the earth, made of dust; **the second Man is the Lord from heaven**. (1 Corinthians 15:47, emphasis added)*

VI.   SON SENT BY THE FATHER

A.   Jesus is presented in the Gospel of John as the only begotten Son of the Father. "Only begotten" is the Greek word "monogenes," which means unique, the only one of its kind or family.

In these passages, too, it might be translated as "the only son of God"; for the emphasis seems to be on His uniqueness, rather than on His sonship, though both ideas are certainly present. He is the son of God in a sense in which no others are. "Monogenes describes the absolutely unique relation of the Son to the Father in His divine nature; prototokos describes the relation of the Risen Christ in His glorified humanity to man" (Westcott on Heb 1:6).[8]

---

8   Rees, T. "Only Begotten." *International Standard Bible Encyclopedia*. Ed. James Orr. Chicago: Howard-Severence Company, 1915. *StudyLight.org*. <http://www.studylight.org/enc/isb/view.cgi?number=T6561>

For God so loved the world that He gave His only begotten Son, that whoever believes in Him should not perish but have everlasting life. (John 3:16)

He who believes in Him is not condemned; but he who does not believe is condemned already, because he has not believed in the name of the only begotten Son of God. (John 3:18)

B.   The New Testament consistently describes Jesus as proceeding forth from, being sent, and being given by the Father.

*Jesus said to them, "If God were your Father, you would love Me, **for I proceeded forth and came from God**; nor have I come of Myself, but **He sent Me**." (John 8:42, emphasis added)*

*And this is eternal life, that they may know You, the only true God, and **Jesus Christ whom You have sent**. (John 17:3, emphasis added)*

*For I have given to them the words which You have given Me; and they have received them, and have known surely that **I came forth from You**; and they have believed that **You sent Me**. (John 17:8, emphasis added)*

***As You sent Me into the world**, I also have sent them into the world. (John 17:18, emphasis added)*

*For what the law could not do in that it was weak through the flesh, **God did by sending His own Son in the likeness of sinful flesh**, on account of sin: He condemned sin in the flesh. (Romans 8:3, emphasis added)*

*But when the fullness of the time had come, **God sent forth His Son, born of a woman**, born under the law. (Galatians 4:4, emphasis added)*

*In this the love of God was manifested toward us, that **God has sent His only begotten Son** into the world, that we might live through Him. In this is love, not that we loved God, but that He loved us and **sent His Son** to be the propitiation for our sins. Beloved, if God so loved us, we also ought to love one another. No one has seen God at any time. If we love one another, God abides in us, and His love has been perfected in us. By this we know that we abide in Him, and He in us, because He has given us of His Spirit. And we have seen and testify that the **Father has sent the Son as Savior of the world**. (1 John 4:9–14, emphasis added)*

VII. OTHER NEW TESTAMENT PASSAGES

A. Glory, love and riches:

*And now, O Father, glorify Me together with Yourself, **with the glory which I had with You before the world was**. (John 17:5, emphasis added)*

*Father, I desire that they also whom You gave Me may be with Me where I am, that they may behold My glory which You have given Me; for **You loved Me before the foundation of the world**. (John 17:24, emphasis added)*

*For you know the grace of our Lord Jesus Christ, that **though He was rich, yet for your sakes He became poor**, that you through His poverty might become rich. (2 Corinthians 8:9, emphasis added)*

B. Before the foundation of the world:

*Jesus said to them, "Most assuredly, I say to you, **before Abraham was, I AM**." (John 8:58, emphasis added)*

Just as He chose us in Him before the foundation of the world, that we should be holy and without blame before Him in love. (Ephesians 1:4)

*But with the precious blood of Christ, as of a lamb without blemish and without spot. He indeed was **foreordained before the foundation of the world**, but was manifest in these last times for you. (1 Peter 1:19–20, emphasis added)*

*All who dwell on the earth will worship him, whose names have not been written in the Book of Life of the Lamb **slain from the foundation of the world**. (Revelation 13:8, emphasis added)*

C. New Testament Christological interpretation:

1. Christ as the Rock in the wilderness: just as the Israelites drank from the rock, now we drink from Christ, the very wisdom of God. Christ is the preexistent, divine wisdom which revealed Himself in Israel's history and now mediates redemption through His life, death, and resurrection.

*Moreover, brethren, I do not want you to be unaware that all our fathers were under the cloud, all passed through the sea, all were baptized into Moses in the cloud and in the sea, all ate the same spiritual food, and all drank the same spiritual drink. For they drank of that spiritual Rock that followed them, and **that Rock was Christ.** (1 Corinthians 10:1–4, emphasis added)*

He is the Rock, His work is perfect; for all His ways are justice, a God of truth and without injustice; righteous and upright is He. *(Deuteronomy 32:4, emphasis added)*

But Jeshurun grew fat and kicked; you grew fat, you grew thick, you are obese! Then he forsook God who made him, and scornfully esteemed the Rock of his salvation. *(Deuteronomy 32:15, emphasis added)*

Of the Rock who begot you, you are unmindful, and have forgotten the God who fathered you. *(Deuteronomy 32:18, emphasis added)*

How could one chase a thousand, and two put ten thousand to flight, unless their Rock had sold them, and the LORD had surrendered them? For their rock is not like our Rock, even our enemies themselves being judges. *(Deuteronomy 32:30–31, emphasis added)*

2. Christ as the Manifestation of God to Moses

*By faith Moses, when he became of age, refused to be called the son of Pharaoh's daughter, choosing rather to suffer affliction with the people of God than to enjoy the passing pleasures of sin, **esteeming the reproach of Christ greater riches than the treasures in Egypt;** for he looked to the reward. (Hebrews 11:24–26, emphasis added)*

Session Three: The Mediator

I. THE GREAT MYSTERY—THE INCARNATION

"Larry King Live" did a story about the one man in history Larry King wanted to interview and what question he would ask him. King picked Jesus Christ and said he wanted to ask Him, "Are you indeed virgin born?" King said, "The answer to that question would explain history to me." [1]

Anyone contemplating the life of Jesus needs to be newly and more deeply aware every day that something scandalous has occurred: that God, in His absolute being, has resolved to manifest Himself in a human life. He must be scandalized by this, he must feel his mind reeling, the very ground giving way beneath his feet; he must at least experience that 'ecstasy' of non-comprehension which transported Jesus' contemporaries (Mark 2:12, 5:42, 6:51).[2]

And without controversy great is the mystery of godliness: God was manifested in the flesh, justified in the Spirit, seen by angels, preached among the Gentiles, believed on in the world, received up in glory. (1 Timothy 3:16, emphasis added)

A. The Incarnation is more than just a doctrine; it is the object of contemplation. It is the place where angels and humans alike stare at a mystery as deep as the Almighty Himself. As soon as understanding enters your mind, cognition loses its grip and recedes into the abyss of non-comprehension. This is true joy—to ponder that which cannot be fully fathomed.

B. Paul emphatically stated that the greatness of the mystery of godliness was incontrovertible. Paul was not speaking as one uninformed. 2 Corinthians 12 tells us that Paul had been to the third heaven. He had seen the Lord. Yet Paul emphatically proclaimed that there was no debate around the magnitude of God becoming a man. No one understands it. Paul declared that both Heaven and Earth are in agreement concerning the God-Man, Jesus Christ. Angels are baffled and long to look into such things (1 Peter 1:12), and humans cannot fathom what God has done.

---

1 Zacharias, Ravi. *Jesus Among Other Gods: The Absolute Claims of the Christian Message* (Nashville, TN: W Publishing Group, 2000), p. 38.
2 Von Balthasar, Hans Urs. *Prayer* (San Francisco, Ignatius, 1986), p. 159.

C.   Great is the mystery of godliness! Have you ever wondered, "What is it about the human frame that pleased Him so much that the One who made all things chose to become human forever?" Jesus is not only your divine King and Maker. Now He is your brother. What has God done in His Son?

D.   What is this desire in the heart of God that resulted in Him taking on flesh for all eternity and governing as a human king? How did such a plan as the incarnation begin and grow in the mind of God? What was the dialogue among the Trinity when, before the foundation of the world, a Lamb was slain in the heart of the majesty of Heaven?

E.   How mysterious is this plan that was birthed in the pure heart of the infinite, holy God, a perfect plan begotten by a perfect God—to have the God-Man sitting on the throne in government. Have you ever thought that right now, within the Trinity, there is a human body? Oh, what grand bliss! The Theandric Union—the God-Man! At the center of the throne a Lamb dwells, a descendant of David, born from the loins of a young Jewish maiden.

F.   The Theandric Union is a mystery because it's designed to bring us to worship, not just comprehension; it's the ecstasy of non-comprehension. This mystery has been the object of great affection throughout Church history. God became man. He took on our frame for the love of us. The Church is unable to explain its depths. Thus, doctrine has rightly sought to give the parameters of defining the Theandric Union.

II.   THEANDRIC UNION—HYPOSTATIC UNION

A.   Four elementary scriptural teachings are essential for understanding the distinctive personhood of Christ: "1. Christ is truly God. 2. He is truly human. 3. He is one person. 4. There are in Him two distinct natures, divine and human."[3] Jesus is the "theanthropos," the "God-Man." Jesus' person is undivided. He is fully God and fully man in one, undivided person.

For in Him dwells all the fullness of the Godhead bodily. (Colossians 2:9)

B.   Without ceasing to be what He has always been, the Eternal Son of God has become the human Jesus; and Jesus, without ceasing to be fully human, is the Eternal Son of God.

---

3   Oden, Thomas C. *The Word of Life, Systematic Theology: Volume Two* (1st Harper Collins paperback ed. San Francisco, HarperSanFrancisco, 1992), p. 164.

Jesus did not "experience" God; he was God. He never at any given moment "became" God; he was God from the start. His life was only the process by which this innate divinity came into its own. His task was to place divine reality and power squarely in the realm of his human consciousness and will; to reflect holy purity in his relation to all things, and to contain infinite love and divinity's boundless plenitude in his heart of flesh and blood.[4]

C.   Prophetic expectation of Immanuel

Therefore the Lord Himself will give you a sign: Behold, the virgin shall conceive and bear a Son, and shall call His name Immanuel. (Isaiah 7:14)

For unto us a Child is born, unto us a Son is given; and the government will be upon His shoulder. And His name will be called Wonderful, Counselor, Mighty God, Everlasting Father, Prince of Peace. Of the increase of His government and peace there will be no end, upon the throne of David and over His kingdom, to order it and establish it with judgment and justice from that time forward, even forever. The zeal of the Lord of hosts will perform this. (Isaiah 9:6)

"Behold, the days are coming," says the Lord, "that I will raise to David a Branch of righteousness; a King shall reign and prosper, and execute judgment and righteousness in the earth. In His days Judah will be saved, and Israel will dwell safely; now this is His name by which He will be called: THE LORD OUR RIGHTEOUSNESS." (Jeremiah 23:5–6)

Now gather yourself in troops, O daughter of troops; He has laid siege against us; they will strike the judge of Israel with a rod on the cheek. "But you, Bethlehem Ephrathah, though you are little among the thousands of Judah, yet out of you shall come forth to Me the One to be Ruler in Israel, whose goings forth are from of old, from everlasting." Therefore He shall give them up, until the time that she who is in labor has given birth; then the remnant of His brethren shall return to the children of Israel. And He shall stand and feed His flock in the strength of the Lord, in the majesty of the name of the Lord His God; and they shall abide, for now He shall be great to the ends of the earth; and this One shall be peace. (Micah 5:1–5)

D.   Jesus is the Mediator. A mediator is one who represents two parties to one another in order to bring about reconciliation.

---

4 Guardini, Romano. *The Lord* (Washington D.C.: Regenery, 1954), p. 20.

The mediator between God and humanity would have to be nothing less than God and nothing less than fully human, otherwise this mediatorship would have been impossible, for how can one mediate a conflict in which one has no capacity to empathize with one or the other side?[5]

If one man sins against another, God will judge him. But if a man sins against the LORD, who will intercede for him? Nevertheless they did not heed the voice of their father, because the LORD desired to kill them. (1 Samuel 2:25)

For there is one God and one Mediator between God and men, the Man Christ Jesus, who gave Himself a ransom for all, to be testified in due time. (1 Timothy 2:5–6)

Now a mediator does not mediate for one only, but God is one (when one person is both parties, they are probably going to agree). (Galatians 3:20, parenthetical statement added)

That in the dispensation of the fullness of the times He might gather together in one all things in Christ, both which are in heaven and which are on earth—in Him. (Ephesians 1:10)

III. PURPOSES OF THE MEDIATION:

A. To reveal God to humanity (John 1:18, 14:7–11). Jesus makes contemplation possible. The only reason we know what God is like is because He has revealed Himself fully in Jesus.

---

5 Oden, Thomas C. *The Word of Life*. Systematic Theology: Volume Two (1ˢᵗ Harper Collins paperback ed. San Francisco, HarperSanFrancisco, 1992), p. 119.

We cannot contemplate God apart from these pathways which lead to Him, and reveal Him to us, for it is thus that He manifests Himself, it is thus that He confronts us. Even in the "unveiled sight" of eternity we shall never see God in any other way but in His sovereign, incomprehensible self-revelation, in which He gives Himself, stepping forth out of His unapproachable Being and bridging the infinite chasm which separates us from Him. Everything is possible to the creature except one thing: it cannot be God. The creature is in root and marrow fundamentally different from Him and will remain so for ever. And the nearer man approaches Him in terms of will and knowledge, the more he experiences the abyss which separates him from the One who is "all" and knows no distinction. . . . It is man's anguish and his glory, his weakness and his dignity, that he must and may relate himself to God in this way; he can only be himself through God, and he can never be God. . . . There is only one way out of the impasse, namely, that infinite, eternal Being should utter its own self in the form of a relative being. That in this epiphany and parousia it should become actually present and give an authoritative interpretation of itself. Then we could hear the infinite Word in the finite, and see the eternal, imageless archetype in the finite form. Now, our contemplation consists of a cautious approach to the mystery of the hypostatic union: the two natures having become one in the Person of the divine Son.[6]

The mystics understood that the gap between God and us (called negative theology) is such that God is so high, there is nothing we can know about Him. But He has become so low in Jesus that we can know everything. This is the paradox of the God-Man.

No one has seen God at any time. The only begotten Son, who is in the bosom of the Father, He has declared Him. (John 1:18)

B. To provide a high priest who is interceding for us and able to sympathize with human weaknesses.

Seeing then that we have a great High Priest who has passed through the heavens, Jesus the Son of God, let us hold fast our confession. For we do not have a High Priest who cannot sympathize with our weaknesses, but was in all points tempted as we are, yet without sin. Let us therefore come boldly to the throne of grace, that we may obtain mercy and find grace to help in time of need. (Hebrews 4:14–16)

---

6 Balthasar, Hans Urs von. *Prayer* (San Francisco, Ignatius, 1986), p. 155-157.

C.   To offer humanity a pattern or example of the fullness of human life (1 Peter 2:21, 1 John 2:6). Jesus stands at the apex of all experience as fully God and fully man. He is not only the highest revelation of the Father sent down to us; He is the highest reaching of a human creature back in worship to God. There are constant cross currents moving and constant winds blowing in His personhood. How great is He who can contain all of what God is and all of what we are, and hold them together in perfect harmony and love? He is awesome! He is a King, and yet He is our Brother. He not only shows us what God is like, He shows us what we're made to be like. This is our inheritance.

He who says he abides in Him ought himself also to walk just as He walked. (1 John 2:6)

D.   To provide a substitutionary sacrifice adequate for the sins of all humanity.

"There is no-one…who can make this satisfaction except God himself… But no-one ought to make it except man; otherwise man does not make satisfaction." Therefore, "it is necessary that one who is God-man should make it."[7]

And every priest stands ministering daily and offering repeatedly the same sacrifices, which can never take away sins. But this Man, after He had offered one sacrifice for sins forever, sat down at the right hand of God. (Hebrews 10:11–12)

E.   To bind up demonic powers. He restored the dominion of humanity on planet Earth. It's the reason He came. He brought back to us our height and our purpose—what we were made to be.

For this purpose the Son of God was manifested, that He might destroy the works of the devil. He who does not honor the Son does not honor the Father who sent Him. Most assuredly, I say to you, he who hears My word and believes in Him who sent Me has everlasting life, and shall not come into judgment, but has passed from death into life. Most assuredly, I say to you, the hour is coming, and now is, when the dead will hear the voice of the Son of God; and those who hear will live. For as the Father has life in Himself, so He has granted the Son to have life in Himself, and has given Him authority to execute judgment also, because He is the Son of Man. (1 John 3:8)

F.   To provide for humanity a final judge at the end of time.

---

7   Stott, John. *The Cross of Christ* (Downers Grove, IL: InterVarsity, 1986), p. 119.

For the Father judges no one, but has committed all judgment to the Son. (John 5:22–27)

And He commanded us to preach to the people, and to testify that it is He who was ordained by God to be Judge of the living and the dead. (Acts 10:42)

Finally, there is laid up for me the crown of righteousness, which the Lord, the righteous Judge, will give to me on that Day, and not to me only but also to all who have loved His appearing. (2 Timothy 4:8)

IV. JESUS' DIVINITY

Quote from Napoleon Bonaparte:

I know men; and I tell you that Jesus Christ is not a man. Superficial minds see a resemblance between Christ and the founders of empires, and the gods of other religions. That resemblance does not exist. There is between Christianity and whatever religions the distance of infinity...

Everything about Christ astonishes me. His spirit overawes me, and His will confounds me. Between Him and whoever else in the world there is no possible term of comparison. He is truly a being by Himself. His ideas and His sentiments, the truth which He announces, his manner of convincing, are not explained either by human organization or by the nature of things.

The nearer I approach, the more carefully I examine, everything is above me; everything remains grand—of a grandeur which overpowers. His religion is a revelation from an intelligence which certainly is not that of man. There is there a profound originality which has created a series of words and of maxims before unknown. Jesus borrowed nothing from our science. One can absolutely find nowhere, but in Him alone, the imitation or the example of His life ... I search in vain in history to find the similar to Jesus Christ, or anything which can approach the gospel. Neither history, nor humanity, nor the ages, nor nature, offer me anything with which I am able to compare it or to explain it. Here everything is extraordinary. The more I consider the gospel, the more I am assured that there is nothing there which is not beyond the march of events, and above the human mind.[8]

A. Wayne Grudem gives three succinct reasons for the necessity of Jesus' deity, other than the fact that it is Scriptural. (You need to know these reasons when talking with Jehovah's Witnesses or Mormons).

---

8 Bonaparte, Napoleon. "I Know Men." *The Book of Jesus: A Treasury of the Greatest Stories & Writings About Christ* (Ed. Calvin Miller. New York: Simon & Schuster, 1998), p. 71-72. Emphasis added.

1. Only someone who is infinitely God could bear the full penalty for all the sins of all those who would believe in Him—any finite creature would have been incapable of bearing that penalty.

2. Salvation is from the Lord (Jonah 2:9), and the whole message of Scripture is designed to show that no human being, no creature, could ever save man—only God Himself could.

3. Only someone who is truly and fully God could be the one mediator between God and man (1 Timothy 2:5), both to bring us back to God and also to reveal God most fully to us (John 14:9).[9]

   "He became 'what we are, that He might bring us to be even what He is Himself.'"[10]

B. John Calvin stated, "Finally, since as God only He could not suffer, and as man only could not overcome death, He united the human nature with the divine, that He might subject the weakness of the one to death as an expiation of sin, and by the power of the other, maintaining a struggle with death, might gain us the victory."[11] Through the weakness of the human nature He could taste death and through the strength of His divine nature, He could overcome it.

C. The Word "God" is used to describe Christ in Scripture. Several passages in the New Testament use "theos," a word reserved for God alone, to refer to Christ.

   In the beginning was the Word, and the Word was with God, and the Word was God ... No one has seen God at any time. The only begotten Son, who is in the bosom of the Father, He has declared Him. (John 1:1,18)

   And Thomas answered and said to Him, "My Lord and my God!" (John 20:28)

   ...of whom are the fathers and from whom, according to the flesh, Christ came, who is over all, the eternally blessed God. Amen. (Romans 9:5)

---

9 Grudem, Wayne. *Systematic Theology: An Introduction to Biblical Doctrine* (Grand Rapids, MI: Zondervan, 1994), p. 553.

10 Oden, Thomas C. *The Word of Life, Systematic Theology: Volume Two* (1st Harper Collins paperback ed. San Francisco, HarperSanFrancisco, 1992), p. 130.

11 Calvin, John. *Institutes of the Christian Religion* (Trans. Henry Beveridge. Grand Rapids, MI: Zondervan, 1989), p. 402.

For the grace of God that brings salvation has appeared to all men, teaching us that, denying ungodliness and worldly lusts, we should live soberly, righteously, and godly in the present age, looking for the blessed hope and glorious appearing of our great God and Savior Jesus Christ, who gave Himself for us, that He might redeem us from every lawless deed and purify for Himself His own special people, zealous for good works. (Titus 2:11–14)

And of the angels He says: "Who makes His angels spirits And His ministers a flame of fire." But to the Son He says: "Your throne, O God, is forever and ever; a scepter of righteousness is the scepter of Your Kingdom." (Hebrews 1:7–8)

Simon Peter, a bondservant and apostle of Jesus Christ, to those who have obtained like precious faith with us by the righteousness of our God and Savior Jesus Christ. (2 Peter 1:1)

D.   Titles given to Jesus—all titles point to His divinity

1.   **Lord (Kyrios):** This word is used 6,814 times in the Septuagint (Greek Old Testament) to translate the Hebrew word for God, "Yahweh." This was early Christianity's most ascribed title to Jesus. After the resurrection, the Christian community boldly proclaimed that Jesus was not only the Messiah, He was also Lord. The word "Lord" did not imply that Jesus was some human master or expert leader. It meant that He was the resurrected sovereign ruler who defeated the power of death, sin, and hell, and was the bearer and executor of the Kingdom of God.

This leads us to the basic significance of the title Kyrios. It is the ascription to Jesus of the functions of deity. If confession of Jesus' Lordship means salvation (Rom. 10:9), the background for this is the Old Testament concept of the calling on the name of Yahweh. Paul himself makes this clear when he quotes from Joel 2:32: "For everyone who calls upon the name of the Lord will be saved" (Rom. 10:13). Thus, we find that the Day of the Lord (1 Corinthians 5:5;11 Thess. 5:2; 2 Thess 2:2) has become the Day of the Lord Jesus (2 Corinthians 1:14), the Day of the Lord Jesus Christ (1 Corinthians 1:8), or even the Day of Christ (Phil. 1:6, 10; 2:16) … As the Lord, the exalted Christ exercises the prerogatives of God. Thus, the judgment seat of God (Rom. 14:10) is also the judgment seat of Christ (2 Corinthians 5:10). God will judge the world through Christ (Rom. 2:16); and until the end of His messianic reign, God rules the world through the exalted Lord. [12]

a. The Gospels:

But why is this granted to me, that the mother of my Lord should come to me? (Luke 1:43)

For this is he who was spoken of by the prophet Isaiah, saying: "The voice of one crying in the wilderness: 'Prepare the way of the LORD; make His paths straight.'" (Matthew 3:3)

(Jesus quoting Psalm 110 about Himself) *He said to them, "How then does David in the Spirit call Him 'Lord,' saying: 'The LORD said to my Lord, "Sit at My right hand, till I make Your enemies Your footstool?"' If David then calls Him 'Lord,' how is He his Son?" (Matthew 22:43–45)*

b. Paul used this title over 250 times in his letters.

That if you confess with your mouth the Lord Jesus and believe in your heart that God has raised Him from the dead, you will be saved. (Romans 10:9)

Yet for us there is one God, the Father, of whom are all things, and we for Him; and one Lord Jesus Christ, through whom are all things, and through whom we live. (1 Corinthians 8:6)

---

12 Ladd, George Eldon. *New Testament Theology* (Grand Rapids, MI: Eerdmans, 1993), p. 456. Emphasis added.

Therefore I make known to you that no one speaking by the Spirit of God calls Jesus accursed, and no one can say that Jesus is Lord except by the Holy Spirit. (1 Corinthians 12:3)

For we do not preach ourselves, but Christ Jesus the Lord, and ourselves your bondservants for Jesus' sake. (2 Corinthians 4:5)

Therefore God also has highly exalted Him and given Him the name which is above every name, that at the name of Jesus every knee should bow, of those in heaven, and of those on earth, and of those under the earth, and that every tongue should confess that Jesus Christ is Lord, to the glory of God the Father. (Philippians 2:9–11)

I charge you therefore before God and the Lord Jesus Christ, who will judge the living and the dead at His appearing and His kingdom. (2 Timothy 4:1)

You, LORD, in the beginning laid the foundation of the earth, and the heavens are the work of Your hands. They will perish, but You remain; and they will all grow old like a garment; like a cloak You will fold them up, and they will be changed. But You are the same, and Your years will not fail. (Hebrews 1:10–12)

   c. Johannine Literature

Now out of His mouth goes a sharp sword, that with it He should strike the nations. And He Himself will rule them with a rod of iron. He Himself treads the winepress of the fierceness and wrath of Almighty God. And He has on His robe and on His thigh a name written: KING OF KINGS AND LORD OF LORDS. (Revelation 19:15–16)

2.   Son of Man: This was Jesus' favorite ascription. In fact, He used it to describe Himself more than sixty-five times. Jesus identified Himself with the heavenly figure of Daniel 7:13–14 who came with the clouds of Heaven and received all authority from the Ancient of Days over all dominions and peoples. The Son was sent to destroy the works of the devil (1 John 3:8).

     a. As the Son of Man, Jesus has the authority to forgive sins (Matthew 9:6; Mark 2:10; Luke 5:24) and is Lord of the Sabbath (Matthew 12:18; Mark 2:27; Luke 6:5).

"But that you may know that the Son of Man has power on earth to forgive sins"—then He said to the paralytic, "Arise, take up your bed, and go to your house." (Matthew 9:6)

And He said to them, "The Sabbath was made for man, and not man for the Sabbath. Therefore the Son of Man is also Lord of the Sabbath." (Mark 2:27–28)

b. Eschatological fulfillment: as the Son of Man, Jesus will come in the glory of His Father with the holy angels. He is seen as sitting at the right hand of power, and will come with the clouds of Heaven (Matthew 16:27, 24:30, 26:64; Mark 8:38, 13:26, 14:62; Luke 9:26, 21:27, 22:69)

For the Son of Man will come in the glory of His Father with His angels, and then He will reward each according to his works. (Matthew 16:27)

Immediately after the tribulation of those days the sun will be darkened, and the moon will not give its light; the stars will fall from heaven, and the powers of the heavens will be shaken. Then the sign of the Son of Man will appear in heaven, and then all the tribes of the earth will mourn, and they will see the Son of Man coming on the clouds of heaven with power and great glory. And He will send His angels with a great sound of a trumpet, and they will gather together His elect from the four winds, from one end of heaven to the other. (Matthew 24:29–31)

But Jesus kept silent. And the high priest answered and said to Him, "I put You under oath by the living God: Tell us if You are the Christ, the Son of God!" Jesus said to him, "It is as you said. Nevertheless, I say to you, hereafter you will see the Son of Man sitting at the right hand of the Power, and coming on the clouds of heaven." (Matthew 26:63-64)

c. It is also worthy to note that Jesus added to the understanding of this heavenly ruling figure of Daniel 7 by highlighting His mission as that of a suffering servant. "The Son of Man is not only a heavenly, pre-existent being; He appears in weakness and humility as a man among human beings to fulfill a destiny of suffering and death. In other words, Jesus poured the content of the Suffering servant into the Son of Man concept."[13]

Behold, we are going up to Jerusalem, and the Son of Man will be betrayed to the chief priests and to the scribes; and they will condemn Him to death and deliver Him to the Gentiles; and they will mock Him, and scourge Him, and spit on Him, and kill Him. And the third day He will rise again. (Mark 10:33–34)

For even the Son of Man did not come to be served, but to serve, and to give His life a ransom for many. (Mark 10:45)

3. Son of God: John stated that the purpose of writing his gospel was "that you may believe that Jesus is the Christ, the Son of God, and that believing you may have life in His name" (20:31). Jesus spoke of God as "the Father" 106 times in John and said "my Father" twenty-four times in John. In John, Jesus is described as the only-begotten, unique Son of God. Even in the synoptic gospels, Jesus is described as the "Beloved Son" who regarded Himself as uniquely able to understand the Father's will and solely able to reveal God (Matthew 3:17, 11:27, 17:5; Luke 10:21–22).

Immediately he preached the Christ in the synagogues, that He is the Son of God. *(Acts 9:20, emphasis added)*

E. The possession of divine attributes

1. His omnipotence

a. Overcame the temptation of Satan in the wilderness— Matthew 4:1–11, Luke 4:1–13

---

13 Ladd, George Eldon. *New Testament Theology* (Grand Rapids, MI: Eerdmans, 1993), p. 155.

Then Jesus said to him, "Away with you, Satan! For it is written, 'You shall worship the LORD your God, and Him only you shall serve.'" Then the devil left Him, and behold, angels came and ministered to Him. (Matthew 4:10–11)

b. Jesus quieted storms

But He said to them, "Why are you fearful, O you of little faith?" Then He arose and rebuked the winds and the sea, and there was a great calm. So the men marveled, saying, "Who can this be, that even the winds and the sea obey Him?" (Matthew 8:26–27)

c. He multiplied the fish and loaves

Then He commanded the multitudes to sit down on the grass. And He took the five loaves and the two fish, and looking up to heaven, He blessed and broke and gave the loaves to the disciples; and the disciples gave to the multitudes. So they all ate and were filled, and they took up twelve baskets full of the fragments that remained. Now those who had eaten were about five thousand men, besides women and children. (Matthew 14:19–21)

d. He cast out a legion of demons

Then they came to Jesus, and saw the one who had been demon-possessed and had the legion, sitting and clothed and in his right mind. And they were afraid. (Mark 5:15)

e. He turned the water into wine

This beginning of signs Jesus did in Cana of Galilee, and manifested His glory; and His disciples believed in Him. (John 2:11)

f. He raised the dead

So he who was dead sat up and began to speak. And He presented him to his mother. (Luke 7:15)

But He put them all outside, took her by the hand and called, saying, "Little girl, arise." Then her spirit returned, and she arose immediately. And He commanded that she be given something to eat. (Luke 8:54–55)

g. He walked on water and enabled Peter to walk with Him.

Now in the fourth watch of the night Jesus went to them, walking on the sea … He said [to Peter], "Come." And when Peter had come down out of the boat, he walked on the water to go to Jesus. (Matthew 14:25,29)

2.   His omniscience: Jesus knew people's thoughts and intentions.

a. He knew the hearts of men.

…He knew all men, and had no need that anyone should testify of man, for He knew what was in man. (John 2:24–25)

b. The disciples declared that Jesus knew all things.

Now we are sure that You know all things, and have no need that anyone should question You. By this we believe that You came forth from God. (John 16:30)

Lord, you know all things; you know that I love you. (John 21:17)

3.   His sovereignty

a. Jesus displayed the authority to forgive sins.

When Jesus saw their faith, He said to the paralytic, "Son, your sins are forgiven you." (Mark 2:5)

b. He uniquely interpreted the law and overrode traditions with the phrase, "But I say to you" (Matthew 5:22,28,32, 34,39,44).

*You have heard that it was said, "You shall love your neighbor and hate your enemy.' **But I say to you**, love your enemies, bless those who curse you, do good to those who hate you, and pray for those who spitefully use you and persecute you. (Matthew 5:43–44, emphasis added)*

c. He boldly proclaimed that the eternal state of every person depended on their belief in Him.

    He who believes in the Son has everlasting life; and he who does not believe the Son shall not see life, but the wrath of God abides on him. (John 3:36)

d. Jesus also claimed to be the sovereign judge of all humanity (Matthew 25:31–46; John 5:24–29). He will display His omnipotence by raising all people at the sound of His voice and then display His sovereignty in deciding their eternal state.

    Most assuredly, I say to you, he who hears My word and believes in Him who sent Me has everlasting life, and shall not come into judgment, but has passed from death into life. Most assuredly, I say to you, the hour is coming, and now is, when the dead will hear the voice of the Son of God; and those who hear will live. For as the Father has life in Himself, so He has granted the Son to have life in Himself, and has given Him authority to execute judgment also, because He is the Son of Man. Do not marvel at this; for the hour is coming in which all who are in the graves will hear His voice and come forth—those who have done good, to the resurrection of life, and those who have done evil, to the resurrection of condemnation. (John 5:24–29)

4. His immortality

    a. Jesus claimed in John 10:17–18 that by His very own power, He would lay down His life and take it up again. In John 2:21–22, Jesus claimed that the temple of His body would be destroyed and that he would raise it up.

Therefore My Father loves Me, because I lay down My life that I may take it again. No one takes it from Me, but I lay it down of Myself. I have power to lay it down, and I have power to take it again. This command I have received from My Father. (John 10:17–18)

b. Hebrews 7:15–16 declares that Jesus has become a priest, not according to a legal requirement concerning bodily descent, but by the power of an indestructible life.

And it is yet far more evident if, in the likeness of Melchizedek, there arises another priest who has come, not according to the law of a fleshly commandment, but according to the power of an endless life. (Hebrews 7:15–16)

5. He received adoration and worship

a. Jesus is the object of worship in the resurrected community and in the heavenly courts. Thomas, after seeing the resurrected Lord, could only respond with worship.

And Thomas answered and said to Him, "My Lord and my God!" (John 20:28)

b. The disciples worshiped Him at His ascension.

Now it came to pass, while He blessed them, that He was parted from them and carried up into heaven. And they worshiped Him, and returned to Jerusalem with great joy. (Luke 24:51–52)

c. The angels and redeemed worship Him alongside His Father in Revelation 5. See John 5:23, 14:13–14, Acts 7:59, 1 Corinthians 11:24–25, Philippians 2:9–11 and Hebrews 1:6.

And every creature which is in heaven and on the earth and under the earth and such as are in the sea, and all that are in them, I heard saying: "Blessing and honor and glory and power be to Him who sits on the throne, and to the Lamb, forever and ever!" Then the four living creatures said, "Amen!" And the twenty-four elders fell down and worshiped Him who lives forever and ever. (Revelation 5:13–14)

F.   Jesus' own claims: in John's gospel, Jesus used "I am" phrases: "I am the bread of life," "I am the good shepherd," "I am the door," "I am the light of the world," "I am the resurrection and the life," "I am the way, the truth, and the life," "I am the true vine."

"Your father Abraham rejoiced to see My day, and he saw it and was glad." Then the Jews said to Him, "You are not yet fifty years old, and have You seen Abraham?" Jesus said to them, "Most assuredly, I say to you, before Abraham was, I AM." Then they took up stones to throw at Him; but Jesus hid Himself and went out of the temple, going through the midst of them, and so passed by. (John 8:56–59)

V.   JESUS' HUMANITY

Standing in awe of God is one thing. Loving Him is quite another thing. You can go through life obedient and struck by His awesomeness, but it's quite another thing to be struck by His tenderness, to be tender towards God. When you know His humanity and tender acquaintance with your frame, your heart feels safe to move towards Him and ask questions you normally would not ask. It is sheer joy to engage with your older Brother in dialogue and in worship, free to love Him with your particular personality. This is joy: to enjoy yourself in enjoying Him.

This is where contemplation sets to work. On the one hand, what the Son is and does is human, and is thus comprehensible … Even the quality of Christ's humanity is so different from all other humanity and from everything that is possible in the world. All the same, the humanity of the Son of Man is human: it is not interfered with, there is no grotesque distortion; it bears the mark of its divine quality just as white-hot iron shows its heat; indeed, the divine reveals its incomparable power in the very fact that what is human is not destroyed. If two magnitudes were of the same order, the greater would of necessity be a threat to the lesser. A tree planted in a flower pot will burst it. Only God can appear in a creature without destroying it. Faith is rendered able to contemplate the divine in creaturely form.[14]

---

14   Von Balthasar, Hans Urs. *Prayer* (San Francisco, Ignatius, 1986), p. 162-163.

The contemplative's gaze continually returns with great attention to the humanity of Jesus. It is the inexhaustible treasure entrusted to us by the heavenly Father. In a true sense he has "despoiled himself" (John 3:16) of him to whom he is always pointing: ipsum audite! (Matthew 17:5). The Son is no floating interstellar body; he is the fruit of the earth and its history; he comes from Mary (who is the exponent of the Old Covenant and of all humanity) just as he comes from the Father. He is grace ascending just as much as grace descending; he is just as much creation's highest response to the Father as he is the Father's Word to creation. He is no God in disguise, acting "as if", simply to give us an example ... No. He is the apex of the world in its strivings towards God, and he cuts a path for all of us, gathering up all men's efforts into Himself the pioneer, the spearhead. He can do this only by being "In every respect tempted as we are, yet without sinning" (Heb. 4:15), by bearing our burdens as the scapegoat (Heb. 13:11), the Lamb brought to the slaughter, slain from the foundation of the world (Revelation 13:8). Thus, he stands at the summit of heaven and earth.[15]

A.   Introduction into fascination:

      1.   He was born. The point of the Incarnation is to make you ponder, to make you marvel, to blow your mind. Marveling is precisely what Mary did.

---

15 *Ibid*, p. 170-171.

Now there were in the same country shepherds living out in the fields, keeping watch over their flock by night. And behold, an angel of the Lord stood before them, and the glory of the Lord shone around them, and they were greatly afraid. Then the angel said to them, "Do not be afraid, for behold, I bring you good tidings of great joy which will be to all people. For there is born to you this day in the city of David a Savior, who is Christ the Lord. And this will be the sign to you: You will find a Babe wrapped in swaddling cloths, lying in a manger." And suddenly there was with the angel a multitude of the heavenly host praising God and saying: "Glory to God in the highest, And on earth peace, goodwill toward men!" So it was, when the angels had gone away from them into heaven, that the shepherds said to one another, "Let us now go to Bethlehem and see this thing that has come to pass, which the Lord has made known to us." And they came with haste and found Mary and Joseph, and the Babe lying in a manger. Now when they had seen Him, they made widely known the saying which was told them concerning this Child. And all those who heard it marveled at those things which were told them by the shepherds. But Mary kept all these things and pondered them in her heart. Then the shepherds returned, glorifying and praising God for all the things that they had heard and seen, as it was told them. (Luke 2:8–20, emphasis added)*

a. Recently, I came across my deceased mother's birth certificate from 1943. On the back of this hospital record were her tiny footprints. Pictures and memories became amazingly familiar. The Lord began speaking to me in this tender moment, and I entered into divine dialogue. He told me, "Allen, I had feet like that." I said, "You're kidding me, Lord! You had feet like this? Tiny feet like my boys now have, feet with toes I love to pull on until they pop?" He answered, "Yes, I did. My toes were just as small and frail as your mother's when she was a baby, with toes as poppable as your sons'." He came as a man.

b. The joy of the Christian life is to gaze upon the mystery of Jesus. Luke 2:7 describes the virgin birth. Mary bore Him in childbirth, brought Him forth with real pain. She brought forth her first-born Son, wrapped Him in swaddling clothes, and laid him in a manger. Then the angels broke out in singing and shepherds paid homage to the newborn king.

c. Look what Mary did after Jesus was born. She was perplexed. She'd given birth to this baby whom angels were praising. In verse nineteen, she pondered: "I know He is God, but I felt real pain and real movements in my belly as He was growing. How could that be? How can it be that angels tell shepherds about this and wise men come to visit Him bearing gifts, and yet He came out of my loins? How can it be that God has my eyes and my nose?" She found the joy of pondering the mystery, and she kept all these things in her heart.

d. *When the Son of God became man for our sake, He could have come on earth as an adult man from the first moment of His human existence. But the sight of little children draws us with an especial attraction to love them, Jesus chose to make His first appearance on earth as a little infant…* "God wished to be born as a little baby," wrote Saint Peter of Chrysologus, "in order that he might teach us to love and not to fear Him." *The prophet Isaiah had long before foretold that the Son of God was to be born as an infant and thus give Himself to us on account of the love He bore us:* "A child is born to us, a son is given to us." ***My Jesus, supreme and true God! What has drawn Thee from heaven to be born in a cold stable, if not the love which Thou bearest us men? What has allured thee from the bosom of Thy Father, to place Thee in a hard manger? What has brought Thee from Thy throne above the stars to lay Thee down on a little straw? What has led Thee from the midst of the nine choirs of angels, to set Thee between two animals? Thou, who inflamest the seraphim with holy fire, art now shivering with cold in this stable! Thou, who settest the stars in the sky in motion, canst not now move unless others carry Thee in their arms! Thou, who givest men and beasts their food, hast need now of a little milk to sustain Thy life! Thou, who art the joy of heaven, dost now whimper and cry in suffering! Tell me who has reduced Thee to such misery?*** *"Love has done it,"* ***says Saint Bernard. The love which Thou bearest us men has brought all this on Thee.***[16]

But when the fullness of the time had come, God sent forth His Son, born of a woman. *(Galatians 4:4, emphasis added)*

---

16 Alphonsus Maria de Liguori, Saint. "God's Love Revealed in His Being Born and Infant." *The Book of Jesus: A Treasury of the Greatest Stories & Writings About Christ* (Ed. Calvin Miller. New York: Simon & Schuster, 1998), pp. 257-58. Emphasis added.

2. Luke tells us that Jesus was not only born with a human body; He grew up. I love to imagine this. What did Jesus' awkward growing stages look like? Can you imagine the time when His ears had outgrown His head and He sat through two more years of rabbinical school before His head caught up? Have you ever thought about that? He was just like you, except without sin. What did it look like when Jesus lost His first tooth and had is first haircut? What was it like? Luke says that the child grew and that Mary was amazed again and again. This is all we know about Jesus until we find Him at age twelve in the temple. He simply grew as a human being.

I look at my little boys all the time and wonder, "Jesus, were you like them? What were You like? What was holy fun like for You, Jesus? Did You ever play a practical joke? What was harmless fun like for You, Jesus?" Oh, it had to be outstanding!

3. Jesus also grew in the Spirit and was filled with wisdom. The grace of God was upon Him. He grew mentally and spiritually. What was it like as He began to discover in stages that He was the unique God-Man? I imagine He sometimes thought to Himself, "Something feels different about Me. I never get in trouble like James does." What was it like when His mental and spiritual capacity got to the point where He began to remember the throne room? What was it like for Him to read the Word as fully human and start to remember speaking it as God? What was it like for Him growing up when He could see all the angels around everybody else?

What was it like on the day when the Father decided that Jesus was ready to see spiritual realities? How would He have responded to His first angelic encounter? I imagine Him trembling with fascination, saying, "I feel like I know you from somewhere. Have we met before?" We seldom think on these things. This is reality. This is your God, and this is your King, and this is your Brother and your Bridegroom! You can fall in love with Him! It's okay. Did you know that? You really can fall in love with Him because of the Incarnation. We've been robbed of Jesus for far too long. It is time to ponder. It is time to enjoy the depths of His mystery and the richness of His shared life.

4. We have so many unfilled blanks; all we know from the Scripture is that He grew (Luke 2). Does He have Mary's cheekbones? He was fully God, yet He grew. He is fully man. I am convinced that we have little information on Jesus' childhood because of His great kindness to cover His family.

B. Virgin birth: in Genesis 3:15, God had promised that through the "Seed" of the woman the serpent would be crushed. He had to come through a family line. God chose to come through the line of Judah and the house of David, and chose Mary to be the favored one. When the Holy Spirit overshadowed Mary, the uniting of full deity and full humanity was made possible in one person (Luke 1:35, Galatians 4:4). In the virgin birth, the humanity of Jesus was established, yet He was without sin. Wayne Grudem points out the doctrinal importance of the virgin birth in three primary ways:

1. It displays that God is the One who initiates and brings salvation. There is no salvation outside of the supernatural intervention of God. Human effort can never save us from the depth of our sin before God.

2. It makes it possible the hypostatic union, the joining of full deity to full humanity.

3. It makes possible for Christ to be truly human, but have no inherited sin. There is not one person in history who has been able to prove that Jesus ever sinned, not one sin, not one moral failure, none, especially those in His own generation.[17]

    And the angel answered and said to her, "The Holy Spirit will come upon you, and the power of the Highest will overshadow you; therefore, also, that Holy One who is to be born will be called the Son of God." (Luke 1:35, emphasis added)

C. Human weaknesses and limitations:

    And the Child grew and became strong in spirit, filled with wisdom; and the grace of God was upon Him. (Luke 2:40)

---

17 Grudem, Wayne. *Systematic Theology: An Introduction to Biblical Doctrine* (Grand Rapids, MI: Zondervan, 1994), pp. 529-30.

Max Lucado's twenty-five questions for Mary: What was it like watching Him pray? How did He respond when He saw other kids giggling during the service at synagogue? When He saw a rainbow, did He ever mention a flood? Did you ever feel awkward teaching Him how He created the world? When He saw a lamb being led to the slaughter, did He act differently? Did you ever see Him with a distant look on His face as if He were listening to someone you couldn't hear? How did He act at funerals? Did the thought ever occur to you that the God to whom you were praying was asleep under your own roof? Did you ever try to count the stars with Him … and succeed? Did He ever come home with a black eye? How did He act when He got His first haircut? Did He have any friends by the name of Judas? Did He do well in school? Did you ever scold Him? Did He ever have to ask a question about Scripture? What do you think He thought when He saw a prostitute offering to the highest bidder the body He made? Did He ever get angry when someone was dishonest with Him? Did you ever catch Him pensively looking at the flesh on His own arm while holding a clod of dirt? Did He ever wake up afraid? Who was His best friend? When someone referred to Satan, how did He act? Did you ever accidentally call Him Father? What did he and His cousin John talk about as kids? Did His other brothers and sisters understand what was happening? Did you ever think, That's God eating my soup?[18]

1. Human body: Jesus was born like all humans in Luke 2:7. In Luke 2:40, we read that Jesus grew up and became strong. He displayed thirst and hunger (John 19:28; Matthew 4:2). He grew tired and slept (Matthew 8:24). At the end of His fast in the wilderness, angels came and attended to Him (Matthew 4:11). He bled and suffered in body greatly throughout the crucifixion event. In fact, in Luke 23:26 Jesus could physically no longer carry the cross. He was fighting for every ounce of composure He could. This weakness endears Him to us. The event culminated with the giving up of His life and the burial of His body in a garden tomb. Kenosis Theory details the relationship between His divine nature and human nature as seen in Philippians 2:5–11: when He came as a man, He laid down operating in His divine nature. He emptied Himself and gave us an example of what it means to trust in the Holy Spirit as a man.

---

18 Lucado, Max. "Twenty-Five Questions for Mary." *The Book of Jesus: A Treasury of the Greatest Stories & Writings about Christ* (Ed. Calvin Miller. New York: Simon & Schuster, 1998), p. 122-23.

2. Mental growth: in His childhood, Jesus grew in both wisdom and stature. Hebrews 5:8 seems to point out His growth even in the area of obedience before His Father. Not that He failed, but that He continued to go to the depths of devotion before His Father, obeying ultimately even to death on a cross.

3. Human soul and human emotions: in John 12:27, Jesus revealed that He is troubled in His soul. He experiences real human emotions and sympathizes with every one of yours. At Gethsemane, He stated, "My soul is very sorrowful, even unto death" (Matthew 26:38). He responded to Mary's grief over Lazarus with weeping (John 11:35). He also wept over Jerusalem's hardness and future destruction (Luke 19:41–44). Yet, in Luke 10:21–24, Jesus rejoiced over the ones to whom He had revealed Himself. What does it look like for Jesus to be "full of joy in the Holy Spirit?" Did He dance? Isaiah 35 says that He will lead the procession into Jerusalem after His second coming, and gladness will overtake us and sorrow will be driven away. What will it look like when He comes into His Kingdom? He is a witty, wonderful, and joyous King. He experiences the depths and heights of human emotions. Therefore, you can approach His throne of grace with boldness. He is your Brother.

    Seeing then that we have a great High Priest who has passed through the heavens, Jesus the Son of God, let us hold fast our confession. For we do not have a High Priest who cannot sympathize with our weaknesses, but was in all points tempted as we are, yet without sin. Let us therefore come boldly to the throne of grace, that we may obtain mercy and find grace to help in time of need. (Hebrews 4:14–16, emphasis added)

D. Jesus maintained His humanity after the Resurrection: He calmed the fears and doubts of the disciples in Luke 24:36–43 by saying, "Behold My hands and My feet, that it is I Myself. Handle Me and see, for a spirit does not have flesh and bones as you see I have" (v. 39). He went on to ask them for food and ate broiled fish and some honeycomb. Thomas stuck his hand into Jesus' side and his fingers into Jesus' hands (John 20:25–28). Later in John 21:1, Jesus ate breakfast with the disciples by the Sea of Tiberias. When you meet Him face to face, He'll have real scars, real experiences, and real emotions to tell you about.

E.   The identification of the Eternal Son with the human Jesus is complete, personal and permanent. The humanity of Jesus isn't visionary or unreal; is genuine and complete. 1 John emphatically establishes the humanity of Jesus and challenges all docetic notions. Docetism is the belief that all physical matter is intrinsically evil, and therefore, Jesus could not have had a human, physical body—His body was an illusion. John shouts "NO!!!" to this belief and declares that anyone who says that Jesus did not come in the flesh is of the Antichrist spirit. Jesus came as a man. The disciples heard Him. They saw Him. They touched Him. And when the hour had come, John watched Him give His life on the cross as an atoning sacrifice for sin.

That which was from the beginning, **which we have heard,** *which* **we have seen** *with our eyes,* **which we have looked upon,** *and* **our hands have handled,** *concerning the Word of life—***the life was manifested,** *and* **we have seen,** *and bear witness, and declare to you that eternal life which was with the Father and was manifested to us—that which* **we have seen and heard** *we declare to you, that you also may have fellowship with us; and truly our fellowship is with the Father and with His Son Jesus Christ. And these things we write to you that your joy may be full. (1 John 1:1–4, emphasis added)*

VI.   HERESIES AND THE CHALCEDON SOLUTION

Heresies of the church always reject either Christ's humanity or deity. He is fully God, fully man; two natures in one person. When you go outside these four parameters, it affects the atonement, and we are still dead in our sin.

A.   Heresies that reject Christ's humanity:

1.   Docetism: Christ did not come fully in the flesh. "The word *docetism* comes from the Greek verb *dokeo*, 'to seem, to appear to be.' Any theological position that says that Jesus was not really a man, but only appeared to be a man, is called a 'docetic' position. Behind docetism is an assumption that the material creation is inherently evil, and therefore the Son of God could not have been united to a true human nature. No prominent church leader ever advocated docetism, but it was a troublesome heresy that had various supporters in the first four centuries of the church."[19]

---

19 Grudem, Wayne. *Systematic Theology: An Introduction to Biblical Doctrine* (Grand Rapids, MI: Zondervan, 1994), p. 540.

2. Apollinarianism: Apollinarius was the bishop of Laodecia about AD 361. He taught that the person of Christ had a human body, but not a human mind or spirit. His mind and spirit were from the eternal Logos. The problem with this view is that the whole human person, body, mind and spirit must be represented in order for redemption to take place.

3. Eutychianism/Monophysitism: Eutyches, a monastic leader in Constantinople in AD 379–454, taught that the human nature of Christ was taken up into and absorbed by the divine nature of Christ, so that both natures changed and a third combined nature came forth. Somehow a metamorphosis took place. The Church rejected this, citing that this view left Jesus as neither fully God nor fully man.

B. Heresies that reject Christ's divinity:

1. Eutychianism/Monophysitism

2. Ebionism: This view challenged the virgin birth, claiming that Jesus was begotten by Joseph.

3. Arianism: In AD 325, Arius, bishop of Alexandria, "taught that God the Son was at one point created by God the Father, and that before that time the Son did not exist, nor did the Holy Spirit, but the Father only."[20] He taught that there was a time when the Son was not. Arius said that the Son was of similar substance (*homoiousios*), but not of the same substance (*homoousios*) as the Father. The Church at the council of Nicea rejected Arius' view and accepted Athanasius' view of the Trinity. The Nicene Creed reads: "We believe in one God, the Father Almighty, Maker of all things visible and invisible. And in one Lord Jesus Christ, the Son of God, begotten of the Father, the only-begotten; that is of the essence of the Father, God of God, Light of Light, very God of very God, begotten not made, being of one substance *(homoousion)* with the Father…"

C. Heresies that reject Christ's personal union:

---

20 Grudem, Wayne. *Systematic Theology: An Introduction to Biblical Doctrine* (Grand Rapids, MI: Zondervan, 1994), p. 243.

1.   Nestorianism: Nestorius was a popular preacher at Antioch and from AD 428 was bishop of Constantinople. He believed that there were two separate persons in Christ—human and divine. The Church rejected this view as being biblically insupportable. Nowhere in the Scriptures is there any indication that two persons were struggling within Christ.

D.   Chalcedon Solution: In AD 451, a large church council convened to answer the arising views concerning the person of Christ. The council decided on the following definition, which guarded against the previous heresies mentioned:

We then, following the holy Fathers, all with one consent, teach men to confess one and the same Son, our Lord Jesus Christ, the same perfect in the Godhead and also perfect in manhood; truly God and truly man, of a reasonable soul and body; consubstantial with the Father according to the Godhead, and consubstantial with us according the Manhood; in all things like unto us, without sin; begotten before all ages of the Father according to the Godhead, and in these latter days, for us and for our salvation, born of the virgin Mary, the Mother of God, according to the Manhood; one and the same Christ, Son, Lord, Only-begotten, to be acknowledged in two natures, inconfusedly, unchangeably, indivisibly, inseparably; the distinction of each nature being preserved, and concurring in one Person and one Subsistence, not parted or divided into two persons, but one and the same Son, and only begotten God, the Word, the Lord Jesus Christ, as the prophets from the beginning have declared concerning Him, and the Lord Jesus Christ Himself has taught us, and the Creed of the holy Fathers has been handed down to us.

VII. SIGNIFICANCE OF THE INCARNATION

(Some of the material presented in this next section comes from my theology professor at Asbury Theological Seminary, Steve Seamands).

A.   The Incarnation secured and guaranteed the Christian revelation of God. Whoever sees the Son sees the Father. The question is not "What is God like?" The better question is, "Is God Christlike?" (Is Christ the full revelation of the Father?)

B.　　E. Stanley Jones, a famous missionary to India, spoke of the divisive nature of the Incarnation: "This verse—'the Word become flesh'—is the great divide. In all other religions it is word become word—a philosophy, a moralism, a system, a technique, but for all time and all men everywhere, 'the word became flesh'—the idea became fact."[21]

C.　　Other religions speculate about what God is like. Christianity shouts, "We know what God is like! 'That which was from the beginning, which we have heard, which we have seen with our eyes, which we have looked upon, and our hands have handled, concerning the Word of life—the life was manifested, and we have seen, and bear witness, and declare to you that eternal life which was with the Father and was manifested to us—that which we have seen and heard we declare to you, that you also may have fellowship with us; and truly our fellowship is with the Father and with His Son Jesus Christ'" (1 John 1:1–3).

D.　　The Incarnation revealed the passionate, zealous, pursuing heart of God. If He will take on the human form and become a man, to what other lengths will He go? The Incarnation demonstrates the unrestrained love of Yahweh. He is the covenant God. He is the consuming fire that both initiated covenantal love and secures it through abandoned, unyielding desire for the objects of His affection. "Love suffers long and is kind; love does not envy; love does not parade itself, is not puffed up; does not behave rudely, does not seek its own, is not provoked, thinks no evil; does not rejoice in iniquity, but rejoices in the truth; bears all things, believes all things, hopes all things, endures all things. Love never fails" (1 Corinthians 13:4–8). His love never gives up, it never gives in, it never quits hoping, it never quits reaching, and it does not stop until you're just like Him and have received the place He purchased for you on Calvary. Love "did not consider it robbery to be equal with God, but made Himself of no reputation, taking the form of a bondservant, and coming in the likeness of men" (Philippians 2:6–7).

Jesus became a human being because God the compassionate One could not suffer and lacked a back to be beaten. God needed a back like our backs on which to receive blows and thereby to perform compassion as well as to preach it.[22]

21　E. Stanley Jones."Introduction." *The Word Became Flesh*. Abingdon Press, New York, 1963. *A Christian Ashram*. <http://www.vaxxine.com/eves/esjbookl.htm#Word>

22　Eckhart, Meister. *The Book of Jesus: A Treasury of the Greatest Stories & Writings about Christ* (Ed. Calvin Miller. New York: Simon & Schuster, 1998), p. 241.

E.   It secured and guaranteed Christian redemption. "God was in Christ reconciling the world to Himself" (2 Corinthians 5:19). When God took on flesh, He was making an emphatic statement that He would redeem humanity. He linked humanity to Himself; our destiny is wrapped up and intertwined in Him. The Incarnation was God's big "YES" to humanity.

F.   It secured and guaranteed the possibility of our regeneration and participation in the divine life. When Christ came into the world, eternal life became embodied in human form and became a fountain of life for all who would receive Him.

To those who have obtained like precious faith with us by the righteousness of our God and Savior Jesus Christ: Grace and peace be multiplied to you in the knowledge of God and of Jesus our Lord, as His divine power has given to us all things that pertain to life and godliness, through the knowledge of Him who called us by glory and virtue, by which have been given to us exceedingly great and precious promises, that through these you may be partakers of the divine nature, having escaped the corruption that is in the world through lust. (2 Peter 1:1–4)

After the bright beam of hot annunciation
fused heaven with dark earth
his searing sharply-focused light
went out for a while
eclipsed in amniotic gloom;
his cool immensity of splendor
his universal grace
small-folded in a warm dim
female space—
the Word stern-sentenced
to be nine months dumb—
infinitely walled in a womb
until the next enormity—the Mighty,
after submission to a woman's pains
helpless on a barn-bare floor
first-tasting bitter earth.
Because eternity
was closeted in time
he is my open door
to forever.
From his imprisonment my freedoms grow,
find wings.

Part of his body, I transcend this flesh.
From his sweet silence my mouth sings.
Out of his dark I glow.
My life, as his,
slips through death's mesh,
time's bars,
joins hands with heaven,
speaks with stars.[23]

G.   The Incarnation alone secured Christian fellowship. The Body of Christ is connected by one mutually shared life. We have One Head, the same Brother. As an anonymous preacher once said, "The Church is that place where someone chose Jesus and got one another." (1 Corinthians 12:12–26; Ephesians 4:1–16; 1 John 1:7, 4:7–11).

But if we walk in the light as He is in the light, we have fellowship with one another, and the blood of Jesus Christ His Son cleanses us from all sin. (1 John 1:7)

Beloved, let us love one another, for love is of God; and everyone who loves is born of God and knows God. He who does not love does not know God, for God is love. In this the love of God was manifested toward us, that God has sent His only begotten Son into the world, that we might live through Him. In this is love, not that we loved God, but that He loved us and sent His Son to be the propitiation for our sins. Beloved, if God so loved us, we also ought to love one another. (1 John 4:7–11)

H.   It secured and guaranteed the Christian meaning and final outcome of history. The Incarnation makes possible a linear understanding of history. The Incarnation is the center of all history. From the sacred point of the Incarnation, faith could look forward and backward. All of human experience matters. It is not cyclical. History is moving us somewhere. It moved us to the Incarnation of Jesus and it will move us towards His return.

Irenaeus' idea of recapitulation: in many world religions, the wheel of life just keeps turning and turning; history repeats itself. Not so with Christianity. Jesus redeemed history! From the time of His conception to the time of His death and resurrection, Jesus was redeeming the human experience at every point. From the lowest depth, Jesus took human experience back up to life. In doing so, Jesus secured the meaning of history. God has joined Himself to humanity and entered into time.

---

23 Shaw, Luci. "Made Flesh". *The Incarnation: An Anthology* *Nelson's Anthology Series. Nashville, TN: Thomas Nelson, 2002), p. 144.

I.   The Incarnation reestablished human dominion on the Earth. God established His government through human beings again. What was lost in the Garden has now been restored by the person of Jesus. A human King came through Judah's line from the House of David, and will have an everlasting dominion. The image bearers, in the Incarnation, are restored to their created place.

Session Four: The Zeal of the Lord of Hosts

I. INTRODUCTION

A. What would move God to become a man? His zeal—the jealous nature of God and the fiery heart of God—moved Him to take on flesh. The Hebrew word for zeal is *qinah*, which is very much associated with covenant, love, and fire. God's *qinah* is the passion that He directs against every internal and external enemy of love, against all hindrances to love.

B. Studying the zeal of the Lord enables us to see the Lord Jesus rightly. We typically see the Father and His Son as stoic, distant and uninvolved—unconcerned with the small details and the day-to-day emotions of our small, unnoticeable lives. God is seen as wise, yet removed. He seems to run the cosmos with ease, yet is restrained from any real intimate connection. God is viewed as the wise Judge who is unemotionally divested from His creation.

C. Yet God is neither stoic nor emotionally detached. The prophets declared "the burden of the word of the Lord" to Israel. This burden was not the wise Judge revealing His words to the prophets in some distant, merely factual presentation. No, the prophets received the burden of the Lord. Their words were charged with the emotions of God, with God's turmoil, compassion, and anger. One of the most fascinating sentences in the Bible is in Isaiah 16:11, where God spoke to Moab through Isaiah: "All my compassion is stirred within me, Moab." In Ezekiel 33:11, God pled with Israel, "Turn, turn from your evil ways! For why should you die, O house of Israel?" He said this because God is not above pleading with the objects of His affections. Zealous and jealous, God is resolute in removing everything that hinders love.

To the prophet, we have noted, God does not reveal himself in an abstract absoluteness, but in a personal and intimate relation to the world. He does not simply command and expect obedience; He is also moved and affected by what happens in the world, and reacts accordingly. Events and human actions arouse in Him joy or sorrow, pleasure or wrath. He is not conceived as judging the world in detachment. He reacts in an intimate and subjective manner, and thus determines the value of events. Quite obviously in the biblical view, man's deeds may move Him, affect Him, grieve Him or, on the other hand, gladden and please Him. This notion that God can be intimately affected, that He possesses not merely intelligence and will, but also pathos, basically defines the prophetic consciousness of God...Pathos denotes, not an idea of goodness, but a living care; not an immutable example, but an outgoing challenge, a dynamic relation between God and man; not mere feeling or passive affection, but an act or attitude composed of various spiritual elements; no mere contemplative survey of the world, but a passionate summons.[1]

D.   Within the human heart is a latent accusation against God—the belief that He is mostly unwilling to care about our lives, or at least is delayed in His sensitivity. This subtle accusation greatly impacts our prayer life and results in anemic prayers. We put more faith in the potency of our culture than the potency of God's fiery passion to come and make wrong things right in our lives. We fail to lay hold of the one thing which is fighting on our behalf—God's great compassion toward us. If we do not understand His zeal for us, we may offer up words, but faith-filled prayer is absent. All we can say are weak words that express our desperate wish for God to listen, instead of prayers that apprehend God's zealous heart and call for Him to come do what He loves to do.

---

1   Heschel, Abraham J. *The Prophets* (Perennial Classics ed. New York: Harper and Row, 2001), p. 289.

E.   Recently, during a Global Bridegroom Fast at the International House of Prayer in Kansas City, the Lord spoke to me in a profound way. "Allen Hood, have you read My résumé?" He said. "Do you know how many cultures I've reduced to nothing in a moment? I tear down kings and I raise them up *(national transformation)*. Cultures are no problem to Me. Do you think your Western culture could somehow stand against the fiery torrent of My heart? Do you know who I am, young man? Do you know what My word does? It is like a hammer that breaks rock and like a fire that burns chaff. Go ask Jerusalem. They killed my Son, and fifty days later My power broke out and began to bring down structures in that city. They killed My Son, yet that failed to stop the moving of My power. Go ask Samaria what My power was like. Go ask Antioch what happened there. Go ask Ephesus of its report of how I brought it down the idol industry. Its entire economy trembled before the word of the Lord. Ask Rome. Ask London what I did there. Ask about the worst time in New York City's history. Ask them what I did in the midst of the stock market on Wall Street—how I caused businessmen to gather for prayer, how revival broke out and hundreds of thousands were saved. Go ask what I did to Kentucky when it was the western frontier of America. Go ask what I did to its 75% alcoholism rate. Go ask them." (To this day some Kentucky counties prohibit the sale of alcohol because of the great revival that began at Cane Ridge.)

The Lord continued, "If you think Freemasonry is so strong, if you think occultism is so strong, go and ask Finney's culture what happened to it. Ask Whitfield of the gospel's power. Look at My résumé, Allen."

F.   As we begin to look at the Incarnation through the lens of God's passion, our emotional chemistry is altered, faith is born, and prayer begins. Might enters our inner man, and we begin to pray from a place of strength—God's strength and our faith in it. We need to ask God to forgive us for our unbelief and our latent accusations concerning His activity in our lives, lest we believe that our culture is stronger than the zeal of the Lord of Hosts. We need an understanding of what happened the day God became man. We need a revelation of what power was loosed on Earth when Jesus was baptized in the river Jordan and the Spirit rested on Him without measure. In Christ, the zeal of the Lord of Hosts has been released in the realm of humanity. We need a glimpse of what was taking place in Christ and what is taking place in us by the indwelling of the Holy Spirit.

II. THE BURNING GOD OF SINAI

A. God established His covenant of love on Mount Sinai. He drew near Israel with tremendous, awesome power, but only after the nation consecrated herself for the covenant. The Lord descended in fire upon the mountain, burning with desire for the covenant of betrothal. At Sinai, He set apart a people for Himself, a people of righteousness, a people of worship for the praise of His glory in the earth. Exodus 20 describes how the Lord gave Israel the Ten Commandments and warned them of His jealous love. In verses 4–6, He commanded them to refrain from idolatry and bowing down to idols. He justified this command by His burning heart of love: "For I, the Lord your God, am a jealous God" (Exodus 20:5). If anyone fell into adultery, He would come with zeal and punish the iniquity of that generation to the fourth generation. However, to those who were faithful in love, He would show mercy and love to them and to thousands of later generations. As God established the Law, He revealed His passionate bridegroom heart, which burns with jealousy over the objects of His affections.

B. From the NIV Study Bible notes on Exodus 20:5:

Jealous God. God will not put up with rivalry or unfaithfulness. Usually His "jealousy" concerned Israel and assumed the covenant relationship (analogous to marriage) and the Lord's exclusive right to possess Israel and to claim her love and allegiance. Actually, jealousy is part of the vocabulary of love. The "jealousy" of God 1) demands exclusive devotion to Himself (see Exodus 34:4; Deuteronomy 4:24; 32:16,21; Joshua 24:19; Psalm 78:58; 1 Corinthians 10:22; James 4:5), 2) delivers judgment to all who oppose Him (see Deuteronomy 29:20; 1 Kings 14:22; Psalm 79:5; Isaiah 42:13; 59:17; Ezekiel 5:13; 16:38; 23:25; 36:5; Nahum 1:2; Zephaniah 1:8; 3:8); and 3) vindicates His people (see 2 Kings 19:31; Isaiah 9:7; 26:11; Ezekiel 39:25; Joel 2:18; Zechariah 1:14; 8:2). This covenant is not easily undone; in fact it is never undone. This covenant He will always have with His people.[2]

C. Later at Sinai, God revealed His glory to Moses by declaring His name: "The Lord, the Lord God, merciful and gracious, longsuffering, and abounding in goodness and truth" (Exodus 34:6). Then the Lord renewed the covenant with Moses and warned Moses of His unrestrained affections towards Israel. He would not share Israel's affections with any other, for His very name is Jealous. "For you shall worship no other god, for the Lord, whose name is Jealous, is a jealous God" (Exodus 34:14).

---

2 Barker, Kenneth, Ed. *NIV Study Bible* (10th anniversary ed. Grand Rapids, MI: Zondervan, 1995), p. 114.

D. Many times in the Law, the word "zeal/jealousy" is used to describe the utter jealousy of a husband when he suspects marital unfaithfulness of his wife (see Numbers 5 for the offering of jealousy—God set up a whole offering devoted to protect women from husbands who got jealous). In fact, Proverbs 6:34 warns a young man not to commit adultery with another man's wife: "Whoever commits adultery with a woman lacks understanding; he who does so destroys his own soul. Wounds and dishonor he will get, and his reproach will not be wiped away. For jealousy is a husband's fury; therefore he will not spare in the day of vengeance. He will accept no recompense, nor will he be appeased though you give many gifts." God's name is Jealous. He is a jealous husband, and in His unbridled passion, He claims sole rights to the hearts of the ones He loves. His zeal moves as a swift witness against everything that hinders divine love. It moves against sin within and without. It struck against the oppression and persecution of Israel's enemies who hindered their worship. He would not and will not allow His love to be scorned. His love is not tamable and it is not easily trampled. It cannot be ignored. "If anyone does not love the Lord Jesus Christ, let him be accursed" (1 Corinthians 16:22). To be indifferent or to ignore Him is to commit the worst offense against God.

E. At the end of Moses' life, he reminded them again in Deuteronomy 4:24 of the covenant and reemphasized the fiery heart of God against idolatry: "For the Lord your God is a consuming fire, a jealous God." Were it not for this love, we would not have had any hope.

F. Joshua 24:19: in his old age, Joshua said farewell to the people and renewed the covenant between them and the Lord. In charging the people to serve the Lord, Joshua told them that the Lord is holy and jealous. If they sinned against Him, He would bring disaster upon them. Holiness and jealousy go together.

III. THE BURNING GOD OF THE PROPHETS

The prophets carried this theme. They looked ahead and pointed back to the covenant and how Israel violated it and how it roused God, both for judgment and redemption.

The prophet is not a mouthpiece, but a person; not an instrument, but a partner, an associate of God ... An analysis of prophetic utterances shows that the fundamental experience of the prophet is a fellowship with the feelings of God, a sympathy with the divine pathos, a communion with the divine consciousness which comes about through the prophet's reflection of, or participation in, the divine pathos ... The emotional experience of the prophet becomes the focal point for the prophet's understanding of God. He lives not only his personal life, but also the life of God. The prophet hears God's voice and feels His heart. He tries to impart the pathos of the message together with its logos. As an imparter his soul overflows, speaking as he does out of the fullness of his sympathy.[3]

A.   The Major Prophets: Isaiah and Ezekiel

Isaiah 9:7: the "zeal of the Lord Almighty" was declared as the primary basis for establishing and upholding the Messianic Kingdom. God's zeal will accomplish the rule of the Messiah.

Isaiah 26:11: God's zeal for His people is like that of a jealous lover. He brings His fiery wrath against the people who refuse holiness and live wickedly. The fiery passion of God removes all hindrances of love between Him and His people.

Isaiah 37:32: The "zeal of the Lord" was the accomplishing agent in battle against King Sennacherib of Assyria. Isaiah prophesied to Hezekiah that Assyria would fail and that the Warrior God would fight on Israel's behalf. The angel of the Lord put 185,000 Assyrian soldiers to death as the Assyrian army slept; the Hebrew actually says they "woke up dead." The jealous love of God for His people would protect them against the onslaught of all enemy forces.

Isaiah 42:13: "The LORD will march out like a mighty man; He shall stir up His zeal like a man of war. He shall cry out, yes, shout aloud; He shall prevail against His enemies." The Lord's zeal was stirred up to establish His Servant, the Messiah, in His Kingdom, and to destroy His enemies. God is zealous and jealous for the establishment of His loving, righteous, and just Kingdom.

---

3   Heschel, Abraham J. *The Prophets*. (Perennial Classics ed. New York: Harper and Row, 2001), p. 30-31.

Isaiah 59:17: God once again came as the Warrior who wraps Himself in zeal as a cloak. His zeal was His jealous love, which refused to accept the unfaithfulness of His people. God as a jealous lover warred against the unfaithful, counting them as His foes. It was precisely the zeal of the Lord that brought judgment upon His people for their adultery and sin, and it is this same zeal which brings destruction upon the enemy forces. Anything that is opposed to the loving covenant between God and His people, whether inside or outside the camp, kindles God's zeal/jealousy and brings forth His fiery wrath.

Isaiah 63:15: Isaiah interceded for the redemption the Lord had promised. He appealed to the zeal of the Lord, asking, "Where are Your zeal and Your might?" The basis for redemption is always found in the Lord's zeal to bring forth a people whom He can love in the splendor of holiness. Isaiah appealed to the character of God and to His zeal for His people when asking for revival.

Ezekiel 5:13: the Lord spoke in His zeal when He promised His wrath against His people for their adulterous love of idols. The jealousy of God was kindled against idolatry. Ezekiel 5:8 says, "Therefore this is what the Sovereign Lord says: I myself am against you, Jerusalem, and I will inflict punishment on you in the sight of the nations. Because of all your detestable idols, I will do to you what I have never done before and will never do again."

Ezekiel 8:3: an idol, a statue of Asherah (the Canaanite goddess of fertility), had been placed in the temple. Ezekiel called it the "idol that provokes to jealousy" or the "idol of jealousy." This jealousy caused God to command that all in Jerusalem who worshipped the statue be marked as idolaters and killed. When Ezekiel saw Jesus, it was as a Man of fire who burned with zeal and jealousy.

Ezekiel 16:38,42: the jealous wrath of God as a Husband comes against the unfaithful prostitution of His wife, Israel. God, in His jealous anger, will use Israel's actual lovers to punish her. Israel despised her covenant of love with the Lord and thus brought upon herself God's jealous wrath.

Ezekiel 23:25: God's jealous anger against His people was evidenced by Babylon's onslaught against Jerusalem.

Ezekiel 35:11: God judged Edom for her anger and envy towards Israel and Judah. Because of His jealousy, God judged His people and also judged those who oppressed His people.

Ezekiel 36:5–6: because Israel was scorned by the nations, God, in His jealous anger, promised judgment upon the oppressing nations.

Ezekiel 38:19: By God's zeal and wrath, He would display His greatness and His holiness in the sight of many nations by destroying the invader from the north, Gog, who would come against Israel.

B. Minor Prophets

Joel 2:18: after a holy fast, sacred assembly, and Israel's repentance, the Lord would be zealous/jealous for His people. This would lead to His pity and manifest blessings upon Zion.

Nahum 1:2: the Lord was jealous and took vengeance against His enemies. God crushed Assyria, who had oppressed Israel.

Zephaniah 1:18: in the fire of God's jealousy, the whole earth will be consumed on the Great Day of the Lord. The fiery jealousy of God will make a sudden end of all who live on the earth. By this time, they will have taken the mark of the beast and worshiped a demonized king.

Zephaniah 3:8: a restatement of Zephaniah 1:18: "The whole world will be consumed by the fire of my jealous anger."

Zechariah 1:14: the word *qana* is used here beside *qinah* to emphasize the Lord's jealous love over His people. It reads "jealous jealous." The Lord Almighty's jealousy for Jerusalem and Zion led Him to vindicate Israel among the nations. If He did not protect the boundaries of love, none of us would make it.

Zechariah 8:2: the word *qana* is again used here beside *qinah* to emphasize the Lord's jealous love over His people. The Lord Almighty is emphatic concerning His jealousy for Zion. In fact, He is burning with jealousy over her, which leads to great blessing for Israel.

IV. THE FIERY ASCENT TO THE THRONE—ISAIAH 9:6–7

"For to us a child is born, to us a son is given, and the government will be on his shoulders. And he will be called Wonderful Counselor, Mighty God, Everlasting Father, Prince of Peace. Of the increase of his government and peace there will be no end. He will reign on David's throne and over his kingdom, establishing and upholding it with justice and righteousness from that time on and forever. The zeal of the LORD Almighty will accomplish this." *(Isaiah 9:6–7, emphasis added)*

A. Assyria kept northern Israel from rebelling against it by either killing all the males or mixing different family groups. For instance, Assyria took some families and sent them to many other parts of the region, then sent other people groups to Northern Israel to intermarry with the remaining Israelites. Intermarriage took away the nation's identity and the resolve to strike back against Assyria. In Jesus' day, the Samaritans were looked upon and despised because their ancestors had intermarried and their faith was mingled. They were the ones who were left after the Northern exile.

B. Isaiah, after prophesying of the oncoming destruction that Assyria would bring on northern Israel, prophesied of a day when the land destroyed by Assyria would be the center of great divine activity. The place of rampant idolatry, oppression of the poor, sexual perversion, and unholy alliances would be the epicenter of the grand, unprecedented activity of the Most High God. The uncreated, holy, beautiful God would send a Son to the nation of Israel, and through this Son He would inaugurate an unparalleled, unshakable kingdom.

C. This Son would be the manifestation of Yahweh's zeal and would establish God's government. The Lord of Hosts, the sovereign ruler of the armies of Heaven, would express His jealous, burning love through the Son. Zeal would overflow the banks of Heaven, take on flesh and defeat the enemies of love. A Man would be filled with the very fire that descended upon Matthew Sinai, and this One would route all the enemies of God. John baptized with water, but He would baptize with the Holy Spirit and fire (Matthew 3:11; Luke 3:16). The affection of the Bridegroom King was stirred. He would march out like a mighty man of war and triumph over His enemies.

D.   Jesus, as a man, came to take back the dominion stolen from humanity in the Garden of Eden. What Adam lost, the embodied zeal of the Lord of Hosts would take back, backed by all the authority of God's passion and power. The grinding of Satan's ancient kingdom came to an end. A human without sin took up authority again. The One who formed the heavens and the earth, the One who gives orders to the hosts of Heaven, assumed flesh. The Second Adam came and will come again to rule.

E.   The zeal of the Lord is not some abstract concept. It's God's heart bringing forth love and restoring human beings to their rightful, created order. Its not just about our redemption, it's about dominion.

V.   YOU SHALL SEE HEAVEN OPEN — JOHN 1:51

*Jesus answered and said to him, "Because I said to you, 'I saw you under the fig tree,' do you believe? You will see greater things than these." And He said to him, "**Most assuredly, I say to you, hereafter you shall see heaven open, and the angels of God ascending and descending upon the Son of Man.**" (John 1:50–51, emphasis added)*

A.   After prophesying to Nathanael, Jesus, blessed by Nathanael's fascinated heart, told him yet more. He said, "Nathanael, you haven't seen anything yet. An open heaven is coming, Nathanael, and you cannot even imagine what is going to take place. Angels ascending and descending on the Son of Man — it is the hour in which the Kingdom of God prevails in the person of His Son."

B.   Jesus referred back to Genesis 28:10–17 when Jacob was running for his life, fleeing from his brother, Esau. After being swindled out of his father's blessing, Esau vowed to murder Jacob once his father died. The prophecy of the younger ruling over the older (Genesis 27:37,40) appeared to be in shambles. The promise in Genesis 3:15 and Genesis 22:18 was now in jeopardy as Jacob fled for his life. After Jacob escaped, he fell asleep and dreamed of an open heaven. He was given the promise that a kingdom would come through his seed and that it would bless all the nations of the earth. He saw the very "gate of heaven," a divine connection where the activity of Heaven was connected with the governing of Earth. Divine agents, called angels, worked to ensure that God's government would be established through the promised lineage in the promised land and among the nations of the earth. Jacob saw the very "house of God." He gazed upon the very Throne of God and the "gate" or "ladder" that connects this Throne to Earth.

C.   Jacob had a divine encounter in which God assured him of divine assistance in carrying out the promises made to his father Isaac and his grandfather Abraham. "Heaven open" is not a figurative expression. When Jesus used it, He was describing the very centerpiece of God's redemptive purposes: the bringing together of Heaven and Earth. Nathanael was so easily fascinated by a word of knowledge, but Jesus declared, "You haven't seen anything yet. Wait until you see the apex of redemptive history, when all things in Heaven and Earth are brought together in the God-man. **Wait until the King of kings, backed by Heaven's resources, brings about an unprecedented hour of God's reign over all the nations. Every sphere of life will be brought under the influence of a King who rules from the Right Hand of the Majesty and has all heavenly resources at His disposal.**"

D.   Though the whole world presently lies under the sway of the evil one, the promised Kingdom of God in His Son will come. In the person of Jesus, the Kingdom is established and will be fully realized. That is why Jesus depicts Himself as the ladder in John 1:51. Jesus is the Mediator of the Kingdom. He is the one who is inaugurating an age of the in-breaking of the Kingdom—the beginning of a glorious day that is the first-fruits of a fuller reign to come in the Millennium. The King has come in the flesh. The divine Son of Man is the ladder. He is the one bringing the divine activity of God to overthrow the kingdom of darkness with the very finger of God. He will progressively bring to pass partial, substantial, and ultimate rule of God.

1.   Stage #1: Partial (good)—His rule now is mostly in the hearts of His people (the Cross, until the Second Coming). Jesus is ruler over the kings of the earth now, but does not manifest His leadership openly except on rare occasions. Currently, Jesus sits at the Right Hand of the Majesty and dispenses the Spirit (Acts 2:33). He infuses the church worldwide with the evidential Word that the kingdom of darkness has come to an end and that a King from David's House rules over all things, judging the living and the dead.

2.   Stage #2: Substantial (better)—His political rule over all the nations (the Millennial Kingdom)

3.   Stage #3: Ultimate (best)—His rule over the New Earth (after the Millennial Kingdom)

VI. REVIVAL AS THE HISTORIC PREFIGURING OF THE MILLENNIUM

A.   Even before Christ's millennial rule is manifested in the natural with the first descent of the New Jerusalem, revival will partially manifest in the natural as a testimony to the coming substantial rule of Jesus from Jerusalem. The New Jerusalem is the manifestation of the Kingdom of God's power, power that renders opposition useless and powerless.

B.   Historic revivals are divine seasons where God manifests His Kingdom in power as a testimony to the coming millennial rule of Jesus Christ. They are divine hours in which Heaven opens and the kingdom of darkness is plundered. In these seasons, God's people are encouraged with the prophetic promise in Genesis 3:15: the Seed of the Woman will crush the head of the seed of the serpent. These seasons remind us of a coming day when evil will be ultimately and finally judged and destroyed. Examples of revival are the Exodus and Conquest, David and Solomon's Reign, Elijah on Mount Carmel, Elisha facing the Syrian army, and Hezekiah.

C.   **Four Important Verses**

1.   *Then the seventy returned with joy, saying, "Lord, even the demons are subject to us in Your name." And He said to them, "I saw Satan fall like lightning from heaven.* **Behold, I give you the authority to trample on serpents and scorpions, and over all the power of the enemy, and nothing shall by any means hurt you.** *Nevertheless do not rejoice in this, that the spirits are subject to you, but rather rejoice because your names are written in heaven." (Luke 10:17–20, emphasis added)*

2.   *On that very day some Pharisees came, saying to Him, "Get out and depart from here, for Herod wants to kill You." And He said to them,* **"Go, tell that fox, 'Behold, I cast out demons and perform cures today and tomorrow, and the third day I shall be perfected.'** *Nevertheless I must journey today, tomorrow, and the day following; for it cannot be that a prophet should perish outside of Jerusalem." (Luke 13:31–33, emphasis added)*

3. *Now as Jesus passed by, He saw a man who was blind from birth. And His disciples asked Him, saying, "Rabbi, who sinned, this man or his parents, that he was born blind?" Jesus answered, "Neither this man nor his parents sinned, but that the works of God should be revealed in him. I must work the works of Him who sent Me **while it is day**; the night is coming when no one can work. As long as I am in the world, I am the light of the world."(John 9:1–5, emphasis added)*

4. *When I was with you daily in the temple, you did not try to seize Me. **But this is your hour, and the power of darkness.** (Luke 22:53, emphasis added)*

VII. REDEFINING REVIVAL IN LIGHT OF THE GOSPEL OF THE KINGDOM

A. This is revival—**the divine season of an open heaven, in which the Kingdom of God breaks in with power, leading to the healing, deliverance, and salvation of multitudes. In this hour, the testimony of the Spirit brings glory to the Father by exalting the Son's rule and reign. Revival is the glimpse of a glorious day to come when God will be all in all.**

B. A vision of the "open heaven" fuels our intercession. This is what we are praying for in Kansas City. We are asking for the season of trampling on scorpions and serpents, for the power of God to break the power of darkness. We are interceding for the hour of light in which God's revelation goes forth with clarity and power.

VIII. ZEAL MANIFEST—THE GALILEAN REVIVAL

Can you picture this? The uncreated, holy, beautiful God sent His Son, and through the Son He will inaugurate an unparalleled, unshakable kingdom. This Son given by God to establish God's government will be the very zeal of Yahweh manifested. What do you do with this beautiful plan from the beautiful God? This is He who said, "Here is how I'm going to get back government. I'm going to take on your form forever and I'm going to fight your battles as your Brother, and you're going to fall madly in love with Me when I do it." How do you stop a King like that?

A. Baptism of Jesus: Luke 3:21–22

B. Dominion over Satan and his demons

1. The contest in the wilderness/the binding of the strong man: Satan tempts Jesus—Matthew 4:1–11; Mark 1:12,13

   Then Jesus, being filled with the Holy Spirit, returned from the Jordan and was led by the Spirit into the wilderness. (Luke 4:1)

   Again, the devil took Him up on an exceedingly high mountain, and showed Him all the kingdoms of the world and their glory. And he said to Him, "All these things I will give You if You will fall down and worship me." Then Jesus said to him, "Away with you, Satan! For it is written, 'You shall worship the LORD your God, and Him only you shall serve.'" Then the devil left Him, and behold, angels came and ministered to Him. (Matthew 4:8–11)

2. The second exodus: demolishing the reigning powers. Power was coming out of Jesus as He was preaching and teaching. God's Word does things in the Spirit; it shifts and moves things. That is why the restoration of preaching is a massive expression of the zeal of the Lord that will come in these days—and it will come not just in churches, but also in the streets, fields and stadiums.

   a. Healing the demoniac on the Sabbath: Mark 1:21–28, Luke 4:31

      And they were astonished at His teaching, for He taught them as one having authority, and not as the scribes. Now there was a man in their synagogue with an unclean spirit. And he cried out, saying, "Let us alone! What have we to do with You, Jesus of Nazareth? Did You come to destroy us? I know who You are—the Holy One of God!" But Jesus rebuked him, saying, "Be quiet, and come out of him!" And when the unclean spirit had convulsed him and cried out with a loud voice, he came out of him. Then they were all amazed, so that they questioned among themselves, saying, "What is this? What new doctrine is this? For with authority He commands even the unclean spirits, and they obey Him." (Mark 1:22–27)

   b. Cast out many demons and healed the multitudes: Matthew 4:23, 12:15, 14:35–36, 15:30–31; Mark 1:34, 3:7–12; Luke 6:17–19

And Jesus went about all Galilee, teaching in their synagogues, preaching the gospel of the kingdom, and healing all kinds of sickness and all kinds of disease among the people. Then His fame went throughout all Syria; and they brought to Him all sick people who were afflicted with various diseases and torments, and those who were demon-possessed, epileptics, and paralytics; and He healed them. (Matthew 4:23–24)

But when Jesus knew it, He withdrew from there. And great multitudes followed Him, and He healed them all. (Matthew 12:15)

And when the men of that place recognized Him, they sent out into all that surrounding region, brought to Him all who were sick, and begged Him that they might only touch the hem of His garment. And as many as touched it were made perfectly well. (Matthew 14:35–36)

   c. Gadarene/Garasene demoniac: Matthew 8:28–34; Mark 5:1–20 (Legion); Luke 8:26–37

Then they came to the other side of the sea, to the country of the Gadarenes. And when He had come out of the boat, immediately there met Him out of the tombs a man with an unclean spirit, who had his dwelling among the tombs; and no one could bind him, not even with chains, because he had often been bound with shackles and chains. And the chains had been pulled apart by him, and the shackles broken in pieces; neither could anyone tame him. And always, night and day, he was in the mountains and in the tombs, crying out and cutting himself with stones. When he saw Jesus from afar, he ran and worshiped Him. And he cried out with a loud voice and said, "What have I to do with You, Jesus, Son of the Most High God? I implore You by God that You do not torment me." For He said to him, "Come out of the man, unclean spirit!" Then He asked him, "What is your name?" And he answered, saying, "My name is Legion; for we are many." Also he begged Him earnestly that He would not send them out of the country. Now a large herd of swine was feeding there near the mountains. So all the demons begged Him, saying, "Send us to the swine, that we may enter them." And at once Jesus gave them permission. Then the unclean spirits went out and entered the swine (there were about two thousand); and the herd ran violently down the steep place into the sea, and drowned in the sea. So those who fed the swine fled, and they told it in the city and in the country. And they went out to see what it was that had happened. Then they came to Jesus, and saw the one who had been demon-possessed and had the legion, sitting and clothed and in his right mind. And they were afraid. (Mark 5:1–15)

d. Mute and blind demoniac: Matthew 9:32–33, 12:22

Then one was brought to Him who was demon-possessed, blind and mute; and He healed him, so that the blind and mute man both spoke and saw. (Matthew 12:22)

e. Epileptic boy: Matthew 17:14–21; Mark 9:14–29; Luke 9:37–42

And when they had come to the multitude, a man came to Him, kneeling down to Him and saying, "Lord, have mercy on my son, for he is an epileptic and suffers severely; for he often falls into the fire and often into the water. So I brought him to Your disciples, but they could not cure him." Then Jesus answered and said, "O faithless and perverse generation, how long shall I be with you? How long shall I bear with you? Bring him here to Me." And Jesus rebuked the demon, and it came out of him; and the child was cured from that very hour. Then the disciples came to Jesus privately and said, "Why could we not cast it out?" So Jesus said to them, "Because of your unbelief; for assuredly, I say to you, if you have faith as a mustard seed, you will say to this mountain, 'Move from here to there,' and it will move; and nothing will be impossible for you. However, this kind does not go out except by prayer and fasting." (Matthew 17:14–21)

    f.   Spirit of infirmity/bent-over woman (eighteen years): Luke 13:10

Now He was teaching in one of the synagogues on the Sabbath. And behold, there was a woman who had a spirit of infirmity eighteen years, and was bent over and could in no way raise herself up. But when Jesus saw her, He called her to Him and said to her, "Woman, you are loosed from your infirmity." (Luke 13:10–12)

C.   Dominion over sickness and infirmity

    1.   The nobleman's son from a distance

The nobleman said to Him, "Sir, come down before my child dies!" Jesus said to him, "Go your way; your son lives." So the man believed the word that Jesus spoke to him, and he went his way. (John 4:49–50)

    2.   Peter's mother-in-law: Matthew 8:14; Mark 1:29; Luke 4:38

Now as soon as they had come out of the synagogue, they entered the house of Simon and Andrew, with James and John. But Simon's wife's mother lay sick with a fever, and they told Him about her at once. So He came and took her by the hand and lifted her up, and immediately the fever left her. And she served them. (Mark 1:29–31)

3.   Leprosy: Matthew 8:1–4; Mark 1:40–42; Luke 5:12, 17:11–19 (ten lepers)

Now a leper came to Him, imploring Him, kneeling down to Him and saying to Him, "If You are willing, You can make me clean." Then Jesus, moved with compassion, stretched out His hand and touched him, and said to him, "I am willing; be cleansed." As soon as He had spoken, immediately the leprosy left him, and he was cleansed. (Mark 1:40–42)

Now it happened as He went to Jerusalem that He passed through the midst of Samaria and Galilee. Then as He entered a certain village, there met Him ten men who were lepers, who stood afar off. And they lifted up their voices and said, "Jesus, Master, have mercy on us!" So when He saw them, He said to them, "Go, show yourselves to the priests." And so it was that as they went, they were cleansed. And one of them, when he saw that he was healed, returned, and with a loud voice glorified God, and fell down on his face at His feet, giving Him thanks. And he was a Samaritan. So Jesus answered and said, "Were there not ten cleansed? But where are the nine? Were there not any found who returned to give glory to God except this foreigner?" And He said to him, "Arise, go your way. Your faith has made you well." (Luke 17:11–19)

4.   Paralysis: Matthew 9:1–8; Mark 2:1–12; Luke 5:17–26

Then behold, they brought to Him a paralytic lying on a bed. When Jesus saw their faith, He said to the paralytic, "Son, be of good cheer; your sins are forgiven you." And at once some of the scribes said within themselves, "This Man blasphemes!" But Jesus, knowing their thoughts, said, "Why do you think evil in your hearts? For which is easier, to say, 'Your sins are forgiven you,' or to say, 'Arise and walk'? But that you may know that the Son of Man has power on earth to forgive sins"—then He said to the paralytic, "Arise, take up your bed, and go to your house." And he arose and departed to his house. Now when the multitudes saw it, they marveled and glorified God, who had given such power to men. (Matthew 9:2–8)

5. Lameness

After this there was a feast of the Jews, and Jesus went up to Jerusalem. Now there is in Jerusalem by the Sheep Gate a pool, which is called in Hebrew, Bethesda, having five porches. In these lay a great multitude of sick people, blind, lame, paralyzed, waiting for the moving of the water. For an angel went down at a certain time into the pool and stirred up the water; then whoever stepped in first, after the stirring of the water, was made well of whatever disease he had. Now a certain man was there who had an infirmity thirty-eight years. When Jesus saw him lying there, and knew that he already had been in that condition a long time, He said to him, "Do you want to be made well?" The sick man answered Him, "Sir, I have no man to put me into the pool when the water is stirred up; but while I am coming, another steps down before me." Jesus said to him, "Rise, take up your bed and walk." And immediately the man was made well, took up his bed, and walked. And that day was the Sabbath. (John 5:1–9)

6. Withered hand: Matthew 12:9–14; Mark 3:1–6; Luke 6:6–11

And He entered the synagogue again, and a man was there who had a withered hand. So they watched Him closely, whether He would heal him on the Sabbath, so that they might accuse Him. And He said to the man who had the withered hand, "Step forward." Then He said to them, "Is it lawful on the Sabbath to do good or to do evil, to save life or to kill?" But they kept silent. And when He had looked around at them with anger, being grieved by the hardness of their hearts, He said to the man, "Stretch out your hand." And he stretched it out, and his hand was restored as whole as the other. Then the Pharisees went out and immediately plotted with the Herodians against Him, how they might destroy Him. (Mark 3:1–6)

7.   Raising the dead

    a.   Widow's son

Now it happened, the day after, that He went into a city called Nain; and many of His disciples went with Him, and a large crowd. And when He came near the gate of the city, behold, a dead man was being carried out, the only son of his mother; and she was a widow. And a large crowd from the city was with her. When the Lord saw her, He had compassion on her and said to her, "Do not weep." Then He came and touched the open coffin, and those who carried him stood still. And He said, "Young man, I say to you, arise." So he who was dead sat up and began to speak. And He presented him to his mother. (Luke 7:11–15)

    b.   Jairus' daughter; the woman with blood: Matthew 9:18–26; Mark 5:21–43; Luke 8:40–56

While He spoke these things to them, behold, a ruler came and worshiped Him, saying, "My daughter has just died, but come and lay Your hand on her and she will live." So Jesus arose and followed him, and so did His disciples. And suddenly, a woman who had a flow of blood for twelve years came from behind and touched the hem of His garment. For she said to herself, "If only I may touch His garment, I shall be made well." But Jesus turned around, and when He saw her He said, "Be of good cheer, daughter; your faith has made you well." And the woman was made well from that hour. When Jesus came into the ruler's house, and saw the flute players and the noisy crowd wailing, He said to them, "Make room, for the girl is not dead, but sleeping." And they ridiculed Him. But when the crowd was put outside, He went in and took her by the hand, and the girl arose. And the report of this went out into all that land. (Matthew 9:18–26)

   c. Lazarus

Then Jesus, again groaning in Himself, came to the tomb. It was a cave, and a stone lay against it. Jesus said, "Take away the stone." Martha, the sister of him who was dead, said to Him, "Lord, by this time there is a stench, for he has been dead four days." Jesus said to her, "Did I not say to you that if you would believe you would see the glory of God?" Then they took away the stone from the place where the dead man was lying. And Jesus lifted up His eyes and said, "Father, I thank You that You have heard Me. And I know that You always hear Me, but because of the people who are standing by I said this, that they may believe that You sent Me." Now when He had said these things, He cried with a loud voice, "Lazarus, come forth!" And he who had died came out bound hand and foot with graveclothes, and his face was wrapped with a cloth. Jesus said to them, "Loose him, and let him go." (John 11:38–44)

8.   Blindness: Matthew 9:27–31; 16:5–12; Mark 8:14–21, 10:46–52; Luke 18:35–43; John 9:1–41

Then He came to Bethsaida; and they brought a blind man to Him, and begged Him to touch him. So He took the blind man by the hand and led him out of the town. And when He had spit on his eyes and put His hands on him, He asked him if he saw anything. And he looked up and said, "I see men like trees, walking." Then He put His hands on his eyes again and made him look up. And he was restored and saw everyone clearly. Then He sent him away to his house, saying, "Neither go into the town, nor tell anyone in the town." (Mark 8:22–26)

Now they came to Jericho. As He went out of Jericho with His disciples and a great multitude, blind Bartimaeus, the son of Timaeus, sat by the road begging. And when he heard that it was Jesus of Nazareth, he began to cry out and say, "Jesus, Son of David, have mercy on me!" Then many warned him to be quiet; but he cried out all the more, "Son of David, have mercy on me!" So Jesus stood still and commanded him to be called. Then they called the blind man, saying to him, "Be of good cheer. Rise, He is calling you." And throwing aside his garment, he rose and came to Jesus. So Jesus answered and said to him, "What do you want Me to do for you?" The blind man said to Him, "Rabboni, that I may receive my sight." Then Jesus said to him, "Go your way; your faith has made you well." And immediately he received his sight and followed Jesus on the road. (Mark 10:46–52)

9.   Blind and lame in the temple: Matthew 21:14; born blind— John 9:1–6

Then the blind and the lame came to Him in the temple, and He healed them. (Matthew 21:14)

Now as Jesus passed by, He saw a man who was blind from birth. And His disciples asked Him, saying, "Rabbi, who sinned, this man or his parents, that he was born blind?" Jesus answered, "Neither this man nor his parents sinned, but that the works of God should be revealed in him. I must work the works of Him who sent Me while it is day; the night is coming when no one can work. As long as I am in the world, I am the light of the world." When He had said these things, He spat on the ground and made clay with the saliva; and He anointed the eyes of the blind man with the clay. (John 9:1–6)

D.   Dominion over sin: He displayed the power to forgive sin.

1.   Paralytic: forgiveness and healing at the same moment: Matthew 9:1–8; Mark 2:1–12; Luke 5:17–26

And again He entered Capernaum after some days, and it was heard that He was in the house. Immediately many gathered together, so that there was no longer room to receive them, not even near the door. And He preached the word to them. Then they came to Him, bringing a paralytic who was carried by four men. And when they could not come near Him because of the crowd, they uncovered the roof where He was. So when they had broken through, they let down the bed on which the paralytic was lying. When Jesus saw their faith, He said to the paralytic, "Son, your sins are forgiven you." And some of the scribes were sitting there and reasoning in their hearts, "Why does this Man speak blasphemies like this? Who can forgive sins but God alone?" But immediately, when Jesus perceived in His spirit that they reasoned thus within themselves, He said to them, "Why do you reason about these things in your hearts? Which is easier, to say to the paralytic, 'Your sins are forgiven you,' or to say, 'Arise, take up your bed and walk'? But that you may know that the Son of Man has power on earth to forgive sins"—He said to the paralytic, "I say to you, arise, take up your bed, and go to your house." Immediately he arose, took up the bed, and went out in the presence of them all, so that all were amazed and glorified God, saying, "We never saw anything like this!" (Mark 2:1–12)

2.   The sinful woman. He pronounced that her sins were forgiven in the presence of the Pharisees.

Then He said to her, "Your sins are forgiven." (Luke 7:48)

3.   The woman caught in adultery

Now early in the morning He came again into the temple, and all the people came to Him; and He sat down and taught them. Then the scribes and Pharisees brought to Him a woman caught in adultery ... He said to her, "Woman, where are those accusers of yours? Has no one condemned you?" She said, "No one, Lord." And Jesus said to her, "Neither do I condemn you; go and sin no more." (John 8:2–3,10–11)

E.   Dominion over nature

1.   Jesus changed water into wine

On the third day there was a wedding in Cana of Galilee, and the mother of Jesus was there. Now both Jesus and His disciples were invited to the wedding. And when they ran out of wine, the mother of Jesus said to Him, "They have no wine." Jesus said to her, "Woman, what does your concern have to do with Me? My hour has not yet come." His mother said to the servants, "Whatever He says to you, do it." Now there were set there six waterpots of stone, according to the manner of purification of the Jews, containing twenty or thirty gallons apiece. Jesus said to them, "Fill the waterpots with water." And they filled them up to the brim. And He said to them, "Draw some out now, and take it to the master of the feast." And they took it. When the master of the feast had tasted the water that was made wine, and did not know where it came from (but the servants who had drawn the water knew), the master of the feast called the bridegroom. And he said to him, "Every man at the beginning sets out the good wine, and when the guests have well drunk, then the inferior. You have kept the good wine until now!" (John 2:1–10)

2.   He caught a great number of fish

When He had stopped speaking, He said to Simon, "Launch out into the deep and let down your nets for a catch." But Simon answered and said to Him, "Master, we have toiled all night and caught nothing; nevertheless at Your word I will let down the net." And when they had done this, they caught a great number of fish, and their net was breaking. (Luke 5:4–6)

3.   He calmed the sea: Matthew 8:23–26; Mark 4:35–41

Now it happened, on a certain day, that He got into a boat with His disciples. And He said to them, "Let us cross over to the other side of the lake." And they launched out. But as they sailed He fell asleep. And a windstorm came down on the lake, and they were filling with water, and were in jeopardy. And they came to Him and awoke Him, saying, "Master, Master, we are perishing!" Then He arose and rebuked the wind and the raging of the water. And they ceased, and there was a calm. (Luke 8:22–24)

4. He fed five thousand and four thousand: Matthew 14:13–21, 15:32–38; Mark 6:30–44, 8:1–9; Luke 9:10–17; John 6:1–14

    But He answered and said to them, "You give them something to eat." And they said to Him, "Shall we go and buy two hundred denarii worth of bread and give them something to eat?" But He said to them, "How many loaves do you have? Go and see." And when they found out they said, "Five, and two fish." Then He commanded them to make them all sit down in groups on the green grass. So they sat down in ranks, in hundreds and in fifties. And when He had taken the five loaves and the two fish, He looked up to heaven, blessed and broke the loaves, and gave them to His disciples to set before them; and the two fish He divided among them all. So they all ate and were filled. And they took up twelve baskets full of fragments and of the fish. Now those who had eaten the loaves were about five thousand men. (Mark 6:37–44)

5. The Transfiguration: Matthew 17:1–9; Mark 9:2; Luke 9:28–29

    Now after six days Jesus took Peter, James, and John his brother, led them up on a high mountain by themselves; and He was transfigured before them. His face shone like the sun, and His clothes became as white as the light. And behold, Moses and Elijah appeared to them, talking with Him. (Matthew 17:1–3)

    Now it came to pass, about eight days after these sayings, that He took Peter, John, and James and went up on the mountain to pray. As He prayed, the appearance of His face was altered, and His robe became white and glistening. (Luke 9:28–29)

6. The cursed fig tree: Matthew 21:18–21; Mark 11:12–14; Luke 19:45

    Now the next day, when they had come out from Bethany, He was hungry. And seeing from afar a fig tree having leaves, He went to see if perhaps He would find something on it. When He came to it, He found nothing but leaves, for it was not the season for figs. In response Jesus said to it, "Let no one eat fruit from you ever again." And His disciples heard it. (Mark 11:12–14)

And Peter, remembering, said to Him, "Rabbi, look! The fig tree which You cursed has withered away." So Jesus answered and said to them, "Have faith in God. For assuredly, I say to you, whoever says to this mountain, 'Be removed and be cast into the sea,' and does not doubt in his heart, but believes that those things he says will be done, he will have whatever he says. Therefore I say to you, whatever things you ask when you pray, believe that you receive them, and you will have them. (Mark 11:21–24)

7.   Jesus walked on water: Matthew 14:22–33; Mark 6:45–51

Therefore when Jesus perceived that they were about to come and take Him by force to make Him king, He departed again to the mountain by Himself alone. Now when evening came, His disciples went down to the sea, got into the boat, and went over the sea toward Capernaum. And it was already dark, and Jesus had not come to them. Then the sea arose because a great wind was blowing. So when they had rowed about three or four miles, they saw Jesus walking on the sea and drawing near the boat; and they were afraid. But He said to them, "It is I; do not be afraid." Then they willingly received Him into the boat, and immediately the boat was at the land where they were going. (John 6:15–21)

F.   Dominion over traditions

1.   Concerning fasting: Mark 2:18–22; Luke 5:33–39

The disciples of John and of the Pharisees were fasting. Then they came and said to Him, "Why do the disciples of John and of the Pharisees fast, but Your disciples do not fast?" And Jesus said to them, "Can the friends of the bridegroom fast while the bridegroom is with them? As long as they have the bridegroom with them they cannot fast. But the days will come when the bridegroom will be taken away from them, and then they will fast in those days. No one sews a piece of unshrunk cloth on an old garment; or else the new piece pulls away from the old, and the tear is made worse. And no one puts new wine into old wineskins; or else the new wine bursts the wineskins, the wine is spilled, and the wineskins are ruined. But new wine must be put into new wineskins." (Mark 2:18–22)

2.   Jesus is Lord of the Sabbath: Matthew 12:1–8; Mark 2:23–3:5

Now it happened on the second Sabbath after the first that He went through the grainfields. And His disciples plucked the heads of grain and ate them, rubbing them in their hands. And some of the Pharisees said to them, "Why are you doing what is not lawful to do on the Sabbath?" But Jesus answering them said, "Have you not even read this, what David did when he was hungry, he and those who were with him: how he went into the house of God, took and ate the showbread, and also gave some to those with him, which is not lawful for any but the priests to eat?" And He said to them, "The Son of Man is also Lord of the Sabbath." (Luke 6:1–5)

3.   Concerning the washing of hands and other traditions: Mark 7:1–23 ("Corban"); Luke 11:37–52 (woe to the Pharisees)

Then the Pharisees and some of the scribes came together to Him, having come from Jerusalem. Now when they saw some of His disciples eat bread with defiled, that is, with unwashed hands, they found fault. For the Pharisees and all the Jews do not eat unless they wash their hands in a special way, holding the tradition of the elders. When they come from the marketplace, they do not eat unless they wash. And there are many other things which they have received and hold, like the washing of cups, pitchers, copper vessels, and couches. Then the Pharisees and scribes asked Him, "Why do Your disciples not walk according to the tradition of the elders, but eat bread with unwashed hands?" He answered and said to them, "Well did Isaiah prophesy of you hypocrites, as it is written: 'This people honors Me with their lips, But their heart is far from Me. And in vain they worship Me, Teaching as doctrines the commandments of men.' For laying aside the commandment of God, you hold the tradition of men—the washing of pitchers and cups, and many other such things you do." He said to them, "All too well you reject the commandment of God, that you may keep your tradition. For Moses said, 'Honor your father and your mother'; and, 'He who curses father or mother, let him be put to death.' But you say, 'If a man says to his father or mother, "Whatever profit you might have received from me is Corban"—'(that is, a gift to God), then you no longer let him do anything for his father or his mother, making the word of God of no effect through your tradition which you have handed down. And many such things you do." When He had called all the multitude to Himself, He said to them, "Hear Me, everyone, and understand: There is nothing that enters a man from outside which can defile him; but the things which come out of him, those are the things that defile a man. If anyone has ears to hear, let him hear!" (Mark 7:1–16)

G.   Dominion over opposition

1.   In Nazareth: John 8:59, 10:39. Whenever a group of people tried to kill Jesus, He somehow passed through the midst of them. Jesus was always passing through the midst of His adversaries without them being able to seize Him.

So all those in the synagogue, when they heard these things, were filled with wrath, and rose up and thrust Him out of the city; and they led Him to the brow of the hill on which their city was built, that they might throw Him down over the cliff. Then passing through the midst of them, He went His way. (Luke 4:28–30)

2. Jesus healed on the Sabbath

And He entered the synagogue again, and a man was there who had a withered hand. So they watched Him closely, whether He would heal him on the Sabbath, so that they might accuse Him. And He sÔm stand? Because you say I cast out demons by Beelzebub. And if I cast out demons by Beelzebub, by whom do your sons cast them out? Therefore they will be your judges. But if I cast out demons with the finger of God, surely the kingdom of God has come upon you. When a strong man, fully armed, guards his own palace, his goods are in peace. But when a stronger than he comes upon him and overcomes him, he takes from him all his armor in which he trusted, and divides his spoils. He who is not with Me is against Me, and he who does not gather with Me scatters." (Luke 11:14–23)

4. He was asked about the temple tax

When they had come to Capernaum, those who received the temple tax came to Peter and said, "Does your Teacher not pay the temple tax?" He said, "Yes." And when he had come into the house, Jesus anticipated him, saying, "What do you think, Simon? From whom do the kings of the earth take customs or taxes, from their sons or from strangers?" Peter said to Him, "From strangers." Jesus said to him, "Then the sons are free. Nevertheless, lest we offend them, go to the sea, cast in a hook, and take the fish that comes up first. And when you have opened its mouth, you will find a piece of money; take that and give it to them for Me and you." (Matthew 17:24–27)

5. He healed the man born blind: John 9

6. The children worshiped Him in the temple

But when the chief priests and scribes saw the wonderful things that He did, and the children crying out in the temple and saying, "Hosanna to the Son of David!" they were indignant and said to Him, "Do You hear what these are saying?" And Jesus said to them, "Yes. Have you never read, 'Out of the mouth of babes and nursing infants You have perfected praise'?" (Matthew 21:15–16)

7. Jesus' authority was questioned

Now when He came into the temple, the chief priests and the elders of the people confronted Him as He was teaching, and said, "By what authority are You doing these things? And who gave You this authority?" But Jesus answered and said to them, "I also will ask you one thing, which if you tell Me, I likewise will tell you by what authority I do these things: The baptism of John—where was it from? From heaven or from men?" And they reasoned among themselves, saying, "If we say, 'From heaven,' He will say to us, 'Why then did you not believe him?' But if we say, 'From men,' we fear the multitude, for all count John as a prophet." So they answered Jesus and said, "We do not know." And He said to them, "Neither will I tell you by what authority I do these things. (Matthew 21:23–27)

8. He was questioned about paying taxes to Caesar

"Tell us, therefore, what do You think? Is it lawful to pay taxes to Caesar, or not?" But Jesus perceived their wickedness, and said, "Why do you test Me, you hypocrites? Show Me the tax money." So they brought Him a denarius. And He said to them, "Whose image and inscription is this?" They said to Him, "Caesar's." And He said to them, "Render therefore to Caesar the things that are Caesar's, and to God the things that are God's." When they had heard these words, they marveled, and left Him and went their way. (Matthew 22:17–22)

9. Jesus turned around their questioning: Matthew 22:34–23:39

10. This list does not even include the run-ins with His mother and brothers or with His disciples.

Session Five: The Sweet Aroma of Meekness

I. MEEKNESS DEFINED

A. David testified to the meek and gentle heart of God after being delivered from the hand of all his enemies. No longer a shepherd boy, but a king, David pointed to the secret of his success: "You have also given me the shield of Your salvation; Your right hand has held me up, **Your gentleness has made me great**" (Psalm 18:35, emphasis added). The strength of God's character is seen in His great humility and meekness.

Mercy and truth preserve the king, and by lovingkindness he upholds his throne. (Proverbs 20:28)

B. Meekness is power under control. It is the restraint of power for the accomplishment of a higher cause. This is not to be confused with weakness. Weakness is the absence of strength and power, a complete lack of options. Meekness is possessing power, yet refraining from using it. Jesus chose to be meek for redemptive purposes, for love. Meekness is also not to be confused with personality traits. A laid-back personality does not equal meekness. An example of meekness versus weakness was clearly seen in the courtroom scene with Jesus and Pontius Pilate just prior to the Cross.

    1. "Then Pilate said to Him, 'Are You not speaking to me? Do You not know that I have power to crucify You, and power to release You?' Jesus answered, 'You could have no power at all against Me unless it had been given you from above'" (John 19:10–11). Jesus refuted Pilate's false assumption.

2.   Many people look at Jesus and say that, in this moment, He was weak. Not so. Jesus had power available to Him far beyond anything we could imagine, yet He restrained Himself from using it. Even at the most crucial hour and the weakest moment, He responded to Pontius Pilate's false review of the situation with the powerful truth. Compared to the status of Jesus as the Captain of the Lord of Hosts, Pilate was the equivalent of Barney Fife in Mayberry, USA. One word from Jesus' lips, and twelve legions of angels would have demolished the whole city. One word—that's all it would have taken. Meek? Yes. Weak? Absolutely not!

3.   Jesus restrained His power for the accomplishment of a higher cause. He was willing to bear reproach for the sake of love. Psalm 36:5 declares, "Your mercy, O LORD, is in the heavens." Mercy and meekness descend only from Heaven and have the amazing power to change the human heart. No one covers frailty and sin but God. On Earth, we exploit weakness and capitalize upon the failures of others. In perfection, Jesus stepped down from Heaven into the broken fray of humanity and refused to exploit us. Instead, He covered us with meekness. He even allowed little itty-bitty creatures with absolutely no power to come together, carry out their kangaroo court, unjustly indict Him, and sentence Him to death. Meekness went further still as tiny, frail men nailed Him to the cross's beam. All the while, love was covering our sin and meekness was restraining divine power. Just think—one command, and twelve legions of angels would have set Him free.

C.   The story of Bart Campolo in an inner-city Philadelphia high school.

D.   The majestic God of Genesis 1 is also the meek and good Shepherd.

The LORD is my shepherd; I shall not want. He makes me to lie down in green pastures; He leads me beside the still waters. He restores my soul; He leads me in the paths of righteousness for His name's sake. Yea, though I walk through the valley of the shadow of death, I will fear no evil; for You are with me; Your rod and Your staff, they comfort me. You prepare a table before me in the presence of my enemies; You anoint my head with oil; my cup runs over. Surely goodness and mercy shall follow me all the days of my life; and I will dwell in the house of the LORD forever. (Psalm 23)

II.   Meekness Resisted

A.   Meekness is the most supernatural gift given to humanity, and thus the most resisted out of all of Heaven's gifts. From the beginning, the sin of pride (bitterness and envy) has manifested itself in violence and oppression.

B.   In Genesis 4, humanity's fallenness was displayed in the violent murder of Abel. Violence continued to spread throughout Earth, until God decided to flood the earth because He saw that the earth was "corrupt … and filled with violence" (Genesis 6:11). Imagine what happened when an individual had a thousand-year lifespan to perfect violence and wickedness.

Now Cain talked with Abel his brother; and it came to pass, when they were in the field, that Cain rose up against Abel his brother and killed him. (Genesis 4:8)

Then the LORD saw that the wickedness of man was great in the earth, and that every intent of the thoughts of his heart was only evil continually. (Genesis 6:5)

The earth also was corrupt before God, and the earth was filled with violence. So God looked upon the earth, and indeed it was corrupt; for all flesh had corrupted their way on the earth. (Genesis 6:11–12)

C.   After the Flood, the seeds of violence remained. Humanity's inclination toward violence was still present, so God made a covenant with Noah concerning immediate recourse for the shedding of human blood. Also, fear and violence were introduced between humanity and the animal world.

And the fear of you and the dread of you shall be on every beast of the earth, on every bird of the air, on all that move on the earth, and on all the fish of the sea. They are given into your hand. Every moving thing that lives shall be food for you. I have given you all things, even as the green herbs. Surely for your lifeblood I will demand a reckoning; from the hand of every beast I will require it, and from the hand of man. From the hand of every man's brother I will require the life of man. Whoever sheds man's blood, by man his blood shall be shed; for in the image of God He made man. And as for you, be fruitful and multiply; bring forth abundantly in the earth and multiply in it. (Genesis 9:2–7)

D. Violence continued to spread as cities and tribes gained power over others. Unchecked perverse practices arose, accompanied by horrible, violent atrocities. Sodom and Gomorrah are a good example of this. Also, look at Chedorlaomer and the allied kings who attacked Lot and carried off all his women and possessions.

And it came to pass in the days of Amraphel king of Shinar, Arioch king of Ellasar, Chedorlaomer king of Elam, and Tidal king of nations, that they made war with Bera king of Sodom, Birsha king of Gomorrah, Shinab king of Admah, Shemeber king of Zeboiim, and the king of Bela (that is, Zoar). All these joined together in the Valley of Siddim (that is, the Salt Sea). Twelve years they served Chedorlaomer, and in the thirteenth year they rebelled … They also took Lot, Abram's brother's son who dwelt in Sodom, and his goods, and departed. (Genesis 14:1–4, 12)

The Angel of the LORD said to her, "Return to your mistress, and submit yourself under her hand." Then the Angel of the LORD said to her, "I will multiply your descendants exceedingly, so that they shall not be counted for multitude." And the Angel of the LORD said to her: "Behold, you are with child, and you shall bear a son. You shall call his name Ishmael, because the LORD has heard your affliction. He shall be a wild man; His hand shall be against every man, and every man's hand against him. And he shall dwell in the presence of all his brethren." (Genesis 16:9–12)

Now before they lay down, the men of the city, the men of Sodom, both old and young, all the people from every quarter, surrounded the house. And they called to Lot and said to him, "Where are the men who came to you tonight? Bring them out to us that we may know them carnally." So Lot went out to them through the doorway, shut the door behind him, and said, "Please, my brethren, do not do so wickedly! See now, I have two daughters who have not known a man; please, let me bring them out to you, and you may do to them as you wish; only do nothing to these men, since this is the reason they have come under the shadow of my roof." And they said, "Stand back!" Then they said, "This one came in to stay here, and he keeps acting as a judge; now we will deal worse with you than with them." So they pressed hard against the man Lot, and came near to break down the door. But the men reached out their hands and pulled Lot into the house with them, and shut the door. And they struck the men who were at the doorway of the house with blindness, both small and great, so that they became weary trying to find the door. (Genesis 19:4–11)

Then the men said to Lot, "Have you anyone else here? Son-in-law, your sons, your daughters, and whomever you have in the city—take them out of this place! For we will destroy this place, because the outcry against them has grown great before the face of the Lord, *and the* Lord *has sent us to destroy it." (Genesis 19:12–13 [Matthew 11:23,24; Luke 17:28–32])*

*For the wrath of God is revealed from heaven against all ungodliness and unrighteousness of men, who suppress the truth in unrighteousness, because what may be known of God is manifest in them, for God has shown it to them. For since the creation of the world His invisible attributes are clearly seen, being understood by the things that are made, even His eternal power and Godhead, so that they are without excuse, because, **although they knew God, they did not glorify Him as God, nor were thankful, but became futile in their thoughts, and their foolish hearts were darkened. Professing to be wise, they became fools, and changed the glory of the incorruptible God into an image made like corruptible man—and birds and four-footed animals and creeping things. Therefore God also gave them up to uncleanness, in the lusts of their hearts,** to dishonor their bodies among themselves, who exchanged the truth of God for the lie, and worshiped and served the creature rather than the Creator, who is blessed forever. Amen. **For this reason God gave them up to vile passions.** For even their women exchanged the natural use for what is against nature. Likewise also the men, leaving the natural use of the woman, burned in their lust for one another, men with men committing what is shameful, and receiving in themselves the penalty of their error which was due. And even as they did not like to retain God in their knowledge, **God gave them over to a debased mind, to do those things which are not fitting; being filled with all unrighteousness, sexual immorality, wickedness, covetousness, maliciousness; full of envy, murder, strife, deceit, evil-mindedness; they are whisperers, backbiters, haters of God, violent, proud, boasters, inventors of evil things, disobedient to parents, undiscerning, untrustworthy, unloving, unforgiving, unmerciful; who, knowing the righteous judgment of God, that those who practice such things are deserving of death,** not only do the same but also approve of those who practice them. (Romans 1:18–32, emphasis added)*

E. The history of humanity, both of God's people and pagan nations, is riddled with violence (Joseph thrown in the pit, Egypt oppressing the Israelites, etc.) So violent and perverse were the pagan nations that God called for their complete annihilation. To mingle with these cultures was to embrace prostitution and, many times, human sacrifice. In fact, God was so angered by King Manasseh's evil practices of killing his son in a pagan ritual that God refused to relent concerning the Babylonian exile (2 Kings 21:16, 24:2–4).

Genesis 25–33

Now it came to pass on the third day, when they were in pain, that two of the sons of Jacob, Simeon and Levi, Dinah's brothers, each took his sword and came boldly upon the city and killed all the males. And they killed Hamor and Shechem his son with the edge of the sword, and took Dinah from Shechem's house, and went out. The sons of Jacob came upon the slain, and plundered the city, because their sister had been defiled. They took their sheep, their oxen, and their donkeys, what was in the city and what was in the field, and all their wealth. All their little ones and their wives they took captive; and they plundered even all that was in the houses. (Genesis 34:25–29)

Now when they saw him afar off, even before he came near them, they conspired against him to kill him. Then they said to one another, "Look, this dreamer is coming! Come therefore, let us now kill him and cast him into some pit; and we shall say, 'Some wild beast has devoured him.' We shall see what will become of his dreams!" But Reuben heard it, and he delivered him out of their hands, and said, "Let us not kill him." And Reuben said to them, "Shed no blood, but cast him into this pit which is in the wilderness, and do not lay a hand on him"—that he might deliver him out of their hands, and bring him back to his father. So it came to pass, when Joseph had come to his brothers, that they stripped Joseph of his tunic, the tunic of many colors that was on him. Then they took him and cast him into a pit. And the pit was empty; there was no water in it. And they sat down to eat a meal. Then they lifted their eyes and looked, and there was a company of Ishmaelites, coming from Gilead with their camels, bearing spices, balm, and myrrh, on their way to carry them down to Egypt. So Judah said to his brothers, "What profit is there if we kill our brother and conceal his blood? Come and let us sell him to the Ishmaelites, and let not our hand be upon him, for he is our brother and our flesh." And his brothers listened. Then Midianite traders passed by; so the brothers pulled Joseph up and lifted him out of the pit, and sold him to the Ishmaelites for twenty shekels of silver. And they took Joseph to Egypt. (Genesis 37:18–28)

Therefore they set taskmasters over them to afflict them with their burdens. And they built for Pharaoh supply cities, Pithom and Raamses. But the more they afflicted them, the more they multiplied and grew. And they were in dread of the children of Israel. So the Egyptians made the children of Israel serve with rigor. And they made their lives bitter with hard bondage—in mortar, in brick, and in all manner of service in the field. All their service in which they made them serve was with rigor. Then the king of Egypt spoke to the Hebrew midwives, of whom the name of one was Shiphrah and the name of the other Puah; and he said, "When you do the duties of a midwife for the Hebrew women, and see them on the birthstools, if it is a son, then you shall kill him; but if it is a daughter, then she shall live." But the midwives feared God, and did not do as the king of Egypt commanded them, but saved the male children alive. So the king of Egypt called for the midwives and said to them, "Why have you done this thing, and saved the male children alive?" And the midwives said to Pharaoh, "Because the Hebrew women are not like the Egyptian women; for they are lively and give birth before the midwives come to them." Therefore God dealt well with the midwives, and the people multiplied and grew very mighty. And so it was, because the midwives feared God, that He provided households for them. So Pharaoh commanded all his people, saying, "Every son who is born you shall cast into the river, and every daughter you shall save alive." (Exodus 1:11–22)

"But in the fourth generation they shall return here, for the iniquity of the Amorites is not yet complete." (Genesis 15:16)

Then the children of Israel did evil in the sight of the LORD. So the LORD delivered them into the hand of Midian for seven years, and the hand of Midian prevailed against Israel. Because of the Midianites, the children of Israel made for themselves the dens, the caves, and the strongholds which are in the mountains. So it was, whenever Israel had sown, Midianites would come up; also Amalekites and the people of the East would come up against them. Then they would encamp against them and destroy the produce of the earth as far as Gaza, and leave no sustenance for Israel, neither sheep nor ox nor donkey. For they would come up with their livestock and their tents, coming in as numerous as locusts; both they and their camels were without number; and they would enter the land to destroy it. So Israel was greatly impoverished because of the Midianites, and the children of Israel cried out to the LORD. (Judges 6:1–6)

*So Samuel told all the words of the L*ORD *to the people who asked him for a king. And he said, "This will be the behavior of the king who will reign over you: He will take your sons and appoint them for his own chariots and to be his horsemen, and some will run before his chariots. He will appoint captains over his thousands and captains over his fifties, will set some to plow his ground and reap his harvest, and some to make his weapons of war and equipment for his chariots. He will take your daughters to be perfumers, cooks, and bakers. And he will take the best of your fields, your vineyards, and your olive groves, and give them to his servants. He will take a tenth of your grain and your vintage, and give it to his officers and servants. And he will take your male servants, your female servants, your finest young men, and your donkeys, and put them to his work. He will take a tenth of your sheep. And you will be his servants. And you will cry out in that day because of your king whom you have chosen for yourselves, and the L*ORD *will not hear you in that day." (1 Samuel 8:10–18)*

*Moreover Manasseh shed very much innocent blood, till he had filled Jerusalem from one end to another, besides his sin by which he made Judah sin, in doing evil in the sight of the L*ORD*. (2 Kings 21:16)*

*Surely at the commandment of the L*ORD *this came upon Judah, to remove them from His sight because of the sins of Manasseh, according to all that he had done, and also because of the innocent blood that he had shed; for he had filled Jerusalem with innocent blood, which the L*ORD *would not pardon. (2 Kings 24:3–4)*

III.   A MEEK KING FORETOLD

A.   Solomon was a king of peace who built the Temple.

*Then he called for his son Solomon, and charged him to build a house for the L*ORD *God of Israel. And David said to Solomon: "My son, as for me, it was in my mind to build a house to the name of the L*ORD *my God; but the word of the L*ORD *came to me, saying, 'You have shed much blood and have made great wars; you shall not build a house for My name, because you have shed much blood on the earth in My sight. Behold, a son shall be born to you, who shall be a man of rest; and I will give him rest from all his enemies all around. His name shall be Solomon, for I will give peace and quietness to Israel in his days. He shall build a house for My name, and he shall be My son, and I will be his Father; and I will establish the throne of his kingdom over Israel forever.'" (1 Chronicles 22:6–10)*

B. Messianic Psalms—the Psalms prophesied of a coming King who would end the violence of the nations, establish justice and righteousness, and bring forth the fruit of peace on the earth.

1. Psalm 2

    Ask of Me, and I will give You the nations for Your inheritance, and the ends of the earth for Your possession. You shall break them with a rod of iron; You shall dash them to pieces like a potter's vessel. (Psalm 2:8–9)

2. Psalm 21

    Your hand will find all Your enemies; Your right hand will find those who hate You. You shall make them as a fiery oven in the time of Your anger; the LORD shall swallow them up in His wrath, and the fire shall devour them. Their offspring You shall destroy from the earth, and their descendants from among the sons of men. For they intended evil against You; they devised a plot which they are not able to perform. Therefore You will make them turn their back; You will make ready Your arrows on Your string toward their faces. (Psalm 21:8–12)

3. Psalm 22

    All the ends of the world shall remember and turn to the LORD, and all the families of the nations shall worship before You. For the kingdom is the LORD's, and He rules over the nations. All the prosperous of the earth shall eat and worship; all those who go down to the dust shall bow before Him, even he who cannot keep himself alive. (Psalm 22:27–29)

4. Psalm 37

    For evildoers shall be cut off; but those who wait on the LORD, they shall inherit the earth. For yet a little while and the wicked shall be no more; indeed, you will look carefully for his place, but it shall be no more. But the meek shall inherit the earth, and shall delight themselves in the abundance of peace. (Psalm 37:9–11)

5. Psalm 45

You are fairer than the sons of men; grace is poured upon Your lips; therefore God has blessed You forever. Gird Your sword upon Your thigh, O Mighty One, with Your glory and Your majesty. And in Your majesty ride prosperously because of truth, humility, and righteousness; and Your right hand shall teach You awesome things. Your arrows are sharp in the heart of the King's enemies; the peoples fall under You. Your throne, O God, is forever and ever; a scepter of righteousness is the scepter of Your kingdom. You love righteousness and hate wickedness; therefore God, Your God, has anointed You with the oil of gladness more than Your companions. (Psalm 45:2–7)

6. Psalm 72

He shall have dominion also from sea to sea, and from the River to the ends of the earth. Those who dwell in the wilderness will bow before Him, and His enemies will lick the dust. The kings of Tarshish and of the isles will bring presents; the kings of Sheba and Seba will offer gifts. Yes, all kings shall fall down before Him; all nations shall serve Him. For He will deliver the needy when he cries, the poor also, and him who has no helper. He will spare the poor and needy, and will save the souls of the needy. He will redeem their life from oppression and violence; and precious shall be their blood in His sight. (Psalm 72:8–14)

7. Psalm 110

The Lord said to my Lord, "Sit at My right hand, till I make Your enemies Your footstool." (Psalm 110:1)

8. Psalm 118

All nations surrounded me, but in the name of the Lord I will destroy them. They surrounded me, yes, they surrounded me; but in the name of the Lord I will destroy them. (Psalm 118:10–11)

I will praise You, for You have answered me, and have become my salvation. The stone which the builders rejected has become the chief cornerstone. This was the Lord's doing; it is marvelous in our eyes. This is the day the Lord has made; we will rejoice and be glad in it. (Psalm 118:21–24)

C.   The Prophets

1.   Isaiah: into the midst of a fallen, violent world came heralds like Isaiah, messengers telling of a coming One who would bring peace to the earth. Isaiah spoke of the Servant of the Lord, who would come forth as the Anointed One of God. He would bring deliverance to Israel and would be a light to the Gentiles. Isaiah 2 states that this One "will judge between the nations and will settle disputes for many peoples. They will beat their swords into plowshares and their spears into pruning hooks. Nation will not take up sword against nation, nor will they train for war anymore." Isaiah 9:6 calls Him the "Prince of Peace."

Isaiah 11 expounds on Isaiah 2 and 9, stating that the Branch of the Lord would be fruitful. The fruit of His righteousness "will be peace, and the effect of righteousness, quietness and assurance forever" (Isaiah 32:17). Under His governance, the curses of violence described in the first nine chapters of Genesis would be reversed. Strife between animals, and between humans and animals, would be broken. The curse of the Fall would be entirely removed with the removal of violence. Isaiah 16:5 declares that this coming throne would not be established through coercive, violent power; love would be its foundation.

Isaiah 42 describes the meekness of the coming Servant King: "Here is my servant, whom I uphold, my chosen one in whom I delight; I will put my Spirit on him and he will bring justice to the nations. He will not shout or cry out, or raise his voice in the streets. A bruised reed he will not break, and a smoldering wick he will not snuff out. In faithfulness he will bring forth justice" (Isaiah 42:1–4, NIV). Then, in grand fashion, Isaiah 52:13–53:12 describes the meek humiliation that God's servant would undergo for the sake of bringing redemption and establishing His rule.

2.   Micah 4:1–5:5

*Now gather yourself in troops, O daughter of troops; He has laid siege against us; they will strike the judge of Israel with a rod on the cheek. "But you, Bethlehem Ephrathah, though you are little among the thousands of Judah, yet out of you shall come forth to Me the One to be Ruler in Israel, whose goings forth are from of old, from everlasting." Therefore He shall give them up, until the time that she who is in labor has given birth; then the remnant of His brethren shall return to the children of Israel. And He shall stand and feed His flock in the strength of the L*ORD*, in the majesty of the name of the L*ORD *His God; and they shall abide, for now He shall be great to the ends of the earth;* **and this One shall be peace.** *(Micah 5:1–5, emphasis added)*

3.   Zechariah: the Anointed One would suffer in meekness, fulfilling the prophecy in Psalm 37:11: "But the meek shall inherit the earth, and shall delight themselves in the abundance of peace." Jesus reaffirmed this prophecy in Matthew 5:5 and entered Jerusalem as the King described in Zechariah 9, meek and riding on a donkey.

Rejoice greatly, O Daughter of Zion! Shout, Daughter of Jerusalem! **See, your king comes to you, righteous and having salvation, gentle and riding on a donkey, on a colt, the foal of a donkey.** *I will take away the chariots from Ephraim and the war-horses from Jerusalem, and the battle bow will be broken.* **He will proclaim peace to the nations.** *His rule will extend from sea to sea and from the River to the ends of the earth.* (Zechariah 9:9–10, emphasis added)

IV.   THE PURSUIT OF MEEKNESS

A.   Meekness is the **magnet** that attracts God's favor.

He gives **more** *grace. Therefore He says: "God…gives grace to the humble." (James 4:6, emphasis added)*

Likewise you younger people, submit yourselves to your elders. Yes, all of you be submissive to one another, and be clothed with humility, for "God resists the proud, but gives grace to the humble." Therefore humble yourselves under the mighty hand of God, that He may exalt you in due time, casting all your care upon Him, for He cares for you. (1 Peter 5:5–7)

*Blessed are the meek, for they shall **inherit** the earth. (Matthew 5:5, emphasis added)*

B.   The pursuit of meekness—three stages

1.   Stage one of meekness: **becoming aware** of the significance of meekness to God's Kingdom.

2.   Stage two of meekness: **setting** of our mind to **pursue** meekness (to **value** it).

3.   Stage three of meekness: **breakthrough** (impartation) of our heart to **possess** meekness (to **enjoy** it).

C.   The beholding principle and the breakthrough of the heart

Now the Lord is the Spirit; and where the Spirit of the Lord is, there is liberty. But we all, with unveiled face, beholding as in a mirror the glory of the Lord, are being transformed into the same image from glory to glory, just as by the Spirit of the Lord. (2 Corinthians 3:17–18)

1.   My story about 1 Corinthians 13:4–8

Love suffers long and is kind; love does not envy; love does not parade itself, is not puffed up; does not behave rudely, does not seek its own, is not provoked, thinks no evil; does not rejoice in iniquity, but rejoices in the truth; bears all things, believes all things, hopes all things, endures all things. Love never fails. But whether there are prophecies, they will fail; whether there are tongues, they will cease; whether there is knowledge, it will vanish away. (1 Corinthians 13:4–8)

2. The most humbling thing one can do is to look upon the meekness of Jesus. His whole life was ordered around this attribute. It was His greatest pursuit. From the moment He was born, the Father contemplated His own humility in the person of His Son. Love would be openly displayed as Jesus went lower and lower, becoming humbler and humbler. Anyone who truly looks upon the man Christ Jesus and His meekness will be left staring at this great mystery: how can One so strong be so tender as He stoops so low?

3. Looking upon Jesus cleanses and sanctifies areas of pride and anger in the human heart. It produces holy tears of longing to be like Him, a longing that cleanses the soul from the trauma of violence and invites the grace of God unto humility.

V. MEEKNESS—DIVINE RESTRAINT DISPLAYED IN JESUS

A. Jesus, as the express image and exact representation of the Father, has always displayed the depths of God's tenderness toward weak, fractured, fallen human beings. John Piper wrote, "Since Christ is the incarnate display of the wealth of the mercies of God, it is not surprising that his life on Earth was a lavish exhibit of mercies to all kinds of people. Every kind of need and pain was touched by the mercies of Jesus in his few years on earth."[1] This tenderness causes wells of love to spring forth in us, for the human heart is quickly pierced by tender mercy. A heart won by tenderness is a heart secured in the tightest grip imaginable; it will not give way in the darkest hours.

B. Jesus' identity

1. As a Man

   We may behold the glory of Christ in His infinite willingness to humble Himself to take this office of mediator on Himself, and uniting our nature to His for that purpose. He did not become mediator by chance. Nor was it imposed on Him against His will … He willingly humbled Himself in order that He might make a righteous peace between God the Judge and man the sinner.[2]

---

1 Piper, John. *Seeing and Savoring Jesus Christ* (Wheaton, IL: Crossway Books, 2004), p. 92.

2 Owen, John. *The Glory of Christ* (Ed. R.J.K. Law. The Puritan Paperback Series. Carlisle, PA: Banner of Truth, 1994), p. 39.

2. As a Servant of men and women

   a. *For even the Son of Man did not come to be served, but to serve, and to give His life a ransom for many. (Mark 10:45)*

   b. *Let nothing be done through selfish ambition or conceit, but in lowliness of mind let each esteem others better than himself. Let each of you look out not only for his own interests, but also for the interests of others. Let this mind be in you which was also in Christ Jesus, who, being in the form of God, did not consider it robbery to be equal with God, but made Himself of no reputation, taking the form of a bondservant, and coming in the likeness of men. And being found in appearance as a man, He humbled Himself and became obedient to the point of death, even the death of the cross. Therefore God also has highly exalted Him and given Him the name which is above every name, that at the name of Jesus every knee should bow, of those in heaven, and of those on earth, and of those under the earth, and that every tongue should confess that Jesus Christ is Lord, to the glory of God the Father. (Philippians 2:3–11)*

   c. *And supper being ended, the devil having already put it into the heart of Judas Iscariot, Simon's son, to betray Him, Jesus, knowing that the Father had given all things into His hands, and that He had come from God and was going to God, rose from supper and laid aside His garments, took a towel and girded Himself. After that, He poured water into a basin and began to wash the disciples' feet, and to wipe them with the towel with which He was girded. (John 13:2–5)*

3. His self-description: Jesus describes Himself as meek and lowly in heart.

   Come to Me, all you who labor and are heavy laden, and I will give you rest. Take My yoke upon you and learn from Me, for I am gentle and lowly in heart, and you will find rest for your souls. For My yoke is easy and My burden is light. (Matthew 11:28–30)

4. He suffered temptation and sympathizes with our weaknesses—Jesus' sympathy made Him deeply compassionate. His compassion for people was displayed in His many acts of healing and deliverance (Matthew 9:36, 14:14, 15:32, 18:27,33, 20:34; Mark 1:41, 5:19, 6:34, 8:2, 9:22; Luke 7:13, 10:33, 15:20).

Seeing then that we have a great High Priest who has passed through the heavens, Jesus the Son of God, let us hold fast our confession. For we do not have a High Priest who cannot sympathize with our weaknesses, but was in all points tempted as we are, yet without sin. Let us therefore come boldly to the throne of grace, that we may obtain mercy and find grace to help in time of need. For every high priest taken from among men is appointed for men in things pertaining to God, that he may offer both gifts and sacrifices for sins. He can have compassion on those who are ignorant and going astray, since he himself is also subject to weakness. (Hebrews 4:14–5:2)

But when He saw the multitudes, He was moved with compassion for them, because they were weary and scattered, like sheep having no shepherd. (Matthew 9:36)

And when Jesus went out He saw a great multitude; and He was moved with compassion for them, and healed their sick. When it was evening, His disciples came to Him, saying, "This is a deserted place, and the hour is already late. Send the multitudes away, that they may go into the villages and buy themselves food." (Matthew 14:14–15)

Now Jesus called His disciples to Himself and said, "I have compassion on the multitude, because they have now continued with Me three days and have nothing to eat. And I do not want to send them away hungry, lest they faint on the way." (Matthew 15:32)

So Jesus had compassion and touched their eyes. And immediately their eyes received sight, and they followed Him. (Matthew 20:34)

Now a leper came to Him, imploring Him, kneeling down to Him and saying to Him, "If You are willing, You can make me clean." Then Jesus, moved with compassion, stretched out His hand and touched him, and said to him, "I am willing; be cleansed." As soon as He had spoken, immediately the leprosy left him, and he was cleansed. (Mark 1:40–42)

And when He got into the boat, he who had been demon-possessed begged Him that he might be with Him. However, Jesus did not permit him, but said to him, "Go home to your friends, and tell them what great things the Lord has done for you, and how He has had compassion on you." And he departed and began to proclaim in Decapolis all that Jesus had done for him; and all marveled. (Mark 5:18–20)

Now it happened, the day after, that He went into a city called Nain; and many of His disciples went with Him, and a large crowd. And when He came near the gate of the city, behold, a dead man was being carried out, the only son of his mother; and she was a widow. And a large crowd from the city was with her. When the Lord saw her, He had compassion on her and said to her, "Do not weep." Then He came and touched the open coffin, and those who carried him stood still. And He said, "Young man, I say to you, arise." So he who was dead sat up and began to speak. And He presented him to his mother. (Luke 7:11–15)

And he arose and came to his father. But when he was still a great way off, his father saw him and had compassion, and ran and fell on his neck and kissed him. And the son said to him, "Father, I have sinned against heaven and in your sight, and am no longer worthy to be called your son." (Luke 15:20–21)

C.   Jesus' glad submission to His Father

1.   His baptism

    a.   The timing: Jesus waited thirty years before He began His public ministry.

    b.   Submitting to John's baptism: in His meekness, Jesus identified with the plight of His people and gladly submitted to all the demands of righteousness.

2.   His mission: Jesus only did and said what He saw His Father saying and doing.

Then Jesus answered and said to them, "Most assuredly, I say to you, the Son can do nothing of Himself, but what He sees the Father do; for whatever He does, the Son also does in like manner. For the Father loves the Son, and shows Him all things that He Himself does; and He will show Him greater works than these, that you may marvel. (John 5:19–20)

I can of Myself do nothing. As I hear, I judge; and My judgment is righteous, because I do not seek My own will but the will of the Father who sent Me. (John 5:30)

3.   Messianic Secret

a. Jesus continually avoided drawing attention to Himself. He did not use the miracles or deliverances as opportunities to gain power. His motivation was obedience to the Father's desire to liberate the sick and oppressed. He did not raise His voice in the streets or draw upon the multitudes to secure political power (Isaiah 42:2; Matthew 12:15–19).

But when Jesus knew it, He withdrew from there. And great multitudes followed Him, and He healed them all. Yet He warned them not to make Him known, that it might be fulfilled which was spoken by Isaiah the prophet, saying: "Behold! My Servant whom I have chosen, My Beloved in whom My soul is well pleased! I will put My Spirit upon Him, and He will declare justice to the Gentiles. He will not quarrel nor cry out, nor will anyone hear His voice in the streets. A bruised reed He will not break, and smoking flax He will not quench, till He sends forth justice to victory; and in His name Gentiles will trust." (Matthew 12:15–21)

b. Jesus did not campaign in order to get human praise/approval or political advantage. He did not entertain the princes or elders of Jerusalem. In fact, He preferred to attend banquets that were hosted by tax collectors and sinners. Compare Matthew's banquet, the suppers at two Pharisees' houses, and the dinner at Zaccheus's house.

(1) Banquet at Matthew's House

After these things He went out and saw a tax collector named Levi (also known as **Matthew**), *sitting at the tax office. And He said to him, "Follow Me." So he left all, rose up, and followed Him. Then Levi gave Him a great feast in his own house. And there were a great number of tax collectors and others who sat down with them. And their scribes and the Pharisees complained against His disciples, saying, "Why do You eat and drink with tax collectors and sinners?" Jesus answered and said to them, "Those who are well have no need of a physician, but those who are sick. I have not come to call the righteous, but sinners, to repentance." (Luke 5:27–32, parenthetical comment added)*

(2) Sinful woman at the Simon the Pharisee's dinner

Then one of the Pharisees asked Him to eat with him. And He went to the Pharisee's house, and sat down to eat. And behold, a woman in the city who was a sinner, when she knew that Jesus sat at the table in the Pharisee's house, brought an alabaster flask of fragrant oil, and stood at His feet behind Him weeping; and she began to wash His feet with her tears, and wiped them with the hair of her head; and she kissed His feet and anointed them with the fragrant oil. Now when the Pharisee who had invited Him saw this, he spoke to himself, saying, "This Man, if He were a prophet, would know who and what manner of woman this is who is touching Him, for she is a sinner." And Jesus answered and said to him, "Simon, I have something to say to you." So he said, "Teacher, say it." "There was a certain creditor who had two debtors. One owed five hundred denarii, and the other fifty. And when they had nothing with which to repay, he freely forgave them both. Tell Me, therefore, which of them will love him more?" Simon answered and said, "I suppose the one whom he forgave more." And He said to him, "You have rightly judged." Then He turned to the woman and said to Simon, "Do you see this woman? I entered your house; you gave Me no water for My feet, but she has washed My feet with her tears and wiped them with the hair of her head. You gave Me no kiss, but this woman has not ceased to kiss My feet since the time I came in. You did not anoint My head with oil, but this woman has anointed My feet with fragrant oil. Therefore I say to you, her sins, which are many, are forgiven, for she loved much. But to whom little is forgiven, the same loves little." Then He said to her, "Your sins are forgiven." (Luke 7:36–48)

(3) Jesus rebuked the Pharisees at a dinner

And as He spoke, a certain Pharisee asked Him to dine with him. So He went in and sat down to eat. When the Pharisee saw it, he marveled that He had not first washed before dinner. Then the Lord said to him, "Now you Pharisees make the outside of the cup and dish clean, but your inward part is full of greed and wickedness. Foolish ones! Did not He who made the outside make the inside also? But rather give alms of such things as you have; then indeed all things are clean to you. But woe to you Pharisees! For you tithe mint and rue and all manner of herbs, and pass by justice and the love of God. These you ought to have done, without leaving the others undone. Woe to you Pharisees! For you love the best seats in the synagogues and greetings in the marketplaces. Woe to you, scribes and Pharisees, hypocrites! For you are like graves which are not seen, and the men who walk over them are not aware of them." Then one of the lawyers answered and said to Him, "Teacher, by saying these things You reproach us also." And He said, "Woe to you also, lawyers! For you load men with burdens hard to bear, and you yourselves do not touch the burdens with one of your fingers. Woe to you! For you build the tombs of the prophets, and your fathers killed them. In fact, you bear witness that you approve the deeds of your fathers; for they indeed killed them, and you build their tombs. Therefore the wisdom of God also said, 'I will send them prophets and apostles, and some of them they will kill and persecute,' that the blood of all the prophets which was shed from the foundation of the world may be required of this generation, from the blood of Abel to the blood of Zechariah who perished between the altar and the temple. Yes, I say to you, it shall be required of this generation. Woe to you lawyers! For you have taken away the key of knowledge. You did not enter in yourselves, and those who were entering in you hindered." (Luke 11:37–52)

(4) Dinner at Zacchaeus' house

Then Jesus entered and passed through Jericho. Now behold, there was a man named Zacchaeus who was a chief tax collector, and he was rich. And he sought to see who Jesus was, but could not because of the crowd, for he was of short stature. So he ran ahead and climbed up into a sycamore tree to see Him, for He was going to pass that way. And when Jesus came to the place, He looked up and saw him, and said to him, "Zacchaeus, make haste and come down, for today I must stay at your house." So he made haste and came down, and received Him joyfully. But when they saw it, they all complained, saying, "He has gone to be a guest with a man who is a sinner." Then Zacchaeus stood and said to the Lord, "Look, Lord, I give half of my goods to the poor; and if I have taken anything from anyone by false accusation, I restore fourfold." And Jesus said to him, "Today salvation has come to this house, because he also is a son of Abraham; for the Son of Man has come to seek and to save that which was lost." (Luke 19:1–10)

c. Often Jesus sent the multitudes away so He could have private times of prayer.

And when He had sent the multitudes away, He went up on the mountain by Himself to pray. Now when evening came, He was alone there. (Matthew 14:23)

However, the report went around concerning Him all the more; and great multitudes came together to hear, and to be healed by Him of their infirmities. So He Himself often withdrew into the wilderness and prayed. (Luke 5:15–16)

d. In John 6:15, Jesus withdrew precisely because the multitudes intended to grab Him by force and make Him king. Later, He emphatically pointed out to Pontius Pilate that if His kingdom were meant to be an earthly kingdom, He would have already established it and would have followers willing to fight for Him unto death.

Therefore when Jesus perceived that they were about to come and take Him by force to make Him king, He departed again to the mountain by Himself alone. (John 6:15)

Jesus answered, "My kingdom is not of this world. If My kingdom were of this world, My servants would fight, so that I should not be delivered to the Jews; but now My kingdom is not from here." Pilate therefore said to Him, "Are You a king then?" Jesus answered, "You say rightly that I am a king." (John 18:36–37)

4. Jesus' prayer life: Luke's Gospel wonderfully illustrates Jesus' prayer life.

When all the people were baptized, it came to pass that Jesus also was baptized; and while He prayed, the heaven was opened. And the Holy Spirit descended in bodily form like a dove upon Him, and a voice came from heaven which said, "You are My beloved Son; in You I am well pleased." (Luke 3:21–22)

However, the report went around concerning Him all the more; and great multitudes came together to hear, and to be healed by Him of their infirmities. So He Himself often withdrew into the wilderness and prayed. (Luke 5:15–16)

Now it came to pass in those days that He went out to the mountain to pray, and continued all night in prayer to God. And when it was day, He called His disciples to Himself; and from them He chose twelve whom He also named apostles... (Luke 6:12–13)

And it happened, as He was alone praying, that His disciples joined Him, and He asked them, saying, "Who do the crowds say that I am?" So they answered and said, "John the Baptist, but some say Elijah; and others say that one of the old prophets has risen again." He said to them, "But who do you say that I am?" Peter answered and said, "The Christ of God." (Luke 9:18–20)

Now it came to pass, about eight days after these sayings, that He took Peter, John, and James and went up on the mountain to pray. As He prayed, the appearance of His face was altered, and His robe became white and glistening. (Luke 9:28–29)

Now it came to pass, as He was praying in a certain place, when He ceased, that one of His disciples said to Him, "Lord, teach us to pray, as John also taught his disciples." So He said to them, "When you pray, say: Our Father in heaven, Hallowed be Your name. Your kingdom come. Your will be done on earth as it is in heaven. Give us day by day our daily bread. And forgive us our sins, for we also forgive everyone who is indebted to us. And do not lead us into temptation, but deliver us from the evil one." (Luke 11:1–4)

And the Lord said, "Simon, Simon! Indeed, Satan has asked for you, that he may sift you as wheat. But I have prayed for you, that your faith should not fail; and when you have returned to Me, strengthen your brethren." (Luke 22:31–32)

Coming out, He went to the Mount of Olives, as He was accustomed, and His disciples also followed Him. When He came to the place, He said to them, "Pray that you may not enter into temptation." And He was withdrawn from them about a stone's throw, and He knelt down and prayed, saying, "Father, if it is Your will, take this cup away from Me; nevertheless not My will, but Yours, be done." Then an angel appeared to Him from heaven, strengthening Him. And being in agony, He prayed more earnestly. Then His sweat became like great drops of blood falling down to the ground. (Luke 22:39–44)

And when they had come to the place called Calvary, there they crucified Him, and the criminals, one on the right hand and the other on the left. Then Jesus said, "Father, forgive them, for they do not know what they do." (Luke 23:33–34)

D.   Jesus' kindness in relationships

1.   Jesus' family: He obeyed Mary in John 2:5 and appeared to James after the Resurrection in 1 Corinthians 15:7.

2.   Jesus' dealing with the disciples: He didn't despise their humble origins. He provided kind teaching and steady patience. He encouraged them in Luke 10 and gave them the keys of the kingdom—explained parables and answered their questions.

a.   Matthew/Levi: Jesus invited a tax collector into the Twelve.

After these things He went out and saw a tax collector named Levi, sitting at the tax office. And He said to him, "Follow Me." So he left all, rose up, and followed Him. (Luke 5:27–28)

b. Judas: Jesus allowed Judas to remain part of the Twelve and to even to oversee the finances.

c. James and John

(1) Jesus answered their desire to eternally rule over all of humanity with Him

Then the mother of Zebedee's sons came to Him with her sons, kneeling down and asking something from Him. And He said to her, "What do you wish?" She said to Him, "Grant that these two sons of mine may sit, one on Your right hand and the other on the left, in Your kingdom." But Jesus answered and said, "You do not know what you ask. Are you able to drink the cup that I am about to drink, and be baptized with the baptism that I am baptized with?" They said to Him, "We are able." So He said to them, "You will indeed drink My cup, and be baptized with the baptism that I am baptized with; but to sit on My right hand and on My left is not Mine to give, but it is for those for whom it is prepared by My Father." (Matthew 20:20–23)

(2) Their desire to call down fire from Heaven to kill the Samaritans

Now it came to pass, when the time had come for Him to be received up, that He steadfastly set His face to go to Jerusalem, and sent messengers before His face. And as they went, they entered a village of the Samaritans, to prepare for Him. But they did not receive Him, because His face was set for the journey to Jerusalem. And when His disciples James and John saw this, they said, "Lord, do You want us to command fire to come down from heaven and consume them, just as Elijah did?" But He turned and rebuked them, and said, "You do not know what manner of spirit you are of. For the Son of Man did not come to destroy men's lives but to save them." And they went to another village. (Luke 9:51–56)

d. Philip: Jesus responded kindly to Philip's unbelief.

Jesus said to him, "I am the way, the truth, and the life. No one comes to the Father except through Me. If you had known Me, you would have known My Father also; and from now on you know Him and have seen Him." Philip said to Him, "Lord, show us the Father, and it is sufficient for us." Jesus said to him, "Have I been with you so long, and yet you have not known Me, Philip? He who has seen Me has seen the Father; so how can you say, 'Show us the Father'? Do you not believe that I am in the Father, and the Father in Me? The words that I speak to you I do not speak on My own authority; but the Father who dwells in Me does the works. Believe Me that I am in the Father and the Father in Me, or else believe Me for the sake of the works themselves." (John 14:6–11)

e. Peter's calling, denial, and restoration

When He had stopped speaking, He said to Simon, "Launch out into the deep and let down your nets for a catch." But Simon answered and said to Him, "Master, we have toiled all night and caught nothing; nevertheless at Your word I will let down the net." And when they had done this, they caught a great number of fish, and their net was breaking. So they signaled to their partners in the other boat to come and help them. And they came and filled both the boats, so that they began to sink. When Simon Peter saw it, he fell down at Jesus' knees, saying, **"Depart from me, for I am a sinful man, O Lord!"** *For he and all who were with him were astonished at the catch of fish which they had taken; and so also were James and John, the sons of Zebedee, who were partners with Simon.* **And Jesus said to Simon, "Do not be afraid. From now on you will catch men." So when they had brought their boats to land, they forsook all and followed Him.** *(Luke 5:4–11, emphasis added)*

Then Jesus said to them, "All of you will be made to stumble because of Me this night, for it is written: 'I will strike the Shepherd, and the sheep will be scattered.' "But after I have been raised, I will go before you to Galilee." **Peter said to Him, "Even if all are made to stumble, yet I will not be."** *Jesus said to him, "Assuredly, I say to you that today, even this night, before the rooster crows twice, you will deny Me three times."* **But he spoke more vehemently, "If I have to die with You, I will not deny You!"** *And they all said likewise. (Mark 14:27–31, emphasis added)*

And the Lord said, **"Simon, Simon! Indeed, Satan has asked for you, that he may sift you as wheat. But I have prayed for you, that your faith should not fail; and when you have returned to Me, strengthen your brethren."** *But he said to Him, "Lord, I am ready to go with You, both to prison and to death." Then He said, "I tell you, Peter, the rooster shall not crow this day before you will deny three times that you know Me." (Luke 22:31–34, emphasis added)*

Then after about an hour had passed, another confidently affirmed, saying, "Surely this fellow also was with Him, for he is a Galilean." But Peter said, "Man, I do not know what you are saying!" Immediately, while he was still speaking, the rooster crowed. And the Lord turned and looked at Peter. Then Peter remembered the word of the Lord, how He had said to him, "Before the rooster crows, you will deny Me three times." So Peter went out and wept bitterly. (Luke 22:59–62)

So when they had eaten breakfast, Jesus said to Simon Peter, "Simon, son of Jonah, do you love Me more than these?" He said to Him, "Yes, Lord; You know that I love You." He said to him, "Feed My lambs." He said to him again a second time, "Simon, son of Jonah, do you love Me?" He said to Him, "Yes, Lord; You know that I love You." He said to him, "Tend My sheep." He said to him the third time, "Simon, son of Jonah, do you love Me?" Peter was grieved because He said to him the third time, "Do you love Me?" And he said to Him, "Lord, You know all things; You know that I love You." Jesus said to him, "Feed My sheep. Most assuredly, I say to you, when you were younger, you girded yourself and walked where you wished; but when you are old, you will stretch out your hands, and another will gird you and carry you where you do not wish." This He spoke, signifying by what death he would glorify God. And when He had spoken this, He said to him, "Follow Me." (John 21:15–19)

f.   Jesus washed the disciples' feet

Now before the Feast of the Passover, when Jesus knew that His hour had come that He should depart from this world to the Father, having loved His own who were in the world, He loved them to the end. And supper being ended, the devil having already put it into the heart of Judas Iscariot, Simon's son, to betray Him, Jesus, knowing that the Father had given all things into His hands, and that He had come from God and was going to God, rose from supper and laid aside His garments, took a towel and girded Himself. After that, He poured water into a basin and began to wash the disciples' feet, and to wipe them with the towel with which He was girded. Then He came to Simon Peter. And Peter said to Him, "Lord, are You washing my feet?" Jesus answered and said to him, "What I am doing you do not understand now, but you will know after this." Peter said to Him, "You shall never wash my feet!" Jesus answered him, "If I do not wash you, you have no part with Me." Simon Peter said to Him, "Lord, not my feet only, but also my hands and my head!" Jesus said to him, "He who is bathed needs only to wash his feet, but is completely clean; and you are clean, but not all of you." For He knew who would betray Him; therefore He said, "You are not all clean." So when He had washed their feet, taken His garments, and sat down again, He said to them, "Do you know what I have done to you? You call Me Teacher and Lord, and you say well, for so I am. If I then, your Lord and Teacher, have washed your feet, you also ought to wash one another's feet. For I have given you an example, that you should do as I have done to you. Most assuredly, I say to you, a servant is not greater than his master; nor is he who is sent greater than he who sent him. If you know these things, blessed are you if you do them. (John 13:1–17)

g. The Eleven's rejection of Jesus on the night of His betrayal

Then Jesus said to them, "All of you will be made to stumble because of Me this night, for it is written: 'I will strike the Shepherd, And the sheep will be scattered.' But after I have been raised, I will go before you to Galilee." Peter said to Him, "Even if all are made to stumble, yet I will not be." Jesus said to him, "Assuredly, I say to you that today, even this night, before the rooster crows twice, you will deny Me three times." But he spoke more vehemently, "If I have to die with You, I will not deny You!" And they all said likewise. (Mark 14:27–31)

Indeed the hour is coming, yes, has now come, that you will be scattered, each to his own, and will leave Me alone. And yet I am not alone, because the Father is with Me. (John 16:32)

h. Thomas' doubt and Jesus' proof

Now Thomas, called the Twin, one of the twelve, was not with them when Jesus came. The other disciples therefore said to him, "We have seen the Lord." So he said to them, "Unless I see in His hands the print of the nails, and put my finger into the print of the nails, and put my hand into His side, I will not believe." And after eight days His disciples were again inside, and Thomas with them. Jesus came, the doors being shut, and stood in the midst, and said, "Peace to you!" Then He said to Thomas, "Reach your finger here, and look at My hands; and reach your hand here, and put it into My side. Do not be unbelieving, but believing." And Thomas answered and said to Him, "My Lord and my God!" Jesus said to him, "Thomas, because you have seen Me, you have believed. Blessed are those who have not seen and yet have believed." (John 20:24–29)

i. Jesus' joy in the disciples' partnership in the work of the Kingdom of God

In that hour Jesus rejoiced in the Spirit and said, "I thank You, Father, Lord of heaven and earth, that You have hidden these things from the wise and prudent and revealed them to babes. Even so, Father, for so it seemed good in Your sight. All things have been delivered to Me by My Father, and no one knows who the Son is except the Father, and who the Father is except the Son, and the one to whom the Son wills to reveal Him." Then He turned to His disciples and said privately, "Blessed are the eyes which see the things you see; for I tell you that many prophets and kings have desired to see what you see, and have not seen it, and to hear what you hear, and have not heard it." (Luke 10:21–24)

3. Jesus' treatment of sinners

   a. The sinful woman: Luke 7:36–50

   b. The Samaritan woman at the well: John 4:5–26

   c. Zacchaeus: Luke 19:1–10

   d. The woman caught in adultery: John 8:11

   e. The daughter of the Samaritan woman: (Mark 7:24–30). "Even the dogs eat the crumbs from the table" (v. 28).

   f. The Centurion's servant

   Now when He concluded all His sayings in the hearing of the people, He entered Capernaum. And a certain centurion's servant, who was dear to him, was sick and ready to die. So when he heard about Jesus, he sent elders of the Jews to Him, pleading with Him to come and heal his servant. And when they came to Jesus, they begged Him earnestly, saying that the one for whom He should do this was deserving, "for he loves our nation, and has built us a synagogue." Then Jesus went with them. And when He was already not far from the house, the centurion sent friends to Him, saying to Him,

"Lord, do not trouble Yourself, for I am not worthy that You should enter under my roof. Therefore I did not even think myself worthy to come to You. But say the word, and my servant will be healed. For I also am a man placed under authority, having soldiers under me. And I say to one, 'Go,' and he goes; and to another, 'Come,' and he comes; and to my servant, 'Do this,' and he does it." When Jesus heard these things, He marveled at him, and turned around and said to the crowd that followed Him, "I say to you, I have not found such great faith, not even in Israel!" And those who were sent, returning to the house, found the servant well who had been sick. (Luke 7:1–10)

g. The rich young ruler

*Now as He was going out on the road, one came running, knelt before Him, and asked Him, "Good Teacher, what shall I do that I may inherit eternal life?" So Jesus said to him, "Why do you call Me good? No one is good but One, that is, God. You know the commandments: 'Do not commit adultery,' 'Do not murder,' 'Do not steal,' 'Do not bear false witness,' 'Do not defraud,' 'Honor your father and your mother.'" And he answered and said to Him, "Teacher, all these things I have kept from my youth." **Then Jesus, looking at him, loved him, and said to him,** "One thing you lack: Go your way, sell whatever you have and give to the poor, and you will have treasure in heaven; and come, take up the cross, and follow Me." But he was sad at this word, and went away sorrowful, for he had great possessions. (Mark 10:17–22, emphasis added)*

4. Jesus' treatment of women

a. *Now it came to pass, afterward, that He went through every city and village, preaching and bringing the glad tidings of the kingdom of God. And the twelve were with Him, and certain women who had been healed of evil spirits and infirmities—Mary called Magdalene, out of whom had come seven demons, and Joanna the wife of Chuza, Herod's steward, and Susanna, and many others who provided for Him from their substance. (Luke 8:1–3)*

b. *Now it happened as they went that He entered a certain village; and a certain woman named Martha welcomed Him into her house. And she had a sister called Mary, who also sat at Jesus' feet and heard His word. But Martha was distracted with much serving, and she approached Him and said, "Lord, do You not care that my sister has left me to serve alone? Therefore tell her to help me."* **And Jesus answered and said to her, "Martha, Martha, you are worried and troubled about many things. But one thing is needed, and Mary has chosen that good part, which will not be taken away from her."** *(Luke 10:38–42, emphasis added)*

c. Healed the widow's only son

Now it happened, the day after, that He went into a city called Nain; and many of His disciples went with Him, and a large crowd. And when He came near the gate of the city, behold, a dead man was being carried out, the only son of his mother; and she was a widow. And a large crowd from the city was with her. When the Lord saw her, He had compassion on her and said to her, "Do not weep." Then He came and touched the open coffin, and those who carried him stood still. And He said, "Young man, I say to you, arise." So he who was dead sat up and began to speak. And He presented him to his mother. Then fear came upon all, and they glorified God, saying, "A great prophet has risen up among us"; and, "God has visited His people." And this report about Him went throughout all Judea and all the surrounding region. (Luke 7:11–17)

5. Jesus' love for children

a. *Then little children were brought to Him that He might put His hands on them and pray, but the disciples rebuked them. But Jesus said,* **"Let the little children come to Me, and do not forbid them; for of such is the kingdom of heaven."** *And He laid His hands on them and departed from there. (Matthew 19:13–15, emphasis added)*

b. *Then they brought little children to Him, that He might touch them; but the disciples rebuked those who brought them. But when Jesus saw it,* **He was greatly displeased** *and said to them, "Let the little children come to Me, and do not forbid them; for of such is the kingdom of God. Assuredly, I say to you, whoever does not receive the kingdom of God as a little child will by no means enter it."* **And He took them up in His arms, laid His hands on them, and blessed them.** *(Mark 10:13–16, emphasis added)*

c. *Then the blind and the lame came to Him in the temple, and He healed them. But when the chief priests and scribes saw the wonderful things that He did, and the children crying out in the temple and saying, "Hosanna to the Son of David!" they were indignant and said to Him, "Do You hear what these are saying?" And* **Jesus said to them, "Yes. Have you never read, 'Out of the mouth of babes and nursing infants You have perfected praise'?"** *(Matthew 21:14–16, emphasis added)*

6. Jesus' gentle handling of the crowds, as displayed in the feeding of the four thousand and five thousand.

Now Jesus called His disciples to Himself and said, "I have compassion on the multitude, because they have now continued with Me three days and have nothing to eat. **And I do not want to send them away hungry, lest they faint on the way."** *(Matthew 15:32, emphasis added)*

7. Jesus' handling of interruptions

a. Jairus' daughter and the bleeding woman

So it was, when Jesus returned, that the multitude welcomed Him, for they were all waiting for Him. And behold, there came a man named Jairus, and he was a ruler of the synagogue. And he fell down at Jesus' feet and begged Him to come to his house, for he had an only daughter about twelve years of age, and she was dying. But as He went, the multitudes thronged Him. Now a woman, having a flow of blood for twelve years, who had spent all her livelihood on physicians and could not be healed by any, came from behind and touched the border of His garment. And immediately her flow of blood stopped. And Jesus said, "Who touched Me?" When all denied it, Peter and those with him said, "Master, the multitudes throng and press You, and You say, 'Who touched Me?'" But Jesus said, "Somebody touched Me, for I perceived power going out from Me." Now when the woman saw that she was not hidden, she came trembling; and falling down before Him, she declared to Him in the presence of all the people the reason she had touched Him and how she was healed immediately. And He said to her, "Daughter, be of good cheer; your faith has made you well. Go in peace." While He was still speaking, someone came from the ruler of the synagogue's house, saying to him, "Your daughter is dead. Do not trouble the Teacher." But when Jesus heard it, He answered him, saying, "Do not be afraid; only believe, and she will be made well." When He came into the house, He permitted no one to go in except Peter, James, and John, and the father and mother of the girl. Now all wept and mourned for her; but He said, "Do not weep; she is not dead, but sleeping." And they ridiculed Him, knowing that she was dead. But He put them all outside, took her by the hand and called, saying, "Little girl, arise." Then her spirit returned, and she arose immediately. And He commanded that she be given something to eat. (Luke 8:40–55)

b. Two blind men healed

When Jesus departed from there, two blind men followed Him, crying out and saying, "Son of David, have mercy on us!" And when He had come into the house, the blind men came to Him. And Jesus said to them, "Do you believe that I am able to do this?" They said to Him, "Yes, Lord." Then He touched their eyes, saying, "According to your faith let it be to you." And their eyes were opened. And Jesus sternly warned them, saying, "See that no one knows it." But when they had departed, they spread the news about Him in all that country. (Matthew 9:27–31)

c. Blind Bartimaeus

Then it happened, as He was coming near Jericho, that a certain blind man sat by the road begging. And hearing a multitude passing by, he asked what it meant. So they told him that Jesus of Nazareth was passing by. And he cried out, saying, "Jesus, Son of David, have mercy on me!" Then those who went before warned him that he should be quiet; but he cried out all the more, "Son of David, have mercy on me!" So Jesus stood still and commanded him to be brought to Him. And when he had come near, He asked him, saying, "What do you want Me to do for you?" He said, "Lord, that I may receive my sight." Then Jesus said to him, "Receive your sight; your faith has made you well." And immediately he received his sight, and followed Him, glorifying God. And all the people, when they saw it, gave praise to God. (Luke 18:35–43)

d. The unending questions of the people and of His disciples

8.   Jesus' reassurance to the disciples

And do not seek what you should eat or what you should drink, nor have an anxious mind. For all these things the nations of the world seek after, and your Father knows that you need these things. But seek the kingdom of God, and all these things shall be added to you. Do not fear, little flock, for it is your Father's good pleasure to give you the kingdom. Sell what you have and give alms; provide yourselves money bags which do not grow old, a treasure in the heavens that does not fail, where no thief approaches nor moth destroys. For where your treasure is, there your heart will be also. (Luke 12:29–34)

Whatever I tell you in the dark, speak in the light; and what you hear in the ear, preach on the housetops. And do not fear those who kill the body but cannot kill the soul. But rather fear Him who is able to destroy both soul and body in hell. Are not two sparrows sold for a copper coin? And not one of them falls to the ground apart from your Father's will. But the very hairs of your head are all numbered. Do not fear therefore; you are of more value than many sparrows. (Matthew 10:27–31)

And again I say to you, it is easier for a camel to go through the eye of a needle than for a rich man to enter the kingdom of God." When His disciples heard it, they were greatly astonished, saying, "Who then can be saved?" But Jesus looked at them and said to them, "With men this is impossible, but with God all things are possible." Then Peter answered and said to Him, "See, we have left all and followed You. Therefore what shall we have?" ***So Jesus said to them, "Assuredly I say to you, that in the regeneration, when the Son of Man sits on the throne of His glory, you who have followed Me will also sit on twelve thrones, judging the twelve tribes of Israel. And everyone who has left houses or brothers or sisters or father or mother or wife or children or lands, for My name's sake, shall receive a hundredfold, and inherit eternal life.*** *(Matthew 19:24–29, emphasis added)*

Let not your heart be troubled; you believe in God, believe also in Me. In My Father's house are many mansions; if it were not so, I would have told you. I go to prepare a place for you. And if I go and prepare a place for you, I will come again and receive you to Myself; that where I am, there you may be also. And where I go you know, and the way you know. (John 14:1–4)

As the Father loved Me, I also have loved you; abide in My love. (John 15:9)

These things I have spoken to you, that in Me you may have peace. In the world you will have tribulation; but be of good cheer, I have overcome the world. (John 16:33)

Session Six: The Crucifixion of Jesus

I.   BORN TO DIE

A.   What kind of King do we have? Imagine the prayers of all the people throughout the ages who groaned for a Messiah. Imagine their surprise at how the events played out. Who could have foreseen this? Who could have known that the inauguration of our King would come as it did? Who could have known how deeply in love with us God is? Who could have known how great His commitment is to holiness, righteousness and justice? Who could have known how greatly He loves mercy? Who could have thought of it? Who but God could have conceived of this plan?

B.   Who could have imagined that Israel's Messiah, who came with the thunder of a thousand angels' voices singing "Glory to God in the highest," would die in a coronation of spit, blood, taunts, scorn and derision? Who would have believed that His innocent flesh would be torn by Roman nails? In the dark hour of Calvary, the brutal truth unfolded. This King was born to die. John the Baptist testified in John 1:29, "Behold! The Lamb of God who takes away the sin of the world!" The herald from the wilderness announced, "Behold your King, the One marked for death, the One designated from birth to be slaughtered for the sins of the world."

Pilate had Jesus beaten, displayed His marred figure with a purple robe and a crown of thorns before the jeering crowd, and announced, "Behold the Man! Behold your King!" But a whisper slowly descended from Heaven: "Not yet. He's still breathing. This King is marked for slaughter. Not long from now, when He is disfigured beyond human appearance, when royal blood stains the cross beam, when the whirlwind of darkness drowns the taunts and jeers, when the Son gropes for His Father's presence, when He breathes His last—then and only then may you behold the Man, the King in all of His glory. This One was born to die." From the very beginning of Jesus' life, He was determined to have His way, and was willing to die to have it.

Father, glorious Father, how could this be? Jesus, precious Jesus, how could it be that You would die for me, that You would ransom my life with Your own precious blood? What kind of love pierces so deeply, stoops so low, and fights so tenaciously, even to the point of death? I am stunned and I am humbled by Your love. Thank you, Father. Thank You, Jesus. Holy Spirit, show me the depths of this humble King, whose origins are from everlasting to everlasting, and whose love would allow His breath to be stolen and His heart to be burst on a Roman tree.

C.	*Such was the life of Jesus on earth. The Gospels tell of a man who was cut off in the flower of His age, His work destroyed just when it should have taken root, His friends scattered, His honor broken, His name a laughingstock. In the words of Isaiah, He was "a worm and not a man, a thing despised and rejected by men, a man of sorrows and familiar with suffering," who experienced the nadir of an agony such as no other man or woman has ever dreamed of. No one has ever died as Jesus died because He was life itself. NO one was ever punished for sin as He was—the sinless One. NO one ever plunged down into the vacuum of evil as did Jesus of Nazareth. Who will ever know the excruciating pain behind His words, "My Father, why have You abandoned Me?" This is the New Testament picture of Jesus—the suffering servant, a man who lives as a lackey and dies in disgrace. He is spurned, avoided, treated as a leper, a born loser. He is one stricken by God, publicly beaten, whipped by disgusted, righteous society. Eliminate Him, they say, He is distasteful. Drive Him across the tracks, out of town, out of society. He is roughly handled, pushed around, taken out, killed, and buried among evil doers. How could it end this way?*[1]

D.	The coronation of this King isn't like any other king's. In Jesus, we find the juxtaposition of royalty and slavery, purity and defilement, glory and rejection. On the hill of Calvary, He took His place as the rightful Ruler of all of humankind. On that day, He ascended the steps to the throne. Who would have thought? From the depths of being despised, rejected, and scorned, our King took a grand stride from death right up to the right hand of God, the Glory, the Majesty of Heaven (Hebrews 1:3). Oh, I tell you, this is our King! The juxtaposition! The tension! The paradox! The Man of sorrow has become the Risen Lord.

---

1   Manning, Brennan. *The Relentless Tenderness of Jesus* (Grand Rapids, MI: Revell, 2004), pp. 83-84.

E.   *Awake now, O my soul, and shake thyself from the dust; and with deeper attention contemplate this wondrous Man, whom, in the glass of the gospel story thou, as it were, gazest upon present before thee. Consider, O my soul, who He is who walketh with the fashion, as it were, of a King, and nevertheless is filled with the confusion of a most despised slave. He goeth crowned, but His very crown is a torture to Him and wounded with a thousand punctures His most glorious head. His cloth is royal purple, yet more is He despised than honored in it. He beareth the scepter in His hand, but with it, His reverent head is beaten. They worship before Him with bowed knee, they hail Him King, but forewith they leap up to spit upon His cheeks lovely to look upon. They smite His jaws with the palms of their hand and dishonor His honorable neck. See further how in all these things He is constrained, spit upon, despised. He is bid to bend His neck beneath the burden of His cross, and He Himself to bear His own ignominy. Brought to the place of punishment, He is given to drink myrrh and gall. He is lifted up upon the cross and He saith, 'Father, forgive them, they know not what they do.' What manner of Man is this, who in all His afflictions never once opened His mouth to utter a word of complaint or pleading, or of threatening or cursing against those accursed dogs, and at last of all poured forth over His enemies a word of blessing? Such has not been heard from the beginning. What more gentle than this Man? What more kind, O my soul, hast thou seen? Gaze on Him, however yet more intently, for He seemeth worthy both of great admiration and of most tender compassion.*

    See Him stripped naked and torn with stripes. Between thieves ignominiously, fixed with nails of iron to the cross. Given vinegar to drink upon the cross, and after death pierced in His side with the spear, and pouring forth plentiful streams of blood from the five wounds of His hands and feet and side. Pour down your tears, mine eyes. Melt, O my soul, with the fire of compassion at the sufferings of that Man of love, whom, in the midst of such gentleness, thou seest afflicted with so bitter griefs.[2]

II.   HISTORICAL FACTS OF JESUS' DEATH

The facts of the story of Jesus' death will cause you to be transformed. The Cross is more than a theological proposition. Once and for all, this event displayed the heart of God to men and made possible the nearness of men's hearts to God. This story has caused men and women from every religious background to give way under its power. It's our privilege forever to ponder the Crucifixion.

---

2 Anselm, Saint. "The Crucifed Christ." *The Book of Jesus: A Treasury of the Greatest Stories and Writings about Christ* (Ed. Calvin Miller. New York: Simon & Schuster, 1998), pp. 414-15.

A.   Predictions of Jesus' death: Mark 8:31–34, 9:30–31, 10:32–34, 10:45

    1.   In Jesus, the two offices of priest and king were made one. The only way He could ascend into His kingly function was through the high priestly ministry of intercession, for the Lord had commanded the crown to be put upon the high priest in Zechariah 6:11. Jesus defined His role as the King—as the Messiah, the Anointed One—through the lens of intercession and atonement. Jesus could only be crowned as King and manifested before the whole earth after He had fulfilled His intercessory function on the Cross as High Priest. This time on the Day of Atonement, the sacrifice wasn't a bull; it was the Lamb of God Himself.

    2.   After Peter confessed that Jesus is the Christ in Caesarea Philippi, Jesus began to teach the disciples of His rejection and suffering.

And He began to teach them that the Son of Man must suffer many things, and be rejected by the elders and chief priests and scribes, and be killed, and after three days rise again. He spoke this word openly. Then Peter took Him aside and began to rebuke Him. But when He had turned around and looked at His disciples, He rebuked Peter, saying, "Get behind Me, Satan! For you are not mindful of the things of God, but the things of men." (Mark 8:31–33)

For He taught His disciples and said to them, "The Son of Man is being betrayed into the hands of men, and they will kill Him. And after He is killed, He will rise the third day." (Mark 9:31)

Now they were on the road, going up to Jerusalem, and Jesus was going before them; and they were amazed. And as they followed they were afraid. Then He took the twelve aside again and began to tell them the things that would happen to Him: "Behold, we are going up to Jerusalem, and the Son of Man will be betrayed to the chief priests and to the scribes; and they will condemn Him to death and deliver Him to the Gentiles; and they will mock Him, and scourge Him, and spit on Him, and kill Him. And the third day He will rise again." (Mark 10:32–34)

B.   The conspiracy to kill Jesus: from the beginning of Jesus' ministry, the members of the religious and political establishments sought to kill Him.

1.   As early as the incident recorded in Mark 3:6, the Pharisees and Herodians worked together, planning to destroy Him.

And when He had looked around at them with anger, being grieved by the hardness of their hearts, He said to the man, "Stretch out your hand." And he stretched it out, and his hand was restored as whole as the other. Then the Pharisees went out and immediately plotted with the Herodians against Him, how they might destroy Him. (Mark 3:5–6)

2.   It was also rumored that King Herod wanted to kill Jesus.

On that very day some Pharisees came, saying to Him, "Get out and depart from here, for Herod wants to kill You." And He said to them, "Go, tell that fox, 'Behold, I cast out demons and perform cures today and tomorrow, and the third day I shall be perfected.' Nevertheless I must journey today, tomorrow, and the day following; for it cannot be that a prophet should perish outside of Jerusalem." (Luke 13:31–33)

3.   Raising Lazarus from the dead put tremendous pressure on the religious establishment to kill Jesus, for many people began to believe in Him as the Messiah after that incident.

Then many of the Jews who had come to Mary, and had seen the things Jesus did, believed in Him. But some of them went away to the Pharisees and told them the things Jesus did. Then the chief priests and the Pharisees gathered a council and said, "What shall we do? For this Man works many signs. If we let Him alone like this, everyone will believe in Him, and the Romans will come and take away both our place and nation." And one of them, Caiaphas, being high priest that year, said to them, "You know nothing at all, nor do you consider that it is expedient for us that one man should die for the people, and not that the whole nation should perish." Now this he did not say on his own authority; but being high priest that year he prophesied that Jesus would die for the nation, and not for that nation only, but also that He would gather together in one the children of God who were scattered abroad. (John 11:45–52)

C.   The betrayal and denial of Jesus

1. Mary of Bethany anointed Jesus for burial (Matthew 26:6–13; Mark 14:3–9; John 12:1–8)

    Judas asked, "Why this waste?" when Mary of Bethany lavished affection on Jesus by pouring costly perfume on Him. But the anointing at Bethany wasn't about the perfume or the fragrance; it was about human love that strengthened Jesus for the Cross. When He saw Mary pouring out her love for Him, it was as though He said, "Father, this is what I desire as a result of my suffering—a heart that loves like this."

2. On the Friday before Passion Week, a dinner was held in Jesus' honor at Simon's house. At that dinner, Mary anointed Jesus with costly perfume for His burial. Satan entered Judas and caused him to make a deal with the Jewish authorities: he would deliver Jesus into their hands for thirty pieces of silver, the sale price of a slave. (Matthew 26:14,25,47, 27:3; Mark 14:10; Luke 22:3,47–48; John 12:4; 13:2,26,29, 18:2,5)

    Now the Feast of Unleavened Bread drew near, which is called Passover. And the chief priests and the scribes sought how they might kill Him, for they feared the people. **Then Satan entered Judas, surnamed Iscariot, who was numbered among the twelve. So he went his way and conferred with the chief priests and captains, how he might betray Him to them. And they were glad, and agreed to give him money.** *So he promised and sought opportunity to betray Him to them in the absence of the multitude. (Luke 22:1–6, emphasis added)*

3. The Last Supper and the confrontation of the betrayer

    a. Jesus ate the Passover Meal with the disciples. He announced that the new covenant would be established through the breaking of His body and the shedding of His blood.

    b. John's gospel deviates from the synoptic gospels in portraying the Last Supper. John wanted to contrast the servanthood of Jesus and the scandal of Judas' betrayal. Jesus reached out publicly to Judas, giving him every opportunity to repent.

        "I do not speak concerning all of you. I know whom I have chosen; but that the Scripture may be fulfilled, ***'He who eats bread with Me has lifted up his heel against Me.'*** *Now I tell*

you before it comes, that when it does come to pass, you may believe that I am He. Most assuredly, I say to you, he who receives whomever I send receives Me; and he who receives Me receives Him who sent Me." **When Jesus had said these things, He was troubled in spirit, and testified and said, "Most assuredly, I say to you, one of you will betray Me."** *Then the disciples looked at one another, perplexed about whom He spoke. Now there was leaning on Jesus' bosom one of His disciples, whom Jesus loved. Simon Peter therefore motioned to him to ask who it was of whom He spoke. Then, leaning back on Jesus' breast, he said to Him, "Lord, who is it?" Jesus answered, "It is he to whom I shall give a piece of bread when I have dipped it." And having dipped the bread, He gave it to Judas Iscariot, the son of Simon.* **Now after the piece of bread, Satan entered him. Then Jesus said to him, "What you do, do quickly."** *But no one at the table knew for what reason He said this to him. For some thought, because Judas had the money box, that Jesus had said to him, "Buy those things we need for the feast," or that he should give something to the poor. Having received the piece of bread, he then went out immediately. And it was night.* (John 13:18–30, emphasis added)

   c.   Only two men are called the "son of perdition" in Scripture: Judas (John 17:12) and the Antichrist (2 Thessalonians 2:3).

   d.   In the midst of the supper, Jesus delivered the message of John 14–16. In order to prepare the disciples for His crucifixion, He promised that His departure would end in great joy for them with the gift of the Holy Spirit.

   e.   After the supper, Jesus and His disciples sang a hymn together. In antiquity, when Jews celebrated the Passover, they traditionally sang Psalms 113–118. Other traditions hold that Jesus sang the Great Hallel of Psalm 136 in antiphonal style.

4.   The Garden of Gethsemane: Matthew 26:30,36–46; Mark 14:26,32–42; Luke 22:39–46; John 18:1–11

   a.   Between the supper and the Garden, Jesus prayed His high priestly prayer of John 17.

b. Jesus entered into a level of intercession never seen before. His spirit was troubled and sorrowful. He was looking for companionship in His hour of sorrow. He wanted friends who would enter into the burden of the Lord. This is a prophetic picture for us. Who will enter into the burdens of the Lord at the same high level of intercession? Who will give their heart to crying out for what is on His heart?

c. The disciples continually fell asleep, although Jesus warned them to pray that they might not enter into temptation.

5. Judas' kiss and the disciples' abandonment: Matthew 26:47–56; Mark 14:43–52; Luke 22:47–53; John 18:2–12. John's gospel describes the power of Jesus, even as the guards arrest Him.

And while He was still speaking, behold, a multitude; and he who was called Judas, one of the twelve, went before them and drew near to Jesus to kiss Him. But Jesus said to him, ***"Judas, are you betraying the Son of Man with a kiss?"*** *When those around Him saw what was going to happen, they said to Him, "Lord, shall we strike with the sword?"* ***And one of them struck the servant of the high priest and cut off his right ear. But Jesus answered and said, "Permit even this."*** *And He touched his ear and healed him. Then Jesus said to the chief priests, captains of the temple, and the elders who had come to Him, "Have you come out, as against a robber, with swords and clubs? When I was with you daily in the temple, you did not try to seize Me. But this is your hour, and the power of darkness." (Luke 22:47–53, emphasis added)*

Jesus therefore, knowing all things that would come upon Him, went forward and said to them, "Whom are you seeking?" They answered Him, "Jesus of Nazareth." Jesus said to them, "I am He." And Judas, who betrayed Him, also stood with them. ***Now when He said to them, "I am He," they drew back and fell to the ground.*** *(John 18:4–6, emphasis added)*

6. Peter's denial: Matthew 26:69–75; Mark 14:66–72; Luke 22:54–62; John 18:15–18,25–27

*But Peter said, "Man, I do not know what you are saying!" Immediately, while he was still speaking, the rooster crowed. **And the Lord turned and looked at Peter.** Then Peter remembered the word of the Lord, how He had said to him, "Before the rooster crows, you will deny Me three times." So Peter went out and wept bitterly. (Luke 22:60–62, emphasis added)*

D. The trial: Jesus' moment of glory. Jesus displays the greatness of His strength.

1. Jesus was brought to the house of Annas, father-in-law of Caiphas, the high priest. (Annas held the office of High Priest before his son-in-law and still wielded the majority of that office's power through Caiaphas). Peter denied Him there, and the men who held Jesus mocked Him and beat Him, saying, "Prophesy! Who is the one who struck You?"

2. Sanhedrin: at daybreak, Caiaphas gathered the Sanhedrin, and they led Jesus to their council. They heard false testimony against Jesus, as well as Jesus' affirmation to the High Priest that He was the Son of God and the Son of Man, and that Caiaphas would see Him sitting at the right hand of Power and coming with the clouds of Heaven.

    But Jesus kept silent. And the high priest answered and said to Him, "I put You under oath by the living God: Tell us if You are the Christ, the Son of God!" Jesus said to him, "It is as you said. Nevertheless, I say to you, hereafter you will see the Son of Man sitting at the right hand of the Power, and coming on the clouds of heaven." Then the high priest tore his clothes, saying, "He has spoken blasphemy! What further need do we have of witnesses? Look, now you have heard His blasphemy! What do you think?" They answered and said, "He is deserving of death." Then they spat in His face and beat Him; and others struck Him with the palms of their hands, saying, "Prophesy to us, Christ! Who is the one who struck You?" (Matthew 26:63–68)

3. Jesus before Pilate: Jesus was then taken before Pilate. The Jews requested that He be put to death for treason and revolt against Caesar. After Pilate discovered Jesus was a Galilean, he gladly sent Jesus over to Herod's Palace in Jerusalem, as Herod held jurisdiction over Galilee.

And they began to accuse Him, saying, "We found this fellow perverting the nation, and forbidding to pay taxes to Caesar, saying that He Himself is Christ, a King." (Luke 23:2)

Then Pilate asked Him, saying, "Are You the King of the Jews?" He answered him and said, "It is as you say." (Luke 23:3)

When Pilate heard of Galilee, he asked if the Man were a Galilean. And as soon as he knew that He belonged to Herod's jurisdiction, he sent Him to Herod, who was also in Jerusalem at that time. (Luke 23:6–7)

4. Jesus before Herod: Herod and his men of war treated Jesus with contempt and mocked Him.

Now when Herod saw Jesus, he was exceedingly glad; for he had desired for a long time to see Him, because he had heard many things about Him, and he hoped to see some miracle done by Him. Then he questioned Him with many words, but He answered him nothing. And the chief priests and scribes stood and vehemently accused Him. Then Herod, with his men of war, treated Him with contempt and mocked Him, arrayed Him in a gorgeous robe, and sent Him back to Pilate. That very day Pilate and Herod became friends with each other, for previously they had been at enmity with each other. (Luke 23:8–12)

5. Jesus sent back to Pilate: Pilate questioned Jesus and found nothing in Jesus worthy of death, so he tried two different approaches to free Jesus. He had Him scourged and offered to release Him in honor of the Passover feast.

    a. Jesus was taken to the Praetorium (the governor's headquarters), where the garrison of soldiers whipped Him, clothed Him in the color of royalty, put a crown of thorns on His head, beat Him over the head with a reed, spat on Him, and mockingly saluted and worshiped Him.

Then the soldiers led Him away into the hall called Praetorium, and they called together the whole garrison. And they clothed Him with purple; and they twisted a crown of thorns, put it on His head, and began to salute Him, "Hail, King of the Jews!" Then they struck Him on the head with a reed and spat on Him; and bowing the knee, they worshiped Him. And when they had mocked Him, they took the purple off Him, put His own clothes on Him, and led Him out to crucify Him. (Mark 15:16–20)

b. The scourging

SCOURGE (skurj), (skur'-jing) (mastix, mastigoo; in Acts 22:25 mastizo, in Mark 15:15 parallel Matthew 27:26 phragelloo): A Roman implement for severe bodily punishment. Horace calls it horrible flagellum. It consisted of a handle, to which several cords or leather thongs were affixed, which were weighted with jagged pieces of bone or metal, to make the blow more painful and effective. It is comparable, in its horrid effects, only with the Russian knout. The victim was tied to a post (Acts 22:25) and the blows were applied to the back and loins, sometimes even, in the wanton cruelty of the executioner, to the face and the bowels. In the tense position of the body, the effect can easily be imagined. So hideous was the punishment that the victim usually fainted and not rarely died under it. Eusebius draws a horribly realistic picture of the torture of scourging (Historia Ecclesiastica, IV, 15).[3]

Eusebius (about 300 AD) described Roman scourging of Christians like this: "At one time they were torn by scourges down to deep-seated veins and arteries, so that the hidden contents of the recesses of their bodies, their entrails and organs, were exposed to sight."[4]

---

3   Dosker, Henry, E. "Scourge, Scourging." *International Standard Bible Encyclopedia*. Chicago: Howard-Severence Company, 1915. *StudyLight.org*. <http://www.studylight.org/enc/isb/view. cgi?number=T7706>

4   Piper, John. *Seeing and Savoring Jesus Christ* (Wheaton, IL: Crossway Books, 2004), p. 74.

c. Pilate found himself in a dilemma. His wife sent a message to him while he was sitting on the judgment seat: "Have nothing to do with that just Man, for I have suffered many things today in a dream because of Him" (Matthew 27:19). The crowds shouted for the release of Barabbas and the crucifixion of Jesus. They applied great pressure to Pilate by saying that to let this supposed king go would be treason to Caesar. Pilate tried one more attempt, saying, "Shall I crucify your King?" Yet, the chief priests answered, "We have no king but Caesar!" Finally, Pilate took the easy way out. He washed his hands of Jesus' death, saying, "I am innocent of the blood of this just Person. You see to it" (Matthew 27:24). Jesus was then given over to be crucified.

E.   The Crucifixion

1.   The way to the Hill (Golgotha/the Skull)

a. Simon of Cyrene: Jesus really needed help by this point. His body was severely beaten and His strength was giving way. Isaiah 52:14 describes Jesus at this point: "Just as many were astonished at you, so His visage was marred more than any man, and His form more than the sons of men."

b. The professional mourners

And a great multitude of the people followed Him, and women who also mourned and lamented Him. But Jesus, turning to them, said, "Daughters of Jerusalem, do not weep for Me, but weep for yourselves and for your children. For indeed the days are coming in which they will say, 'Blessed are the barren, wombs that never bore, and breasts which never nursed!' Then they will begin 'to say to the mountains, "Fall on us!" and to the hills, "Cover us!"' For if they do these things in the green wood, what will be done in the dry?" (Luke 23:27–31)

c. Spurgeon described the Crucifixion this way: "Consider him further still. Do you mark him in your imagination nailed to yonder cross! O eyes! ye are full of pity, with tears standing thick! Oh! how I mark the floods gushing down his checks! Do you see his hands bleeding, and his feet too, gushing gore? Behold him! The bulls of Bashan gird him round, and the dogs are hounding him to death! Hear him! 'Eloi, Eloi, lama sabachthani?' The earth startles with affright. A God is groaning on a cross!"[5]

2. Description of crucifixion

The prisoner would first be publicly humiliated by being stripped naked. He was then laid on his back on the ground, while his hands were either nailed or roped to the horizontal wooden beam, and his feet to the vertical pole. The cross was then hoisted to an upright position and dropped into a socket which had been dug for it in the ground. Usually a peg or rudimentary seat was provided to take some of the weight of the victim's body and prevent it from being torn loose. But there he would hang, helplessly exposed to intense physical pain, public ridicule, daytime heat and nighttime cold. The torture would last several days.[6]

At every turn, Jesus intentionally volunteered for the next step. At every step, His will said "yes" to another nail. It would have been impossible to have penetrated His flesh or to have struck His jaw unless He willingly consented. He said to Pilate, "You could have no power over Me unless it had been given you from above" (John 19:11). His love for us strengthened His heart to say "yes" again and again.

3. The time of the Crucifixion: six hours

Third hour = 9 a.m.   Sixth hour = Noon   Ninth hour = 3 p.m.

4. Jesus' last words

a. Third hour

---

5 Spurgeon, Charles. "The Exaltation of Christ." *The Spurgeon Archive*. 2001. <http://www.spurgeon. org/sermons/0101.htm> Sec. 2, par. 8.

6 Stott, John. *The Cross of Christ* (Downers Grove, IL: InterVarsity, 1986), p. 48.

(1) *"Father, forgive them, for they do not know what they do." (Luke 32:34)*

(2) *"Woman, behold your son! ... [Son,] behold your mother!" (John 19:26, 27)*

(3) *"Assuredly, I say to you, today you will be with Me in Paradise." (Luke 23:43)*

The words of Jesus in the third to the sixth hour were filled with mercy and compassion. Forgiveness was first upon His lips: "Father, forgive them." Care for His mother and mercy for the penitent flowed from a heart that was undefiled from the background noise of taunts and jeers. Truly, Jesus' greatness is shown here. In the hours of His greatest weakness, He showed the greatest amount of restraint and revealed His true colors. He loves at all times.

b. Sixth hour: darkness covered the land until the ninth hour

(1) *"My God, my God, why have You forsaken me?" (Matthew 27:46; Mark 15:34)*

Jesus cried this when He began to bear the wrath of God that came against the corporate sin of all humanity. Only the God-Man could have borne this weight.

(2) *"I thirst!" (John 19:28)*

(3) *"It is finished!" (John 19:30)*

(4) *"Father, 'into Your hands I commit My spirit.'" (Luke 23:46)*

From the sixth to the ninth hour, Jesus bore the penalty of sin and was crushed by the wrath of God. He voiced the cry of dereliction and thirsted for relief. He became the Lamb of God who takes away the sin of the world. Faithful and true, Jesus finished the task of the Servant by bearing the sins of many and making intercession for transgressors (Isaiah 53:12).

c. Ninth hour: death

(1) Jesus yielded up His spirit to the Father.

And Jesus cried out again with a loud voice, and yielded up His spirit. Then, behold, the veil of the temple was torn in two from top to bottom; and the earth quaked, and the rocks were split, and the graves were opened; and many bodies of the saints who had fallen asleep were raised; and coming out of the graves after His resurrection, they went into the holy city and appeared to many. So when the centurion and those with him, who were guarding Jesus, saw the earthquake and the things that had happened, they feared greatly, saying, "Truly this was the Son of God!" (Matthew 27:50–54)

(2) The soldiers broke the legs of the two thieves in order to speed the dying process up, yet in fulfillment of Psalm 34:20, Jesus' legs were not broken.

Then the soldiers came and broke the legs of the first and of the other who was crucified with Him. But when they came to Jesus and saw that He was already dead, they did not break His legs. But one of the soldiers pierced His side with a spear, and immediately blood and water came out. And he who has seen has testified, and his testimony is true; and he knows that he is telling the truth, so that you may believe. For these things were done that the Scripture should be fulfilled, "Not one of His bones shall be broken." And again another Scripture says, "They shall look on Him whom they pierced." (John 19:32–37)

He guards all his bones; not one of them is broken. (Psalm 34:20)

(3) The aftermath of Jesus' death: Jesus cried out with a loud voice, yielded up His Spirit, and certain anomalies took place.

(a) The Temple veil was torn from top to bottom.

(b) The earth quaked and rocks split.

(c) Graves were opened, and many saints were raised from the dead. These raised saints went about the holy city, appearing to many.

(d) The centurion testified, "Truly this was the Son of God!"

III. THE QUESTION OF WHO KILLED JESUS

Now it was about the sixth hour, and there was darkness over all the earth until the ninth hour. Then the sun was darkened, and the veil of the temple was torn in two. And when Jesus had cried out with a loud voice, He said, "Father, 'into Your hands I commit My spirit.'" Having said this, He breathed His last. So when the centurion saw what had happened, he glorified God, saying, "Certainly this was a righteous Man!" And the whole crowd who came together to that sight, seeing what had been done, beat their breasts and returned. (Luke 23:44–48, emphasis added)

The madness began to wane. Compulsion turned to sorrow as the crowd realized in the deep darkness that something scandalous had occurred. Staring at the dead body of Jesus, the centurion broke the silence and added to the guilt of the moment: "This was a righteous man!" The once jeering, mocking crowd fell silent, but they could not stop the internal voices of condemnation. In a failed attempt at removing their shame, they beat their breasts, but the voices continued. "Who did this? What happened here? The veil was torn in two, the earth is shaking, and once-dead holy men are walking around Jerusalem. Something went wrong. Something went dead wrong, and someone is guilty. Someone has blood on their hands. Who?"

A. Judas, after Satan entered him, betrayed Jesus for thirty pieces of silver.

B. The chief priests and elders, along with the Jewish people

Pilate said to them, "What then shall I do with Jesus who is called Christ?" They all said to him, "Let Him be crucified!" Then the governor said, "Why, what evil has He done?" But they cried out all the more, saying, "Let Him be crucified!" When Pilate saw that he could not prevail at all, but rather that a tumult was rising, he took water and washed his hands before the multitude, saying, "I am innocent of the blood of this just Person. You see to it." And all the people answered and said, "His blood be on us and on our children." (Matthew 27:22–25)

> *Then Pilate said to Him, "Are You not speaking to me? Do You not know that I have to crucify You, and power to release You?" Jesus answered, "You could have no power at all against Me unless it had been given you from above. Therefore the one who delivered Me to you has the greater sin." (John 19:10–11)*

C.   Pontius Pilate and the Roman authorities

> *Behold, we are going up to Jerusalem, and the Son of Man will be betrayed to the chief priests and to the scribes; and they will condemn Him to death and deliver Him to the Gentiles; and they will mock Him, and scourge Him, and spit on Him, and kill Him. And the third day He will rise again. (Mark 10:33–34)*

> *For He will be delivered to the Gentiles and will be mocked and insulted and spit upon. They will scourge Him and kill Him. And the third day He will rise again. (Luke 18:32–33)*

D.   Our sin

1.   *The crucifixion of Christ was the crowning sin of our race. In his death we shall find all the sins of mankind uniting in foul conspiracy. Envy and pride and hate are there, with covetousness, falsehood, and blasphemy, eager to rush on to cruelty, revenge, and murder. The devil roused around the seed of the woman the iniquities of us all: they compassed the Lord about, yea, they compassed him about like bees. All the evils of human hearts of all ages were concentrated around the cross: even as all the rivers run into the sea, and as all the clouds empty themselves upon the earth, so did all the crimes of man gather to the slaying of the Son of God. It seemed as if hell held a levee, and all the various forms of sin came flocking to the rendezvous; army upon army, they hastened to the battle. As the vultures hasten to the body, so came the flocks of sins to make the Lord their prey. By all the assembled troops of sins there was consummated the foulest crime which the sun has ever beheld. By wicked hands they did crucify and slay the Saviour of the world.[7]*

---

7   "Pilate and Ourselves Guilty of the Savior's Death." *Spurgeon's Encyclopedia of Sermons.* CD-ROM. Seattle, WA: Biblesoft, 1997.

2.   Before we can see the Cross as something done for us, we have to see it as something done by us. Indeed, "only the man who is prepared to own his share in the guilt of the Cross," wrote Canon Peter Green, "may claim his share in its grace."[8]

3.   Horatius Bonar (1808–1889):Scottish Hymn Writer

Twas I that shed the sacred blood;
I nailed Him to the tree;
I crucified the Christ of God;
I joined the mockery.

Of all that shouting multitude
I fell that I am one;
And in that din of voices rude
I recognize my own.

Around the cross the throng I see,
Mocking the Sufferer's groan;
Yet still my voice it seems to be,
As if I mocked alone.[9]

E.   The Son laid down His own life and the Father bruised the Son.

No one takes it from Me, but I lay it down of Myself. I have power to lay it down, and I have power to take it again. This command I have received from My Father. (John 10:18)

I have been crucified with Christ; it is no longer I who live, but Christ lives in me; and the life which I now live in the flesh I live by faith in the Son of God, who loved me and gave Himself for me. (Galatians 2:20)

And walk in love, as Christ also has loved us and given Himself for us, an offering and a sacrifice to God for a sweet-smelling aroma. (Ephesians 5:2)

Therefore I will divide Him a portion with the great, and He shall divide the spoil with the strong, because He poured out His soul unto death, and He was numbered with the transgressors, and He bore the sin of many, and made intercession for the transgressors. (Isaiah 53:12)

---

8   Stott, John. *The Cross of Christ* (Downers Grove, IL: InterVarsity, 1986), p. 60.
9   *Ibid,* p. 60.

F. Octavius Winslow summed it up in a neat statement: *"Who delivered up Jesus to die? Not Judas, for money; not Pilate, for fear; not the Jews, for envy;—but the Father, for love!"… On the human level, Judas gave Him up to the priests, who gave Him up to Pilate, who gave Him up to the soldiers, who crucified Him. But on the divine level, the Father gave Him up, and He gave Himself up, to die for us. As we face the cross, then, we can say to ourselves both "I did it, my sins sent Him there" and "He did it, His love took Him there."[10]*

---

10 Stott, John. *The Cross of Christ* (Downers Grove, IL: InterVarsity, 1986), p. 61. Emphasis added.

Session Seven: The Cross—The Heart of the Matter

I. THE PROBLEM OF FORGIVENESS

A. In today's pristine theological discourse, there is little room for the Cross. Modern minds consider the need for atonement barbaric and antiquated. The Cross is the last vestige of an angry God from a darkened age. Lawlessness is an ancient concept. Atonement is cast aside for the language of liberation of an oppressed inner humanity. What the Bible declares as lawless and iniquitous, the modern person views as liberation. At the first Re-imagining Conference in Minneapolis, women from mainline denominations gathered to re-imagine the concept of God:

Delores Williams, a [Presbyterian] professor at Union Theological Seminary in New York, boldly suggested, "I don't think we need a theory of atonement at all ... atonement has to do so much with death ... I don't think we need folks hanging on crosses, and blood dripping, and weird stuff ... we just need to listen to the god within." Another speaker, Virginia Mollenkott, who serves on the National Council of Churches, claimed that the death of Jesus was the ultimate in child abuse. She said that the commonly accepted view of Christ's atonement pictures God as an abusive parent, and Jesus as an obedient child.[1]

At a later re-imaging conference, Williams called the removal of the Cross from a church's sanctuary "life giving."[2]

B. Regardless of the modern attempt to re-imagine or replace the orthodox view of God, the biblical witness testifies that the separation of God and man is more than an enlightenment issue. The solution to humanity's lack of God will not come by getting in touch with some inner spiritual force. The heart of the problem is that a breach has occurred between God and humanity. The issue is not that humanity has difficulty finding God and articulating how we are to properly relate to Him; the issue is that humanity has rebelled against God and hates His ways. Thus, there is a divine collision between the sinfulness of humanity and the perfection of God's holy love. They are incompatible.

---

1 "The WCC Solidarity with Women Minneapolis Conference." *BRF Witness*. May/June 1994. Brethern Revival Fellowship. <http://www.brfwitness.org/Articles/1994v29n3.htm>.
2 "Sophia upstages Jesus at ReImagining Revival." *The Presbyterian Layman*. <http://www.layman. org/layman/news/reimagining-revival.htm.>

C. Before we can understand the greatness of the salvation worked at the Cross, we must first understand from whom and what we were saved. If the Cross is to ever produce the fruit of humility and gratitude, we must understand the gravity of human sin. The crucifixion of Christ was the crowning sin of the human race. The means by which we are saved is also the display of our great depravity. The Crucifixion clearly displays the heart of humanity, the greatness of God, and the means necessary to acquit a guilty race.

1. Archbishop Anselm stated that if anybody imagines that God can simply forgive us as we forgive others, that person has not considered two realities: "the seriousness of sin" and "the majesty of God."[3] Humans, through willful disobedience of and rebellion against their Creator, have highly offended God's honor.

2. Emil Brunner said, "Sin is a defiance, arrogance, the desire to be equal with God ... the assertion of human independence over and against God ... the constitution of the autonomous reason, morality, and culture."[4]

D. The holiness/wrath of God and the love/mercy of God: that God is holy is foundational to biblical religion. So is the corollary that sin is incompatible with His holiness. His eyes are too pure to look on evil and He cannot tolerate wrong (Isaiah 59:2; Habakkuk 1:13). Therefore, our sins effectively separate us from Him; His face is hidden from us and He refuses to listen to our prayers. In consequence, the biblical authors clearly understood that no human being could ever set eyes on God and survive the experience. God's wrath, in the words of Leon Morris, is His "personal divine revulsion to evil" and His "personal vigorous opposition" to it.[5] God loves us, but He is in opposition to us.

1. *For the wrath of God is revealed from heaven against all ungodliness and unrighteousness of men, who suppress the truth in unrighteousness, because what may be known of God is manifest in them, for God has shown it to them. For since the creation of the world His invisible attributes are clearly seen, being understood by the things that are made, even His eternal power and Godhead, so that they are without excuse, because, although they knew God, they did not glorify Him as God, nor were thankful, but became futile in their thoughts, and their foolish hearts were darkened. Professing to be wise, they became*

---

3 Stott, John. *The Cross of Christ* (Downers Grove IL: InterVarsity, 1986), p. 88.
4 *Ibid*, p. 90.
5 *Ibid*, pp. 102, 105.

fools, and changed the glory of the incorruptible God into an image made like corruptible man—and birds and four-footed animals and creeping things. Therefore God also gave them up to uncleanness, in the lusts of their hearts, to dishonor their bodies among themselves, who exchanged the truth of God for the lie, and worshiped and served the creature rather than the Creator, who is blessed forever. Amen. For this reason God gave them up to vile passions. For even their women exchanged the natural use for what is against nature. Likewise also the men, leaving the natural use of the woman, burned in their lust for one another, men with men committing what is shameful, and receiving in themselves the penalty of their error which was due. And even as they did not like to retain God in their knowledge, God gave them over to a debased mind, to do those things which are not fitting; being filled with all unrighteousness, sexual immorality, wickedness, covetousness, maliciousness; full of envy, murder, strife, deceit, evil-mindedness; they are whisperers, backbiters, haters of God, violent, proud, boasters, inventors of evil things, disobedient to parents, undiscerning, untrustworthy, unloving, unforgiving, unmerciful; who, knowing the righteous judgment of God, that those who practice such things are deserving of death, not only do the same but also approve of those who practice them. Therefore you are inexcusable, O man, whoever you are who judge, for in whatever you judge another you condemn yourself; for you who judge practice the same things. (Romans 1:16–2:1)

2. *What then? Are we better than they? Not at all. For we have previously charged both Jews and Greeks that they are all under sin. As it is written: "There is none righteous, no, not one; there is none who understands; there is none who seeks after God. They have all turned aside; they have together become unprofitable; there is none who does good, no, not one." "Their throat is an open tomb; with their tongues they have practiced deceit"; "The poison of asps is under their lips"; "Whose mouth is full of cursing and bitterness." "Their feet are swift to shed blood; destruction and misery are in their ways; and the way of peace they have not known." "There is no fear of God before their eyes." ... For all have sinned and fall short of the glory of God ... (Romans 3:9–18, 23)*

3. *For the wages of sin is death, but the gift of God is eternal life in Christ Jesus our Lord. (Romans 6:23)*

4. *Therefore be imitators of God as dear children. And walk in love, as Christ also has loved us and given Himself for us, an offering and a sacrifice to God for a sweet-smelling aroma. But fornication and all uncleanness or covetousness, let it not even be named among you, as is fitting for saints; neither filthiness, nor foolish talking, nor coarse jesting, which are not fitting, but rather giving of thanks. For this you know, that no fornicator, unclean person, nor covetous man, who is an idolater, has any inheritance in the kingdom of Christ and God. **Let no one deceive you with empty words, for because of these things the wrath of God comes upon the sons of disobedience. Therefore do not be partakers with them.** (Ephesians 5:1–7, emphasis added)*

E. The Cross is the place where perfect mercy and perfect justice meet and embrace one another, where divine holiness and divine love find perfect expression, and where righteousness and peace kiss each other (Psalm 85:10–11).

I really don't believe it is possible to grasp the central drama of the Bible until we begin to feel this tension. Until the coming of Jesus Christ, the Bible is like a piece of music whose dissonance begs for some final resolution into harmony…The death and resurrection of Jesus Christ is the resolution of the symphony of history. In the death of Jesus the two themes of God's love for His glory and His love for sinners are resolved.[6]

II. SATISFACTION FOR SIN

A. Who is satisfied by Jesus' sacrifice?

1. Did it satisfy the Devil?

2. Did it satisfy God's law?

3. Did it satisfy God's honor?

4. Did it satisfy God Himself?

---

6 Piper, John. *The Pleasures of God* (Portland, OR: Multnomah, 1991), p. 162.

B.   One speaks of the overthrow of the devil by satisfying his demands, others of satisfying God's law, honour or justice, and the last of satisfying the moral order of the world. In differing degrees all these formulations are true. The limitation they share is that, unless they are very carefully stated, they represent God as being subordinate to something outside and above Himself which controls His actions, to which he is accountable, and from which he cannot free Himself. Satisfaction is an appropriate word, providing we realize that it is He Himself in His inner being who needs to be satisfied, and not something external to Himself. Talk of law, honour, justice, and the moral order is true only in so far as these are seen as expressions of God's own character. Atonement is a necessity because it arises from within God Himself.[7]

C.   God is provoked by, burns with righteous indignation over, and breaks out against sin. God's holy justice had to be satisfied. Sin in His universe had to be accounted for; it had to be punished. He was willing to strike His Son for man's sin.

1.   Scriptures about the provocation of God:

They provoked Him to jealousy with foreign gods; with abominations they provoked Him to anger. (Deuteronomy 32:16, emphasis added)

Then the children of Israel did evil in the sight of the Lord, and served the Baals; and they forsook the Lord God of their fathers, who had brought them out of the land of Egypt; and they followed other gods from among the gods of the people who were all around them, and they bowed down to them; and they provoked the Lord to anger. They forsook the Lord and served Baal and the Ashtoreths. (Judges 2:11–13, emphasis added)

Because of the sins of Jeroboam, which he had sinned and by which he had made Israel sin, because of his provocation with which he had provoked the Lord God of Israel to anger. (1 Kings 15:30, emphasis added)

---

7   Stott, John. *The Cross of Christ* (Downers Grove, IL: InterVarsity, 1986), p. 123.

So Ahab said to Elijah, "Have you found me, O my enemy?" And he answered, "I have found you, because you have sold yourself to do evil in the sight of the LORD: 'Behold, I will bring calamity on you. I will take away your posterity, and will cut off from Ahab every male in Israel, both bond and free. I will make your house like the house of Jeroboam the son of Nebat, and like the house of Baasha the son of Ahijah, because of the provocation with which you have provoked Me to anger, and made Israel sin.' And concerning Jezebel the LORD also spoke, saying, 'The dogs shall eat Jezebel by the wall of Jezreel.'" (1 Kings 21:20–23, emphasis added)

Because the children of Israel and the children of Judah have done only evil before Me from their youth. For the children of Israel have provoked Me only to anger with the work of their hands,' says the LORD. For this city has been to Me a provocation of My anger and My fury from the day that they built it, even to this day; so I will remove it from before My face. (Jeremiah 32:30–31, emphasis added)

He stretched out the form of a hand, and took me by a lock of my hair; and the Spirit lifted me up between earth and heaven, and brought me in visions of God to Jerusalem, to the door of the north gate of the inner court, where the seat of the image of jealousy was, which provokes to jealousy. (Ezekiel 8:3, emphasis added)

Ephraim provoked Him to anger most bitterly; therefore his Lord will leave the guilt of his bloodshed upon him, and return his reproach upon him. (Hosea 12:14, emphasis added)

2.   Scriptures about God's burning anger:

But the children of Israel committed a trespass regarding the accursed things, for Achan the son of Carmi, the son of Zabdi, the son of Zerah, of the tribe of Judah, took of the accursed things; so the anger of the LORD burned against the children of Israel. (Joshua 7:1, emphasis added)

When you have transgressed the covenant of the LORD your God, which He commanded you, and have gone and served other gods, and bowed down to them, then the anger of the LORD will burn against you, and you shall perish quickly from the good land which He has given you. (Joshua 23:16, emphasis added)

> *Now Satan stood up against Israel, and moved David to number Israel. So David said to Joab and to the leaders of the people, "Go, number Israel from Beersheba to Dan, and bring the number of them to me that I may know it." And Joab answered, "May the LORD make His people a hundred times more than they are. But, my lord the king, are they not all my lord's servants? Why then does my lord require this thing? Why should he be a cause of guilt in Israel?" Nevertheless the king's word prevailed against Joab. Therefore Joab departed and went throughout all Israel and came to Jerusalem. Then Joab gave the sum of the number of the people to David. All Israel had one million one hundred thousand men who drew the sword, and Judah had four hundred and seventy thousand men who drew the sword. But he did not count Levi and Benjamin among them, for the king's word was abominable to Joab. (1 Chronicles 21:1–6, emphasis added)*

> *Again the anger of the LORD was aroused against Israel, and He moved David against them to say, "Go, number Israel and Judah." (2 Samuel 24:1, emphasis added)*

> *Your calf is rejected, O Samaria! My anger is aroused against them—how long until they attain to innocence? (Hosea 8:5, emphasis added)*

3. Scriptures of God breaking out against sin: we need to praise Him for this. God is committed to forever removing sin from human beings so that humans would not suffer the same fate as Satan and his demons.

> *Circumcise yourselves to the LORD, and take away the foreskins of your hearts, you men of Judah and inhabitants of Jerusalem, lest My fury come forth like fire, and burn so that no one can quench it, because of the evil of your doings. (Jeremiah 4:4)*

> *And concerning the house of the king of Judah, say, "Hear the word of the LORD, O house of David! Thus says the LORD: 'Execute judgment in the morning; and deliver him who is plundered out of the hand of the oppressor, lest My fury go forth like fire and burn so that no one can quench it, because of the evil of your doings.' (Jeremiah 21:11–12)*

4. Scriptures of God's covenantal love and self-satisfaction

a. Hosea 3: God commanded Hosea to go again and love Gomer, a prostitute whom God had commanded him to marry (Hosea 1:2–3). She was enslaved by another lover, but God told Hosea to go again and buy her back. Was she worthy? Did she deserve it? No! But that is not the issue. The real issue is God's great mercy to forgive and great passion to restore. God brought Hosea into the whirlwind of His great love and commanded, "Go again, Hosea. The same passion which causes me to be provoked by Israel's sin is the same passion which leads Me to love and pursue Israel even to the depths. Go again, Hosea. Discover this kind of love."

b. *Come, and let us return to the LORD; for He has torn, but He will heal us; He has stricken, but He will bind us up. (Hosea 6:1)*

c. *How can I give you up, Ephraim? How can I hand you over, Israel? How can I make you like Admah? How can I set you like Zeboiim? My heart churns within Me; My sympathy is stirred. I will not execute the fierceness of My anger; I will not again destroy Ephraim. For I am God, and not man, the Holy One in your midst; and I will not come with terror. (Hosea 11:8–9)*

d. *Say to them: "As I live," says the Lord GOD, "I have no pleasure in the death of the wicked, but that the wicked turn from his way and live. Turn, turn from your evil ways! For why should you die, O house of Israel?" (Ezekiel 33:11)*

e. In Isaiah 49, God asked the question, "Can a mother forget her child?" to illustrate that He would not forget His people:

But Zion said, "The LORD has forsaken me, and my Lord has forgotten me." "Can a woman forget her nursing child, and not have compassion on the son of her womb? Surely they may forget, yet I will not forget you. See, I have inscribed you on the palms of My hands; Your walls are continually before Me. (Isaiah 49:14–16)

D. God's holy covenantal love moved Him to satisfy His own desire for justice and for love by sacrificing His Son. The Cross is the perfect expression, the perfect harmony of both justice and love; it represents the perfect balance and symmetry of the beautiful God.

E.   *So then, the cross of Christ "is the event in which God makes known His holiness and His love simultaneously, in one event, in an absolute manner" (p. 450). "The cross is the only place where the loving, forgiving merciful God is revealed in such a way that we perceive that His holiness and His love are equally infinite" (p. 470). In fact, "the objective aspect of the atonement … may be summed up thus: it consists in the combination of inflexible righteousness, with its penalties, and transcendent love" (p. 520).[8]*

F.   The Son stands in the gap as the ultimate intercessor of the ages. In His very person, He pleads the cause of God and the cause of humanity. In Christ, the very justice and mercy of God find solace. He is the ultimate intercessor!

Between the sovereignty of God and the destiny of man, one finds the intercessor. There, in the great chasm between God's blazing righteousness and man's fallenness, an intercessor is found waiting. There, love waits and wrestles for God to be heard and man to be pitied. **The courageous are found there, fighting for God to be adored and man to be accepted. In this holy place, one enters into the suffering heart of the Mediator, Jesus, who vindicates His Father's glorious name and atones for the rebellion. This is a holy place, a divine meeting where doors open to deep caverns of divine paradox, where God's emotions and economy lead to groans and pleas for triumph and redemption. Blessed is the man who waits here.**

Blessed is the man who enters secret chambers where justice and mercy give birth to love in action. Blessed is the one who enters into the divine unity of God's own nature. Justice demands sentence on the trespassers. Blazing righteousness zeroes in on the defiled. Mercy reaches to cover sin, and kindness moves to adorn ugliness. **In the swirl of God's own passions, the intercessor is beckoned to enter the place where God prays to God, where the Son asks His Father to forgive them—and the Father agrees, crushing the Son with the burden of the masses. The intercessor meets the crucified Jesus at Golgotha's triumph and finds fullness there: God's fullness and our acceptance into it!**

III.   GOD'S SELF-SUBSTITUTION

---

8   Stott, John. *The Cross of Christ* (Downers Grove, IL: InterVarsity, 1986), p. 131

A.   *God, because in His mercy He willed to forgive sinful men, and, being truly merciful, willed to forgive them righteously, that is, without in any way condoning their sin, purposed to direct against His own very self in the person of His Son the full weight of that righteous wrath which they deserved.*[9]

Therefore purge out the old leaven, that you may be a new lump, since you truly are unleavened. For indeed Christ, our Passover, was sacrificed for us. (1 Corinthians 5:7)

Grace to you and peace from God the Father and our Lord Jesus Christ, who gave Himself for our sins, that He might deliver us from this present evil age, according to the will of our God and Father. (Galatians 1:3–4)

And walk in love, as Christ also has loved us and given Himself for us, an offering and a sacrifice to God for a sweet-smelling aroma. But fornication and all uncleanness or covetousness, let it not even be named among you, as is fitting for saints. (Ephesians 5:2–3)

But Christ came as High Priest of the good things to come, with the greater and more perfect tabernacle not made with hands, that is, not of this creation. Not with the blood of goats and calves, but with His own blood He entered the Most Holy Place once for all, having obtained eternal redemption. For if the blood of bulls and goats and the ashes of a heifer, sprinkling the unclean, sanctifies for the purifying of the flesh, how much more shall the blood of Christ, who through the eternal Spirit offered Himself without spot to God, cleanse your conscience from dead works to serve the living God? And for this reason He is the Mediator of the new covenant, by means of death, for the redemption of the transgressions under the first covenant, that those who are called may receive the promise of the eternal inheritance. (Hebrews 9:11–15)

For Christ has not entered the holy places made with hands, which are copies of the true, but into heaven itself, now to appear in the presence of God for us; not that He should offer Himself often, as the high priest enters the Most Holy Place every year with blood of another—He then would have had to suffer often since the foundation of the world; but now, once at the end of the ages, He has appeared to put away sin by the sacrifice of Himself. And as it is appointed for men to die once, but after this the judgment. (Hebrews 9:24–27)

Previously saying, "Sacrifice and offering, burnt offerings, and offerings for sin You did not desire, nor had pleasure in them" (which are offered

---

9   Stott, John. *The Cross of Christ* (Downers Grove, IL: InterVarsity, 1986), p. 134.

according to the law), then He said, "Behold, I have come to do Your will, O God." He takes away the first that He may establish the second. By that will we have been sanctified through the offering of the body of Jesus Christ once for all. And every priest stands ministering daily and offering repeatedly the same sacrifices, which can never take away sins. But this Man, after He had offered one sacrifice for sins forever, sat down at the right hand of God, from that time waiting till His enemies are made His footstool. For by one offering He has perfected forever those who are being sanctified. But the Holy Spirit also witnesses to us; for after He had said before. (Hebrews 10:8–15)

B.   Foreshadowed in the sacrificial system in the Old Testament

  1.   *Two basic and complementary notions of sacrifice [were shown] in God's Old Testament revelation. The first expressed the sense human beings have of belonging to God by right, and the second their sense of alienation from God because of their sin and guilt. Characteristics of the first were the peace or fellowship offering which was often associated with thanksgiving (Leviticus 7:12), the burnt offering and the ritual of the three annual harvest festivals (Exodus 23:14–17). Characteristics of the second were the sin offering and the guilt offering, in which the need for atonement was clearly acknowledged.*[10]

  2.   The sacrificial system pointed to the two realities of the holiness and love of God. Jesus satisfied the requirements of both sacrifices on the Cross. Not only did He die as a guilt offering/sin offering, He died as an offering to bring us into fellowship with God.

  3.   In the Old Testament ritual of animal sacrifice, the worshiper brought the offering, laid hands on it (signifying that the animal took the worshiper's place), and killed it. Then the priest applied the blood, burned some of the flesh, and consumed the remainder of the animal.

  4.   Atonement in the Old Testament came through the spilling of blood. "For the life of the flesh is in the blood, and I have given it to you upon the altar to make atonement for your souls; for it is the blood that makes atonement for the soul." (Leviticus 17:11)

C.   Passover: Exodus 12:2–28

---

10   Stott, John. *The Cross of Christ* (Downers Grove, IL: InterVarsity, 1986), p. 135.

1.   Actual event: Yahweh displayed as Judge, Redeemer, and Covenant Maker.[11] Christ is seen as the fulfillment of Passover: John 1:29–30,36, 13:1, 18:28–29, 19:14,31; 1 Corinthians 5:6–8.

The next day John saw Jesus coming toward him, and said, "Behold! **The Lamb of God who takes away the sin of the world!** *This is He of whom I said, 'After me comes a Man who is preferred before me, for He was before me.' (John 1:29–30, emphasis added)*

Again, the next day, John stood with two of his disciples. And looking at Jesus as He walked, he said, **"Behold the Lamb of God!"** *(John 1:35–36, emphasis added)*

Now before the Feast of the Passover, when Jesus knew that His hour had come that He should depart from this world to the Father, *having loved His own who were in the world, He loved them to the end. (John 13:1, emphasis added)*

Then they led Jesus from Caiaphas to the Praetorium, and it was early morning. But they themselves did not go into the Praetorium, lest they should be defiled, **but that they might eat the Passover.** *Pilate then went out to them and said, "What accusation do you bring against this Man?" (John 18:28–29, emphasis added)*

Now it was the Preparation Day of the Passover, *and about the sixth hour. And he said to the Jews, "Behold your King!" (John 19:14, emphasis added)*

Your glorying is not good. Do you not know that a little leaven leavens the whole lump? Therefore purge out the old leaven, that you may be a new lump, since you truly are unleavened. **For indeed Christ, our Passover, was sacrificed for us.** *Therefore let us keep the feast, not with old leaven, nor with the leaven of malice and wickedness, but with the unleavened bread of sincerity and truth. (1 Corinthians 5:6–8, emphasis added)*

D.   Christ is the Sin-Bearer. Christ, in His body, bore the punishment for our sin. (See Isaiah 53.)

---

11   Stott, John. *The Cross of Christ* (Downers Grove, IL: InterVarsity, 1986), p. 40.

When we are united to Christ a mysterious exchange takes place: He took our curse, so that we may receive His blessing; He became sin with our sin, so that we may become righteous with His righteousness.[12]

Christ has redeemed us from the curse of the law, having become a curse for us (for it is written, "Cursed is everyone who hangs on a tree"), that the blessing of Abraham might come upon the Gentiles in Christ Jesus, that we might receive the promise of the Spirit through faith. (Galatians 3:13–14)

For He made Him who knew no sin to be sin for us, that we might become the righteousness of God in Him. (2 Corinthians 5:21)

So Christ was offered once to bear the sins of many. To those who eagerly wait for Him He will appear a second time, apart from sin, for salvation. (Hebrews 9:28)

Who Himself bore our sins in His own body on the tree, that we, having died to sins, might live for righteousness—by whose stripes you were healed. For you were like sheep going astray, but have now returned to the Shepherd and Overseer of your souls. (1 Peter 2:24–25)

E. God was in Christ: God Himself in Christ was our substitute for sin

　　1. *Our substitute who took our place and died our death on the cross, was neither Christ alone (since that would make Him a third party thrust in between God and us), nor God alone (since that would undermine the historical incarnation), but God in Christ, who was truly and fully both God and man, and who on that account was uniquely qualified to represent both God and man to mediate between them.[13]*

　　2. *"There is no-one…who can make this satisfaction except God himself … But no-one ought to make it except man; otherwise man does not make satisfaction." Therefore, "it is necessary that one who is God-man should make it."[14]*

---

12 Stott, John. *The Cross of Christ* (Downers Grove, IL: InterVarsity, 1986), p. 148.
13 *Ibid*, p. 156.
14 *Ibid*, p. 119.

*Now all things are of God, who has reconciled us to Himself through Jesus Christ, and has given us the ministry of reconciliation, that is, that **God was in Christ reconciling the world to Himself,** not imputing their trespasses to them, and has committed to us the word of reconciliation. Now then, we are ambassadors for Christ, as though God were pleading through us: we implore you on Christ's behalf, be reconciled to God. For He made Him who knew no sin to be sin for us, that we might become the righteousness of God in Him. (2 Corinthians 5:18–21, emphasis added)*

*For it pleased the Father that in Him all the fullness should dwell, and **by Him to reconcile all things to Himself, by Him, whether things on earth or things in heaven, having made peace through the blood of His cross.** And you, who once were alienated and enemies in your mind by wicked works, yet now He has reconciled. (Colossians 1:19–21, emphasis added)*

*Therefore take heed to yourselves and to all the flock, among which the Holy Spirit has made you overseers, to shepherd the church of God which **He purchased with His own blood**. (Acts 20:28, emphasis added)*

3.   *For the essence of sin is man substituting himself for God, while the essence of salvation is God substituting Himself for man. **Man asserts himself against God and puts himself where only God deserves to be; God sacrifices Himself for man and puts Himself where only man deserves to be.** Man claims prerogatives which belong to God alone; God accepts penalties which belong to man alone.*[15]

---

15   Stott, John. *The Cross of Christ* (Downers Grove, IL: InterVarsity, 1986), p. 160. Emphasis added.

4.   *It is this outstanding fact which differentiates the scriptural concept of propitiation from unworthy heathen notions of celestial bribery and demonstrates that in Scripture propitiation means not 'to make gracious' but 'to enable to be gracious'. God is already gracious in intention, and is making a way for his mercy to operate without prejudice to his justice and truth. Sin is the cause and sinners are the objects of his wrath, and in substitutionary atonement God turns away his wrath by expressing upon the substitute, as a sacrifice for sin, all his holy indignation against sin, visiting upon it the full penalty due to it from divine justice. Thus God himself provides the atonement for sin – both symbolically in the institution of the Old Testament sacrifices and actually in the delivering up to sacrificial death of his own Son.*[16]

---

16 Lewis, Peter. *The Glory of Christ* (Paternoster Press: Great Britain, reprinted 2004) p. 266-267.

Session Eight: The Cross—The Manifold Beauty of Salvation

I.   SALVATION OF SINNERS

We were in great need, and God sent His Son in the fullness of time to save sinners. Jesus' very name means "God Saves." The Cross is the place where sinners find refuge. Language throughout biblical record testifies to this. The Cross is like a diamond seen in differing brilliance from many different angles, each facet worthy of one's full attention. The biblical writers portrayed the Cross with a wide variety of language—ritual, marketplace, legal, and covenantal/familial terms. The work of Calvary is vast, with a breadth as endless as the sky. This six-hour moment on Golgotha when God was glorified and humanity saved will be the object of contemplation forever. Even in the coming ages, the saints will ponder the Lamb, searching for more revelation of the One slain from the foundations of the world. The Cross is our access to our future, all contained in that once-and-for-all time event.

   A.   Propitiation: ritual language. Propitiation is the language of sacrifice and ministry. To propitiate means to placate wrath, to appease God's righteous indignation against sin. God is not simply bothered by sin. Sin is not a mere nuisance to God. God is provoked by sin; it provokes His jealousy for our love. The justice of God must strike out and eradicate iniquity. At the Cross, God satisfied His own wrath by pouring it out on Christ. When Jesus cried out, "My God, why have You forsaken Me?" He was bearing the wrath of God. Can you imagine the frame of a man and the soul of a man enduring the potent wrath of God? In the sin-bearing of Jesus, we begin to see the strength of the God-Man.

        1.   *In Pauline thought, man is alienated from God by sin and God is alienated from man by wrath. It is in the substitutionary death of Christ that sin is overcome and wrath averted, so that God can look on man without displeasure and man can look on God without fear. Sin is expiated and God is propitiated.*[1]

        2.   Propitiation means "a sacrifice that bears God's wrath to the end and in so doing changes God's wrath toward us into favor."[2]

---

1   Stott, John. *The Cross of Christ* (Downers Grove, IL: InterVarsity, 1986), p. 175.

2   Grudem, Wayne. *Systematic Theology: An Introduction to Biblical Doctrine* (Grand Rapids, MI: Zondervan, 1994), p. 575.

B.   Redemption: marketplace language. Redemption is the language of the marketplace and trade. The Bible testifies that Jesus' blood bought us. To redeem means to buy back or to purchase from slavery. Christ Jesus purchased us for God. The New Testament stops short of telling us to whom the price was paid, yet it is quite clear that the ransom for the guilt of our sin was paid to God Himself. Many confuse this language by saying that Jesus paid sin-debt to Satan. This view is not accurate. God did not owe Satan anything. The debt that had to be paid was owed to God by sinful humanity. Jesus came and paid a debt because we could not pay it.

Christ has redeemed us from the curse of the law, having become a curse for us (for it is written, "Cursed is everyone who hangs on a tree"), that the blessing of Abraham might come upon the Gentiles in Christ Jesus, that we might receive the promise of the Spirit through faith. (Galatians 3:13–14)

But when the fullness of the time had come, God sent forth His Son, born of a woman, born under the law, to redeem those who were under the law, that we might receive the adoption as sons. (Galatians 4:4–5)

"For even the Son of Man did not come to be served, but to serve, and to give His life a ransom for many." (Mark 10:45)

Knowing that you were not redeemed with corruptible things, like silver or gold, from your aimless conduct received by tradition from your fathers, but with the precious blood of Christ, as of a lamb without blemish and without spot. (1 Peter 1:18–19)

Being justified freely by His grace through the redemption that is in Christ Jesus, whom God set forth as a propitiation by His blood, through faith, to demonstrate His righteousness, because in His forbearance God had passed over the sins that were previously committed, to demonstrate at the present time His righteousness, that He might be just and the justifier of the one who has faith in Jesus. (Romans 3:24–26)

Therefore take heed to yourselves and to all the flock, among which the Holy Spirit has made you overseers, to shepherd the church of God which He purchased with His own blood. (Acts 20:28)

Now when He had taken the scroll, the four living creatures and the twenty-four elders fell down before the Lamb, each having a harp, and golden bowls full of incense, which are the prayers of the saints. And they sang a new song, saying: "You are worthy to take the scroll, and to open its seals; for You were slain, and have redeemed us to God by Your blood out of every tribe and tongue and people and nation. (Revelation 5:8–9)

C.   Justification: courtroom/legal language. Justification means to be righteous before God. In Christ, we stand acquitted and justified before God. God sent His Son as both the defense attorney and the One who stood in our place to take the punishment that we deserved.

    1.   *When God justifies sinners, He is not declaring bad people to be good, or saying that they are not sinners after all; He is pronouncing them legally righteous, free from any liability to the broken law, because He Himself in His Son has borne the penalty of their law-breaking.[3]*

    2.   *God's grace is the source and Christ's blood is the ground of our justification; faith is only the means by which we are united to Christ.[4]*

    3.   We are justified by grace through faith and thus brought into the community. From this faith, works then proceed.

D.   Reconciliation: familial language. Reconciliation is the language of covenant and personal relationship. Two parties were at odds, but in Christ the family is restored. Using this language, the Father is pictured as removing enmity, drawing us near, and being at peace with His children through the shed blood of His Son.

Much more then, having now been justified by His blood, we shall be saved from wrath through Him. For if when we were enemies we were reconciled to God through the death of His Son, much more, having been reconciled, we shall be saved by His life. And not only that, but we also rejoice in God through our Lord Jesus Christ, through whom we have now received the reconciliation. (Romans 5:9–11)

---

3   Stott, John. *The Cross of Christ* (Downers Grove, IL: InterVarsity, 1986), p. 190.
4   *Ibid.*

Now all things are of God, who has reconciled us to Himself through Jesus Christ, and has given us the ministry of reconciliation, that is, that God was in Christ reconciling the world to Himself, not imputing their trespasses to them, and has committed to us the word of reconciliation. Now then, we are ambassadors for Christ, as though God were pleading through us: we implore you on Christ's behalf, be reconciled to God. For He made Him who knew no sin to be sin for us, that we might become the righteousness of God in Him. (2 Corinthians 5:18–21)

For it pleased the Father that in Him all the fullness should dwell, and by Him to reconcile all things to Himself, by Him, whether things on earth or things in heaven, having made peace through the blood of His cross. And you, who once were alienated and enemies in your mind by wicked works, yet now He has reconciled in the body of His flesh through death, to present you holy, and blameless, and above reproach in His sight. (Colossians 1:19–22)

But now in Christ Jesus you who once were far off have been brought near by the blood of Christ. For He Himself is our peace, who has made both one, and has broken down the middle wall of separation, having abolished in His flesh the enmity, that is, the law of commandments contained in ordinances, so as to create in Himself one new man from the two, thus making peace, and that He might reconcile them both to God in one body through the cross, thereby putting to death the enmity. And He came and preached peace to you who were afar off and to those who were near. For through Him we both have access by one Spirit to the Father. (Ephesians 2:13–18)

E. **Summary Statement:** *Propitiation* (ritual language) *underscores the wrath of God upon us, redemption* (marketplace language) *our captivity to sin, justification* (courtroom language) *our guilt, and reconciliation* (familial language) *our enmity against God and alienation from Him.*[5]

II.   THE REVELATION OF GOD

A.   The glory of God: what did the Cross accomplish? Glory! The Cross glorified the harmony, balance, and perfection of the divine excellencies of God. The Cross is all of His virtues wrapped up in one holy event—a declaration to the ages. This is what your God is like; this is the beauty of God. Because of the Cross, we have no doubts about His nature.

---

5   Stott, John.*The Cross of Christ* (Downers Grove, IL: InterVarsity, 1986), p. 202. Parenthetical comments added.

> *"Now My soul is troubled, and what shall I say? 'Father, save Me from this hour'? But for this purpose I came to this hour. Father, glorify Your name." Then a voice came from heaven, saying, "I have both glorified it and will glorify it again." (John 12:27–28, emphasis added)*

> *Jesus spoke these words, lifted up His eyes to heaven, and said: "Father, the hour has come. Glorify Your Son, that Your Son also may glorify You, as You have given Him authority over all flesh, that He should give eternal life to as many as You have given Him." (John 17:1–2, emphasis added)*

B.   Thomas Dubay commented on the glory of the Cross of Jesus: "Consummate splendor in monstrous horror: the Passion and crucifixion of the Lord of glory … Far beyond all the created beauties is the divine glory that shines out from this unsurpassable love found in the torture of the Holy Week: Perfection Himself whipped to blood, crowned with thorns, mocked, spit upon, ridiculed, nailed, pierced—all because He loves you and me, who have in return sinned against Him."[6]

C.   The justice of God

1.   In God's economy, love will not be scorned. Righteousness will preserve the dignity of love, and holy justice will move against all that desires to pervert the love of God. Sin will be judged. It will not continue to exist in God's economy.

2.   How committed is God to removing sin from the universe? How committed is God to judging sin and removing it from His economy? Committed enough to kill His Son. We need to understand that the Cross demonstrates God's wholehearted commitment to judge all that is unholy. Jesus bore the wrath of God for you, but if you do not accept His sacrifice, He will dispense that wrath upon you on the Last Day.

D.   The love of God: true, pure love was displayed at the Cross. The depth of God's compassion and empathy were displayed at Calvary.

---

6   Dubay, Thomas. *The Evidential Power of Beauty* (San Francisco: Ignatius, 1999), p. 310-311.

Nothing is more precious to the Christian believer than a personal awareness of the love of God. Without his love his holiness would terrify us, his power would crush us and his eternity (and ours) would be our greatest nightmare. But the knowledge that God is love, and that in Christ God has in love committed himself to us to dace us from our sin and to reconcile us to himself for evermore, brings us both peace and joy. In Christ, God's power is our protection, his justice is our justification and his eternity our glorious destiny: the eternal God is our dwelling place, and underneath are the everlasting arms (Deut. 33:27).[7]

1.   Scriptures:

Being justified freely by His grace through the redemption that is in Christ Jesus, whom God set forth as a propitiation by His blood, through faith, to demonstrate His righteousness, because in His forbearance God had passed over the sins that were previously committed. (Romans 3:24–25)

Therefore, in all things He had to be made like His brethren, that He might be a merciful and faithful High Priest in things pertaining to God, to make propitiation for the sins of the people. (Hebrews 2:17)

My little children, these things I write to you, so that you may not sin. And if anyone sins, we have an Advocate with the Father, Jesus Christ the righteous. And He Himself is the propitiation for our sins, and not for ours only but also for the whole world. (1 John 2:1–2)

In this is love, not that we loved God, but that He loved us and sent His Son to be the propitiation for our sins. Beloved, if God so loved us, we also ought to love one another. (1 John 4:10–11)

But God demonstrates His own love toward us, in that while we were still sinners, Christ died for us. Much more then, having now been justified by His blood, we shall be saved from wrath through Him. For if when we were enemies we were reconciled to God through the death of His Son, much more, having been reconciled, we shall be saved by His life. And not only that, but we also rejoice in God through our Lord Jesus Christ, through whom we have now received the reconciliation. (Romans 5:8–11)

---

7   Lewis, Peter. *The Glory of Christ*. Great Britain: Paternoster Press, reprinted 2004. p. 255.

Knowing that a man is not justified by the works of the law but by faith in Jesus Christ, even we have believed in Christ Jesus, that we might be justified by faith in Christ and not by the works of the law; for by the works of the law no flesh shall be justified. But if, while we seek to be justified by Christ, we ourselves also are found sinners, is Christ therefore a minister of sin? Certainly not! (Galatians 2:16–17)

For God so loved the world that He gave His only begotten Son, that whoever believes in Him should not perish but have everlasting life. (John 3:16)

But God, who is rich in mercy, because of His great love with which He loved us, even when we were dead in trespasses, made us alive together with Christ (by grace you have been saved), and raised us up together, and made us sit together in the heavenly places in Christ Jesus, that in the ages to come He might show the exceeding riches of His grace in His kindness toward us in Christ Jesus. For by grace you have been saved through faith, and that not of yourselves; it is the gift of God, not of works, lest anyone should boast. (Ephesians 2:4–9)

I have been crucified with Christ; it is no longer I who live, but Christ lives in me; and the life which I now live in the flesh I live by faith in the Son of God, who loved me and gave Himself for me. I do not set aside the grace of God; for if righteousness comes through the law, then Christ died in vain. (Galatians 2:20–21)

In this the love of God was manifested toward us, that God has sent His only begotten Son into the world, that we might live through Him. In this is love, not that we loved God, but that He loved us and sent His Son to be the propitiation for our sins. (1 John 4:9–10)

And from Jesus Christ, the faithful witness, the firstborn from the dead, and the ruler over the kings of the earth. To Him who loved us and washed us from our sins in His own blood, and has made us kings and priests to His God and Father, to Him be glory and dominion forever and ever. Amen. (Revelation 1:5–6)

For Christ did not send me to baptize, but to preach the gospel, not with wisdom of words, lest the cross of Christ should be made of no effect. For the message of the cross is foolishness to those who are perishing, but to us who are being saved it is the power of God. For it is written: "I will destroy the wisdom of the wise,

And bring to nothing the understanding of the prudent." Where is the wise? Where is the scribe? Where is the disputer of this age? Has not God made foolish the wisdom of this world? For since, in the wisdom of God, the world through wisdom did not know God, it pleased God through the foolishness of the message preached to save those who believe. For Jews request a sign, and Greeks seek after wisdom; but we preach Christ crucified, to the Jews a stumbling block and to the Greeks foolishness, but to those who are called, both Jews and Greeks, Christ the power of God and the wisdom of God. Because the foolishness of God is wiser than men, and the weakness of God is stronger than men. For you see your calling, brethren, that not many wise according to the flesh, not many mighty, not many noble, are called. But God has chosen the foolish things of the world to put to shame the wise, and God has chosen the weak things of the world to put to shame the things which are mighty; and the base things of the world and the things which are despised God has chosen, and the things which are not, to bring to nothing the things that are, that no flesh should glory in His presence. But of Him you are in Christ Jesus, who became for us wisdom from God—and righteousness and sanctification and redemption—that, as it is written, "He who glories, let him glory in the LORD." And I, brethren, when I came to you, did not come with excellence of speech or of wisdom declaring to you the testimony of God. For I determined not to know anything among you except Jesus Christ and Him crucified. I was with you in weakness, in fear, and in much trembling. And my speech and my preaching were not with persuasive words of human wisdom, but in demonstration of the Spirit and of power, that your faith should not be in the wisdom of men but in the power of God. (1 Corinthians 1:17–2:5)

For I am not ashamed of the gospel of Christ, for it is the power of God to salvation for everyone who believes, for the Jew first and also for the Greek. For in it the righteousness of God is revealed from faith to faith; as it is written, "The just shall live by faith." (Romans 1:16–17)

To me, who am less than the least of all the saints, this grace was given, that I should preach among the Gentiles the unsearchable riches of Christ, and to make all see what is the fellowship of the mystery, which from the beginning of the ages has been hidden in God who created all things through Jesus Christ; to the intent that now the manifold wisdom of God might be made known by the church to the principalities and powers in the heavenly places, according to the eternal purpose which He accomplished in Christ Jesus our Lord, in whom we have boldness and access with confidence through faith in Him. (Ephesians 3:8–12)

For I want you to know what a great conflict I have for you and those in Laodicea, and for as many as have not seen my face in the flesh, that their hearts may be encouraged, being knit together in love, and attaining to all riches of the full assurance of understanding, to the knowledge of the mystery of God, both of the Father and of Christ, in whom are hidden all the treasures of wisdom and knowledge. (Colossians 2:1–3)

2. Moral influence theory: As Peter Abelard (1079–1142) stated, "How cruel and wicked it seems that anyone should demand the blood of an innocent person as the price for anything, or that it should in any way please Him that an innocent man should be slain—still less that God should consider the death of His Son so agreeable that by it He should be reconciled to the whole world!"[8] Abelard saw Jesus primarily as our teacher and our example. The Son's voluntary giving of His own life should move us to respond to God in contrition and love.

E. The wisdom and power of God

1. First Corinthians

2. When Paul went to Mars Hill, he preached the gospel and tried to make it relevant to the culture. Afterwards, three people came to Christ. This was a defeat compared to the response in the other towns he had just visited; it was not an effective crusade. Once in Corinth, he went back to preaching the simple message of the Cross, and God birthed a whole church. Jesus said in John 5 that He didn't need man's witness. Instead, we men need the witness of heaven to verify our words with signs and wonders. "But you shall receive power when the Holy Spirit has come upon you; and you shall be witnesses to Me in Jerusalem, and in all Judea and Samaria, and to the end of the earth." (Acts 1:8)

> *But in the grace that rescued man*
> *His brightest form of glory shines;*
> *Here, on the cross, 'tis fairest drawn,*
> *In precious blood and crimson lines.*

---

8 Stott, John. *The Cross of Christ* (Downers Grove, IL: InterVarsity, 1986), p. 217.

Here His whole name appears complete;
Nor wit can guess, nor reason prove,
Which of the letters best is writ,
The power, the wisdom, or the love.[9]

III.   THE CONQUEST OF EVIL

A.   The atonement is also viewed as having destroyed the works of the devil and as setting humanity free from the grip and slavery of the enemy. The enemy of God, who deceived us in the Garden usurped our authority over creation, loses his authority over humanity. Sin is atoned, and power is given to humanity to overcome temptation and sin.

B.   Gustav Aulen's Classical Theory of Atonement: This view asserts that Christ on the cross did battle with the powers of evil and gained victory over them. He asserts that this was the predominant view of the Church for the first thousand years.[10]

The sting of death is sin, and the strength of sin is the law. But thanks be to God, who gives us the victory through our Lord Jesus Christ. (1 Corinthians 15:56–57)

Yet in all these things we are more than conquerors through Him who loved us. For I am persuaded that neither death nor life, nor angels nor principalities nor powers, nor things present nor things to come, nor height nor depth, nor any other created thing, shall be able to separate us from the love of God which is in Christ Jesus our Lord. (Romans 8:37–39)

Now thanks be to God who always leads us in triumph in Christ, and through us diffuses the fragrance of His knowledge in every place. (2 Corinthians 2:14)

And you, being dead in your trespasses and the uncircumcision of your flesh, He has made alive together with Him, having forgiven you all trespasses, having wiped out the handwriting of requirements that was against us, which was contrary to us. And He has taken it out of the way, having nailed it to the cross. Having disarmed principalities and powers, He made a public spectacle of them, triumphing over them in it. (Colossians 2:13–15)

---

9 Watts, Isaac. "Hymn 10: Christ crucified, the wisdom and power of God." *Psalms and Hymns of Isaac Watts*. Christian Classics Ethereal Library. <http://www.ccel.org/ccel/watts/psalmshymns.ii.iii.x.html>

10 Stott, John. *The Cross of Christ* (Downers Grove, IL: InterVarsity, 1986), p. 228.

- In the Greek, "disarmed" is used in the sense that He stripped the enemy bare. He disarmed him.

And they overcame him by the blood of the Lamb and by the word of their testimony, and they did not love their lives to the death. (Revelation 12:11)

He who sins is of the devil, for the devil has sinned from the beginning. For this purpose the Son of God was manifested, that He might destroy the works of the devil. (1 John 3:8)

Inasmuch then as the children have partaken of flesh and blood, He Himself likewise shared in the same, that through death He might destroy him who had the power of death, that is, the devil, and release those who through fear of death were all their lifetime subject to bondage. For indeed He does not give aid to angels, but He does give aid to the seed of Abraham. Therefore, in all things He had to be made like His brethren, that He might be a merciful and faithful High Priest in things pertaining to God, to make propitiation for the sins of the people. For in that He Himself has suffered, being tempted, He is able to aid those who are tempted. (Hebrews 2:14–18)

A.   *The weapon of soul-destroying sin and guilt is taken out of Satan's hand. He is disarmed of the single weapon that can condemn us—unforgiven sin … only unforgiven sin can condemn the soul and make death a door to hell, not heaven.*[11]

B.   In Revelation 1:17–18, Jesus was saying to John, "John, don't be afraid. I have the keys of death and hell. I've conquered and vanquished the foe. I've stolen the right. I now possess the access for human beings so that when they die, they go right to God. I've stripped the power of Sheol. The abode of the dead has been stripped. Don't fear, John. You will never die!"

---

11   Piper, John. *Seeing and Savoring Jesus Christ* (Wheaton, IL: Crossway Books, 2004), p. 83.

C. There is a famous, common saying: "On the back of Satan's neck is a nail-scarred footprint." Can you imagine when the hour of darkness reigned, when the enemy convinced Jerusalem and Israel and the leadership and the people to kill the Son? But in that moment, when holy blood was spilled on that beam, a tremor was loosed through the powers of darkness. The hordes of hell realized that the blood of Jesus was interceding for the forgiveness of humanity's sin. When the Son of Man, the military general, was lifted up, He sized up the battlefield from the high ground—from the vantage point of Calvary. In that moment, when His holy, precious blood touched the ground and atonement was made, the battle was won. The Cross is a military victory! And He did this in meekness. The first battle was won by the Lamb in meekness. The next battle will be won by the Lion of the Tribe of Judah in an open display of power as He binds Satan and sets the captives free!

Session Nine: The Cross—The Relentless Pursuit of the Bridegroom

I. THE BRIDAL PARDIGM

A. Bride of Christ: this term qualifies and describes the type of affection that God has for His people. Positionally, we are the sons of God. As the redeemed, we are the aristocracy of heaven, co-heirs with Christ; we were made by God in His image to rule and reign with Him forever. Yet, the Bible not only describes our function in God's created order; it also describes the quality of our relationship with Him. Our relationship goes beyond contractual agreement and faithful obedience. It is to be typified by fervent, ardent love and longing, the way a bridegroom and a bride long for and love one another. This is precisely why the Bible begins and ends with a wedding. Love is what we were made for, and we do not work right any other way.

B. If we are not living passionately, then we are susceptible to the worst tormenters of the soul: (1) spiritual boredom and (2) harsh legalism. We become susceptible to all manner of sin and unrighteousness when passion and ardent love are not at the center of our relationship with God.

II. VIEWING THE CROSS THROUGH THE BRIDAL PARADIGM

A. The Cross was more than legal acquittal. It was more than penal substitution. The Cross was a glorious event, evidence of the extravagant heart of a lovely Groom who was willing to fight for the Bride promised to Him by His Father. Before time began, the Father promised His Son a companion: a wife equally yoked in light and love, adorned with the virtue of the Deity Himself. This Bride would share the very affections of the Godhead. She would be clothed with holiness and adorned with the fiery passion of a lovesick worshiper. She would love the Son like the Father loves the Son. She would love the Father like the Son loves the Father. This story is the romance story of the ages.

B. Two themes of literature arrest the human heart and awaken stirrings of love. The human heart yearns for the return of true love. The heart craves and thirsts to find the place of intimacy lost in a garden long ago.

1. The first theme is that of a king who loves his people, humbles himself and fights for the people's freedom. The movie *Braveheart* is a classic example of this. *First Knight* is another. We love a king who will not sell out his people for wealth and power, but who will humbly serve the people, even unto the death.

2. The second theme is that of a husband who fights for the heart, honor, and nobility of his bride, even to the point of death. *Les Miserable* and *The Man from LaManchais* are examples. Jesus restores His bride's dignity to her; this is what your Groom is like. Many times we push Him away, but the statement of the Cross is "You're the one I want." There is something about a husband who speaks forth that which his wife is not, but that which she shall be (Romans 4:17).

C. Revelation 19:1–9: the Wedding Supper of the Lamb

1. In order to fully understand the Cross, one has to first understand the final product of redemption. Redemption finds its consummation in a hallelujah chorus, a wedding feast, and a queen dressed in white. It is consummated at the marriage supper of the Lamb.

2. At the end of the day, the saints will not primarily be identified as the acquitted; rather, the redeemed will be presented as the wife of the Lamb. The once-unfaithful prostitute will have become the Lamb's wife. In the end, you and I will be established in an identity we can't even imagine.

3. This wedding in the heart and mind of God is the blueprint from which the Godhead has operated since the very beginning. It's the reason He formed atonement the way He did. It's the reason He determined the shedding of blood to be the method of sacrifice for sins. It's the reason He would demonstrate such depths of sacrificial love to win over a bride. God the Father is moving all things towards the wedding, toward giving a companion to His Son. The Son, in His death and resurrection, secured that which the Father promised, and the Spirit now fills the betrothed ones and brings them to completion.

4. The dowry was the payment that secured a bride based on social standing. The Cross was our dowry. The glory and beauty of the bride was equated to the price of the dowry. You can't get any higher price than God giving all of Himself for love. This is what you are worth to God—the equivalent of His Son shedding His blood on a tree. From the Cross we hear the Son shouting, "With all that I have and all that I am, I honor you."

III. **GLIMPSES OF A COMING BRIDEGROOM; GLIMPSES OF A GROOM WHO FIGHTS FOR HIS BRIDE UNTO DEATH; THE RANSOM OF A BRIDEGROOM KING**

A. Genesis 2:1–25

And the LORD God caused a deep sleep to fall on Adam, and he slept; and He took one of his ribs, and closed up the flesh in its place. Then the rib which the LORD God had taken from man He made into a woman, and He brought her to the man. And Adam said: "This is now bone of my bones and flesh of my flesh; she shall be called Woman, because she was taken out of Man." Therefore a man shall leave his father and mother and be joined to his wife, and they shall become one flesh. (Genesis 2:21–24)

1. From the beginning, God foreshadowed the glorious day to come when the second Adam (Jesus) would be put to sleep and a beautiful bride would come forth out of His side.

2. The formation of man was not like the heavens—it came through a simple creative word. The very hand of the Word Himself worked this masterpiece, and His very breath ushered in a living soul. The very breath and life-force of God fashioned and formed the heart of man. God left His indelible mark upon Adam, His holy breath filling a treasured soul.

3. From the beginning, God defined reality for man in this garden. God desired a companion for Adam. This was not an alternative plan to a debunked system. This was the clarifying of reality for man and was the prophetic foreshadowing of the nature of things for the second Adam to come. Just as God desired to create in His image and join humanity unto Himself in the person of His Son, so God desired that the first Adam be joined to a companion.

4.   God used loneliness to cultivate something in the heart of Adam. God created longing in his heart and made Adam endure a rigorous process of recognizing his lacking. Loneliness became the birthplace for longing and desire. Loneliness presupposes desire and longing. Without loneliness, longing for something else is impossible. Adam bore the weight of naming all that is created, while his heart was noticing that something was missing and also that something was being kindled. Desire for a companion was growing. God was setting forth the ultimate object lesson for Adam to understand something of himself. He was a creature of desire and intimacy, made in the image of His Creator. The longing in God's heart for communion is stamped on the very nature on human beings.

5.   This was the design of God: to create longing and passion in the heart of man. Man, like no other creature, was designed to feel the longing of love, the relentless pursuit of the heart for another person. Humanity would share in the experience of God with longing love.

6.   The foreshadowing of the Cross of Christ: the Bride of both the first and second Adam would come forth through the suffering love of the Groom. The wise God established the story of His Son and His Bride from the very first. Adam longed for a companion. In His longing, the Heavenly Father satisfied his heart, first putting him to sleep. From Adam's broken side, God fashioned a beautiful spouse for His beautiful son and brought her to Adam. It is the story of the ages. The wedding of the ages is set forth from the very beginning in the DNA of humanity.

7.   This is a picture of the divine betrothal God has planned for His Son. It will take a supernatural intervention of God to pull off this wedding. The Son yearns for a companion, the Father puts Him to sleep and forms her from the Son's wounded side, and the Spirit brings the beautiful Spouse to the Son with great joy.

8.   God would structure all of society around the reality of a man and a woman longing to be together in order to show us to the greatest longing of all: the human heart's yearning to be joined to its Maker and King.

B.   Covenantal language: a covenant of love. God is portrayed as a jealous husband who will share us with no other.

"Now therefore, if you will indeed obey My voice and keep My covenant, then you shall be a special treasure to Me above all people; for all the earth is Mine. And you shall be to Me a kingdom of priests and a holy nation." These are the words which you shall speak to the children of Israel. (Exodus 19:5–6)

You shall not make for yourself a carved image—any likeness of anything that is in heaven above, or that is in the earth beneath, or that is in the water under the earth; you shall not bow down to them nor serve them. ***For I, the LORD your God, am a jealous God, visiting the iniquity of the fathers upon the children to the third and fourth generations of those who hate Me.*** *(Exodus 20:4–5, emphasis added)*

Nor shall you make marriages with them. You shall not give your daughter to their son, nor take their daughter for your son. For they will turn your sons away from following Me, to serve other gods; so the anger of the LORD will be aroused against you and destroy you suddenly. But thus you shall deal with them: you shall destroy their altars, and break down their sacred pillars, and cut down their wooden images, and burn their carved images with fire. For you are a holy people to the LORD your God; the LORD your God has chosen you to be a people for Himself, a special treasure above all the peoples on the face of the earth. The LORD did not set His love on you nor choose you because you were more in number than any other people, for you were the least of all peoples; but because the LORD loves you, and because He would keep the oath which He swore to your fathers, the LORD has brought you out with a mighty hand, and redeemed you from the house of bondage, from the hand of Pharaoh king of Egypt. Therefore know that the LORD your God, He is God, the faithful God who keeps covenant and mercy for a thousand generations with those who love Him and keep His commandments. (Deuteronomy 7:3–9)

Indeed heaven and the highest heavens belong to the LORD your God, also the earth with all that is in it. The LORD delighted only in your fathers, to love them; and He chose their descendants after them, you above all peoples, as it is this day. (Deuteronomy 10:14–15)

C.   Psalm 45

D.   The Book of Hosea: Hosea was one of the first prophets.

1.   Prophets bear the burden of God's heart concerning His people.

        The prophet is not a mouthpiece, but a person; not an instrument, but a partner, an associate of God … An analysis of prophetic utterances shows that the fundamental experience of the prophet is a fellowship with the feelings of God, a sympathy with the divine pathos, a communion with the divine the consciousness which comes about through the prophet's reflection of, or participation in, the divine pathos.[1]

2.   The Cross is the moment when the glory and love of God are displayed like no other. This is what glory is like. It is the abandonment of one's own life in pursuit to save another. It is shameless humbling for love. We would expect this sacrifice from a nobleman for his fair maiden. Yet, for a king to choose disgrace, suffering, humiliation, and dishonor for a prostitute is unheard of in royal chronicles. A king's life for a seasoned harlot? Insanity! Do not be ridiculous! But Heaven calls this scandalous act an act of glory.

3.   The Cross is the outworking of what God spoke to the prophet Hosea long before. "Go again, love a woman who is loved by a lover and is committing adultery, just like the love of the LORD for the children of Israel, who look to other gods and love the raisin cakes of the pagans" (Hosea 3:1). Hosea had married the prostitute Gomer. Gomer continued to chase other lovers, committing adultery after adultery, and finally ended up as another man's love slave. And for the same price as Judas' betrayal fee, Hosea bought her back. The Cross is the great "go again" of God. It is the refusal of love to give up on the object of its affection. How far will love go? As far as it takes, even to hillsides in faraway places, where arms are stretched, joints are torn, blood is spilled, and faint whispers reach upward, saying, "Father, forgive them; for they know not what they do" (Luke 23:34, KJV).

        Then the LORD said to me, "Go again, love a woman who is loved by a lover and is committing adultery, just like the love of the LORD for the children of Israel, who look to other gods and love the raisin cakes of the pagans." (Hosea 3:1, emphasis added)

---

1   Abraham J. Heschel, *The Prophets* (New York: Harper and Row, Perennial Classics Edition 2001), p. 30-31.

E.   Isaiah 53–54

F.   *For Zion's sake I will not hold My peace, and for Jerusalem's sake I will not rest, until her righteousness goes forth as brightness, and her salvation as a lamp that burns. The Gentiles shall see your righteousness, and all kings your glory. You shall be called by a new name, which the mouth of the LORD will name. You shall also be a crown of glory in the hand of the LORD, and a royal diadem in the hand of your God. You shall no longer be termed Forsaken, nor shall your land any more be termed Desolate; but* **you shall be called Hephzibah, and your land Beulah; for the LORD delights in you, and your land shall be married. For as a young man marries a virgin, so shall your sons marry you; and as the bridegroom rejoices over the bride, so shall your God rejoice over you.** *(Isaiah 62:1–5, emphasis added)*

G.   Jeremiah 2–3:1: The prophets do not give sterile, prophetic utterances. Prophets bear the very burden of the Lord. The Lord's burden was charged with the anguish of emotional investment. Do we know what God feels?

H.   Ezekiel 16: "The Bridegroom is here; He will display His passion to win you over." That is the message of this passage.

IV.   UNRELENTING BRIDEGROOM

A.   John testified that the coming of Jesus was like a bridegroom coming for a bride.

He who has the bride is the bridegroom; but the friend of the bridegroom, who stands and hears him, rejoices greatly because of the bridegroom's voice. Therefore this joy of mine is fulfilled. (John 3:29)

B.   Matthew 22:1–14 and 25:1–13: in Matthew 22, Jesus set the context for what was taking place in Jerusalem during Holy Week. Among the glory of the Temple, the regalia of the elders and religious leaders, and the fickleness of the multitudes, Jesus revealed that all this was part of His Father's plan to arrange a wedding for His Son. Determined to gain His Bride, Jesus paid the dowry a few days later.

And Jesus answered and spoke to them again by parables and said: "The kingdom of heaven is like a certain king who arranged a marriage for his son." (Matthew 22:1–2)

C. The High Priestly prayer of Jesus, the hour before the Cross—John 17. We are the object of His affections. He longs for a companion. The Bible begins with a wedding and ends with the wedding supper of the Lamb. In fact, at the end of the book of Revelation it is us as the Bride of Christ who cry out, "Maranatha! Come Lord Jesus." God cannot be a bystander in the affairs of men; they are the object of His affections. Apathy and indifference are not options for God towards humanity. He cannot simply create the earth and all that is in it and let it play out its natural course. He has set His affections upon us.

*Father, I desire that they also **whom You gave Me may be with Me where I am,** that they may behold My glory which You have given Me; for You loved Me before the foundation of the world. O righteous Father! The world has not known You, but I have known You; and these have known that You sent Me. And I have declared to them Your name, and will declare it, **that the love with which You loved Me may be in them, and I in them.** (John 17:24–26, emphasis added)*

1. We are the one creatures made in the image of God for God, created to be an eternal companion and co-heir with Christ forever. Beloved, Jesus is human even now. He will maintain a resurrected human body forever. He has forever joined Himself to us.

2. The Father and Son are in agreement. The Father wants to give His Son a Bride and the Son wants an eternal companion with Him where He, is in full partnership with Him and adorned with His beauty. This prayer of agreement seals the demise of Satan and his oppression of humanity. This prayer sends shock waves through the demonic kingdom

D. Paul interpreted his whole ministry as that of preparing a bride for the Bridegroom.

For I am jealous for you with godly jealousy. For I have betrothed you to one husband, that I may present you as a chaste virgin to Christ. (2 Corinthians 11:2)

E. In Ephesians 5, Paul was exhorting the church on marital relationships. Suddenly, he slipped into the grand mystery of God wanting to join Himself to humanity in Christ.

For we are members of His body, of His flesh and of His bones. "For this reason a man shall leave his father and mother and be joined to his wife, and the two shall become one flesh." This is a great mystery, but I speak concerning Christ and the church. (Ephesians 5:30–32)

F.   The Book of Revelation unveils Christ's holy desire to restore all things to their created purpose. The Bride is the focal point of His affections. In Revelation, we see Jesus' leadership bring the Church, His Bride, to wholehearted love and purity at the deepest levels possible while removing iniquity and judging sin.

Grace to you and peace from Him who is and who was and who is to come, and from the seven Spirits who are before His throne, and from Jesus Christ, the faithful witness, the firstborn from the dead, and the ruler over the kings of the earth. To Him who loved us and washed us from our sins in His own blood, and has made us kings and priests to His God and Father, to Him be glory and dominion forever and ever. Amen. (Revelation 1:4–6)

And the Spirit and the bride say, "Come!" And let him who hears say, "Come!" And let him who thirsts come. Whoever desires, let him take the water of life freely. (Revelation 22:17)

V.   THE CROSS: THE FITTING PRICE OF LOVE

Behold what manner of love the Father has bestowed on us, that we should be called children of God! *(1 John 3:1, emphasis added)*

A.   Who made up the rules for atonement? Have you ever wondered who decided that blood must be shed for atonement? Is there some book in Heaven about atonement that God had to consult?

B.   Some seem to imagine that the Fall of Man caught God by surprise. "Oh, no, they fell! Somebody get the atonement book. Yahweh needs to know what to do next." Perhaps the seraphim found the rule book on redemption in some niche of Heaven and brought it to the Father, telling Him, "It seems to say in this book that only by the shedding of blood can atonement be made." Others do not ask the question at all, but think that the whole concept of sacrifice seems a little bit strange, even slightly barbaric.

C.   The atoning sacrifice is neither a dictate forced upon God nor a strange, archaic approach to the salvation of humanity. In fact, it is essential that we understand that there is no standard outside of God by which God must conform. God is the standard. Atonement came through sacrifice because God set up the system that way in order to show us two dramatic points.

D.   First, sin is costly. The sacrificial system reminds us of the high-priced nature of our sin. Atonement can only be made by the costly spilling of blood. Sin is not laissez-faire and casual. Sin is costly and has separated the whole race from intimate communion with God. The sacrificial system reminds us that the "wages of sin is death." Our sin cost Jesus much.

E.   Second, God desired to display the depths of His suffering, tenacious love. How far will God go for love? God established atonement in precisely this way because of the depths of love within His own heart. His love makes Him willing to pour Himself out, even to the point of self surrender and self-sacrifice. His depths must be seen. He not only made provision for atonement, but He designed it so that it displays both the greatness of His love and the tenacity of His heart in fulfilling it. The Apostle John told us to behold this manner of love. By doing so, we fall madly in love with our Bridegroom King. This is why we call Him Wonderful Counselor, Almighty God, Everlasting Father, and Prince of Peace (Isaiah 9:6). Can you hear His vows from Calvary? He says, "With all that I have and all that I am, I honor you."

Session Ten: The Cross—The Delight of the Saints

I. THE DELIGHT OF THE SAINTS

A. How does the Cross affect behavior? What are the responses the Cross elicits in the heart of a believer? How do you draw upon it? What does it encourage and sustain in the human heart?

B. God created the atonement in such a way that it causes us to love Him and causes our hearts to respond. He did not simply establish a sterile atonement where we follow some guidelines. God, in His creative brilliance, designed atonement to elicit a response of love in the human heart. In the Cross, we see the greatness of love and give way to all its implications.

II. THE CROSS ENGENDERS GREATNESS IN THE HEART OF THE BELIEVER

A. The Cross is God's big "YES!" to humanity. The Cross is a statement of God's desire for and commitment to human beings. It is the official stamp of His love. It is the place where humanity was eternally affirmed in the heart of God and before the eyes of all.

Greater love has no one than this, than to lay down one's life for his friends. (John 15:13)

For when we were still without strength, in due time Christ died for the ungodly. For scarcely for a righteous man will one die; yet perhaps for a good man someone would even dare to die. But God demonstrates His own love toward us, in that while we were still sinners, Christ died for us. Much more then, having now been justified by His blood, we shall be saved from wrath through Him. (Romans 5:6–9)

B. The Cross produces great affection in the heart of the individual believer. To ponder the excellencies of Christ on Calvary is to find the wellspring of all charitable emotion. The Cross becomes the object of meditation for the tenderizing of the heart. See how much He loved us! See it! Look upon it! Look what God has done! Look how far His love will go to secure our love, our salvation!

C.   The divine wound

1.   What is the divine wound? It is when the heart crumbles, pierced by the arrow of God's love. God's strategy is to bring forth voluntary love from a freely-given heart of longing. Thus, He reveals Himself to the vessel in such a way that leaves the vessel helpless against the affections of God. The divine wound is but the initial awakening of the heart left in the pain of its incompletion. It is the heart starved for consummation. Once awakened by the Great Lover, the heart has enough life to long for the promise of fullness brought in the first touch.

2.   Jesus' heart cry in John 17 is that we would be with Him where He is, behold His glory, and fall madly in love with Him in the way the Father loves Him.

*Father, I desire that they also whom You gave Me may be with Me where I am, that they may behold My glory which You have given Me; for You loved Me before the foundation of the world. O righteous Father! The world has not known You, but I have known You; and these have known that You sent Me. And I have declared to them Your name, and will declare it, **that the love with which You loved Me may be in them, and I in them.** (John 17:24–26, emphasis added)*

3.   His tenderness wounds us. The heart is defenseless against two things: undeserved mercy and unreserved kindness. Jesus overcomes the heart and leaves it rent asunder by loving us where we are. We are used to setting up shadows and putting forth illusions in order for others to give us their love. All the while, these others speak to the fortresses in which we hide. But they never reach our heart, alone in its lowly condition. Jesus moves through the veneer of illusions to speak directly to the heart. Upon the reception of such kindness, the heart has no more defenses. It collapses, only to be caught by the gentle Lover who shares Himself, transforming us at the deepest levels.

4.   The Cross creates bondservants who have been wounded by love and will do anything to get Him back. Apostolic preaching flows from apostolic wounding. The love of Christ compels them. They are set apart by love for Him and Him alone. Above function, above place and position, they want Jesus and want Him manifest in their lives. They are madly in love with Jesus. What transforms the son of thunder into the Apostle of love? John would tell you, "The Cross." He said, "Behold what manner of love the Father has bestowed on us, that we should be called children of God!" (1 John 3:1)

Paul, a bondservant of Jesus Christ, called to be an apostle, separated to the gospel of God which He promised before through His prophets in the Holy Scriptures. (Romans 1:1–2)

Paul, a bondservant of God and an apostle of Jesus Christ, according to the faith of God's elect and the acknowledgment of the truth which accords with godliness, in hope of eternal life which God, who cannot lie, promised before time began, but has in due time manifested His word through preaching, which was committed to me according to the commandment of God our Savior. (Titus 1:1–3)

James, a bondservant of God and of the Lord Jesus Christ, to the twelve tribes which are scattered abroad: Greetings. (James 1:1)

Simon Peter, a bondservant and apostle of Jesus Christ, to those who have obtained like precious faith with us by the righteousness of our God and Savior Jesus Christ. (2 Peter 1:1)

Jude, a bondservant of Jesus Christ, and brother of James, to those who are called, sanctified by God the Father, and preserved in Jesus Christ. (Jude 1)

Paul and Timothy, bondservants of Jesus Christ, to all the saints in Christ Jesus who are in Philippi, with the bishops and deacons. (Philippians 1:1)

The Revelation of Jesus Christ, which God gave Him to show His servants—things which must shortly take place. And He sent and signified it by His angel to His servant John, who bore witness to the word of God, and to the testimony of Jesus Christ, to all things that he saw. (Revelation 1:1–2)

I, John, both your brother and companion in the tribulation and kingdom and patience of Jesus Christ, was on the island that is called Patmos for the word of God and for the testimony of Jesus Christ. (Revelation 1:9)

5.   The Cross sanctifies people for Christ. They exude the fragrance of love for Jesus. They long for Him more than the prestige of their platform or ministry. They follow in the path of Jesus, who made Himself of no reputation. They consider the honor and delight of loving Him and knowing Him to be above all earthly honors and joys. They labor only to bring Him back to the Earth, for it would be better if He were there.

Repent therefore and be converted, that your sins may be blotted out, so that times of refreshing may come from the presence of the Lord, and that He may send Jesus Christ, who was preached to you before, whom heaven must receive until the times of restoration of all things, which God has spoken by the mouth of all His holy prophets since the world began. (Acts 3:19–21)

For to me, to live is Christ, and to die is gain. But if I live on in the flesh, this will mean fruit from my labor; yet what I shall choose I cannot tell. For I am hard-pressed between the two, having a desire to depart and be with Christ, which is far better. Nevertheless to remain in the flesh is more needful for you. And being confident of this, I know that I shall remain and continue with you all for your progress and joy of faith. (Philippians 1:21–25)

Though I also might have confidence in the flesh. If anyone else thinks he may have confidence in the flesh, I more so: circumcised the eighth day, of the stock of Israel, of the tribe of Benjamin, a Hebrew of the Hebrews; concerning the law, a Pharisee; concerning zeal, persecuting the church; concerning the righteousness which is in the law, blameless. But what things were gain to me, these I have counted loss for Christ. Yet indeed I also count all things loss for the excellence of the knowledge of Christ Jesus my Lord, for whom I have suffered the loss of all things, and count them as rubbish, that I may gain Christ and be found in Him, not having my own righteousness, which is from the law, but that which is through faith in Christ, the righteousness which is from God by faith; that I may know Him and the power of His resurrection, and the fellowship of His sufferings, being conformed to His death, if, by any means, I may attain to the resurrection from the dead. Not that I have already attained, or am already perfected; but I press on, that I may lay hold of that for which Christ Jesus has also laid hold of me. Brethren, I do not count myself to have apprehended; but one thing I do, forgetting those things which are behind and reaching forward to those things which are ahead. (Philippians 3:4–13)

All the brethren greet you. Greet one another with a holy kiss. The salutation with my own hand—Paul's. If anyone does not love the Lord Jesus Christ, let him be accursed. O Lord, come! The grace of our Lord Jesus Christ be with you. My love be with you all in Christ Jesus. Amen. (1 Corinthians 16:20–24)

Peace to the brethren, and love with faith, from God the Father and the Lord Jesus Christ. Grace be with all those who love our Lord Jesus Christ in sincerity. Amen. (Ephesians 6:23–24)

And the Spirit and the bride say, "Come!" And let him who hears say, "Come!" And let him who thirsts come. Whoever desires, let him take the water of life freely. (Revelation 22:17)

He who testifies to these things says, "Surely I am coming quickly." Amen. Even so, come, Lord Jesus! (Revelation 22:20)

D.   Quotes and Scriptures

1.   *Hence that great lover of Jesus Christ, Saint Paul, once said: "The love of Christ compels us" (2 Corinthians 5:14). Listen to what Saint Francis de Sales says on this text from Corinthians: "Knowing that Jesus Christ, true God, has loved us so that He suffered death, and death on a cross, for us, doesn't that put our hearts in a vise, and make them feel its force, and squeeze love from them, but with a power that, the stronger it is, the more delightful it is." He goes on to say, "When then, don't we cast ourselves on Jesus crucified, to die on the Cross with Him, who has chosen to die for love of us? I will hold Him and I will never let Him go; I will die with Him, and will be consumed in the flames of His love. One flame will consume this divine Creator and His wretched creature. Jesus gives Himself unreservedly to me, and I give myself unreservedly to Him. I will live and die in His loving arms; neither life nor death shall ever separate me from Him. O eternal love, my soul longs after You, and chooses You forever. Come, Holy Spirit, and inflame our hearts in love. O to love! O to die! To die to all other loves, and to live only for the love of Jesus Christ! O Redeemer of our souls, grant that we may eternally sing, long live Jesus, whom I love. I love Jesus, who lives for ever and ever."*[1]

2.   All of Psalm 72 proclaims, "Long live Jesus," speaking of the Millennial reign. The people of the earth will shout, "Ever bless Him!" and "Long may He live!"

3.   *For unto us a Child is born, unto us a Son is given; and the government will be upon His shoulder. And His name will be called Wonderful, Counselor, Mighty God, Everlasting Father, Prince of Peace. (Isaiah 9:6)*

4.   Philippians 2: how is the government going to be placed upon Jesus' shoulders? He humbled Himself even to the point of death on a Cross. So the government is going to be put on His shoulders through the Cross.

---

1   Liguori, Saint Alphonsus. *The Practice of the Love of Jesus Christ* (Liguori, MO: Liguori, 1997), p. 5.

> *Let this mind be in you which was also in Christ Jesus, who, being in the form of God, did not consider it robbery to be equal with God, but made Himself of no reputation, taking the form of a bondservant, and coming in the likeness of men. And being found in appearance as a man, He humbled Himself and became obedient to the point of death, even the death of the cross. Therefore God also has highly exalted Him and given Him the name which is above every name, that at the name of Jesus every knee should bow, of those in heaven, and of those on earth, and of those under the earth, and that every tongue should confess that Jesus Christ is Lord, to the glory of God the Father. (Philippians 2:5–11, emphasis added)*

5. The Apostle John: from a Son of Thunder to the Apostle of Love

   > *Behold what manner of love the Father has bestowed on us, that we should be called children of God! (1 John 3:1, emphasis added)*

6. *If anyone does not love the Lord Jesus Christ, let him be accursed. O Lord, come! (1 Corinthians 16:22)*

III. THE CROSS ENABLES US TO BE DEAD TO SIN AND ALIVE TO GOD

A. Through the work of the Cross, we are brought into a new relationship with God. We are put in right standing as dearly beloved sons and daughters of God, co-heirs with Christ; children of light and love who walk no longer according to the traditions of men and the deeds of darkness.

   > *Therefore, brethren, having boldness to enter the holiest by the blood of Jesus, by a new and living way which He consecrated for us, through the veil, that is, His flesh, and having a High Priest over the house of God, let us draw near with a true heart in full assurance of faith, having our hearts sprinkled from an evil conscience and our bodies washed with pure water. (Hebrews 10:19–22)*

B. Paul saw Christian baptism as an entrance into Christ's death and resurrection where we no longer live for the flesh. We die to sin and become alive in Christ.

1. We are baptized into the death of Christ that we may no longer live for sin. The death of Christ breaks both the guilt and the power of sin. The Cross gives us strength to say no to sin, to resist sin, even unto the shedding of our blood (Hebrews 12:4).

   Therefore we were buried with Him through baptism into death, that just as Christ was raised from the dead by the glory of the Father, even so we also should walk in newness of life. For if we have been united together in the likeness of His death, certainly we also shall be in the likeness of His resurrection, knowing this, that our old man was crucified with Him, that the body of sin might be done away with, that we should no longer be slaves of sin. For he who has died has been freed from sin. Now if we died with Christ, we believe that we shall also live with Him, knowing that Christ, having been raised from the dead, dies no more. Death no longer has dominion over Him. For the death that He died, He died to sin once for all; but the life that He lives, He lives to God. Likewise you also, reckon yourselves to be dead indeed to sin, but alive to God in Christ Jesus our Lord. (Romans 6:4–11)

2. We live Christianity like it is a natural religion. We see the Cross as a "once in time" event, not a "once for all time" event, all the while thinking, "That is what He did so that we can get into Heaven; it's up to us by moral strength, aptitude and tenacity of will to live out the Christian life." It is, however, a mystical union. We are brought through faith into His life. When we are baptized, we are entering into His death and resurrection. Jesus Himself sums up all of humanity. Irenaeus called it "recapitulation," where, from the moment He was born all the way through His death and resurrection, Jesus was redeeming humanity. We join ourselves with Christ in His commitment against sin—in the place where God judged it and rendered it powerless, once and for all. You must be a participant, entering in by faith to a divine flow, a divine power, a divine strength, a supernatural enabling, where the Holy Spirit fills you in the inner man, where the death and resurrection of Jesus Christ are made effective in you by the Holy Spirit.

In Him you were also circumcised with the circumcision made without hands, by putting off the body of the sins of the flesh, by the circumcision of Christ, buried with Him in baptism, in which you also were raised with Him through faith in the working of God, who raised Him from the dead. And you, being dead in your trespasses and the uncircumcision of your flesh, He has made alive together with Him, having forgiven you all trespasses, having wiped out the handwriting of requirements that was against us, which was contrary to us. And He has taken it out of the way, having nailed it to the cross. Having disarmed principalities and powers, He made a public spectacle of them, triumphing over them in it. (Colossians 2:11–15)

IV. THE CROSS BECKONS US INTO SELF-SACRIFICE

A. Dietrich Bonheoffer described it well when he said, "When Christ calls a man, he bids him come and die."[2] God wins our hearts by love and then invites us into the delight of laying down our lives so that others may live. The Cross becomes the pattern of life for the believer, whereby he or she walks in the steps of Jesus, surrendered even unto death to the Father's will.

B. In John 12:12–36, at Jesus' greatest point of public ministry, He chose the road less traveled, the way of humility. Calvary became His coronation path into glory. He said that all His servants are to choose the same path, and the Father validated that statement from Heaven with His own voice. The Father declared from Heaven that the only path to glory is the Cross.

But Jesus answered them, saying, "The hour has come that the Son of Man should be glorified. Most assuredly, I say to you, unless a grain of wheat falls into the ground and dies, it remains alone; but if it dies, it produces much grain. He who loves his life will lose it, and he who hates his life in this world will keep it for eternal life. If anyone serves Me, let him follow Me; and where I am, there My servant will be also. If anyone serves Me, him My Father will honor." (John 12:23–26)

---

2 Bonhoeffer, Dietrich. *The Cost of Discipleship*. (New York, Touchstone, 1995), p. 89.

So when He had washed their feet, taken His garments, and sat down again, He said to them, "Do you know what I have done to you? You call Me Teacher and Lord, and you say well, for so I am. If I then, your Lord and Teacher, have washed your feet, you also ought to wash one another's feet. For I have given you an example, that you should do as I have done to you. Most assuredly, I say to you, a servant is not greater than his master; nor is he who is sent greater than he who sent him. If you know these things, blessed are you if you do them." (John 13:12–17)

Husbands, love your wives, just as Christ also loved the church and gave Himself for her, that He might sanctify and cleanse her with the washing of water by the word, that He might present her to Himself a glorious church, not having spot or wrinkle or any such thing, but that she should be holy and without blemish. So husbands ought to love their own wives as their own bodies; he who loves his wife loves himself. (Ephesians 5:25–28)

Let each of you look out not only for his own interests, but also for the interests of others. Let this mind be in you which was also in Christ Jesus, who, being in the form of God, did not consider it robbery to be equal with God, but made Himself of no reputation, taking the form of a bondservant, and coming in the likeness of men. And being found in appearance as a man, He humbled Himself and became obedient to the point of death, even the death of the cross. Therefore God also has highly exalted Him and given Him the name which is above every name, that at the name of Jesus every knee should bow, of those in heaven, and of those on earth, and of those under the earth, and that every tongue should confess that Jesus Christ is Lord, to the glory of God the Father. (Philippians 2:4–11)

By this we know love, because He laid down His life for us. And we also ought to lay down our lives for the brethren. But whoever has this world's goods, and sees his brother in need, and shuts up his heart from him, how does the love of God abide in him? (1 John 3:16–17)

C.   Chris, an acquaintance of mine from seminary, told me of his story with Mother Theresa. He worked with her one summer in the House for the Dying. In this house, workers take in those who are terminally ill and care for them in their last days as a display of Christ's great love for people. Chris' job was to bury the bodies. He would bury people by the hundreds that summer. Before Mother Theresa allowed him to start this job, she asked him, "Chris, do you really love Jesus?" Over and over, she continued to ask him, "Chris, do you really love Jesus? Are you sure you love Jesus?" Chris was saddened that she continued her line of questioning. She finally relented, saying, "Chris, only someone who loves Jesus can do this."

V.   THE CROSS ENCOURAGES US IN THE MIDST OF PERSECUTION AND SUFFERING

A.   The apostles continually encouraged persecuted churches by pointing them to the perseverance of Jesus on the Cross. They reminded them of Jesus' words: that just as He suffered in this life, so would His disciples. They pointed them to the Cross and reminded them of the glorious resurrection.

The Spirit Himself bears witness with our spirit that we are children of God, and if children, then heirs—heirs of God and joint heirs with Christ, if indeed we suffer with Him, that we may also be glorified together. (Romans 8:16–17)

For to you it has been granted on behalf of Christ, not only to believe in Him, but also to suffer for His sake. (Philippians 1:29)

Yes, and all who desire to live godly in Christ Jesus will suffer persecution. (2 Timothy 3:12)

You have put all things in subjection under his feet. For in that He put all in subjection under him, He left nothing that is not put under him. But now we do not yet see all things put under him. But we see Jesus, who was made a little lower than the angels, for the suffering of death crowned with glory and honor, that He, by the grace of God, might taste death for everyone. (Hebrews 2:8–9)

For consider Him who endured such hostility from sinners against Himself, lest you become weary and discouraged in your souls. You have not yet resisted to bloodshed, striving against sin. (Hebrews 12:3–4)

B.   Mistreatment and opposition are both the context and fruit of a fallen world. Everyone suffers. Everyone is hurt, betrayed, abused, taken advantage of, oppressed. Yet enduring mistreatment can count only for the redeemed. Even suffering can be used by God to produce fruitfulness and wholeheartedness in the redeemed.

   1.   Saint Augustine stated that "the same miseries send some to heaven and others to hell."[3] The test of suffering separates the wheat from the chaff in the Church of God during times of tribulation: those who humble themselves to the will of God are wheat for paradise; those who grow haughty and enraged, and so forsake God, are chaff for hell.

   2.   Saint Alphonsus Ligouri said, "The condition of the saints on the earth is to suffer as they love; the condition of the saints in heaven (in the next age) is to enjoy as they love."[4]

C.   We need to break the fantasy that "I was the 'one' wronged." Everyone is mistreated. Everyone right now is either being mistreated, or is about to be mistreated, or is mistreating someone else. We expect suffering from unbelievers outside the church. But in regard to the Church, we often believe the lie that as we mature, we should suffer less mistreatment in the Church.

D.   Why does mistreatment exist? It exposes the great enemy of our soul—pride manifesting in anger. The crucible places pressures on the human heart that expose the fault lines underneath the surface. Mistreatment and opposition touch places of pride that otherwise go unnoticed in our controlled environments. This is why marriage can be, if the couple cooperates with it, a great sanctifier of the human heart. When I was single, I could control my environment in such a way as to keep my sin undisturbed in hidden places. In marriage, you can run, but you cannot hide. Opposition and mistreatment are part of the unspoken vows: "In sickness and in health, in opposition and mistreatment, until death do us part or until we kill each other." I thought I was holy when I was single, but I found out quickly there is a difference between being holy and being undisturbed.

---

3   Liguori, Saint Alphonsus. *The Practice of the Love of Jesus Christ* (Liguori, MO: Liguori Publications, 1997), p. 43.

4   *Ibid*, p. 49. Parenthetical comment added.

E.   Receive mistreatment and suffering as from the hand of a loving Father, which brings forth a greater work of sanctification in you. Redemptive suffering counts! You see, mistreatment is not only the test of meekness. The test contains within itself the avenues for reform and transformation. The pressures expose and, if responded to rightly, can produce meekness in the heart. Understanding how to grow in meekness in the midst of mistreatment produces the opportunity for dependence, faith, and trust. If we knew the divine exchange rate and what the next age holds for those who embrace meekness in the midst of trial, we would not dare waste a good opportunity to receive correction from the Lord's hand. We would not throw away the eternal currency of forgiving and doing good to those who have wronged us. There is something better than being right in this life. It is being free!

But when you do good and suffer, if you take it patiently, this is commendable before God. For to this you were called, because Christ also suffered for us, leaving us an example, that you should follow His steps: "Who committed no sin, nor was deceit found in His mouth" who, when He was reviled, did not revile in return; when He suffered, He did not threaten, but committed Himself to Him who judges righteously; who Himself bore our sins in His own body on the tree, that we, having died to sins, might live for righteousness—by whose stripes you were healed. (1 Peter 2:20–24)

VI.   THE CROSS DEMANDS THAT WE FORGIVE OUR ENEMIES

A.   In the Sermon on the Mount, Jesus called us to be perfect just as the Father in Heaven is perfect. This was in the context of loving and forgiving our enemies. We are to be perfect in love by forgiving those who sin against us. The extravagant, undeserved forgiveness extended to each of us at the Cross undermines any of our rights to hold offense; it demands that we show a relatively small amount of forgiveness towards our enemies, compared to the vast amount of forgiveness the Lord has shown us. We are all equal at the foot of the Cross.

B.   There is nothing you can add to the Cross; freedom comes when you comprehend this truth. When you discover this, you can love the weak, you begin to love yourself, you quit striving and you rest there. The Cross demands that we forgive our enemies.

C.   This is seen as early as the first martyr, Stephen. He forgave his killers just as Christ forgave His killers when they crucified Him on the Cross. Saul saw something of another world that day. You can only forgive your enemies if you know Jesus. My theory is that Stephen's death was the intercession for Saul to come into the kingdom as the apostle to the Gentiles. Saul was a zealous man! Yet how many times do you think Stephen debated Saul and rendered him useless?

When they heard these things they were cut to the heart, and they gnashed at him with their teeth. But he, being full of the Holy Spirit, gazed into heaven and saw the glory of God, and Jesus standing at the right hand of God, and said, "Look! I see the heavens opened and the Son of Man standing at the right hand of God!" Then they cried out with a loud voice, stopped their ears, and ran at him with one accord; and they cast him out of the city and stoned him. And the witnesses laid down their clothes at the feet of a young man named Saul. And they stoned Stephen as he was calling on God and saying, "Lord Jesus, receive my spirit." Then he knelt down and cried out with a loud voice, "Lord, do not charge them with this sin." And when he had said this, he fell asleep. (Acts 7:54–60)

VII.   THE CROSS INVITES US INTO A TRANSCENDENT LIFE

A.   In the Cross, we find the freedom to look death in the face and resist the urge to sell out to fear, sin, and oppression. The Cross empowers the heart to live out of the well of another world, an eternal dwelling place in God.

B.   At the Cross, we cry out with Moses, "You have been our dwelling place" (Psalm 90:1). At Calvary, we are freed from placating the power brokers of society. We sneer at the powers of this age who cannot steal our lives through intimidation, fear, or coercion. The forces of this life use the threat of death to hold people in bondage. Their leverage is pain and oppression. Disciples of the Cross laugh at the hollowness of the enemy's position. From a transcendent foundation, we cry "No!" to the systems of oppression and torment.

C. Broken free from the vain strivings of power, ambition, and vain glory, the saints of light are free to love the weak, to search out the lost and broken. True power is granted when the saints are free from the fear of death. Thus, the saints live from the vantage point of Calvary, from the high and lofty place where love can flow, where trust in God brings a fountain of life to all who are weak and weary of heart. From this place of the Cross, the believer scans the world and is free to love with Christ there. When you live in bondage to rulers, power brokers and coercion, no matter what the relationship is, you're not free to love the weak and the poor. If you give your life for the weak and the poor, you are exalted with Him in heavenly places. There is only one way to love the weak: from the vantage point of the Cross. Freedom to love is power.

D. The story of the Nigerian evangelist when he was attacked by Muslim extremists.

E. *Consider him further still. Do you mark him in your imagination nailed to yonder cross! O eyes! ye are full of pity, with tears standing thick! Oh! how I mark the floods gushing down his cheeks! Do you see his hands bleeding, and his feet too, gushing gore? Behold him! The bulls of Bashan gird him round, and the dogs are hounding him to death! Hear him! 'Eloi, Eloi, lama sabachthani?' The earth startles with affright. A God is groaning on a cross! What! Does not this dishonour Christ? No; it honours him! Each of the thorns becomes a brilliant in his diadem of glory; the nails are forged into his sceptre, and his wounds do clothe him with the purple of empire. The treading of the wine-press hath stained his garments, but not with stains of scorn and dishonour. The stains are embroideries upon his royal robes for ever. The treading of that wine-press hath made his garments purple with the empire of a world; and he is the Master of a universe for ever. O Christian! sit down and consider that thy Master did not mount from earth's mountains into heaven, but from her valleys. It was not from heights of bliss on earth that he strode to bliss eternal, but from depths of woe he mounted up to glory. Oh! what a stride was that, when, at one mighty step from the grave to the throne of The Highest, the man Christ, the God, did gloriously ascend.*[5]

---

5 Spurgeon, Charles. "The Exaltation of Christ." *The Spurgeon Archive*. 2001. <http://www.spurgeon. org/sermons/0101.htm.>

Session Eleven: The Risen Lord

I. THE HISTORIC IMPORTANCE OF THE RESURRECTION

A. The Resurrection is at the very core of the Christian faith. Inasmuch as the Resurrection can be validated and set forth, Christianity stands or falls. We are the resurrection people; we believe in the resurrection from the dead. If you were to name the four global religions that are based on a personality, not just a code of ethics or philosophical construct, only one of those four has a founder who claimed that He would rise from the dead—and did. There is only one reason we propagate a faith as outlandish as this, only one reason we can claim that God came in the flesh, in the form of a man, and died on a Cross for forgiveness of sin: because the founder came out of the grave and stayed out forever.

B. The birth of the Church is dependent on Christ's resurrection from the dead. Without the empty tomb and the appearances of Jesus, no disciples would have left their fishing boats ever again, and no one would ever have gathered in the upper room. What took place early on the third day after the Crucifixion sealed the beginning of a historic shift in world history.

Without it (The Resurrection) Christianity would have been still-born, for a living faith cannot survive a dead saviour.[1]

C. Some quotes from Josh McDowell's *Evidence That Demands a Verdict*:

1. William Lane Craig: *It is difficult to exaggerate what a devastating effect the crucifixion must have had on the disciples. They had no conception of a dying, much less a rising, Messiah, for the Messiah would reign forever. Without prior belief in the resurrection, belief in Jesus as Messiah would have been impossible in light of his death. The resurrection turned catastrophe into victory…it was His resurrection that enabled Jesus' shameful death to be interpreted in salvific terms. Without it, Jesus' death would have meant only humiliation and accursedness by God; but in view of the resurrection it could be seen to be the event by which forgiveness of sins was obtained. Without the resurrection, the Christian Way could never have come into being.*[2]

---

1 Lewis, Peter. *The Glory of Christ.* (Great Britain: Paternoster Press, reprinted 2004), p. 339.
2 McDowell, Josh. *Evidence That Demands A Verdict: Volume 1* (Nashville, TN: Nelson Reference, 1999), p. 207.

2.   Michael Green: *Christianity does not hold the resurrection to be one among many tenets of belief. Without faith in the resurrection there would be no Christianity at all. The Christian church would never have begun; the Jesus-movement would have fizzled out like a damp squib with His execution. Christianity stands or falls with the truth of the resurrection.*[3]

D.   Jesus staked His own claims upon the Resurrection. Jesus foretold His own death and stated that the evidence of His identity would be based upon His rising from the dead. He is the ultimate risk-taker. Imagine the audacity of someone saying, "Do you want to know what validates my messianic identity? I have power over death!" No other religion has a founder basing the veracity of his claims, as well as his ethics, upon an empty tomb and upon post-death appearances in a physical body. Mohammad, Buddha, and Joseph Smith all have grave sites with bones in them— dead, decaying bones.

1.   *So the Jews answered and said to Him, "What sign do You show to us, since You do these things?" Jesus answered and said to them, "Destroy this temple, and in three days I will raise it up." Then the Jews said, "It has taken forty-six years to build this temple, and will You raise it up in three days?" But He was speaking of the temple of His body. Therefore, when He had risen from the dead, His disciples remembered that He had said this to them; and they believed the Scripture and the word which Jesus had said. (John 2:18–22)*

The proof of His resurrection after three days in the grave would be similar to Jonah being released from the belly of a whale after three days. When you begin to see Jonah in light of Jesus' resurrection, you begin to see God's brilliance.

2.   R. M'Cheyne Edgar: *Here is a teacher of religion and He calmly professes to stake His entire claims upon His ability, after having been done to death, to rise again from the grave. We may safely assume that there never was, before or since, such a proposal made. To talk of this extraordinary test being invented by mystic students of the prophecies, and inserted in the way it has been into the gospel narratives, is to lay too great a burden on our credulity. He who was ready to stake everything on His ability to come back from the tomb stands before us as the most original of all teachers, one who shines in His own self-evidencing life!*[4]

3   McDowell, Josh. *Evidence That Demands A Verdict: Volume 1* (Nashville, TN: Nelson Reference, 1999), p. 208.

4   *Ibid*, p. 207.

3. Wilbur M. Smith: *It was this same Jesus, the Christ who, among many other remarkable things, said and repeated something which, proceeding from any other being would have condemned him at once as either a bloated egotist or a dangerously unbalanced person. That Jesus said He was going up to Jerusalem to die is not so remarkable, though all the details He gave about that death, weeks and months before He died, are together a prophetic phenomenon. But when He said that He himself would rise again from the dead, the third day after He was crucified, he said something that only a fool would dare say, if he expected longer the devotion of any disciples—unless He was sure He was going to rise. No founder of any world religion known to men ever dared say a thing like that!*[5]

4. One of the greatest arguments for the Resurrection is the story of the Apostle Paul's conversion. How do you explain a man who gave his life to killing Christians, but, in one moment, turned around and joined the very ones he was killing, even giving his own life for them? What happened on the road to Damascus? Your arguments against Christianity can be foolproof and your position can be strong. Yet, there is no defense against a risen Lord who shows up the way He showed up to Saul of Tarsus on that day.

II. OLD TESTAMENT PROPHECIES CONCERNING THE RESURRECTION

Jesus did not create a new religion. Rather, He brought forth a new season in redemptive history for the people of God. The Old Testament prophesied of the coming Messiah's death and resurrection.

A. Abrahamic Covenant: in Genesis, God promised to Abraham that he would inherit the land. If you read Genesis 15 and 17 quickly, you may be tempted to quickly categorize Abraham's inheritance as being progressively received through his descendants. Yet, several times in the book of Genesis, God directly promised that Abraham himself would inherit the land. Abraham believed that promise, and it was accredited to him as righteousness. The New Testament specifically states that Abraham never inherited the land; that he was waiting for a city not built by human hands, but whose architect and builder is God (Hebrews 11:8–10).

---

5   McDowell, Josh. *Evidence That Demands A Verdict: Volume 1* (Nashville, TN: Nelson Reference, 1999), p. 209.

B.   So if he never inherited the land in his day and he is dead in the grave, then what does the promise mean? What city is he going to receive? Revelation 21 tells us that the New Jerusalem will come down out of Heaven. Beloved, this is a literal city that God has prepared for the joining of Heaven and Earth in the person of His Son. Many Christians think we are leaving this Earth to have some spiritual, ethereal, and abstract existence with God somewhere out there in space. This may be the gospel of George Lucas, but it is not the testimony of the Bible. It may be *Star Wars*, but it is not Christianity. I do not want to become one with the Force. I want a physical resurrected body with which to commune with God. The gospel of *Star Wars* has done much to warp and twist our Christian thinking of eternity. God's highest plan for you is not to drift through eternity in an ethereal state of existence. God is not trying to get you to escape this life or to enable your atman become one with Brahman. Christians are not looking to escape the cycle of life. Christians are looking to receive an inheritance on this planet from which humanity came, and we will physically experience our inheritance with a resurrected, glorified body that will never die. God has promised to renew created order. He will create a new Heaven and a new Earth, and He will build an eternal city in which a resurrected humanity will forever dwell with Him.

1.   Hebrews 11:13 states that "these all died in faith, not having received the promises but having seen them far off, were assured of them and embraced them and confessed that they were strangers and pilgrims on the earth." In other words, Abraham knew that he would not taste of the promise in his day, but he saw the big picture and trusted God.

2.   The passage goes on to say that the test of offering up Isaac was in regard to Abraham's belief in the resurrection. "…Therefore God is not ashamed to be called their God, for He has prepared a city for them. By faith Abraham, when he was tested, offered up Isaac…" (Hebrews 11:16–17). In other words, God was asking, "Abraham, you saw the big picture; do you really trust Me? Do you really trust what I showed you?" The testing of Abraham was not arbitrary testing by a harsh God. God had revealed His plan to Abraham when He appeared to him in His glory. Thus, He tested Abraham's belief. "Abraham, do you believe me? If you believe me, offer up your son Isaac. If you believe in the resurrection I showed you, Abraham, offer him up."

> *By faith Abraham, when he was tested, offered up Isaac, and he who had received the promises offered up his only begotten son, of whom it was said, "In Isaac your seed shall be called," concluding that God was able to raise him up, even from the dead, from which he also received him in a figurative sense.*
> (Hebrews 11:17–19, emphasis added)

C. Abraham himself is going to receive the promise with the rest of his descendents in a resurrected body. He will inherit the land in his resurrected body at the Second Coming of Jesus. He will enjoy the fruit of the land as a member of the New Jerusalem, the celestial city that comes to Earth.

> *Then He brought him outside and said, "Look now toward heaven, and count the stars if you are able to number them." And He said to him, "So shall your descendants be." And he believed in the LORD, and He accounted it to him for righteousness. Then He said to him, "I am the LORD, who brought you out of Ur of the Chaldeans, to give you this land to inherit it."* (Genesis 15:5–7, emphasis added)

> *And I will establish My covenant between Me and you and your descendants after you in their generations, for an everlasting covenant, to be God to you and your descendants after you.* **Also I give to you** *and your descendants after you the land in which you are a stranger, all the land of Canaan, as an everlasting possession; and I will be their God."* (Genesis 17:7–8, emphasis added)

Genesis 22

> *By faith Abraham obeyed when he was called to go out to the place which he would receive as an inheritance. And he went out, not knowing where he was going. By faith he dwelt in the land of promise as in a foreign country, dwelling in tents with Isaac and Jacob, the heirs with him of the same promise; for he waited for the city which has foundations, whose builder and maker is God. By faith Sarah herself also received strength to conceive seed, and she bore a child when she was past the age, because she judged Him faithful who had promised. Therefore from one man, and him as good as dead, were born as many as the stars of the sky in multitude — innumerable as the sand which is by the seashore.* **These all died in faith, not having received the promises, but having seen them afar off were assured of them, embraced them and confessed that they were strangers and pilgrims on the earth.** *For those who say such things declare plainly that they seek a homeland. And truly if they had called to mind that country from which they had come out, they*

would have had opportunity to return. But now they desire a better, that is, a heavenly country. Therefore God is not ashamed to be called their God, for He has prepared a city for them. **By faith Abraham, when he was tested, offered up Isaac, and he who had received the promises offered up his only begotten son, of whom it was said, "In Isaac your seed shall be called," concluding that God was able to raise him up, even from the dead,** *from which he also received him in a figurative sense. (Hebrews 11:8–19, emphasis added)*

And **God gave him no inheritance in it, not even enough to set his foot on.** *But even when Abraham had no child, He promised to give it to him for a possession and to his descendants after him. (Acts 7:5, emphasis added)*

D.   The New Testament indicates that Abraham knew more about the plan of redemption than we realize at first. Galatians tells us that the Gospel was preached to Abraham. In fact, Jesus stated in John 8:56 that Abraham saw His day and was glad. The Jews asked how Abraham, who is dead, could have seen Jesus in the present. Jesus answered by pointing to His pre-existence. In other words, Jesus revealed that it was He who appeared to Abraham and explained the plan of redemption to him. Our modern minds have clouded our understanding of the extent to which God had revealed His plan to the patriarchs and the prophets.

"Most assuredly, I say to you, if anyone keeps My word he shall never see death." Then the Jews said to Him, "Now we know that You have a demon! Abraham is dead, and the prophets; and You say, 'If anyone keeps My word he shall never taste death.' Are You greater than our father Abraham, who is dead? And the prophets are dead. Who do You make Yourself out to be?" Jesus answered, "If I honor Myself, My honor is nothing. It is My Father who honors Me, of whom you say that He is your God. Yet you have not known Him, but I know Him. And if I say, 'I do not know Him,' I shall be a liar like you; but I do know Him and keep His word. **Your father Abraham rejoiced to see My day, and he saw it and was glad."** *Then the Jews said to Him, "You are not yet fifty years old, and have You seen Abraham?" Jesus said to them, "Most assuredly, I say to you, before Abraham was, I AM." (John 8:51–58, emphasis added)*

And the Scripture, foreseeing that God would justify the Gentiles by faith, **preached the gospel to Abraham beforehand,** *saying, "In you all the nations shall be blessed." (Galatians 3:8, emphasis added)*

E.   In fact, Jesus used Abraham as the Old Testament argument for the resurrection from the dead. Jesus answered the question of the resurrection with what seemed to be a statement concerning eternal existence and immortality, not resurrection of the body. However, Jesus clearly meant this statement as an example of the resurrection of the dead. In other words, Jesus was not saying that right now Abraham is immortal. Jesus was not answering the question of immortal existence. He was answering the question of physical resurrection from the dead.

F.   Jesus used God's identification to Moses as "the God of your father—the God of Abraham, Isaac and Jacob." We know from the text that it was in fact Jesus as the Angel of Yahweh who was communicating to Moses at the burning bush. Jesus explained to the Sadducees that the promise from the beginning of creation was resurrection from the dead: God is going to have a kingdom, and that kingdom is going to be filled with resurrected people. God is the God of the living, not the dead. All who trust in Him will never die. They will live, and they will receive resurrected bodies.

"Therefore, in the resurrection, whose wife does she become? For all seven had her as wife." Jesus answered and said to them, "The sons of this age marry and are given in marriage. But those who are counted worthy to attain that age, and the resurrection from the dead, neither marry nor are given in marriage; nor can they die anymore, for they are equal to the angels and are sons of God, being sons of the resurrection. **But even Moses showed in the burning bush passage that the dead are raised, when he called the Lord 'the God of Abraham, the God of Isaac, and the God of Jacob.' For He is not the God of the dead but of the living, for all live to Him."** *(Luke 20:33–38, emphasis added)*

G.   Psalms

1.   *O Lord, You are the portion of my inheritance and my cup; you maintain my lot. The lines have fallen to me in pleasant places; yes, I have a good inheritance. I will bless the Lord who has given me counsel; my heart also instructs me in the night seasons. I have set the Lord always before me; because He is at my right hand I shall not be moved. Therefore my heart is glad, and my glory rejoices; my flesh also will rest in hope. For You will not leave my soul in Sheol, nor will You allow Your Holy One to see corruption. You will show me the path of life; in Your presence is fullness of joy; at Your right hand are pleasures forevermore. (Psalms 16:5–11)*

This whole Psalm is a prophetic cry for deliverance from the grave. David is entering into a prophetic cry and a statement of faith that God will not abandon him to the grave. Jesus was silent before His hearers on the Cross, on the way to the Cross, and on trial before Pilate and the Sanhedrin, but you can bet that in His inner man He was saying, "You will not abandon Me to Sheol."

2. Psalm 22 is a cry of dereliction. At verse 21, there is a change of faith: "Save Me from the lion's mouth and from the horns of the wild oxen! You have answered Me" (Psalm 22:21).

   All the prosperous of the earth shall eat and worship; all those who go down to the dust shall bow before Him, even he who cannot keep himself alive. *(Psalm 22:29, emphasis added)*

3. Psalm 37

4. *You have ascended on high, You have led captivity captive; You have received gifts among men, even from the rebellious, that the* LORD *God might dwell there. Blessed be the Lord, who daily loads us with benefits, the God of our salvation! Selah. Our God is the God of salvation; and to* GOD *the Lord belong escapes from death.* (Psalm 68:18–20)

5. Psalm 116

6. Psalm 118

   I shall not die, but live, and declare the works of the LORD. *(Psalm 118:17, emphasis added)*

   The stone which the builders rejected has become the chief cornerstone. This was the LORD's *doing; it is marvelous in our eyes.* (Psalm 118:22–23)

H. *Set me as a seal upon your heart, as a seal upon your arm; for love is as strong as death, jealousy as cruel as the grave; its flames are flames of fire, a most vehement flame. Many waters cannot quench love, nor can the floods drown it. If a man would give for love all the wealth of his house, it would be utterly despised. (Song 8:6–7)*

I.   Isaiah

And in this mountain the Lord of hosts will make for all people a feast of choice pieces, a feast of wines on the lees, of fat things full of marrow, of well-refined wines on the lees. And He will destroy on this mountain the surface of the covering cast over all people, and the veil that is spread over all nations. He will swallow up death forever, and the Lord God will wipe away tears from all faces; the rebuke of His people He will take away from all the earth; for the Lord has spoken. And it will be said in that day: "Behold, this is our God; we have waited for Him, and He will save us. This is the Lord; we have waited for Him; we will be glad and rejoice in His salvation." (Isaiah 25:6–9)

"Then I said, 'I have labored in vain, I have spent my strength for nothing and in vain; yet surely my just reward is with the Lord, and my work with my God.'" "And now the Lord says, who formed Me from the womb to be His Servant, to bring Jacob back to Him, so that Israel is gathered to Him (for I shall be glorious in the eyes of the Lord, and My God shall be My strength), indeed He says, 'It is too small a thing that You should be My Servant to raise up the tribes of Jacob, and to restore the preserved ones of Israel; I will also give You as a light to the Gentiles, that You should be My salvation to the ends of the earth.'" Thus says the Lord, the Redeemer of Israel, their Holy One, to Him whom man despises, to Him whom the nation abhors, to the Servant of rulers: "Kings shall see and arise, princes also shall worship, because of the Lord who is faithful, the Holy One of Israel; and He has chosen You." (Isaiah 49:4–7)

The Lord God has given Me the tongue of the learned, that I should know how to speak a word in season to him who is weary. He awakens Me morning by morning, He awakens My ear to hear as the learned. The Lord God has opened My ear; and I was not rebellious, nor did I turn away. I gave My back to those who struck Me, ad My cheeks to those who plucked out the beard; I did not hide My face from shame and spitting. For the Lord God will help Me; therefore I will not be disgraced; therefore I have set My face like a flint, and I know that I will not be ashamed. He is near who justifies Me; who will contend with Me? Let us stand together. Who is My adversary? Let him come near Me. Surely the Lord God will help Me; who is he who will condemn Me? Indeed they will all grow old like a garment; the moth will eat them up. Who among you fears the Lord? Who obeys the voice of His Servant? Who walks in darkness and has no light? Let him trust in the name of the Lord and rely upon his God. (Isaiah 50:4–10)

Behold, My Servant shall deal prudently; He shall be exalted and extolled and be very high. Just as many were astonished at you, so His visage was marred more than any man, and His form more than the sons of men; so shall He sprinkle many nations. Kings shall shut their mouths at Him; for what had not been told them they shall see, and what they had not heard they shall consider. (Isaiah 52:13–15)

Kings did not shut their mouths because of Jesus' death; they shut their mouths because they could not keep Him dead. No king on the earth has ever had any reason to fear someone they have killed, unless that someone refuses to remain dead.

Yet it pleased the LORD to bruise Him; He has put Him to grief. When You make His soul an offering for sin, He shall see His seed, He shall prolong His days, and the pleasure of the LORD shall prosper in His hand. He shall see the labor of His soul, and be satisfied. By His knowledge My righteous Servant shall justify many, for He shall bear their iniquities. Therefore I will divide Him a portion with the great, and He shall divide the spoil with the strong, because He poured out His soul unto death, and He was numbered with the transgressors, and He bore the sin of many, and made intercession for the transgressors. (Isaiah 53:10–12)

J.   Hosea

After two days He will revive us; on the third day He will raise us up, that we may live in His sight. (Hosea 6:2)

I will ransom them from the power of the grave; I will redeem them from death. O Death, I will be your plagues! O Grave, I will be your destruction! Pity is hidden from My eyes. (Hosea 13:14)

K.   *Now gather yourself in troops, O daughter of troops; He has laid siege against us; they will strike the judge of Israel with a rod on the cheek. "But you, Bethlehem Ephrathah, though you are little among the thousands of Judah, yet out of you shall come forth to Me the One to be Ruler in Israel, whose goings forth are from of old, from everlasting." Therefore He shall give them up, until the time that she who is in labor has given birth; then the remnant of His brethren shall return to the children of Israel. And He shall stand and feed His flock in the strength of the LORD, in the majesty of the name of the LORD His God; and they shall abide, for now He shall be great to the ends of the earth; and this One shall be peace. When the Assyrian comes into our land, and when he treads in our palaces, then we will raise against him seven shepherds and eight princely men. (Micah 5:1–5)*

III. PREDICTIONS OF THE RESURRECTION FROM THE LIPS OF JESUS

A.   John 2:19: in the gospel of John, Jesus' first proclamation after cleansing the Temple was to prophesy of His own death and resurrection. The Jews asked Him for a sign to give proof of His authority to do the things He did in the cleansing of the Temple. Jesus announced the sign: "Destroy this Temple and in three days I will raise it up." The sign of His authority would be His death and resurrection.

B.   In the gospel of Mark, after the disciples' retreat to Caesarea Philippi and Peter's confession that Jesus was the Christ, Jesus clearly spoke to the disciples at least three times concerning His death and resurrection. (Mark 8:31–32, 9:31–32, 10:33–34)

   1.   *And He began to teach them that the Son of Man must suffer many things, and be rejected by the elders and chief priests and scribes, and be killed, and after three days rise again. (Mark 8:31)*

   2.   *For He taught His disciples and said to them, "The Son of Man is being betrayed into the hands of men, and they will kill Him. And after He is killed, He will rise the third day." But they did not understand this saying, and were afraid to ask Him. (Mark 9:31–32)*

C.   The Lord's Supper: Matthew 26:26–30; Mark 14:22–26; Luke 22:14–20

   When the hour had come, He sat down, and the twelve apostles with Him. Then He said to them, "With fervent desire I have desired to eat this Passover with you before I suffer; for I say to you, I will no longer eat of it until it is fulfilled in the kingdom of God." Then He took the cup, and gave thanks, and said, "Take this and divide it among yourselves; for I say to you, I will not drink of the fruit of the vine until the kingdom of God comes." And He took bread, gave thanks and broke it, and gave it to them, saying, "This is My body which is given for you; do this in remembrance of Me." Likewise He also took the cup after supper, saying, "This cup is the new covenant in My blood, which is shed for you. But behold, the hand of My betrayer is with Me on the table. And truly the Son of Man goes as it has been determined, but woe to that man by whom He is betrayed!" Then they began to question among themselves, which of them it was who would do this thing. (Luke 22:14–23)

D. After the Crucifixion, Jesus' enemies requested that his body be guarded precisely because of Jesus' predictions of the Resurrection.

On the next day, which followed the Day of Preparation, the chief priests and Pharisees gathered together to Pilate, saying, "Sir, we remember, while He was still alive, how that deceiver said, 'After three days I will rise.' Therefore command that the tomb be made secure until the third day, lest His disciples come by night and steal Him away, and say to the people, 'He has risen from the dead.' So the last deception will be worse than the first." Pilate said to them, "You have a guard; go your way, make it as secure as you know how." (Matthew 27:62–65)

IV. THE RESURRECTION ACCOUNTS

A. The resurrection of Jesus took place early on the third day. Darkness remained, but light was on the horizon.

B. Angelic activity

C. Jesus' appearances

1. Mary Magdalene (John 20). Who would you choose to appear to first if you were Jesus? Perhaps Herod? Pontius Pilate? The Sanhedrin? Caesar? Jesus chose the weakest one who had found life in His presence, the one who washed His feet with her tears and hair. Mary had been forgiven much and had learned to love much.

   Now when He rose early on the first day of the week, He appeared first to Mary Magdalene, out of whom He had cast seven demons. (Mark 16:9, emphasis added)

   Our lovely King is so different from us. He longed to visit the most fragile among them, the one most devastated. Mary Magdalene had had seven demons and most likely lived a life of prostitution before Jesus delivered her and changed her whole life. Her thoughts after the Crucifixion must have been, "Was any of this real? Did any of this really change anything?" She was absolutely devastated. Jesus must have said to Himself, "I think I'll go to her. I think I'll see her." This decision is a theological statement of what your God is like: "I want to see Mary. I want to see the weakest among them." Let's revisit the story and meet Jesus there.

Mary went to the tomb to pay her respects to the Man with whom she fell in love. She was on her way early in the morning; it was still dark when she noticed the stone was rolled back from the entrance. Many men had put it in place a few days before. Frightened, she ran to Simon Peter and to the other disciple whom Jesus loved and said to them, "They have taken away the Lord out of the tomb…" (John 20:2). The disciples did not understand what had happened. In fact, the Gospels indicate that the disciples did not understand the Resurrection until afterwards.

Mary assumed someone has taken the Lord's body and desecrated it. "She…said to them, 'They have taken away the Lord from the tomb and we do not know where they have laid Him.' Peter therefore went out, and the other disciple, and were going to the tomb. So they both ran together, and the other disciple outran Peter and came to the tomb first" (v. 2–4). I love John's inclusion of the fact that he outran Peter. Boys will be boys, even at the resurrection site.

John goes on to display his humility by admitting that he did not, for whatever reason, go into the tomb. "And he, stooping down, and looking in, saw the linen cloths lying there; yet he did not go in" (v. 25). Then Simon Peter finally caught up, went into the tomb, and saw the linen cloths lying there.

"Then the other disciple, who came to the tomb first, went in also; and he saw and believed. For as yet they did not know the Scripture, that He must rise again from the dead" (v. 8–9). John believed! Peter was uncertain. Mary simply stood outside the tomb, weeping. She was devastated. The three of them were at the empty tomb. Who would Jesus choose to reveal Himself to first? The future pillars of the faith? Or a girl from the wrong side of the tracks who had learned what forgiveness and love were all about?

"And she saw two angels in white sitting, one at the head and the other at the feet, where the body of Jesus had lain. Then they said to her, 'Woman, why are you weeping?' She said to them, 'Because they have taken away my Lord, and I do not know where they have laid Him'" (v. 12–13). She believed that someone had stolen the body of Jesus. "They've taken away my Lord!" She was groaning and crying. This was the absolute travail of her soul.

The angels were trying to pull something out of her by asking the question, "Why are you weeping?" They were drawing a response out of her: "Because I love Him, and He's dead, and now they have done the absolute worst thing—they've taken His body. I can't even pay homage to Him. I do not know where they have laid Him."

"Now when she had said this, she turned around and saw Jesus standing there, and did not know that He was Jesus" (v.14). Now here's what's interesting. She found herself at His feet again. The last time she was at His feet, she walked into a Pharisee's home and she wept over Him, washing His feet with her hair.

Interesting enough, Jesus asked the same question as the angels, but extended it further to include, "Whom are you seeking?" (v.14). This tells you something about Jesus. He loves to know that you desire Him. Jesus longs to hear you say it. He knew Mary's heart. He knew everything, but He longed to hear her say it. Why? The reality was true in her heart, right? Isn't that enough?

Some people ask me about prayer, wondering, "Do I have to say it out loud?" I always reply, "No, you don't have to, but something about saying it out loud moves God's heart in a way unlike any other." I often pray quietly, yet something happens in my meditation when I begin to say the words out loud. I am escorted to another place of communion.

Jesus likes to draw out the articulation of the heart. In the process of articulating the desire, love is awakened in greater measure. Jesus was drawing the articulation out of Mary. "'Woman, why are you weeping? Whom are you seeking?' She, supposing Him to be the gardener, said to Him, 'Sir, if you have carried Him away, tell me where You have laid Him, and I will take Him away'" (v. 15). I wonder what her tone of voice was. Was it begging? Was it hopeful? Or was it, "I'll break your legs, gardener, if you don't give me back this body"? Think about Mary—she was a rough gal. I wonder how it was. We'll have to ask her one day.

Jesus was looking at her and hearing her voice. Then He broke in: "Mary!" (v. 16) He couldn't take it any longer. Hide and seek was over. He could not wait to go to His Father, but He wanted to be found right away by the one who longed for Him so. Her longing was not based upon future aspirations of ministry and destiny. Her only motive was love. She missed the One she had come to love and hope in.

He called her name. "Mary!" Immediately, she recognized the voice. "She turned and said to Him, 'Rabboni!' Jesus said, 'Do not cling to Me, for I am not yet ascended to my Father; but go to My brethren and say to them, 'I am ascending to My Father and your Father, to My God and your God'" (v. 16–17).

In the moment of rejoicing, Jesus required her to not cling to Him. In other words, He was saying, "Mary, do not touch Me or you'll die! There's so much power on My body after the Resurrection. Don't touch Me. It is not that I don't want you to touch Me, but it will kill you. There's real power on My body." Ephesians 1:19–20 tells us that it was the exceeding greatness of God's power. "Don't cling to me, Mary!"

Jesus had drawn out her heart. She had articulated her longing, and Jesus preempted protocol for the sake of love: "Forget it! Mary! It's Me, Mary! It's okay. It's okay, Mary. Redemption is going to stick this time. You are going all the way, and the demons that you were delivered from are never coming back. I'm here, and I am here to stay! Mary, it's not over. It has only just begun."

2.   The women

3.   The race to the tomb: Peter and John raced to the tomb to verify the women's report. John beat Peter to the tomb, yet stopped at the entrance as Peter rushed in, finding the linen neatly folded.

4.   The road to Emmaus (Luke 24): Jesus appeared to two disciples on the road to Emmaus. As Jesus led them through the Law of Moses, the Prophets, and the Psalms, the disciples moved into a supernatural understanding of Scripture. Their eyes were able to see both the suffering and the glory of the Messiah.

5.   Thomas

> *Then He said to Thomas, "Reach your finger here, and look at My hands; and reach your hand here, and put it into My side. Do not be unbelieving, but believing." And Thomas answered and said to Him, "My Lord and my God!" Jesus said to him, "Thomas, because you have seen Me, you have believed. Blessed are those who have not seen and yet have believed."* (John 20:27–29, emphasis added)

6.   By the sea of Tiberias (John 21)

7.   To James, the five hundred, and to Paul (1 Corinthians 15)

> *For I delivered to you first of all that which I also received: that Christ died for our sins according to the Scriptures, and that He was buried, and that He rose again the third day according to the Scriptures, and that He was seen by Cephas, then by the twelve. After that He was seen by over five hundred brethren at once, of whom the greater part remain to the present, but some have fallen asleep. After that He was seen by James, then by all the apostles. Then last of all He was seen by me also, as by one born out of due time.* (1 Corinthians 15:3–8, emphasis added)

V.   A HISTORICAL EVENT

A.   Christianity claims that the Resurrection was not a mere spiritual resurrection in the hearts of the disciples for some philosophical or theological construct. It claims that Jesus, in real time and space, rose from the dead with a physical body and appeared in the flesh to real people. You can believe in the Resurrection or not, inasmuch as the evidence points to the truth of the Resurrection.

1.   The Gospel writers testified that the tomb was empty and that Jesus appeared to the disciples over a period of forty days. In those encounters, the disciples and the women held on to His feet and touched His hands and side. Jesus also ate with the disciples.

2.   *Now as they said these things, Jesus Himself stood in the midst of them, and said to them, "Peace to you." But they were terrified and frightened, and supposed they had seen a spirit. And He said to them, "Why are you troubled? And why do doubts arise in your hearts? Behold My hands and My feet, that it is I Myself. Handle Me and see, for a spirit does not have flesh and bones as you see I have." (Luke 24:36–39)*

B.   Ignatius:

*Ignatius (A.D. c. 50–115), bishop of Antioch, a native of Syria and pupil of the apostle John, is said to have "been thrown to the wild beasts in the colosseum at Rome. His epistles were written during his journey from Antioch to his martyrdom" (**Moyer, Who Was Who in Church History**, p. 209). At a time when he would undoubtedly have been very sober of mind, he says of Christ: "He was crucified and died under Pontius Pilate. He really, and not merely in appearance, was crucified, and died, in the sight of beings in heaven, and on earth, and under the earth. He also rose again in three days…On the day of the preparation, then, at the third hour, he received the sentence from Pilate, the Father permitting that to happen; at the sixth hour He was crucified; at the ninth hour he gave up the ghost; and before sunset he was buried. During the Sabbath he continued under the earth in the tomb in which Joseph of Arimathaea had laid Him. He was carried in the womb, even as we are, for the usual period of time, and was really born, as we also are; and was in reality nourished with milk, and partook of common meat and drink, even as we do. And when He had lived among men for thirty years, He was baptized by John, really and not in appearance; and when He had preached the gospel three years, and done signs and wonders, he who was Himself the Judge was judged by the Jews, falsely so called, and by Pilate the governor; was scourged, was smitten on the cheek, was spit upon; He wore a crown of thorns and a purple robe; he was condemned: He was crucified in reality, and not in appearance, not in imagination, not in deceit. He really died, and was buried, and rose from the dead."* [6]

C.   The Jewish historian Josephus (the veracity of this Josephus quote is debated):

---

6 McDowell, Josh. *Evidence That Demands A Verdict: Volume 1* (Nashville, TN: Nelson Reference, 1999), p. 211-12.

Now there was about this time Jesus, a wise man, if it be lawful to call him man; for he was a doer of wonderful works, a teacher of such men as receive the truth with pleasure. He drew over to him many Jews, and also many of the Greeks. This man was the Christ. And when Pilate had condemned him to the Cross, upon his impeachment by the principal man among us, those who had loved him from the first did not forsake him, for he appeared to them alive on the third day, the divine prophets having spoken these and thousands of other wonderful things about him. And even now, the race of Christians, so named from him, has not died out.[7]

D.   Story of witnessing to a lady at the haunted house.

VI.   THE EVIDENCE

A.   The empty tomb stands as a proof of the Resurrection.

1.   All it would have taken to dispel the "myth" and to squash the beginning of this upstart religion would have been to produce Jesus' body from the tomb. One body from Joseph's tomb, and the testimony would have been over.

Tom Anderson (the former president of the California Trial Lawyers Association):

Let's assume that the written accounts of His appearances to hundreds of people are false. I want to pose a question. With an event so well publicized don't you think it's reasonable that one historian, one eye witness, one antagonist would record for all time that he had seen Christ's body? The silence of history is deafening when it comes to the testimony against the resurrection. As we will see, His opponents don't even argue the fact the tomb was empty. They concede it.[8]

2.   It is important to note that even the enemies of the Gospel admit to the empty tomb and do not try to dissuade people from believing in an empty tomb. Rather, they spread the rumor that the disciples stole the body and paid off the guards to say the same.

---

7   Josephus. *The Works of Josephus* (Trans. William Whiston. Peabody, MA: Hendrickson, 1987), p. 480.

8   Zukeran, Patrick. "The Resurrection: Fact or Fiction?" Probe Ministries. 1997. <http://www.probe. org/theology-and-philosophy/theology---christ/the-resurrection-fact-or-fiction.html.>

B.   The changed lives of the apostles

    1.   Their newly-found faith: the Gospels are clear that the disciples were in a state of disillusionment when the Resurrection occurred. The Gospels testify that the disciples had not understood Jesus' prophecies about His death and resurrection. Confused and broken, they were returning home after His death. The road to Emmaus demonstrated their shattered faith. Even after the empty tomb, some did not believe until they had seen the risen Lord. It is clear that Thomas did not believe. Before the Resurrection, James, John, Simon and Andrew had returned to fishing, and Matthew had returned to collecting taxes. John Stott says, "Perhaps the transformation of the disciples of Jesus is the greatest evidence of all for the resurrection."[9]

    2.   Their quick change in courage: the apostles moved from denial, dispersement, and disillusionment to bold declaration of Jesus' resurrection from the dead. For instance, Peter had been moved to denial out of fear from a young girl's question. Shortly after, Peter was boldly proclaiming the resurrection of Christ in the face of death.

    3.   Their self-sacrifice: the apostles moved from argument over who was the greatest to self-surrender and sacrifice for the witness of Christ. After the Resurrection, a moral shift took place among the Twelve. By Acts 15, the reader is not sure who was in charge. Was it Peter? Was it James? Humility permeated the scene of the early Church. This is a weighty argument for the Resurrection. How could men who preached and lived lives of the highest moral standards have based their moral construct on such an outlandish and intentional deception? How could they have stolen His body and then said He had risen from the dead? Their transformed lives speak to the veracity of their claims concerning the Resurrection.

    4.   Their martyrdom: even scholars who do not believe in the bodily resurrection of Jesus admit that something powerful had to have happened for the disciples to be willing to die for the witness to the Resurrection—powerful enough to make them willing to die the most gruesome and torturous deaths imaginable.

---

9 McDowell, Josh. *Evidence That Demands A Verdict: Volume 1* (Nashville, TN: Nelson Reference, 1999), p. 252.

C.   Preaching in Jerusalem

1.   The disciples immediately preached the message of the Resurrection in the very town where all the events described had happened in plain sight of everyone. Not enough time had transpired for legends or myths to be circulated and believed, for the events they were proclaiming had happened just weeks before. Creating legends and myths about Jesus in the same town where He had been killed a few weeks earlier would have been impossible.

2.   John Warwick Montgomery: *Note that when the disciples of Jesus proclaimed the resurrection, they did so as eyewitnesses and they did so while people were still alive who had contact with the events they spoke of. In 56 A.D. Paul wrote that over 500 people had seen the risen Jesus and that most of them were still alive (1 Corinthians 15:6 ff.). It passes the bounds of credibility that the early Christians could have manufactured such a tale and then preached it among those who might easily have refuted it simply by producing the body of Jesus.*[10]

D.   Conversion of Saul of Tarsus to Paul the Apostle

1.   In order to dispute the claims of Christianity and the resurrection of Jesus, one must explain the dramatic conversion of Saul of Tarsus. In Acts 7:58 and 8:1, Saul was found on the scene of Stephen's martyrdom, giving consent to and assisting in his execution by holding the stone throwers' clothes.

2.   Acts 8 and 9 describe Saul's great hatred towards believers in Jesus. Acts 9:1 states that Saul was constantly breathing threats and murder against the disciples of the Lord.

3.   Saul was suddenly encountered on the road to Damascus by the risen Lord and was changed to Paul the Apostle. After that encounter, Paul lived a life of self-sacrifice and persecution. From that day onward, Paul endured out of love for the disciples the very persecution he had once dispensed.

---

10   McDowell, Josh. *Evidence That Demands A Verdict: Volume 1* (Nashville, TN: Nelson Reference, 1999), p. 249.

4. Paul gave the reason for his startling shift in belief and behavior before the Sanhedrin in Jerusalem (Acts 22). He declared that he had met the risen Lord. Before King Agrippa in Acts 26, Paul again gave the reason for his change. He had met the risen Lord, Jesus the Messiah.

*"Brethren and fathers, hear my defense before you now." And when they heard that he spoke to them in the Hebrew language, they kept all the more silent. Then he said: "I am indeed a Jew, born in Tarsus of Cilicia, but brought up in this city at the feet of Gamaliel, taught according to the strictness of our fathers' law, and was zealous toward God as you all are today. I persecuted this Way to the death, binding and delivering into prisons both men and women, as also the high priest bears me witness, and all the council of the elders, from whom I also received letters to the brethren, and went to Damascus to bring in chains even those who were there to Jerusalem to be punished. **Now it happened, as I journeyed and came near Damascus at about noon, suddenly a great light from heaven shone around me. And I fell to the ground and heard a voice saying to me, 'Saul, Saul, why are you persecuting Me?' So I answered, 'Who are You, Lord?' And He said to me, 'I am Jesus of Nazareth, whom you are persecuting.'"** (Acts 22:1–8, emphasis added)*

*Indeed, I myself thought I must do many things contrary to the name of Jesus of Nazareth. This I also did in Jerusalem, and many of the saints I shut up in prison, having received authority from the chief priests; and when they were put to death, I cast my vote against them. And I punished them often in every synagogue and compelled them to blaspheme; and being exceedingly enraged against them, I persecuted them even to foreign cities. **While thus occupied, as I journeyed to Damascus with authority and commission from the chief priests, at midday, O king, along the road I saw a light from heaven, brighter than the sun, shining around me and those who journeyed with me. And when we all had fallen to the ground, I heard a voice speaking to me and saying in the Hebrew language, "Saul, Saul, why are you persecuting Me? It is hard for you to kick against the goads." So I said, "Who are You, Lord?" And He said, "I am Jesus, whom you are persecuting. But rise and stand on your feet; for I have appeared to you for this purpose, to make you a minister and a witness both of the things which you have seen and of the things which I will yet reveal to you."** (Acts 26:9–16, emphasis added)*

VII. ALTERNATIVE EXPLANATIONS FOR THE RESURRECTION

A. **The wrong tomb theory:** This position holds that because it was dark, the women went to the wrong tomb. Having found the wrong tomb empty, they rushed back with joy to tell the disciples, and thus what had been a rumor was presented as truth.

Argument against the wrong tomb theory:

1. Everyone knew where the tomb was. Peter and John verified the women's account later and found the grave clothes folded in the empty tomb.

2. Jesus' enemies knew where the empty tomb was and could have easily produced the body to silence the young movement.

B. **The stolen body theory:** This theory states that either the Roman or Jewish authorities stole the body.

Argument against the stolen body theory:

1. In light of the trouble that the apostles' preaching about the Resurrection caused for both the Jewish and Roman authorities, this view is unthinkable. One cannot imagine the authorities would have hidden the very object that would have dispelled all rumors of the Resurrection.

2. The production of Jesus' dead body would have ended all the contention.

C. **The swoon theory:** This theory holds that Jesus did not actually die on the cross. While appearing to die, He actually swooned. Supposedly, His injuries left Him in shock but still alive, and the coolness of the tomb revived Him in such a way that He was able to come forth from the grave on the third day.

Argument against the swoon theory:

1. It is clear that Jesus was dead. No one could have survived those injuries, especially without aid or assistance. Also, the blood and water that flowed from His side clearly indicated that Jesus was dead.

2.   The soldiers were experts at crucifixion. They made sure and testified that Jesus was dead. They did not break His legs due to their certainty of His death, but proceeded to stick a spear in His side to ensure their findings were correct.

3.   Jesus was covered with burial clothes and eighty pounds of spices after the Crucifixion. How could Jesus have lived for three days without food or water while being completely wrapped from head to toe in linen and covered by eighty pounds of spices?

4.   How could have Jesus revived, unwrapped himself, rolled away a great stone that took many men to put in place, fought off a Roman guard, and then walked several miles on the road to Emmaus while dialoguing with two disciples?

5.   How could Jesus have disappeared for the next forty or more years without a trace while the disciples died for a propagated lie? Moreover, why would He have done such a thing?

D.   **The hallucination theory:** This theory holds that the Resurrection took place in the minds of the disciples. Dr. William McNeil articulates this position:

The Roman authorities in Jerusalem arrested and crucified Jesus ... But soon afterwards the dispirited Apostles gathered in an upstairs room and suddenly felt again the heartwarming presence of their master. This seemed absolutely convincing evidence that Jesus' death on the cross had not been the end but the beginning ... The Apostles bubbled over with excitement and tried to explain to all who would listen all that had happened.[11]

---

11   Zukeran, Patrick. "The Resurrection: Fact or Fiction?" Probe Ministries. 1997. <http://www.probe. org/theology-and-philosophy/theology---christ/the-resurrection-fact-or-fiction.html.>

Argument against the hallucination theory:

1. Hallucinations of this kind can only happen if certain conditions are met. People who experience hallucinations fit a certain psychological profile. They have a nervous, imaginative and high-strung nature. There were many types of psychological profiles among the disciples.

2. Also, hallucinations are perceived by only individuals, not groups, and are very subjective. Entire groups of people saw the risen Jesus, and they all saw the same thing.

3. The disciples did not claim to have seen a vision. They testified to touching Him and eating with Him.

    Now as they said these things, Jesus Himself stood in the midst of them, and said to them, "Peace to you." But they were terrified and frightened, and supposed they had seen a spirit. And He said to them, "Why are you troubled? And why do doubts arise in your hearts? Behold My hands and My feet, that it is I Myself. Handle Me and see, for a spirit does not have flesh and bones as you see I have." (Luke 24:36–39, emphasis added)

4. Also, hallucinations are very restricted as to when, where, and how often they occur. The resurrection appearances happened in several different environments and at different times.

5. Hallucinations occur when a person is hopeful and expecting something to happen. The disciples were not in a hopeful, expecting state. Rather, they were disillusioned and in despair. Jesus showed up unannounced and suddenly.

E. **The theft theory:** This theory is the most popular and was the one the Jews circulated in attempting to discredit and squelch the Apostles' ministry in Jerusalem.

Now while they were going, behold, some of the guard came into the city and reported to the chief priests all the things that had happened. When they had assembled with the elders and consulted together, they gave a large sum of money to the soldiers, saying, "Tell them, 'His disciples came at night and stole Him away while we slept.' And if this comes to the governor's ears, we will appease him and make you secure." So they took the money and did as they were instructed; and this saying is commonly reported among the Jews until this day. (Matthew 28:11–15)

Argument against the theft theory:

1. If the Romans were sleeping, how did they know it was the disciples who stole the body?

2. The possibility of a Roman guard sleeping was highly unlikely. Falling asleep on a night watch was punishable by death for a Roman soldier.

3. It is highly unlikely that the disciples would have gathered in one place to strategize such a plot. Their lives were in danger, and they were in hiding.

4. Even if they had gathered and formulated such a plan, the tomb was also secured with a Roman seal, and the punishment for breaking that seal was death. It is unimaginable that the disciples would have risked their lives for their dead master when they had not been willing to risk their lives for their master when He was alive.

5. If the disciples had overcome their cowardice, broken the Roman seal, rolled the large ("great") stone uphill without waking the soldiers, and stolen the body, why would they have taken the time to unwrap Jesus and leave His grave clothes nicely folded in the tomb?

VIII. THE SIGNIFICANCE OF THE RESURRECTION

A. The Resurrection confirmed the identity of Jesus as the Messiah, the Divine Son of God, and the Lord. Jesus is the Lord, the resurrected Christ, and we are the people who testify to the Resurrection. He is going to judge the human race based on what we believe concerning the Resurrection.

So the Jews answered and said to Him, "What sign do You show to us, since You do these things?" Jesus answered and said to them, "Destroy this temple, and in three days I will raise it up." Then the Jews said, "It has taken forty-six years to build this temple, and will You raise it up in three days?" But He was speaking of the temple of His body. Therefore, when He had risen from the dead, His disciples remembered that He had said this to them; and they believed the Scripture and the word which Jesus had said. (John 2:18–22)

Acts: the messages in this book all center around the Resurrection. The eternal destiny of human beings does not lie in the balance because we have some needs; it is based on whether we believe in our hearts and confess with our mouths that Jesus rose from the dead. It's what we believe about who He said He was and what He did on that third day. We must preach the Gospel again. So many people think the Gospel is academically deficient, but many of the greatest minds in the world have believed that this Man rose from the dead. The average Western believer accepts the shame of the false belief that we have a second-class place in the realm of academia. We needlessly buy into this deception because we don't know the information.

1. *Therefore, of these men who have accompanied us all the time that the Lord Jesus went in and out among us, beginning from the baptism of John to that day when He was taken up from us, one of these must become a witness with us of His resurrection. (Acts 1:21–22)*

2. *This Jesus God has raised up, of which we are all witnesses. Therefore being exalted to the right hand of God, and having received from the Father the promise of the Holy Spirit, He poured out this which you now see and hear. For David did not ascend into the heavens, but he says himself: "The LORD said to my Lord, 'Sit at My right hand, till I make Your enemies Your footstool.'" Therefore let all the house of Israel know assuredly that God has made this Jesus, whom you crucified, both Lord and Christ. (Acts 2:32–36)*

3. *The God of our fathers raised up Jesus whom you murdered by hanging on a tree. Him God has exalted to His right hand to be Prince and Savior, to give repentance to Israel and forgiveness of sins. And we are His witnesses to these things, and so also is the Holy Spirit whom God has given to those who obey Him. (Acts 5:30–32)*

4. *Then certain Epicurean and Stoic philosophers encountered him. And some said, "What does this babbler want to say?" Others said, "He seems to be a proclaimer of foreign gods," because he preached to them Jesus and the resurrection. (Acts 17:18)*

5. *Therefore, having obtained help from God, to this day I stand, witnessing both to small and great, saying no other things than those which the prophets and Moses said would come—that the Christ would suffer, that He would be the first to rise from the dead, and would proclaim light to the Jewish people and to the Gentiles. (Acts 26:22–23)*

6. *Paul, a bondservant of Jesus Christ, called to be an apostle, separated to the gospel of God which He promised before through His prophets in the Holy Scriptures, concerning His Son Jesus Christ our Lord, who was born of the seed of David according to the flesh, and declared to be the Son of God with power according to the Spirit of holiness, by the resurrection from the dead. Through Him we have received grace and apostleship for obedience to the faith among all nations for His name, among whom you also are the called of Jesus Christ. (Romans 1:1–6)*

7. *That the God of our Lord Jesus Christ, the Father of glory, may give to you the spirit of wisdom and revelation in the knowledge of Him, the eyes of your understanding being enlightened; that you may know what is the hope of His calling, what are the riches of the glory of His inheritance in the saints, and what is the exceeding greatness of His power toward us who believe, according to the working of His mighty power which He worked in Christ when He raised Him from the dead and seated Him at His right hand in the heavenly places, far above all principality and power and might and dominion, and every name that is named, not only in this age but also in that which is to come. And He put all things under His feet, and gave Him to be head over all things to the church, which is His body, the fullness of Him who fills all in all. (Ephesians 1:17–23)*

8.   *And being found in appearance as a man, He humbled Himself and became obedient to the point of death, even the death of the cross. Therefore God also has highly exalted Him and given Him the name which is above every name, that at the name of Jesus every knee should bow, of those in heaven, and of those on earth, and of those under the earth, and that every tongue should confess that Jesus Christ is Lord, to the glory of God the Father. (Philippians 2:8–11)*

B.   The Resurrection vindicates the righteousness of Christ and the righteousness of God.

    1.   My professor Stephen Seamands used to quote E. Stanley Jones: "If Good Friday raised the question, Easter Sunday raised the man, and the raised man is the answer to all the raised questions."

    2.   God was vindicated as the righteous judge of sin, and Jesus was vindicated as the sinless acceptable sacrifice. In God's economy, sin had to be judged. At the same time, He provided a way for weak humans to come back into relationship with God through the atoning sacrifice of Jesus Christ.

C.   We share in the resurrection power of Christ. His resurrected life indwells every believer, releasing divine might and power unto transformation. The resurrection life of Jesus breaks the power of sin in our lives and makes us into a new creation. There is a new life working in us. The law of sin and death no longer prevails in our mortal bodies. The resurrection power enables us to live the crucified life as it produces a glorious new creation within us. We are a supernatural people—resurrection people. We testify to the resurrected Christ who now dwells in us by His Spirit. The workings of Christ and the Holy Spirit are inseparable.

After they had come to Mysia, they tried to go into Bithynia, but the Spirit did not permit them. So passing by Mysia, they came down to Troas. And a vision appeared to Paul in the night. A man of Macedonia stood and pleaded with him, saying, "Come over to Macedonia and help us." Now after he had seen the vision, immediately we sought to go to Macedonia, concluding that the Lord had called us to preach the gospel to them. (Acts 16:7–10)

Of this salvation the prophets have inquired and searched carefully, who prophesied of the grace that would come to you, searching what, or what manner of time, the Spirit of Christ who was in them was indicating when He testified beforehand the sufferings of Christ and the glories that would follow. (1 Peter 1:10–11)

Much more then, having now been justified by His blood, we shall be saved from wrath through Him. For if when we were enemies we were reconciled to God through the death of His Son, much more, having been reconciled, we shall be saved by His life. And not only that, but we also rejoice in God through our Lord Jesus Christ, through whom we have now received the reconciliation. (Romans 5:9–11)

D.   Paul teaches the Resurrection as more than just an historical event; it was an eschatological event. It was the first fruits of a transition in the human experience. Just as Christ was raised from the dead, so you shall be raised from the dead when He appears. However, between His resurrection and your resurrection, you have access to His resurrected life by the Spirit. The first fruits of a harvest is when a selection of the crop is taken out to see if the harvest is done. It's the first fruit you enjoy before the whole crop is harvested. Jesus' resurrection was the beginning of an eschatological resurrection of the whole human race at the end of the age, but the resurrection has started in this age through the Spirit.

For if we have been united together in the likeness of His death, certainly we also shall be in the likeness of His resurrection, knowing this, that our old man was crucified with Him, that the body of sin might be done away with, that we should no longer be slaves of sin. (Romans 6:5–6)

But if the Spirit of Him who raised Jesus from the dead dwells in you, He who raised Christ from the dead will also give life to your mortal bodies through His Spirit who dwells in you. (Romans 8:11)

And what is the exceeding greatness of His power toward us who believe, according to the working of His mighty power which He worked in Christ when He raised Him from the dead and seated Him at His right hand in the heavenly places, far above all principality and power and might and dominion, and every name that is named, not only in this age but also in that which is to come. (Ephesians 1:19–21)

But God, who is rich in mercy, because of His great love with which He loved us, even when we were dead in trespasses, made us alive together with Christ (by grace you have been saved), and raised us up together, and made us sit together in the heavenly places in Christ Jesus, (Ephesians 2:4–6)

If then you were raised with Christ, seek those things which are above, where Christ is, sitting at the right hand of God. Set your mind on things above, not on things on the earth. For you died, and your life is hidden with Christ in God. When Christ who is our life appears, then you also will appear with Him in glory. Therefore put to death your members which are on the earth: fornication, uncleanness, passion, evil desire, and covetousness, which is idolatry. (Colossians 3:1–5)

That I may know Him and the power of His resurrection, and the fellowship of His sufferings, being conformed to His death, if, by any means, I may attain to the resurrection from the dead. (Philippians 3:10–11)

Blessed be the God and Father of our Lord Jesus Christ, who according to His abundant mercy has begotten us again to a living hope through the resurrection of Jesus Christ from the dead, to an inheritance incorruptible and undefiled and that does not fade away, reserved in heaven for you, who are kept by the power of God through faith for salvation ready to be revealed in the last time. (1 Peter 1:3–5)

Now may the God of peace who brought up our Lord Jesus from the dead, that great Shepherd of the sheep, through the blood of the everlasting covenant, make you complete in every good work to do His will, working in you what is well pleasing in His sight, through Jesus Christ, to whom be glory forever and ever. Amen. (Hebrews 13:20–21)

E.   The Resurrection announced the destruction of death.

Jesus said to her, "I am the resurrection and the life. He who believes in Me, though he may die, he shall live. And whoever lives and believes in Me shall never die. Do you believe this?" (John 11:25–26)

Behold, I tell you a mystery: We shall not all sleep, but we shall all be changed—in a moment, in the twinkling of an eye, at the last trumpet. For the trumpet will sound, and the dead will be raised incorruptible, and we shall be changed. For this corruptible must put on incorruption, and this mortal must put on immortality. So when this corruptible has put on incorruption, and this mortal has put on immortality, then shall be brought to pass the saying that is written: "Death is swallowed up in victory." "O Death, where is your sting? O Hades, where is your victory?" The sting of death is sin, and the strength of sin is the law. But thanks be to God, who gives us the victory through our Lord Jesus Christ. (1 Corinthians 15:51–57)

F. The Resurrection testifies to a coming resurrection of the dead where Christ, the first fruits, will judge between the wicked and righteous. The righteous will rise unto eternal life and the wicked will rise unto eternal destruction.

And you will be blessed, because they cannot repay you; for you shall be repaid at the resurrection of the just. (Luke 14:14)

"Therefore, in the resurrection, whose wife does she become? For all seven had her as wife." Jesus answered and said to them, "The sons of this age marry and are given in marriage. But those who are counted worthy to attain that age, and the resurrection from the dead, neither marry nor are given in marriage; nor can they die anymore, for they are equal to the angels and are sons of God, being sons of the resurrection. But even Moses showed in the burning bush passage that the dead are raised, when he called the Lord 'the God of Abraham, the God of Isaac, and the God of Jacob.' For He is not the God of the dead but of the living, for all live to Him." (Luke 20:33–38)

For as the Father raises the dead and gives life to them, even so the Son gives life to whom He will. For the Father judges no one, but has committed all judgment to the Son, that all should honor the Son just as they honor the Father. He who does not honor the Son does not honor the Father who sent Him. Most assuredly, I say to you, he who hears My word and believes in Him who sent Me has everlasting life, and shall not come into judgment, but has passed from death into life. Most assuredly, I say to you, the hour is coming, and now is, when the dead will hear the voice of the Son of God; and those who hear will live. For as the Father has life in Himself, so He has granted the Son to have life in Himself, and has given Him authority to execute judgment also, because He is the Son of Man. Do not marvel at this; for the hour is coming in which all who are in the graves will hear His voice and come forth—those who have done good, to the resurrection of life, and those who have done evil, to the resurrection of condemnation. I can of Myself do nothing. As I hear, I judge; and My judgment is righteous, because I do not seek My own will but the will of the Father who sent Me. (John 5:21–30)

Now as they spoke to the people, the priests, the captain of the temple, and the Sadducees came upon them, being greatly disturbed that they taught the people and preached in Jesus the resurrection from the dead. (Acts 4:1–2)

And we are witnesses of all things which He did both in the land of the Jews and in Jerusalem, whom they killed by hanging on a tree. Him God raised up on the third day, and showed Him openly, not to all the people, but to witnesses chosen before by God, even to us who ate and drank with Him after He arose from the dead. And He commanded us to preach to the people, and to testify that it is He who was ordained by God to be Judge of the living and the dead. To Him all the prophets witness that, through His name, whoever believes in Him will receive remission of sins. (Acts 10:39–43)

Truly, these times of ignorance God overlooked, but now commands all men everywhere to repent, because He has appointed a day on which He will judge the world in righteousness by the Man whom He has ordained. He has given assurance of this to all by raising Him from the dead. (Acts 17:30–31)

But when Paul perceived that one part were Sadducees and the other Pharisees, he cried out in the council, "Men and brethren, I am a Pharisee, the son of a Pharisee; concerning the hope and resurrection of the dead I am being judged!" (Acts 23:6)

I have hope in God, which they themselves also accept, that there will be a resurrection of the dead, both of the just and the unjust. This being so, I myself always strive to have a conscience without offense toward God and men. (Acts 24:15–16)

Or else let those who are here themselves say if they found any wrongdoing in me while I stood before the council, unless it is for this one statement which I cried out, standing among them, "Concerning the resurrection of the dead I am being judged by you this day." (Acts 24:20–21)

For since by man came death, by Man also came the resurrection of the dead. For as in Adam all die, even so in Christ all shall be made alive. But each one in his own order: Christ the firstfruits, afterward those who are Christ's at His coming. Then comes the end, when He delivers the kingdom to God the Father, when He puts an end to all rule and all authority and power. For He must reign till He has put all enemies under His feet. The last enemy that will be destroyed is death. For "He has put all things under His feet." But when He says "all things are put under Him," it is evident that He who put all things under Him is excepted. Now when all things are made subject to Him, then the Son Himself will also be subject to Him who put all things under Him, that God may be all in all. (1 Corinthians 15:21–28)

But the rest of the dead did not live again until the thousand years were finished. This is the first resurrection. Blessed and holy is he who has part in the first resurrection. Over such the second death has no power, but they shall be priests of God and of Christ, and shall reign with Him a thousand years. (Revelation 20:5–6)

Then I saw a great white throne and Him who sat on it, from whose face the earth and the heaven fled away. And there was found no place for them. And I saw the dead, small and great, standing before God, and books were opened. And another book was opened, which is the Book of Life. And the dead were judged according to their works, by the things which were written in the books. The sea gave up the dead who were in it, and Death and Hades delivered up the dead who were in them. And they were judged, each one according to his works. Then Death and Hades were cast into the lake of fire. This is the second death. And anyone not found written in the Book of Life was cast into the lake of fire. (Revelation 20:11–15)

G.   The Resurrection of Jesus displayed what characteristics our renewed, glorified human bodies will have.

So also is the resurrection of the dead. The body is sown in corruption, it is raised in incorruption. It is sown in dishonor, it is raised in glory. It is sown in weakness, it is raised in power. It is sown a natural body, it is raised a spiritual body. There is a natural body, and there is a spiritual body. And so it is written, "The first man Adam became a living being." The last Adam became a life-giving spirit. (1 Corinthians 15:42–45)

Behold what manner of love the Father has bestowed on us, that we should be called children of God! Therefore the world does not know us, because it did not know Him. Beloved, now we are children of God; and it has not yet been revealed what we shall be, but we know that when He is revealed, we shall be like Him, for we shall see Him as He is. And everyone who has this hope in Him purifies himself, just as He is pure. (1 John 3:1–3)

Session Twelve: The Ascension and Session of Christ

I. **THE SESSION**

A. Psalm 110 describes Jesus' session: He sits at the Lord's right hand and waits for the Father to make all His enemies a footstool underneath His feet. Jesus is waiting for the day of His wrath. In Revelation 6, when the sun grows dark, the stars begin to fall from the sky and the earth starts to quake, all the peoples of the earth will hide in caves and say, "Let the mountains fall on us." The Kingdom has come, but it is not yet fully consummated. Until that time, Jesus sits at the right hand of the Father and leads human history. Everything is leading up to the day when He will break in with His power, execute His wrath upon His enemies and release His vengeance. What He is in heaven will be displayed on earth.

B. He said, "I will not drink of this fruit of the vine from now on until that day when I drink it new with you in My Father's kingdom"(Matthew 26:29). Jesus is fasting the Lord's Supper—that communal meal, that meal of intimacy—until the day He returns and drinks of the fruit of the vine in His kingdom with us. He won't enter into the joy alone. He intercedes for us. He brings about things on the earth up to the coming of His return.

1. Right now, at the right hand of the Father, the second Person of the Trinity has a human body. You have a Brother, a Man, who is ruling in heaven at the right hand of the Father. Human history is guaranteed to continue because there is a Man, a human King, sitting at the Father's right hand.

2. *But the true Christian's heart leapeth for joy, even when cast down by divers sorrows and temptations, at the remembrance that Christ is exalted, for in that he finds enough cheer to his own heart...He feels that Jesus Christ, the glorified "Prince of the kings of the earth," is his brother. While he reverences Him as God, he admires Him as the man-Christ, bone of his bone, and flesh of his flesh, and he delights, in his calm and placid moments of communion with Jesus, to say to Him, "O Lord, thou art my brother." His song is, "My beloved is mine, and I am His." It is his joy to sing— "In ties of blood with sinners one," Christ Jesus is; for He is man, even as we are: and He is no less and no more man than we are, save only sin. Surely when we feel we are related to Christ, His exaltation is the source of the greatest joy to our spirits: we take a delight in it, seeing it is one of our family that is exalted. It is the Elder Brother of the great one family of God in heaven and earth; it is the Brother to whom all of us are related.[1]*

C.   The event on Earth: Luke 24:44–52, Acts 1:1–11

Then He said to them, "These are the words which I spoke to you while I was still with you, that all things must be fulfilled which were written in the Law of Moses and the Prophets and the Psalms concerning Me." And He opened their understanding, that they might comprehend the Scriptures. Then He said to them, "Thus it is written, and thus it was necessary for the Christ to suffer and to rise from the dead the third day, and that repentance and remission of sins should be preached in His name to all nations, beginning at Jerusalem. And you are witnesses of these things. Behold, I send the Promise of My Father upon you; but tarry in the city of Jerusalem until you are endued with power from on high." And He led them out as far as Bethany, and He lifted up His hands and blessed them. Now it came to pass, while He blessed them, that He was parted from them and carried up into heaven. And they worshiped Him, and returned to Jerusalem with great joy, and were continually in the temple praising and blessing God. Amen. (Luke 24:44–53)

---

1   Spurgeon, Charles. "The Exaltation of Christ." *The Spurgeon Archive.* 2001. <http://www.spurgeon. org/sermons/0101.htm.>

The former account I made, O Theophilus, of all that Jesus began both to do and teach, until the day in which He was taken up, after He through the Holy Spirit had given commandments to the apostles whom He had chosen, to whom He also presented Himself alive after His suffering by many infallible proofs, being seen by them during forty days and speaking of the things pertaining to the kingdom of God. And being assembled together with them, He commanded them not to depart from Jerusalem, but to wait for the Promise of the Father, "which," He said, "you have heard from Me; for John truly baptized with water, but you shall be baptized with the Holy Spirit not many days from now." Therefore, when they had come together, they asked Him, saying, "Lord, will You at this time restore the kingdom to Israel?" And He said to them, "It is not for you to know times or seasons which the Father has put in His own authority. But you shall receive power when the Holy Spirit has come upon you; and you shall be witnesses to Me in Jerusalem, and in all Judea and Samaria, and to the end of the earth." Now when He had spoken these things, while they watched, He was taken up, and a cloud received Him out of their sight. And while they looked steadfastly toward heaven as He went up, behold, two men stood by them in white apparel, who also said, "Men of Galilee, why do you stand gazing up into heaven? This same Jesus, who was taken up from you into heaven, will so come in like manner as you saw Him go into heaven." (Acts 1:1–11)

D.   The reality in Heaven: Revelation 4–5. Paul declared that believers are seated in heavenly places with Christ Jesus (Ephesians 2:6). We must see the Ascension from the heavenly perspective. In fact, Stephen witnessed Jesus at the Father's right hand when he was being martyred for the gospel (Acts 7:55–56). Looking from Heaven's perspective, we tremble before the majesty of Heaven, as did the apostle John in the Book of Revelation. Revelation 4 and 5 shows us why Jesus can open the seals, as well as why He has the authority to execute all of human history and close out the end of the age.

1.   The four living creatures began to address the reality of God's holiness: "Holy, Holy, Holy is the Lord God Almighty" (Revelation 4:8). They pointed out that He always has been, always will be, and still is holy. He is unlike anything else. None compares to His brilliance, His potency, and His purity. They gave witness to the highness, the perfection, and the consummation of all the attributes of God working together in perfect symmetry. Can you imagine what it is like to have perfect mercy, perfect justice, perfect kindness, perfect soberness and perfect wisdom operating all at once?

2. He is not compromised in one facet of His nature. He is the beautiful God, lovely and perfect. The only word the Bible can use to describe this is "Holy."

    We must not think of God as highest in an ascending order of beings, starting with the single cell and going on up from the fish to the bird to the animal to man to angel to cherub to God. This would be to grant God eminence, even pre-eminence, but that is not enough; we must grant Him transcendence in the fullest meaning of that word. Forever God stands apart, in light unapproachable. He is as high above an archangel as above a caterpillar, for the gulf that separates the archangel from the caterpillar is but finite, while the gulf between God and the archangel is infinite. The caterpillar and the archangel, though far removed from each other in the scale of created things, are nevertheless one in that they are alike created.[2]

    He is totally "other than," beyond our comprehension. He never dissipates; the only thing He feeds Himself on is Himself. He replenishes Himself.

3. John saw the Holy, and now the dilemma was set. How would sinful humanity ever span the gap between themselves and the Holy? Who was going to ensure that the human race could have a relationship with this holy Being? In Revelation 5:2, the strong angel raised the issue: "Who is worthy to open the scroll and loose its seals?" The Greek text highlights the fact that this was a challenge being made to all of creation. Who is worthy? Who can make it past the strong angel, and who can make it through the inapproachable glory of the One who sits on the throne? Who will secure human history? Who is worthy? John wept because no one in all of creation was found worthy. Suddenly, one of the elders charged John not to weep. Weeping was not necessary, for One had been found worthy to open the scrolls and loose it seals. "The Lion of the Tribe of Judah, the Root of David, has prevailed" (Revelation 5:5). John watched as Jesus walked past the angel and through the inapproachable light. Given all authority, Jesus took the scroll from the right hand of the Father.

---

2 Tozer, A.W. *The Knowledge of the Holy* (San Francisco: HarperSanFrancisco, 1961), p. 70.

4. Psalm 72 describes the rule of Jesus in the Millennial Reign. The psalmist begins by saying, "Give the king your judgments, O God." This is precisely what happens in Revelation 5. Jesus was given all authority at the Ascension, and one day the Father will release Him to loose God's judgments upon the earth, ushering in the eternal Kingdom of God on the earth.

II. THE SIGNIFICANCE OF CHRIST'S ASCENSION AND SESSION

A. Presence

1. Christ exists now as the God-Man in the Holy of Holies, and we are there with Him. Jesus sits at the Father's right hand. God in a human frame intercedes to God, asking for us to be filled with the Holy Spirit and matured in righteousness.

   Even when we were dead in trespasses, made us alive together with Christ (by grace you have been saved), and raised us up together, and made us sit together in the heavenly places in Christ Jesus. (Ephesians 2:5–6)

2. He is present in the outpouring of the Holy Spirit

   If you love Me, keep My commandments. And I will pray the Father, and He will give you another Helper, that He may abide with you forever—the Spirit of truth, whom the world cannot receive, because it neither sees Him nor knows Him; but you know Him, for He dwells with you and will be in you. I will not leave you orphans; I will come to you. (John 14:15–18)

Nevertheless I tell you the truth. It is to your advantage that I go away; for if I do not go away, the Helper will not come to you; but if I depart, I will send Him to you. And when He has come, He will convict the world of sin, and of righteousness, and of judgment: of sin, because they do not believe in Me; of righteousness, because I go to My Father and you see Me no more; of judgment, because the ruler of this world is judged. I still have many things to say to you, but you cannot bear them now. However, when He, the Spirit of truth, has come, He will guide you into all truth; for He will not speak on His own authority, but whatever He hears He will speak; and He will tell you things to come. He will glorify Me, for He will take of what is Mine and declare it to you. All things that the Father has are Mine. Therefore I said that He will take of Mine and declare it to you. (John 16:7–15)

Now as the people were in expectation, and all reasoned in their hearts about John, whether he was the Christ or not, John answered, saying to all, "I indeed baptize you with water; but One mightier than I is coming, whose sandal strap I am not worthy to loose. He will baptize you with the Holy Spirit and fire. His winnowing fan is in His hand, and He will thoroughly clean out His threshing floor, and gather the wheat into His barn; but the chaff He will burn with unquenchable fire." (Luke 3:15–17)

Behold, I send the Promise of My Father upon you; but tarry in the city of Jerusalem until you are endued with power from on high. (Luke 24:49)

And being assembled together with them, He commanded them not to depart from Jerusalem, but to wait for the Promise of the Father, "which," He said, "you have heard from Me; for John truly baptized with water, but you shall be baptized with the Holy Spirit not many days from now." Therefore, when they had come together, they asked Him, saying, "Lord, will You at this time restore the kingdom to Israel?" And He said to them, "It is not for you to know times or seasons which the Father has put in His own authority. But you shall receive power when the Holy Spirit has come upon you; and you shall be witnesses to Me in Jerusalem, and in all Judea and Samaria, and to the end of the earth." (Acts 1:4–8)

Therefore being exalted to the right hand of God, and having received from the Father the promise of the Holy Spirit, He poured out this which you now see and hear. (Acts 2: 33)

He who descended is also the One who ascended far above all the heavens, that He might fill all things. (Ephesians 4:10)

3. As a man, Jesus can only be in one place, so by the outpouring of the Holy Spirit His ministry continues in the saints. You have power and virtue in your inner man. This is bridal partnership. It's what Jesus purchased. The Spirit is the seal. It's the first fruits, a Promise who is the guarantee of our inheritance until the redemption at the end of the age. Jesus is now in all places in the hearts of the believers by the Holy Spirit.

    In Him you also trusted, after you heard the word of truth, the gospel of your salvation; in whom also, having believed, you were sealed with the Holy Spirit of promise, who is the guarantee of our inheritance until the redemption of the purchased possession, to the praise of His glory. (Ephesians 1:13–14)

B. Power: Jesus now sits at the right hand of the Almighty. The right hand of God is synonymous with the full extent of God's power and authority. As the risen Lord and ascended King, Christ has full access to and command of all of Heaven's resources.

    1. As the God-Man, He will rule with all power. He will complete the plan of redemption in human history. At the right hand of the Father, Jesus has all power over all things—demonic forces, sicknesses, weather patterns, etc. Because we are seated with Christ, we rule with Him from that vantage point, commanding demons to go, sickness to leave, bodies to be made whole, and doors to open for the Gospel.

God, who at various times and in various ways spoke in time past to the fathers by the prophets, has in these last days spoken to us by His Son, whom He has appointed heir of all things, through whom also He made the worlds; who being the brightness of His glory and the express image of His person, and upholding all things by the word of His power, when He had by Himself purged our sins, sat down at the right hand of the Majesty on high, having become so much better than the angels, as He has by inheritance obtained a more excellent name than they. (Hebrews 1:1–4)

The LORD said to my Lord, "Sit at My right hand, till I make Your enemies Your footstool." The LORD shall send the rod of Your strength out of Zion. Rule in the midst of Your enemies! Your people shall be volunteers in the day of Your power; in the beauties of holiness, from the womb of the morning, You have the dew of Your youth. The LORD has sworn and will not relent, "You are a priest forever according to the order of Melchizedek." The Lord is at Your right hand; He shall execute kings in the day of His wrath. He shall judge among the nations, He shall fill the places with dead bodies, He shall execute the heads of many countries. He shall drink of the brook by the wayside; therefore He shall lift up the head. (Psalm 110:1–7)

2. Paul prayed for the believers to have the eyes of their understanding enlightened so that they might know the exceeding greatness of His power towards us who believe. We must understand the revelation that Christ is above all things, and we are with Him.

> *[I] do not cease to give thanks for you, making mention of you in my prayers: that the God of our Lord Jesus Christ, the Father of glory, may give to you the spirit of wisdom and revelation in the knowledge of Him, the eyes of your understanding being enlightened; that you may know what is the hope of His calling, what are the riches of the glory of His inheritance in the saints, and what is the exceeding greatness of His power toward us who believe,* according to the working of His mighty power which He worked in Christ when He raised Him from the dead and seated Him at His right hand in the heavenly places, far above all principality and power and might and dominion, and every name that is named, not only in this age but also in that which is to come. And He put all things under His feet, and gave Him to be head over all things to the church, which is His body, the fullness of Him who fills all in all. (Ephesians 1:16–23, emphasis added)

C.   Intercession: this is Jesus' eternal glory, to ask His Father for things forever.

   1.   Jesus will forever rule through intercession. His blood is interceding for your atonement, and His prayers are interceding for your completion. He is constantly asking the Father to give Him the nations as His inheritance (Psalm 2:8). He ever lives to make intercession before His Father (Hebrews 7:25). Even the God-Man has to ask the Father for the kingdom. It's a reflection of the way He made human beings.

   2.   We are the only creatures in Heaven and Earth who get to ask God for things. This is a dignity far beyond anything that we can imagine. What other creature gets to approach the eternal King of Glory and ask for things? To ask is an honor far beyond our fathoming. We ask, God hears, and angels are dispatched with divine decrees. How unthinkable. Weak human beings lift their voices, and the God of Heaven hears and releases His governmental decrees to change planet Earth.

   3.   Intercession is rooted in our design. God designed us in His image and gave us the governmental delight of asking Him for things. God has forever connected government and intimacy; our dominion is forever linked with our dependency upon intimacy and asking. Governmental decisions are never outside the context of intimacy, love, and fascination. God loves to be asked, He

loves to hear, and He loves to thrill us with the answers. This is life—to forever lean upon our Bridegroom God and ask Him for decisions on the earth. Intercession is at the foundation of what it means to be human and made in the image of the living God. Government in God's kingdom is never about simply making decisions with a given set of facts. It is always indelibly marked with leaning on, communing with, and asking for things from the King. Government is more than enforcing divine order. It is filled with intimacy, light, and love. It is the fascinated interplay of human asking and divine answering unto worship, wonder, and whispers of love.

Therefore He is also able to save to the uttermost those who come to God through Him, since He always lives to make intercession for them. (Hebrews 7:25)

Ask of Me, and I will give You the nations for Your inheritance, and the ends of the earth for Your possession. (Psalm 2:8)

III. THE GROUND OF POWERFUL PREACHING IN THE EARLY CHURCH

A. The Resurrection and Ascension of Christ do not only form an intricate part of the preaching of the Gospel; they give great boldness in the actual proclamation of the Gospel.

1. *So then, after the Lord had spoken to them, He was received up into heaven, and sat down at the right hand of God. And they went out and preached everywhere, the Lord working with them and confirming the word through the accompanying signs. Amen.(Mark 16:19–20)*

2. Acts 2:32: Peter, the denier, became emblazoned with boldness after the Resurrection.

    This Jesus God has raised up, of which we are all witnesses. Therefore being exalted to the right hand of God, and having received from the Father the promise of the Holy Spirit, He poured out this which you now see and hear. (Acts 2:32–33)

3. Acts 4:23–33: both the Resurrection of Jesus and His resurrection power in their midst gave great boldness to the apostles.

4.   Acts 5:29–32: boldness before the Sanhedrin.

> *And when they had brought them, they set them before the council. And the high priest asked them, saying, "Did we not strictly command you not to teach in this name? And look, you have filled Jerusalem with your doctrine, and intend to bring this Man's blood on us!" But Peter and the other apostles answered and said: "We ought to obey God rather than men. The God of our fathers raised up Jesus whom you murdered by hanging on a tree. Him God has exalted to His right hand to be Prince and Savior, to give repentance to Israel and forgiveness of sins. And we are His witnesses to these things, and so also is the Holy Spirit whom God has given to those who obey Him." (Acts 5:27–32)*

5.   *When they heard these things they were cut to the heart, and they gnashed at him with their teeth. But he, being full of the Holy Spirit, gazed into heaven and saw the glory of God, and Jesus standing at the right hand of God, and said, "Look! I see the heavens opened and the Son of Man standing at the right hand of God!" Then they cried out with a loud voice, stopped their ears, and ran at him with one accord; and they cast him out of the city and stoned him. And the witnesses laid down their clothes at the feet of a young man named Saul. And they stoned Stephen as he was calling on God and saying, "Lord Jesus, receive my spirit." Then he knelt down and cried out with a loud voice, "Lord, do not charge them with this sin." And when he had said this, he fell asleep. (Acts 7:54–60)*

6.   Acts 9:1–22: Paul meets the resurrected and ascended Lord.

    a.   Acts 22

    b.   Acts 23

    c.   Acts 24

    d.   Acts 26

B.   Psalms 2 and 110 are the backdrop to the early Church's understanding of its nature and mission. By the Resurrection and Ascension, God has set His King on His holy hill. He will sit, enthroned in power, until all His enemies will be put underneath His feet.

C.   When you get an understanding of the Ascension and Session of Jesus, you have three things: presence, power and prayer. You have the Holy Spirit in you to destroy the works of darkness. You pray from a higher ground. You don't have to ask God as if to convince Him. When you pray, you are seated with Him, praying His will into the earth. You're functioning in government as you're seated at the right hand of God in heavenly places.

D.   The Ascension changes everything. Now everything as a believer counts for good, even your suffering. He will answer your prayers. If you want to break the power of sin and boredom in the Church of this age and of this land, proclaim the knowledge of God.

Session Thirteen: The Return of the King

I. **OUR BLESSED HOPE**

   A. In Matthew 9:14, Jesus spoke of a time when He would no longer be with the disciples, and in that time they would fast out of longing to be with Him. Jesus' great leadership development strategy consisted of raising up leaders who were pierced, struck, fascinated and overcome by the strength and power of His personhood. After He seized their hearts in the first three years, they would labor for the Kingdom in a sacrificial way. They would long for Jesus. They would give all to work for His return. Thus, the apostles spoke with great affection of the Second Coming of their Savior and King. They longed for His appearing. Their sacrificial labor, diligence, and mission were born out of a deep desire to see the return of their Master and Friend.

   B. Peter appealed to Jerusalem to repent. If they repented, the times of refreshing would come, and God would send Jesus back (Acts 3:19–20). We were made for the presence of Jesus, specifically designed for intimate communion with the God-Man; when He's not here, we feel it. Jesus' leadership development strategy was to addict them to His presence so that they would do anything to get Him back.

   Repent therefore and be converted, that your sins may be blotted out, so that times of refreshing may come from the presence of the Lord, and that He may send Jesus Christ, who was preached to you before, whom heaven must receive until the times of restoration of all things, which God has spoken by the mouth of all His holy prophets since the world began. For Moses truly said to the fathers, "The LORD your God will raise up for you a Prophet like me from your brethren. Him you shall hear in all things, whatever He says to you." (Acts 3:19–22)

Blessed be the God and Father of our Lord Jesus Christ, who according to His abundant mercy has begotten us again to a living hope through the resurrection of Jesus Christ from the dead, to an inheritance incorruptible and undefiled and that does not fade away, reserved in heaven for you, who are kept by the power of God through faith for salvation ready to be revealed in the last time. In this you greatly rejoice, though now for a little while, if need be, you have been grieved by various trials, that the genuineness of your faith, being much more precious than gold that perishes, though it is tested by fire, may be found to praise, honor, and glory at the revelation of Jesus Christ, whom having not seen you love. Though now you do not see Him, yet believing, you rejoice with joy inexpressible and full of glory, receiving the end of your faith—the salvation of your souls. (1 Peter 1:3–9)

C.   Paul called the second coming of the Lord Jesus the Church's blessed hope.

For the grace of God that brings salvation has appeared to all men, teaching us that, denying ungodliness and worldly lusts, we should live soberly, righteously, and godly in the present age, looking for the blessed hope and glorious appearing of our great God and Savior Jesus Christ, who gave Himself for us, that He might redeem us from every lawless deed and purify for Himself His own special people, zealous for good works. (Titus 2:11–14)

To them God willed to make known what are the riches of the glory of this mystery among the Gentiles: which is Christ in you, the hope of glory. Him we preach, warning every man and teaching every man in all wisdom, that we may present every man perfect in Christ Jesus. (Colossians 1:27–28)

Paul, a bondservant of God and an apostle of Jesus Christ, according to the faith of God's elect and the acknowledgment of the truth which accords with godliness, in hope of eternal life which God, who cannot lie, promised before time began, but has in due time manifested His word through preaching, which was committed to me according to the commandment of God our Savior. (Titus 1:1–3)

For we through the Spirit eagerly wait for the hope of righteousness by faith. (Galatians 5:5)

D.   Paul, at the close of his life, promised the crown of righteousness to all who longed for and loved the Lord's appearing.

Finally, there is laid up for me the crown of righteousness, which the Lord, the righteous Judge, will give to me on that Day, and not to me only but also to all who have loved His appearing. (2 Timothy 4:8)

E.   Wayne Grudem states, "To some extent, then, the degree to which we actually long for Christ's return is a measure of the spiritual condition of our own lives at the moment."[1] Many times when I was growing up, I hoped Jesus would not come back before certain things would happen: receiving my driver's license, getting married, or having children. The return of Jesus was merely a doctrine. It was not personal for me. The second coming of Jesus was highly personal for the disciples and soon will be for the church worldwide. Revelation 22:17 speaks of a time when the Spirit and the Bride will be in complete unity in their desire for Jesus to return and rule on the earth. At the end of the age, the heart cry of believers will be one of longing for their King and their God. God will release revelation about His Son that will produce the highest expressions of longing and love from the Church. John closed Revelation with this divine dialogue. Jesus gives the revelation of His coming; John receives the revelation and responds back with the cry of yearning, the heart given to love: "Come, Jesus! I miss you!"

He who testifies to these things says, "Surely I am coming quickly." Amen. Even so, come, Lord Jesus!" (Revelation 22:20)

II.   WHY PEOPLE DRAW BACK FROM THE STUDY OF THE END TIMES

A.   "I cannot understand anyway because no one really understands it."

   1.   **A common lie**: There's not much biblical information on the subject.

   2.   **A common fear**: The fear of facing the mountain of evidence and the multitude of opinions.

B.   The fear of man is seeking to be politically correct. End-time prophecy is not politically correct. A man-pleasing spirit does not go along with the study of end-time prophecy.

   A common accusation: People who study the End Times get weird.

---

1   Grudem, Wayne. Systematic Theology (Grand Rapids, MI: Zondervan, 1994), p. 1093.

C.   Wrong ideas about how it will minimize the work of the kingdom.

A common misconception: Study of the End Times will divert the Church's attention from the primary call of the Church to fulfill the Great Commission.

D.   "Jesus discourages us from seeking to understand the details. In fact, He tells us that we cannot know the day or hour and should not seek to know the times and the seasons set by the Father."

A common deception: Jesus told us not to be overly concerned and caught up with the End Times.

E.   The enemy's mocking strategy is to keep us from peering into those things which are freely given to us by the Holy Spirit for the building up of the Church. In fact, most of the Church today has unknowingly given in to that strategy. You hear common phraseology that excuses their need to be biblically informed. One example is when people state that they are neither pre-millennial or post-millennial. They are simply pan-millennial—they believe everything will "pan" out in the end. I must admit that this is quite the cute saying, yet it is very harmful. The real question is not if everything will pan out in the end. Of course it will! God is sovereign. He sits in the heavens and does whatever He pleases. He is the Lord who executes all of human history according to His will and the greatness of His power. The true question is, "Will it pan out well for you? Your family? Your community?" Will you be prepared? Will you recognize the hour in which you live, or will you be like the five unwise virgins who did not have enough oil in their lamps when the Bridegroom came?

Beloved, I now write to you this second epistle (in both of which I stir up your pure minds by way of reminder), that you may be mindful of the words which were spoken before by the holy prophets, and of the commandment of us, the apostles of the Lord and Savior, knowing this first: **that scoffers will come in the last days, walking according to their own lusts, and saying, "Where is the promise of His coming? For since the fathers fell asleep, all things continue as they were from the beginning of creation." For this they willfully forget: that by the word of God the heavens were of old, and the earth standing out of water and in the water.** *(2 Peter 3:1–5, emphasis added)*

III.   **THE NATURE OF HIS RETURN**

Now when He had spoken these things, while they watched, He was taken up, and a cloud received Him out of their sight. And while they looked steadfastly toward heaven as He went up, behold, two men stood by them in white apparel, who also said, "Men of Galilee, why do you stand gazing up into heaven? This same Jesus, who was taken up from you into heaven, will so come in like manner as you saw Him go into heaven." Then they returned to Jerusalem from the mount called Olivet, which is near Jerusalem, a Sabbath day's journey. (Acts 1:9–12, emphasis added)

A.   Luke testifies in Acts 1:9–11 that Jesus ascended into heaven, and that two men in white apparel (angels) referred to Him as "this same Jesus." The messengers confirm that it is Jesus, the man from Nazareth, who is coming again. This detail is very important. The bodiless Second Person of the Trinity is not coming back into our hearts at His Second Coming. The God-Man is returning in a glorified human body to physically rule on the earth.

B.   Secondly, Jesus is coming back to the same place. Jesus gave his famous discourse from the Mount of Olives and ascended from that very mountain. Zechariah 14:4 states that He will come back to Jerusalem and will come to the Mount of Olives at some point in His return. Jesus is going to rule from Jerusalem, the city of the Great King.

*Then the LORD will go forth and fight against those nations, as He fights in the day of battle. **And in that day His feet will stand on the Mount of Olives**, which faces Jerusalem on the east. And the Mount of Olives shall be split in two, from east to west, making a very large valley; half of the mountain shall move toward the north and half of it toward the south. (Zechariah 14:3–4)*

C.   There will be some differences between the Ascension and the Second Coming. He will come with great power when He comes again. The sky will grow dark, the stars will fall, and the heavens will shake. Then we will hear three piercing sounds. Jesus will shout, the voice of the Archangel will ring out, and the trumpet shall sound. The sky will roll back like a scroll as Jesus appears in the sky, coming with great power and with the clouds of Heaven. He will be accompanied by all the angels and met by the saints in the air. Every eye will see Him, and He will destroy the forces of darkness by the brightness of His appearing.

Immediately after the tribulation of those days the sun will be darkened, and the moon will not give its light; the stars will fall from heaven, and the powers of the heavens will be shaken. 30 Then the sign of the Son of Man will appear in heaven, and then all the tribes of the earth will mourn, and they will see the Son of Man coming on the clouds of heaven with power and great glory. And He will send His angels with a great sound of a trumpet, and they will gather together His elect from the four winds, from one end of heaven to the other. (Matthew 24:29–31)

For as the lightning that flashes out of one part under heaven shines to the other part under heaven, so also the Son of Man will be in His day. But first He must suffer many things and be rejected by this generation. And as it was in the days of Noah, so it will be also in the days of the Son of Man. (Luke 17:24–26)

For this we say to you by the word of the Lord, that we who are alive and remain until the coming of the Lord will by no means precede those who are asleep. For the Lord Himself will descend from heaven with a shout, with the voice of an archangel, and with the trumpet of God. And the dead in Christ will rise first. Then we who are alive and remain shall be caught up together with them in the clouds to meet the Lord in the air. And thus we shall always be with the Lord. Therefore comfort one another with these words. (1 Thessalonians 4:15–18)

And then the lawless one will be revealed, whom the Lord will consume with the breath of His mouth and destroy with the brightness of His coming. The coming of the lawless one is according to the working of Satan, with all power, signs, and lying wonders. (2 Thessalonians 2:8–9)

Behold, He is coming with clouds, and every eye will see Him, even they who pierced Him. And all the tribes of the earth will mourn because of Him. Even so, Amen. (Revelation 1:7)

Now I saw heaven opened, and behold, a white horse. And He who sat on him was called Faithful and True, and in righteousness He judges and makes war. His eyes were like a flame of fire, and on His head were many crowns. He had a name written that no one knew except Himself. He was clothed with a robe dipped in blood, and His name is called The Word of God. And the armies in heaven, clothed in fine linen, white and clean, followed Him on white horses. Now out of His mouth goes a sharp sword, that with it He should strike the nations. And He Himself will rule them with a rod of iron. He Himself treads the winepress of the fierceness and wrath of Almighty God. And He has on His robe and on His thigh a name written: KING OF KINGS AND LORD OF LORDS. Then I saw an angel standing in the sun; and he cried with a loud voice, saying to all the birds that fly in the midst of heaven, "Come and gather together for the supper of the great God, that you may eat the flesh of kings, the flesh of captains, the flesh of mighty men, the flesh of horses and of those who sit on them, and the flesh of all people, free and slave, both small and great." And I saw the beast, the kings of the earth, and their armies, gathered together to make war against Him who sat on the horse and against His army. Then the beast was captured, and with him the false prophet who worked signs in his presence, by which he deceived those who received the mark of the beast and those who worshiped his image. These two were cast alive into the lake of fire burning with brimstone. And the rest were killed with the sword which proceeded from the mouth of Him who sat on the horse. And all the birds were filled with their flesh. (Revelation 19:11–21)

IV. WHEN IS JESUS RETURNING?

A. Can we know the time? The Scriptures set up a wondrous tension.

1. Many passages seem to indicate that the hour of His coming cannot be known and that He could come suddenly at any time, like a thief in the night or as in the days of Noah. Jesus told His disciples that only the Father knows the hour of His coming (Matthew 24:36). He also exhorted them to watch and pray, for they did not know the hour of His coming. He told them at the Ascension that it was not for them "to know the times or seasons which the Father has put in His own authority" (Acts 1:7).

Watch therefore, for you do not know what hour your Lord is coming. But know this, that if the master of the house had known what hour the thief would come, he would have watched and not allowed his house to be broken into. Therefore you also be ready, for the Son of Man is coming at an hour you do not expect. (Matthew 24:42–44)

Watch therefore, for you know neither the day nor the hour in which the Son of Man is coming. (Matthew 25:13)

But of that day and hour no one knows, not even the angels in heaven, nor the Son, but only the Father. Take heed, watch and pray; for you do not know when the time is. It is like a man going to a far country, who left his house and gave authority to his servants, and to each his work, and commanded the doorkeeper to watch. Watch therefore, for you do not know when the master of the house is coming—in the evening, at midnight, at the crowing of the rooster, or in the morning— lest, coming suddenly, he find you sleeping. And what I say to you, I say to all: Watch! (Mark 13:32–37)

For you yourselves know perfectly that the day of the Lord so comes as a thief in the night. For when they say, "Peace and safety!" then sudden destruction comes upon them, as labor pains upon a pregnant woman. And they shall not escape. (1 Thessalonians 5:2–3)

2. On the other hand, Jesus told us many signs of His coming. He stated that He told us these things beforehand, so that when they begin to happen, we can know that our redemption draws near. Paul told the Thessalonians that they were to be prepared, not caught off guard like those who practice darkness. Also, both Jesus and Paul gave clear conditions that must take place before Jesus' return so that the Church would be able to identify the season.

But take heed; see, I have told you all things beforehand. (Mark 13:23)

See, I have told you beforehand. (Matthew 24:25)

But concerning the times and the seasons, brethren, you have no need that I should write to you. For you yourselves know perfectly that the day of the Lord so comes as a thief in the night. For when they say, "Peace and safety!" then sudden destruction comes upon them, as labor pains upon a pregnant woman. And they shall not escape. But you, brethren, are not in darkness, so that this Day should overtake you as a thief. You are all sons of light and sons of the day. We are not of the night nor of darkness. (1 Thessalonians 5:1–5)

Now when these things begin to happen, look up and lift up your heads, because your redemption draws near. (Luke 21:28)

Now, brethren, concerning the coming of our Lord Jesus Christ and our gathering together to Him, we ask you, not to be soon shaken in mind or troubled, either by spirit or by word or by letter, as if from us, as though the day of Christ had come. Let no one deceive you by any means; for that Day will not come unless the falling away comes first, and the man of sin is revealed, the son of perdition, who opposes and exalts himself above all that is called God or that is worshiped, so that he sits as God in the temple of God, showing himself that he is God. Do you not remember that when I was still with you I told you these things? And now you know what is restraining, that he may be revealed in his own time. For the mystery of lawlessness is already at work; only He who now restrains will do so until He is taken out of the way. (2 Thessalonians 2:1–7)

B. Possible solutions

1. One such solution is proposed by those who hold to a pre-Tribulation rapture view. In this position, there are two distinct comings of Jesus in the Second Coming. The first is for believers and can happen at any moment. The believers will meet the Lord in the air and be taken to heaven. Next, a seven-year period of tribulation will take place on the earth. The conditions and signs Jesus spoke of will take place in these seven years, leading to the destruction of the Antichrist and his forces, as well as to the salvation of Israel. The period will culminate with Christ's return to rule in the Millennial Kingdom.

2. Another solution is to take the passages of His imminent return as an admonition for unbelievers. The passages pertaining to signs and conditions for His Coming are supposed to strengthen believers for persecution and prevent them from falling into deception.

3. The passages about His imminent return address something in the human frame that needs the urgency of the hour in order to passionately walk in obedience and holiness. Humans are designed for passion. Urgency empowers and impassions people to live wholeheartedly. In addition, there is great comfort in knowing what is coming. **Knowing our frame, God created the heart to live from the place of urgency without torment. The urgency gives us moral courage and focus, and the signs give us comfort that God is in control and is directing all things.**

V. CAN WE KNOW WHEN THE END TIMES OCCUR?

A. Many people use Jesus' statement in Matthew 24:36 to make the claim that believers cannot know the day or the hour of the end. They use this verse to justify their lack of study of the End Times and their unfamiliarity with biblical prophecy.

But of that day and hour no one knows, not even the angels of heaven, but My Father only. But as the days of Noah were, so also will the coming of the Son of Man be. For as in the days before the flood, they were eating and drinking, marrying and giving in marriage, until the day that Noah entered the ark, and did not know until the flood came and took them all away, so also will the coming of the Son of Man be. Then two men will be in the field: one will be taken and the other left. Two women will be grinding at the mill: one will be taken and the other left. Watch therefore, for you do not know what hour your Lord is coming. But know this, that if the master of the house had known what hour the thief would come, he would have watched and not allowed his house to be broken into. Therefore you also be ready, for the Son of Man is coming at an hour you do not expect. (Matthew 24:36–44)

B. When one looks closely at this verse, a few important points must be made.

1. The verse simply states that no one knows the day and the hour but the Father. It does not say that we cannot and will not know the day and the hour in the future, or that we will not know the season or the conditions surrounding the Second Coming. In fact, in the preceding verses, Jesus explained the conditions with profound clarity and detail. Jesus said in Luke's account of the Olivet Discourse, "Now when these things begin to happen, look up and lift up your heads, because your redemption draws near" (Luke 21:28).

2. Jesus compared the time frame of the Second Coming to the days of Noah. In the days of Noah, the people of God knew what was coming. God had prophesied since the days of Enoch of the coming judgment of God. Noah knew 120 years before the Flood (Genesis 6:3), when God told him to build the Ark. In Genesis 7:4, God warned Noah again that He was sending the flood in seven days. The remnant knew the plans of God in detail: that in seven days, the rains would come for forty days and forty nights. In fact, Hebrews 11:5 and 2 Peter 2:5 tell us that Noah preached to his generation concerning what was coming, condemning them in their refusal to receive the witness.

    By faith Noah, being divinely warned of things not yet seen, moved with godly fear, prepared an ark for the saving of his household, by which he condemned the world and became heir of the righteousness which is according to faith. (Hebrews 11:7)

    *For if God did not spare the angels who sinned, but cast them down to hell and delivered them into chains of darkness, to be reserved for judgment; and did not spare the ancient world, but saved Noah, one of eight people, **a preacher of righteousness**, bringing in the flood on the world of the ungodly. (2 Peter 2:4–5, emphasis added)*

3. The Scriptures clearly tell us that Noah knew, and that the unrepentant choose not to heed the warnings which Noah very clearly presented to them. So it will be in the End Times. Matthew 24:36 tells us that only the Father knows the day and the hour. It does not state that believers will not know the season, nor does it state that the Father will not reveal the specifics to the end-time Church. The nature of prophecy in the Bible teaches us clearly that God reveals specific warnings concerning His coming judgments in order to prepare His people and bring salvation to

the multitude of unbelievers. **Every major biblical calamity was prophesied with detailed accuracy to the generation it affected**.

Surely the Lord God does nothing, unless He reveals His secret to His servants the prophets. A lion has roared! Who will not fear? The Lord God has spoken! Who can but prophesy? (Amos 3:7–8, emphasis added)

a.   The Flood

*And the LORD said, "My Spirit shall not strive with man forever, for he is indeed flesh; yet his days shall be **one hundred and twenty years**." (Genesis 6:3, emphasis added)*

And God said to Noah, "The end of all flesh has come before Me, for the earth is filled with violence through them; and behold, I will destroy them with the earth. (Genesis 6:13)

*For **after seven more days** I will cause it to rain on the earth forty days and forty nights, and I will destroy from the face of the earth all living things that I have made. (Genesis 7:4, emphasis added)*

b.   Sojourn in Egypt

*Then He said to Abram: "Know certainly that your descendants will be strangers in a land that is not theirs, and will serve them, and **they will afflict them four hundred years**. And also the nation whom they serve I will judge; afterward they shall come out with great possessions. Now as for you, you shall go to your fathers in peace; you shall be buried at a good old age. But in the fourth generation they shall return here, for the iniquity of the Amorites is not yet complete." (Genesis 15:13–16, emphasis added)*

*Now the sojourn of the children of Israel who lived in Egypt was **four hundred and thirty years**. And it came to pass at the end of the **four hundred and thirty years—on that very same day**—it came to pass that all the armies of the LORD went out from the land of Egypt. (Exodus 12:40–41, emphasis added)*

c. The destruction of Nineveh

Arise, go to Nineveh, that great city, and cry out against it; for their wickedness has come up before Me. (Jonah 1:2)

*And Jonah began to enter the city on the first day's walk. Then he cried out and said, "**Yet forty days, and Nineveh shall be overthrown!**" (Jonah 3:4, emphasis added)*

*But the LORD said, "You have had pity on the plant for which you have not labored, nor made it grow, which came up in a night and perished in a night. **And should I not pity Nineveh, that great city, in which are more than one hundred and twenty thousand persons who cannot discern between their right hand and their left—and much livestock?**" (Jonah 4:10–11, emphasis added)*

d. The fall of Northern Israel

*And say to him: "Take heed, and be quiet; do not fear or be fainthearted for these two stubs of smoking firebrands, for the fierce anger of Rezin and Syria, and the son of Remaliah. Because Syria, Ephraim, and the son of Remaliah have plotted evil against you, saying, "Let us go up against Judah and trouble it, and let us make a gap in its wall for ourselves, and set a king over them, the son of Tabel"—thus says the Lord GOD: "It shall not stand, nor shall it come to pass. For the head of Syria is Damascus, and the head of Damascus is Rezin. **Within sixty-five years Ephraim will be broken, so that it will not be a people.** (Isaiah 7:4–8, emphasis added)*

*Therefore the Lord Himself will give you a sign: Behold, the virgin shall conceive and bear a Son, and shall call His name Immanuel. Curds and honey He shall eat, that He may know to refuse the evil and choose the good. For **before the Child shall know to refuse the evil and choose the good, the land that you dread will be forsaken by both her kings.** The LORD will bring the king of Assyria upon you and your people and your father's house—days that have not come since the day that Ephraim departed from Judah." (Isaiah 7:14–17, emphasis added)*

e. The fall of Judah and the exile to Babylon

*From the thirteenth year of Josiah the son of Amon, king of Judah, even to this day, this is the twenty-third year in which the word of the LORD has come to me; and I have spoken to you, rising early and speaking, but you have not listened. And the LORD has sent to you all His servants the prophets, rising early and sending them, but you have not listened nor inclined your ear to hear … And this whole land shall be a desolation and an astonishment, and these nations **shall serve the king of Babylon seventy years. "Then it will come to pass, when seventy years are completed, that I will punish the king of Babylon** and that nation, the land of the Chaldeans, for their iniquity," says the LORD; "and I will make it a perpetual desolation. (Jeremiah 25:3–4, 11–12, emphasis added)*

f. The first advent: Gabriel, Anna, Simeon, John the Baptist

g. World-wide famine of Acts 11:27–28

And in these days prophets came from Jerusalem to Antioch. Then one of them, named Agabus, stood up and showed by the Spirit that there was going to be a great famine throughout all the world, which also happened in the days of Claudius Caesar. (Acts 11:27–28)

h. Destruction of Jerusalem

i. The Antichrist and the Great Tribulation

j. The Second Coming: How much more will God warn the billions of people who will be in danger of eternal damnation at His Second Coming?

4. Also, Jesus was using this illustration to combat lethargy and slowness in understanding the signs of the times. **People use this verse to empower the very thing which Jesus is speaking against.** Jesus uses lack of knowledge in order to produce a watchful spirit, an active posture in discerning the season. In other words, He does not want us to be like the unbelieving in the days of Noah. He is saying, "Know this: I am coming, and you should be watchful like Noah." Jesus demanded that the disciples be ready.

5. The context of these verses exhorts us to be watchful and to know the season, to be familiar with the conditions surrounding Jesus' coming. In fact, in the parable of the wise and faithful servant, Jesus said that it is the wise servant who gives the household food in due season. He then equated those who think He is delaying and do not give them food in due season to the evil servant who beats the other servants of the household.

    Now learn this parable from the fig tree: When its branch has already become tender and puts forth leaves, you know that summer is near. So you also, when you see all these things, know that it is near—at the doors! Assuredly, I say to you, this generation will by no means pass away till all these things take place. Heaven and earth will pass away, but My words will by no means pass away. (Matthew 24:32–35)

    "Who then is a faithful and wise servant, whom his master made ruler over his household, to give them food in due season? *Blessed is that servant whom his master, when he comes, will find so doing. Assuredly, I say to you that he will make him ruler over all his goods.* ***But if that evil servant says in his heart, 'My master is delaying his coming,'*** *and begins to beat his fellow servants, and to eat and drink with the drunkards, the master of that servant will come on a day when he is not looking for him and at an hour that he is not aware of, and will cut him in two and appoint him his portion with the hypocrites. There shall be weeping and gnashing of teeth. (Matthew 24:45–51, emphasis added)*

VI.   SHOULD WE KNOW WHEN THE END TIME IS?

A.   After using Matthew 24:36 to conclude that knowing when Jesus is returning is impossible, people use Acts 1:7 to decide that we should not be concerned with knowing the season. Again, this attitude is reflected in the statement, "I am neither pre-mil nor post-mil. I am pan-mil. It will all pan out in the end." Yes, it will all pan out in the end. **But remember, that is not the real question. The real question is, "Will it pan out well for you?"** Will you be prepared, and will you have prepared others?

And He said to them, "It is not for you to know times or seasons which the Father has put in His own authority. But you shall receive power when the Holy Spirit has come upon you; and you shall be witnesses to Me in Jerusalem, and in all Judea and Samaria, and to the end of the earth." (Acts 1:7–8)

B.   Again, several important points must be made from this passage in Acts.

1.   Jesus was not saying that the last generation should not know the season or the times. He simply stated that it was not for the apostles to know these times and seasons appointed by the Father. Jesus had already taught them of the Kingdom of God for forty days after the Resurrection. They knew its details and conditions. That was why they asked if the kingdom would be restored to Israel at this time.

2.   This was a smart question. It was not misplaced nationalism. Jesus had clearly taught them concerning the salvation of the nation of Israel. However, Jesus knew that before this can happen, the Gospel must go forth to the nations. Jesus refocused them from thinking about national glory to thinking about the task of being a witness. He reminded them of their apostolic function/mandate. They were to receive power from on high in order to take the Gospel to Jerusalem, Judea, Samaria, and to the end of the earth. Their question was, "Jesus, are you going to restore the kingdom to Israel before the Gospel is taken to the nations?"

3.   Jesus reoriented them and told them not to be concerned with this, but to focus on the great task at hand in the promulgation of the Gospel. We know they struggled with this, for God had to raise up Phillip and allow persecution in order to cause the apostles to take the Gospel beyond Jerusalem. And in Acts 10, Peter had to have a vision in order to witness to Gentiles.

C.   We are told clearly in Scripture that we should be aware of the season and the time. Jesus wept over Jerusalem because she did not recognize the hour of her visitation. He taught that the people of God would come under judgment for not knowing the time of visitation.

Now as He drew near, He saw the city and wept over it, saying, "If you had known, even you, especially in this your day, the things that make for your peace! But now they are hidden from your eyes. For days will come upon you when your enemies will build an embankment around you, surround you and close you in on every side, and level you, and your children within you, to the ground; and they will not leave in you one stone upon another, **because you did not know the time of your visitation.***" (Luke 19:41–44)*

O Jerusalem, Jerusalem, the one who kills the prophets and stones those who are sent to her! How often I wanted to gather your children together, as a hen gathers her chicks under her wings, **but you were not willing!** *(Matthew 23:35–37)*

1.   The Olivet discourse

2.   *Then He also said to the multitudes, "Whenever you see a cloud rising out of the west, immediately you say, 'A shower is coming'; and so it is. And when you see the south wind blow, you say, 'There will be hot weather'; and there is. Hypocrites! You can discern the face of the sky and of the earth, but how is it you do not discern this time?" (Luke 12:54–56)*

3. *Of this salvation the prophets have inquired and searched carefully, who prophesied of the grace that would come to you, searching what, or what manner of time, the Spirit of Christ who was in them was indicating when He testified beforehand the sufferings of Christ and the glories that would follow. To them it was revealed that, not to themselves, but to us they were ministering the things which now have been reported to you through those who have preached the gospel to you by the Holy Spirit sent from heaven—things which angels desire to look into. (1 Peter 1:10–12)*

4. *But concerning the times and the seasons, brethren, you have no need that I should write to you. For you yourselves know perfectly that the day of the Lord so comes as a thief in the night. For when they say, "Peace and safety!" then sudden destruction comes upon them, as labor pains upon a pregnant woman. And they shall not escape. But you, brethren, are not in darkness, so that this Day should overtake you as a thief. You are all sons of light and sons of the day. We are not of the night nor of darkness. Therefore let us not sleep, as others do, but let us watch and be sober. For those who sleep, sleep at night, and those who get drunk are drunk at night. But let us who are of the day be sober, putting on the breastplate of faith and love, and as a helmet the hope of salvation. For God did not appoint us to wrath, but to obtain salvation through our Lord Jesus Christ, who died for us, that whether we wake or sleep, we should live together with Him. (1 Thessalonians 5:1–10)*

5. *Now, brethren, concerning the coming of our Lord Jesus Christ and our gathering together to Him, we ask you, not to be soon shaken in mind or troubled, either by spirit or by word or by letter, as if from us, as though the day of Christ had come. Let no one deceive you by any means; for that Day will not come unless the falling away comes first, and the man of sin is revealed, the son of perdition, who opposes and exalts himself above all that is called God or that is worshiped, so that he sits as God in the temple of God, showing himself that he is God. Do you not remember that when I was still with you I told you these things? (2 Thessalonians 2:1–5)*

6.   *Beloved, I now write to you this second epistle (in both of which I stir up your pure minds by way of reminder), that you may be mindful of the words which were spoken before by the holy prophets, and of the commandment of us, the apostles of the Lord and Savior, knowing this first: that scoffers will come in the last days, walking according to their own lusts, and saying, "Where is the promise of His coming? For since the fathers fell asleep, all things continue as they were from the beginning of creation." For this they willfully forget: that by the word of God the heavens were of old, and the earth standing out of water and in the water, by which the world that then existed perished, being flooded with water. But the heavens and the earth which are now preserved by the same word, are reserved for fire until the day of judgment and perdition of ungodly men. (2 Peter 3:1–7)*

7.   *And to the angel of the church in Sardis write, "These things says He who has the seven Spirits of God and the seven stars: 'I know your works, that you have a name that you are alive, but you are dead. Be watchful, and strengthen the things which remain, that are ready to die, for I have not found your works perfect before God. Remember therefore how you have received and heard; hold fast and repent. Therefore if you will not watch, I will come upon you as a thief, and you will not know what hour I will come upon you. You have a few names even in Sardis who have not defiled their garments; and they shall walk with Me in white, for they are worthy. He who overcomes shall be clothed in white garments, and I will not blot out his name from the Book of Life; but I will confess his name before My Father and before His angels.'" (Revelation 3:1–5)*

VII. HOW CAN WE KNOW THAT WE ARE LIVING IN THE LAST GENERATION?

Jesus established two clear conditions for His return that enable anyone who believes the Bible to recognize the generation of His return. One generation will simultaneously witness both the salvation of Israel and the Gospel being preached to all nations. Both of these events are possible for the first time since AD 70. After 1,900 years, Israel is back in their land with their language and religious customs intact. This miraculous event is taking place simultaneously with the existence of the first generation since Pentecost that can fulfill the Great Commission: to preach the Gospel to every people group on the earth. This is not coincidence. This is the beginning of the fulfillment of the simultaneous two conditions for the Messiah's return, as set forth by Jesus Himself.

A.   Matthew 23:37: Jesus declared to the religious leadership of His day that Jerusalem would not see Him again until they said, "Blessed is he who comes in the name of the Lord." We see Jesus' commitment to this when He had the disciples meet Him in Galilee after the Resurrection. His return to Jerusalem will not happen until the Jewish leadership receives Him as the Messiah.

B.   Matthew 24:14: the timing of the end is tied to world-wide evangelism.

And this gospel of the kingdom will be preached in all the world as a witness to all the nations, and then the end will come. (Matthew 24:14)

1.   Present situation

2.   Revelation 5:9 and 7:9 tell us that a remnant will come forth from every tribe, tongue, people and nation.

And they sang a new song, saying: "You are worthy to take the scroll, and to open its seals; for You were slain, and have redeemed us to God by Your blood out of every tribe and tongue and people and nation. (Revelation 5:9)

After these things I looked, and behold, a great multitude which no one could number, of all nations, tribes, peoples, and tongues, standing before the throne and before the Lamb, clothed with white robes, with palm branches in their hands. (Revelation 7:9)

3.   Revelation 11:9–10 reveals that the two witnesses at the end of the age will prophesy to the whole world for 1,260 days.

And I will give power to my two witnesses, and they will prophesy one thousand two hundred and sixty days, clothed in sackcloth. (Revelation 11:3)

When they finish their testimony, the beast that ascends out of the bottomless pit will make war against them, overcome them, and kill them. And their dead bodies will lie in the street of the great city which spiritually is called Sodom and Egypt, where also our Lord was crucified. Then those from the peoples, tribes, tongues, and nations will see their dead bodies three-and-a-half days, and not allow their dead bodies to be put into graves. And those who dwell on the earth will rejoice over them, make merry, and send gifts to one another, because these two prophets tormented those who dwell on the earth. Now after the three-and-a-half days the breath of life from God entered them, and they stood on their feet, and great fear fell on those who saw them. (Revelation 11:7–11)

4.   Revelation 14:6–7 reveals that an angel will be released to proclaim the everlasting Gospel to every nation, tribe, tongue and people.

Then I saw another angel flying in the midst of heaven, having the everlasting gospel to preach to those who dwell on the earth—to every nation, tribe, tongue, and people—saying with a loud voice, "Fear God and give glory to Him, for the hour of His judgment has come; and worship Him who made heaven and earth, the sea and springs of water." (Revelation 14:6–7)

5. In light of the end of the age activity by the two witnesses and the angel who will preach the everlasting gospel, Matthew 24:14 may not necessarily have to be complete by the Great Tribulation. Perhaps the preaching is fulfilled by the two witnesses during the Great Tribulation. This means that the end of the age scenario could begin any time now. However, Revelation 5:9 seems to indicate that there is a remnant from every tribe, tongue, people, and nation at Jesus' initiation of God's end-time purposes in that chapter. My guess is that the preaching of the Gospel will be completed by the Church in the three-and-a-half year period before the Great Tribulation, and it will be one of the major factors that triggers Jesus' taking of the scroll from the Father and loosing its seals. Thus, the two witnesses in Revelation 11 become a prophetic witness against the nations which have already heard the Gospel and are without excuse.

VIII. THE SIGNS OF CHRIST'S RETURN

A. **Gathering of Israel**: The Bible speaks of gathering Israel in the land for a time of tribulation which will lead to her salvation and the overcoming of rebellious nations.

The word that came to Jeremiah from the LORD, saying, "Thus speaks the LORD God of Israel, saying: 'Write in a book for yourself all the words that I have spoken to you. For behold, the days are coming,' says the LORD, 'that I will bring back from captivity My people Israel and Judah,' says the LORD.' And I will cause them to return to the land that I gave to their fathers, and they shall possess it.'" Now these are the words that the LORD spoke concerning Israel and Judah. "For thus says the LORD: 'We have heard a voice of trembling, Of fear, and not of peace. Ask now, and see, whether a man is ever in labor with child? So why do I see every man with his hands on his loins like a woman in labor, and all faces turned pale? Alas! For that day is great, so that none is like it; and it is the time of Jacob's trouble, but he shall be saved out of it. (Jeremiah 30:1–7)

B. **Covenant of peace with Israel**: Daniel's 70th week begins with a covenant of peace confirmed with Israel by the Antichrist.

Then he shall confirm a covenant with many for one week; but in the middle of the week He shall bring an end to sacrifice and offering. And on the wing of abominations shall be one who makes desolate, even until the consummation, which is determined, is poured out on the desolate. (Daniel 9:27)

C.   **Universal preaching of the Gospel**: Jesus tells us that the Gospel will be preached in all nations and then the end will come.

And this gospel of the kingdom will be preached in all the world as a witness to all the nations, and then the end will come. (Matthew 24:14)

And the gospel must first be preached to all the nations. But when they arrest you and deliver you up, do not worry beforehand, or premeditate what you will speak. But whatever is given you in that hour, speak that; for it is not you who speak, but the Holy Spirit. (Mark 13:10–11)

D.   **Series of tribulations**

    1.   **Birth pangs**

        a. Wars and rumors of wars

        b. Various troubles—social and civil disorder and breakdown

        c. Famines

        d. Pestilences

        e. Earthquakes

        f. Fearful sights and great signs

    2.   **The Great Tribulation**: initiated by the man of lawlessness (2 Thessalonians 2:8–9) when he exalts himself as God in the Temple. This is a time of severe persecution, famine, plagues and conflict as the judgments of God strike the earth and strike the rebellious.

3.   Revelation 12: It is clear that in that moment the dragon (Satan) and his angels will fight against Michael and his angels. Michael will be victorious, and they will cast Satan out of heaven and onto the earth. For a three-and-a-half year period, he will go after the woman who has twelve stars around her head—the nation of Israel. He will begin to persecute the woman who gave birth to the child, but she will flee to the wilderness and be nourished for three and a half years. When Michael throws Satan out of heaven, that will be the hour in which Satan will fully inhabit this man, the Antichrist. His strategy will now become focused in a man on earth, because he has been thrown out of heaven.

4.   When this man of lawlessness stands in God's holy temple and exalts himself as God, watch out, because the seal judgments will then be loosed. Have you ever read about people who exalted themselves against God, such as Nebuchadnezzar or Herod? When the son of perdition (2 Thessalonians 2:3) does this, the Lion of the Tribe of Judah will open the seals and loose the scroll.

E.   **The judgments of God**: Revelation 6–19: seals, trumpets and bowls.

F.   **Two witnesses appear in Jerusalem**: Revelation 11. None of us currently understand the weight of this verse; the closest comparison is when Moses and Aaron effortlessly brought Egypt to its knees. During the whole time the two witnesses prophesy, the heavens will be shut up worldwide. There will be no rain. Moses and Aaron foreshadowed these two witnesses in the Exodus. Many believe Moses and Elijah will return as these two witnesses.

G.   **Extraordinary disturbances in nature**

And there will be signs in the sun, in the moon, and in the stars; and on the earth distress of nations, with perplexity, the sea and the waves roaring; men's hearts failing them from fear and the expectation of those things which are coming on the earth, for the powers of the heavens will be shaken. Then they will see the Son of Man coming in a cloud with power and great glory. (Luke 21:25–27)

H.   **Extreme depravity and the pretense of security**

But know this, that in the last days perilous times will come: for men will be lovers of themselves, lovers of money, boasters, proud, blasphemers, disobedient to parents, unthankful, unholy, unloving, unforgiving, slanderers, without self-control, brutal, despisers of good, traitors, headstrong, haughty, lovers of pleasure rather than lovers of God, having a form of godliness but denying its power. And from such people turn away! For of this sort are those who creep into households and make captives of gullible women loaded down with sins, led away by various lusts, always learning and never able to come to the knowledge of the truth. Now as Jannes and Jambres resisted Moses, so do these also resist the truth: men of corrupt minds, disapproved concerning the faith. (2 Timothy 3:1–8)

And because lawlessness will abound, the love of many will grow cold. But he who endures to the end shall be saved. (Matthew 24:12–13)

For you yourselves know perfectly that the day of the Lord so comes as a thief in the night. For when they say, "Peace and safety!" then sudden destruction comes upon them, as labor pains upon a pregnant woman. And they shall not escape. But you, brethren, are not in darkness, so that this Day should overtake you as a thief. (1 Thessalonians 5:2–4)

Now the Spirit expressly says that in latter times some will depart from the faith, giving heed to deceiving spirits and doctrines of demons, speaking lies in hypocrisy, having their own conscience seared with a hot iron, forbidding to marry, and commanding to abstain from foods which God created to be received with thanksgiving by those who believe and know the truth. For every creature of God is good, and nothing is to be refused if it is received with thanksgiving; for it is sanctified by the word of God and prayer. (1 Timothy 4:1–5)

1 Timothy 4:1–5 is a strange passage. A time is coming when blatant sexual immorality is allowed, marriage is not, and spirituality is based upon what food one eats. There is a form of godliness and an appearance of spirituality based upon foods, but there is a total absence of Christian morality.

I. **False prophets and messiahs**: Jesus began His discourse with a strong warning against deception. Jesus warned us three times (v. 4, 11, 23) against deception that will happen during this time period and during the period of Great Tribulation. This is the key issue—deception. False christs will come.

Then I saw another beast coming up out of the earth, and he had two horns like a lamb and spoke like a dragon. And he exercises all the authority of the first beast in his presence, and causes the earth and those who dwell in it to worship the first beast, whose deadly wound was healed. He performs great signs, so that he even makes fire come down from heaven on the earth in the sight of men. And he deceives those who dwell on the earth by those signs which he was granted to do in the sight of the beast, telling those who dwell on the earth to make an image to the beast who was wounded by the sword and lived. He was granted power to give breath to the image of the beast, that the image of the beast should both speak and cause as many as would not worship the image of the beast to be killed. He causes all, both small and great, rich and poor, free and slave, to receive a mark on their right hand or on their foreheads, and that no one may buy or sell except one who has the mark or the name of the beast, or the number of his name. Here is wisdom. Let him who has understanding calculate the number of the beast, for it is the number of a man: His number is 666. (Revelation 13:11–18)

J.   **The Apostasy**

And then many will be offended, will betray one another, and will hate one another. Then many false prophets will rise up and deceive many. (Matthew 24:10–11)

Not to be soon shaken in mind or troubled, either by spirit or by word or by letter, as if from us, as though the day of Christ had come. **Let no one deceive you by any means; for that Day will not come unless the falling away comes first,** *and the man of sin is revealed, the son of perdition. (2 Thessalonians 2:2–3, emphasis added)*

Now the Spirit expressly says that in latter times some will depart from the faith, *giving heed to deceiving spirits and doctrines of demons, speaking lies in hypocrisy, having their own conscience seared with a hot iron, forbidding to marry, and commanding to abstain from foods which God created to be received with thanksgiving by those who believe and know the truth. (1 Timothy 4:1–3, emphasis added)*

Preach the word! Be ready in season and out of season. Convince, rebuke, exhort, with all longsuffering and teaching. For the time will come when they will not endure sound doctrine, but according to their own desires, because they have itching ears, they will heap up for themselves teachers; and they will turn their ears away from the truth, and be turned aside to fables. (2 Timothy 4:2–4)

K. **The Lawless One revealed with the abomination of desolation:**
Daniel 9:27, 11:31,36–37, 12:11

Then he shall confirm a covenant with many for one week; but in the middle of the week He shall bring an end to sacrifice and offering. And on the wing of abominations shall be one who makes desolate, even until the consummation, which is determined, is poured out on the desolate. (Daniel 9:27)

And forces shall be mustered by him, and they shall defile the sanctuary fortress; then they shall take away the daily sacrifices, and place there the abomination of desolation ... Then the king shall do according to his own will: he shall exalt and magnify himself above every god, shall speak blasphemies against the God of gods, and shall prosper till the wrath has been accomplished; for what has been determined shall be done. He shall regard neither the God of his fathers nor the desire of women, nor regard any god; for he shall exalt himself above them all. (Daniel 11:31,36–37)

And from the time that the daily sacrifice is taken away, and the abomination of desolation is set up, there shall be one thousand two hundred and ninety days. (Daniel 12:11)

Therefore when you see the "abomination of desolation," spoken of by Daniel the prophet, standing in the holy place (whoever reads, let him understand), then let those who are in Judea flee to the mountains. Let him who is on the housetop not go down to take anything out of his house. (Matthew 24:15–17)

So when you see the "abomination of desolation," spoken of by Daniel the prophet, standing where it ought not (let the reader understand), then let those who are in Judea flee to the mountains. Let him who is on the housetop not go down into the house, nor enter to take anything out of his house. (Mark 13:14–15)

But when you see Jerusalem surrounded by armies, then know that its desolation is near. Then let those who are in Judea flee to the mountains, let those who are in the midst of her depart, and let not those who are in the country enter her. For these are the days of vengeance, that all things which are written may be fulfilled. (Luke 21:20–22)

Let no one deceive you by any means; for that Day will not come unless the falling away comes first, and the man of sin is revealed, the son of perdition, who opposes and exalts himself above all that is called God or that is worshiped, so that he sits as God in the temple of God, showing himself that he is God. (2 Thessalonians 2:3–4)

The coming of the lawless one is according to the working of Satan, with all power, signs, and lying wonders, and with all unrighteous deception among those who perish, because they did not receive the love of the truth, that they might be saved. And for this reason God will send them strong delusion, that they should believe the lie, that they all may be condemned who did not believe the truth but had pleasure in unrighteousness. (2 Thessalonians 2:9–12)

Then I stood on the sand of the sea. And I saw a beast rising up out of the sea, having seven heads and ten horns, and on his horns ten crowns, and on his heads a blasphemous name. Now the beast which I saw was like a leopard, his feet were like the feet of a bear, and his mouth like the mouth of a lion. The dragon gave him his power, his throne, and great authority. And I saw one of his heads as if it had been mortally wounded, and his deadly wound was healed. And all the world marveled and followed the beast. So they worshiped the dragon who gave authority to the beast; and they worshiped the beast, saying, "Who is like the beast? Who is able to make war with him?" And he was given a mouth speaking great things and blasphemies, and he was given authority to continue for forty-two months. Then he opened his mouth in blasphemy against God, to blaspheme His name, His tabernacle, and those who dwell in heaven. It was granted to him to make war with the saints and to overcome them. And authority was given him over every tribe, tongue, and nation. All who dwell on the earth will worship him, whose names have not been written in the Book of Life of the Lamb slain from the foundation of the world. (Revelation 13:1–8)

IX. THE EFFECTS OF HIS COMING

A. The deliverance and glorifying of the saints

When Christ who is our life appears, then you also will appear with Him in glory. (Colossians 3:4)

Finally, there is laid up for me the crown of righteousness, which the Lord, the righteous Judge, will give to me on that Day, and not to me only but also to all who have loved His appearing. (2 Timothy 4:8)

Beloved, now we are children of God; and it has not yet been revealed what we shall be, but we know that when He is revealed, we shall be like Him, for we shall see Him as He is. And everyone who has this hope in Him purifies himself, just as He is pure. (1 John 3:2–3)

So Christ was offered once to bear the sins of many. To those who eagerly wait for Him He will appear a second time, apart from sin, for salvation. (Hebrews 9:28)

In Him you also trusted, after you heard the word of truth, the gospel of your salvation; in whom also, having believed, you were sealed with the Holy Spirit of promise, who is the guarantee of our inheritance until the redemption of the purchased possession, to the praise of His glory. (Ephesians 1:13–14)

And to give you who are troubled rest with us when the Lord Jesus is revealed from heaven with His mighty angels, in flaming fire taking vengeance on those who do not know God, and on those who do not obey the gospel of our Lord Jesus Christ. These shall be punished with everlasting destruction from the presence of the Lord and from the glory of His power, when He comes, in that Day, to be glorified in His saints and to be admired among all those who believe, because our testimony among you was believed. (2 Thessalonians 1:7–10)

Revelation 19

B.   **The salvation of Israel**

*Indeed the L*ᴏʀᴅ *has proclaimed to the end of the world: "**Say to the daughter of Zion, 'Surely your salvation is coming; behold, His reward is with Him, and His work before Him.'**" And they shall call them The Holy People, The Redeemed of the L*ᴏʀᴅ*; and you shall be called Sought Out, A City Not Forsaken. (Isaiah 62:11–12, emphasis added)*

*For I do not desire, brethren, that you should be ignorant of this mystery, lest you should be wise in your own opinion, that blindness in part has happened to Israel until the fullness of the Gentiles has come in. **And so all Israel will be saved, as it is written: "The Deliverer will come out of Zion, and He will turn away ungodliness from Jacob; for this is My covenant with them, when I take away their sins."** Concerning the gospel they are enemies for your sake, but concerning the election they are beloved for the sake of the fathers. For the gifts and the calling of God are irrevocable. For as you were once disobedient to God, yet have now obtained mercy through their disobedience, even so these also have now been disobedient, that through the mercy shown you they also may obtain mercy. For God has committed them all to disobedience, that He might have mercy on all. (Romans 11:25–32, emphasis added)*

And I will pour on the house of David and on the inhabitants of Jerusalem the Spirit of grace and supplication; then they will look on Me whom they pierced. Yes, they will mourn for Him as one mourns for his only son, and grieve for Him as one grieves for a firstborn. In that day there shall be a great mourning in Jerusalem, like the mourning at Hadad Rimmon in the plain of Megiddo. (Zechariah 12:10–11)

In that day a fountain shall be opened for the house of David and for the inhabitants of Jerusalem, for sin and for uncleanness. (Zechariah 13:1)

*Behold, He is coming with clouds, and every eye will see Him, **even they who pierced Him**. And all the tribes of the earth will mourn because of Him. Even so, Amen. (Revelation 1:7, emphasis added)*

C.   **The destruction of the powers of darkness**: Genesis 3:15, Revelation 19–20

And I will put enmity between you and the woman, and between your seed and her Seed; He shall bruise your head, and you shall bruise His heel. (Genesis 3:15)

For when they say, "Peace and safety!" then sudden destruction comes upon them, as labor pains upon a pregnant woman. And they shall not escape. But you, brethren, are not in darkness, so that this Day should overtake you as a thief. (1 Thessalonians 5:3–4)

So that we ourselves boast of you among the churches of God for your patience and faith in all your persecutions and tribulations that you endure, which is manifest evidence of the righteous judgment of God, that you may be counted worthy of the kingdom of God, for which you also suffer; since it is a righteous thing with God to repay with tribulation those who trouble you, and to give you who are troubled rest with us when the Lord Jesus is revealed from heaven with His mighty angels, in flaming fire taking vengeance on those who do not know God, and on those who do not obey the gospel of our Lord Jesus Christ. These shall be punished with everlasting destruction from the presence of the Lord and from the glory of His power, when He comes, in that Day, to be glorified in His saints and to be admired among all those who believe, because our testimony among you was believed. (2 Thessalonians 1:4–10)

And then the lawless one will be revealed, whom the Lord will consume with the breath of His mouth and destroy with the brightness of His coming. (2 Thessalonians 2:8)

D. **The condemnation of the wicked:** Matthew 25:31, 2 Timothy 4:14, Revelation 20:13, Daniel 12:2, John 5:28–29

When the Son of Man comes in His glory, and all the holy angels with Him, then He will sit on the throne of His glory. (Matthew 25:31)

Alexander the coppersmith did me much harm. May the Lord repay him according to his works. (2 Timothy 4:14)

The sea gave up the dead who were in it, and Death and Hades delivered up the dead who were in them. And they were judged, each one according to his works. (Revelation 20:13)

And many of those who sleep in the dust of the earth shall awake, some to everlasting life, some to shame and everlasting contempt. (Daniel 12:2)

Do not marvel at this; for the hour is coming in which all who are in the graves will hear His voice and come forth—those who have done good, to the resurrection of life, and those who have done evil, to the resurrection of condemnation. (John 5:28–29)

E. **The rewarding of the righteous**: Daniel 12:2, 1 Corinthians 3:13, John 5:28–29

And many of those who sleep in the dust of the earth shall awake, some to everlasting life, some to shame and everlasting contempt. (Daniel 12:2)

Now if anyone builds on this foundation with gold, silver, precious stones, wood, hay, straw, each one's work will become clear; for the Day will declare it, because it will be revealed by fire; and the fire will test each one's work, of what sort it is. If anyone's work which he has built on it endures, he will receive a reward. If anyone's work is burned, he will suffer loss; but he himself will be saved, yet so as through fire. (1 Corinthians 3:12–15)

Do not marvel at this; for the hour is coming in which all who are in the graves will hear His voice and come forth—those who have done good, to the resurrection of life, and those who have done evil, to the resurrection of condemnation. (John 5:28–29)

F. **The deliverance of the created order from the effects of sin**

For the earnest expectation of the creation eagerly waits for the revealing of the sons of God. (Romans 8:19)

The wolf also shall dwell with the lamb, the leopard shall lie down with the young goat, the calf and the young lion and the fatling together; and a little child shall lead them. The cow and the bear shall graze; their young ones shall lie down together; and the lion shall eat straw like the ox. The nursing child shall play by the cobra's hole, and the weaned child shall put his hand in the viper's den. They shall not hurt nor destroy in all My holy mountain, for the earth shall be full of the knowledge of the LORD as the waters cover the sea. (Isaiah 11:6–9)

Then He who sat on the throne said, "Behold, I make all things new." And He said to me, "Write, for these words are true and faithful." (Revelation 21:5)

G. **The establishment of the Kingdom of God on Earth forever**: 1 Corinthians 15, Revelation 20–22.

1. Jesus will initiate the Millennial Reign and begin to restore all things under His leadership. For one thousand years, He will reign on the earth to fulfill all the promises of the Word of God. He will disciple the nations and will establish the Kingdom of God in every sphere of human life (political, social, agricultural, economic, spiritual, educational, etc.). In this period of blessing initiated at Jesus' second coming, Satan will be bound and Jesus will rule the earth with a rod of iron (Deuteronomy 8, 28; Psalm 2:6–12, 110:1–7; Isaiah 2:1–4, 9:6–9, 11:1–16, 51:1–8, 60–62, 65:17–25; Matthew 5:5, 6:10, 17:11, 19:28, 28:19; Acts 1:6, 3:21; Revelation 19:11–21, 20:1–6).

2. The result of Jesus' rule will be a thousand-year period of peace, righteousness, prosperity, and unprecedented blessing for the whole earth as Jesus restores life to the conditions seen in the **Garden of Eden**. Jesus, as the King of kings, will govern a worldwide Kingdom from Jerusalem. He will reign in partnership with resurrected saints who rule with Him, establishing a biblically-based social order (Daniel 2:44–45; Matthew 19:28, 25:23; Luke 22:29–30; 1 Corinthians 6:2–3, 15:23–28; 2 Timothy 2:12; Revelation 2:26–27, 3:21, 5:10, 20:4–6, 20:1–6, 22:5).

You watched while a stone was cut out without hands, which struck the image on its feet of iron and clay, and broke them in pieces. Then the iron, the clay, the bronze, the silver, and the gold were crushed together, and became like chaff from the summer threshing floors; the wind carried them away so that no trace of them was found. And the stone that struck the image became a great mountain and filled the whole earth. (Daniel 2:34–35)

And in the days of these kings the God of heaven will set up a kingdom which shall never be destroyed; and the kingdom shall not be left to other people; it shall break in pieces and consume all these kingdoms, and it shall stand forever. Inasmuch as you saw that the stone was cut out of the mountain without hands, and that it broke in pieces the iron, the bronze, the clay, the silver, and the gold—the great God has made known to the king what will come to pass after this. The dream is certain, and its interpretation is sure. (Daniel 2:44–45)

But each one in his own order: Christ the firstfruits, afterward those who are Christ's at His coming. Then comes the end, when He delivers the kingdom to God the Father, when He puts an end to all rule and all authority and power. For He must reign till He has put all enemies under His feet. The last enemy that will be destroyed is death. For "He has put all things under His feet." But when He says "all things are put under Him," it is evident that He who put all things under Him is excepted. Now when all things are made subject to Him, then the Son Himself will also be subject to Him who put all things under Him, that God may be all in all. (1 Corinthians 15:23–28)

Then I saw an angel coming down from heaven, having the key to the bottomless pit and a great chain in his hand. He laid hold of the dragon, that serpent of old, who is the Devil and Satan, and bound him for a thousand years; and he cast him into the bottomless pit, and shut him up, and set a seal on him, so that he should deceive the nations no more till the thousand years were finished. But after these things he must be released for a little while. And I saw thrones, and they sat on them, and judgment was committed to them. Then I saw the souls of those who had been beheaded for their witness to Jesus and for the word of God, who had not worshiped the beast or his image, and had not received his mark on their foreheads or on their hands. And they lived and reigned with Christ for a thousand years. But the rest of the dead did not live again until the thousand years were finished. This is the first resurrection. Blessed and holy is he who has part in the first resurrection. Over such the second death has no power, but they shall be priests of God and of Christ, and shall reign with Him a thousand years. (Revelation 20:1–6)

3. The work of Calvary and the ministry of the Holy Spirit prepared the earth for the Lord's return. In the same way, the earthly rule of Jesus with the full power of the Holy Spirit will prepare the earth for the coming of the Father, when Heaven and Earth will be fully joined together. Before this takes place, God will release Satan for one final testing of the nations at the end of the thousand years. This conflict will end with the casting of Satan, the wicked, and Hell itself into the lake of fire. Then all things will be made new, and God will dwell with men.

Then I saw an angel coming down from heaven, having the key to the bottomless pit and a great chain in his hand. He laid hold of the dragon, that serpent of old, who is the Devil and Satan, and bound him for a thousand years; and he cast him into the bottomless pit, and shut him up, and set a seal on him, so that he should deceive the nations no more till the thousand years were finished. But after these things he must be released for a little while. And I saw thrones, and they sat on them, and judgment was committed to them. Then I saw the souls of those who had been beheaded for their witness to Jesus and for the word of God, who had not worshiped the beast or his image, and had not received his mark on their foreheads or on their hands. And they lived and reigned with Christ for a thousand years. But the rest of the dead did not live again until the thousand years were finished. This is the first resurrection. Blessed and holy is he who has part in the first resurrection. Over such the second death has no power, but they shall be priests of God and of Christ, and shall reign with Him a thousand years. Now when the thousand years have expired, Satan will be released from his prison and will go out to deceive the nations which are in the four corners of the earth, Gog and Magog, to gather them together to battle, whose number is as the sand of the sea. They went up on the breadth of the earth and surrounded the camp of the saints and the beloved city. And fire came down from God out of heaven and devoured them. The devil, who deceived them, was cast into the lake of fire and brimstone where the beast and the false prophet are. And they will be tormented day and night forever and ever. Then I saw a great white throne and Him who sat on it, from whose face the earth and the heaven fled away. And there was found no place for them. And I saw the dead, small and great, standing before God, and books were opened. And another book was opened, which is the Book of Life. And the dead were judged according to their works, by the things which were written in the books. The sea gave up the dead who were in it, and Death and Hades delivered up the dead who were in them. And they were judged, each one according to his works. Then Death and Hades were cast into the lake of fire. This is the second death. And anyone not found written in the Book of Life was cast into the lake of fire. Now I saw a new heaven and a new earth, for the first heaven and the first earth had passed away. Also there was no more sea. Then I, John, saw the holy city, New Jerusalem, coming down out of heaven from God, prepared as a bride adorned for her husband. And I heard a loud voice from heaven saying, "Behold, the tabernacle of God is with men, and He will dwell with them, and they shall be His people. God Himself will be with them and be their God. And God will wipe away every tear from their eyes; there shall be no more death, nor sorrow, nor crying. There

shall be no more pain, for the former things have passed away."
Then He who sat on the throne said, "Behold, I make all things
new." And He said to me, "Write, for these words are true and
faithful." And He said to me, "It is done! I am the Alpha and the
Omega, the Beginning and the End. I will give of the fountain
of the water of life freely to him who thirsts. He who overcomes
shall inherit all things, and I will be his God and he shall be
My son. But the cowardly, unbelieving, abominable, murderers,
sexually immoral, sorcerers, idolaters, and all liars shall have
their part in the lake which burns with fire and brimstone, which
is the second death." (Revelation 20–21:8)

Session Fourteen: The Fury of the Bridegroom

I.   THE LAST GENERATION—AN APPOINTED END

A.   Matthew 23:37–39 and 24:14 as the two conditions for the Second Coming.

O Jerusalem, Jerusalem, the one who kills the prophets and stones those who are sent to her! How often I wanted to gather your children together, as a hen gathers her chicks under her wings, but you were not willing! See! Your house is left to you desolate; for I say to you, you shall see Me no more till you say, "Blessed is He who comes in the name of the Lᴏʀᴅ!" (Matthew 23:37–39, emphasis added)

And this gospel of the kingdom will be preached in all the world as a witness to all the nations, and then the end will come. (Matthew 24:14, emphasis added)

B.   This generation will witness God's full opposition against the world, the flesh, and the devil. This generation will see the Lord in the fullness of His compassion and love as He vindicates the saints with the resurrection from the dead and saves Israel in their darkest hour. They will meet the Bridegroom King in all of His passion and fury—passion towards those who are His; fury towards those who have scorned His love, refused His tender affections, and embraced the ugly, perverted, wicked thirst for rebellion and iniquity. God has appointed an end, a time when He will drive the usurper out. Our Bridegroom will come as a lion of sheer force and power against wickedness.

But when the king heard about it, he was furious. And he sent out his armies, destroyed those murderers, and burned up their city. (Matthew 22:7, emphasis added)

C. The Day of the Lord displays the various tensions of God's love in a single event that will forever change the course of human history and usher us into the next age. It is the hour when God's nature of love will be fully manifest and clarified before the whole world. In the person of Christ, the world will watch God declare His name—His mercy, compassion, deliverance, protection, righteousness and justice. Jesus will declare His Father's name again and again as He delivers the saints, protects and saves Israel, destroys the wicked, and binds Satan in the bottomless pit. All His manifold glory will be displayed as He vindicates His loving nature, as He saves and removes wickedness from the Earth.

Behold, the Lord God shall come with a strong hand, and His arm shall rule for Him; behold, His reward is with Him, and His work before Him. He will feed His flock like a shepherd; He will gather the lambs with His arm, and carry them in His bosom, and gently lead those who are with young. (Isaiah 40:10–11)

Behold, the Lord comes with ten thousands of His saints, to execute judgment on all, to convict all who are ungodly among them of all their ungodly deeds which they have committed in an ungodly way, and of all the harsh things which ungodly sinners have spoken against Him. (Jude 14–15)

D. The mystery of iniquity

1. You cannot understand the Second Coming of Christ and the events which surround it without first staring at the mystery of iniquity—humanity's stubborn refusal to submit to God's laws and leadership and their active aggression to cast off all of God's restraints (Psalm 2:1–2). Even as Jesus returns in the sky, marches on land, and releases the last of the bowl judgments, people will still be blaspheming God and gathering together to fight against Him. This is unthinkable to us, but true nonetheless. When all is visible, all is manifest, humanity will still resist God. Not only will they resist, they will violently oppose Jesus' rule.

2.   For three and a half years, the earth will witness the disastrous rule of the Antichrist. His rule will be the epitome of human strength and ingenuity, yet it will release the greatest amounts of devastation in human history. The earth will also witness the hand of God opposing and preserving humanity through His manifest judgments. Even as the earth is in full-fledged rebellion, God is working to dismantle darkness, break delusions, and bring as many people as possible to the saving knowledge of Jesus while using the least severe means possible. Yet, at the end of the trumpet judgments and throughout the bowl judgments, the people will refuse to repent. Instead, they will blaspheme God.

*But the rest of mankind, who were not killed by these plagues, **did not repent of the works of their hands, that they should not worship demons, and idols of gold, silver, brass, stone, and wood, which can neither see nor hear nor walk. And they did not repent of their murders or their sorceries or their sexual immorality or their thefts.** (Revelation 9:20–21, emphasis added)*

*And men were scorched with great heat, and **they blasphemed the name of God** who has power over these plagues; and **they did not repent and give Him glory**. Then the fifth angel poured out his bowl on the throne of the beast, and his kingdom became full of darkness; and they gnawed their tongues because of the pain. **They blasphemed the God of heaven because of their pains and their sores, and did not repent of their deeds.** (Revelation 16:9–11, emphasis added)*

***These will make war with the Lamb**, and the Lamb will overcome them, for He is Lord of lords and King of kings; and those who are with Him are called, chosen, and faithful. (Revelation 17:14, emphasis added)*

3.   At the last trumpet, Jesus will return. He will deliver the saints, release the vengeance of God against all iniquity, destroy the Antichrist's armies, and gather the remnant of Israel. Jesus is resolute in His desire to bring the saints to consummation and to rid the earth of all evil. On the great Day of the Lord, the earth will witness a face of Jesus that they have never seen. He came the first time as the Lamb of God to save sinners. He will come the second time as a Lion to destroy all the forces of darkness and save the earth from Satan's rule.

*And as it is appointed for men to die once, but after this the judgment, so Christ was offered once to bear the sins of many. To those who eagerly wait for Him **He will appear a second time, apart from sin, for salvation**. (Hebrews 9:27–28, emphasis added)*

E. ***The memory of this event will impact the social, emotional, legal, and economic decisions in the earth*** *the next one thousand years (Revelation 20). The memory will live on and the power of it will affect generation after generation. They will tell the story to their offspring and to their descendants, the story of this zealous King who killed all of His enemies with His own hand! The vivid memory of this display of Divine zeal will cause the nations of the earth to say of the King reigning in Jerusalem, "O, you do not want disobey Him! I was there when He took the rod of iron and smashed the nations!" This one event will re-align the emotional "DNA" of the earth for a thousand years! The story will be told to the generations because God desires voluntary lovers all over the earth who tremble at His majesty![1]*

*Now therefore, be wise, O kings; be instructed, you judges of the earth. **Serve the Lord with fear, and rejoice with trembling. Kiss the Son**, lest He be angry, and you perish in the way, when His wrath is kindled but a little. Blessed are all those who put their trust in Him. (Psalm 2:10–12, emphasis added)*

II. THE FURY OF THE BRIDEGROOM

A. In the last days, we will see the fury of the Bridegroom as He removes the power of Satan from the planet. The Lion of the tribe of Judah will triumph over all the works of darkness. This is the premeditated and predetermined plan of God. The fury of the Bridegroom is not an outburst of rage from a weak-willed man. **This is a calculated strike against the kingdom of darkness. God's passion and power explodes against darkness with His full control and wise administration of perfect justice.** God has prophesied about this event for six thousand years; the Bible pictures Him as a Lion ready to pounce upon His prey. Jesus alone has the resolve and the courage to do what is necessary to completely remove evil from the human experience.

And I will put enmity between you and the woman, and between your seed and her Seed; He shall bruise your head, and you shall bruise His heel. (Genesis 3:15)

---

1 Bickle, Mike. *Studies in Joel* (Kansas City, MO: Forerunner Books, 2005), p. 144. Emphasis added.

The scepter shall not depart from Judah, nor a lawgiver from between his feet, until Shiloh comes; and to Him shall be the obedience of the people. (Genesis 49:10)

I see Him, but not now; I behold Him, but not near; a Star shall come out of Jacob; a Scepter shall rise out of Israel, and batter the brow of Moab, and destroy all the sons of tumult. (Numbers 24:17)

Surely the Lord GOD does nothing, unless He reveals His secret to His servants the prophets. A lion has roared! Who will not fear? The Lord GOD has spoken! Who can but prophesy? (Amos 3:7–8)

B. The Bible reveals that Jesus will be viewed on that day as a lion devouring His prey and crushing His enemies. He will be seen as a great King, and all the nations shall worship Him.

Judah is a lion's whelp; from the prey, my son, you have gone up. He bows down, he lies down as a lion; and as a lion, who shall rouse him? The scepter shall not depart from Judah, nor a lawgiver from between his feet, until Shiloh comes; and to Him shall be the obedience of the people. (Genesis 49:9–10)

His king shall be higher than Agag, and his kingdom shall be exalted. God brings him out of Egypt; He has strength like a wild ox; He shall consume the nations, his enemies; He shall break their bones and pierce them with his arrows. "He bows down, he lies down as a lion; and as a lion, who shall rouse him?" Blessed is he who blesses you, and cursed is he who curses you ... I see Him, but not now; I behold Him, but not near; a Star shall come out of Jacob; a Scepter shall rise out of Israel, and batter the brow of Moab, and destroy all the sons of tumult. (Numbers 24:7–9,17)

The king's wrath is like the roaring of a lion, but his favor is like dew on the grass. (Proverbs 19:12)

The wrath of a king is like the roaring of a lion; whoever provokes him to anger sins against his own life. (Proverbs 20:2)

Therefore prophesy against them all these words, and say to them: "The Lᴏʀᴅ will roar from on high, and utter His voice from His holy habitation; He will roar mightily against His fold. He will give a shout, as those who tread the grapes, against all the inhabitants of the earth. A noise will come to the ends of the earth—for the Lᴏʀᴅ has a controversy with the nations; He will plead His case with all flesh. He will give those who are wicked to the sword," says the Lᴏʀᴅ ... He has left His lair like the lion; for their land is desolate because of the fierceness of the Oppressor, and because of His fierce anger." (Jeremiah 25:30–31,38)

Multitudes, multitudes in the valley of decision! For the day of the Lᴏʀᴅ is near in the valley of decision. The sun and moon will grow dark, and the stars will diminish their brightness. The Lᴏʀᴅ also will roar from Zion, and utter His voice from Jerusalem; the heavens and earth will shake; but the Lᴏʀᴅ will be a shelter for His people, and the strength of the children of Israel. (Joel 3:14–16)

Surely the Lord Gᴏᴅ does nothing, unless He reveals His secret to His servants the prophets. A lion has roared! Who will not fear? The Lord Gᴏᴅ has spoken! Who can but prophesy? (Amos 3:7–8)

C.   The terrifying language concerning the Day of the Lord: Jesus is not coming to discipline the nations. He is coming to punish them. This is the day of His wrath. Jesus is coming to liberate the Jews and bring retribution upon the nations that have gathered against them.

*He who sits in the heavens shall laugh; the Lᴏʀᴅ shall hold them in derision. Then He shall speak to them in His wrath, **and distress them in His deep displeasure ... You shall break them with a rod of iron; You shall dash them to pieces like a potter's vessel.** (Psalm 2:4,5,9, emphasis added)*

*The Lᴏʀᴅ shall send the rod of Your strength out of Zion. Rule in the midst of Your enemies! ... The Lord is at Your right hand; **He shall execute kings in the day of His wrath.** He shall judge among the nations, **He shall fill the places with dead bodies,** He shall execute the heads of many countries. (Psalm 110:2,5,6, emphasis added)*

The chariots of God are twenty thousand, even thousands of thousands; the Lord is among them as in Sinai, in the Holy Place. You have ascended on high, You have led captivity captive; You have received gifts among men, even from the rebellious, that the LORD God might dwell there ...But **God will wound the head of His enemies,** *the hairy scalp of the one who still goes on in his trespasses. The Lord said, "I will bring back from Bashan, I will bring them back from the depths of the sea,* **that your foot may crush them in blood, and the tongues of your dogs may have their portion from your enemies."** *(Psalm 68:17–23, emphasis added)*

They shall go into the holes of the rocks, and into the caves of the earth, from the terror of the LORD and the glory of His majesty, when He arises to shake the earth mightily. (Isaiah 2:19)

The noise of a multitude in the mountains, like that of many people! A tumultuous noise of the kingdoms of nations gathered together! The LORD of hosts musters the army for battle. They come from a far country, from the end of heaven—the LORD and His weapons of indignation, to destroy the whole land. Wail, for the day of the LORD is at hand! It will come as destruction from the Almighty. Therefore all hands will be limp, every man's heart will melt, and they will be afraid. Pangs and sorrows will take hold of them; they will be in pain as a woman in childbirth; they will be amazed at one another; their faces will be like flames. Behold, the day of the LORD comes, cruel, with both wrath and fierce anger, to lay the land desolate; and He will destroy its sinners from it. For the stars of heaven and their constellations will not give their light; the sun will be darkened in its going forth, and the moon will not cause its light to shine. **"I will punish the world for its evil, and the wicked for their iniquity; I will halt the arrogance of the proud, and will lay low the haughtiness of the terrible. I will make a mortal more rare than fine gold, a man more than the golden wedge of Ophir.** *Therefore I will shake the heavens, and the earth will move out of her place, in the wrath of the LORD of hosts and in the day of His fierce anger." (Isaiah 13:4–13, emphasis added)*

Come, my people, enter your chambers, and shut your doors behind you; hide yourself, as it were, for a little moment, until the indignation is past. For behold, **the LORD comes out of His place to punish the inhabitants of the earth for their iniquity; the earth will also disclose her blood, and will no more cover her slain.** *(Isaiah 26:20–21, emphasis added)*

Your eyes will see the King in His beauty; they will see the land that is very far off. Your heart will meditate on terror: "Where is the scribe? Where is he who weighs? Where is he who counts the towers?" (Isaiah 33:17–18)

*Come near, you nations, to hear; and heed, you people! Let the earth hear, and all that is in it, the world and all things that come forth from it. For the **indignation of the Lord is against all nations, and His fury against all their armies; He has utterly destroyed them, He has given them over to the slaughter. Also their slain shall be thrown out; their stench shall rise from their corpses, and the mountains shall be melted with their blood.** (Isaiah 34:1–3, emphasis added)*

"The sword of the Lord is filled with blood … For the Lord has a sacrifice in Bozrah, and a great slaughter in the land of Edom … Their land shall be soaked with blood, and their dust saturated with fatness." For it is the day of the Lord's vengeance, the year of recompense for the cause of Zion. Its streams shall be turned into pitch, and its dust into brimstone; its land shall become burning pitch. (Isaiah 34:6–9)

I have trodden the winepress alone, and from the peoples no one was with Me. For I have trodden them in My anger, and trampled them in My fury; their blood is sprinkled upon My garments, and I have stained all My robes. For the day of vengeance is in My heart, and the year of My redeemed has come. (Isaiah 63:3–4)

*When you see this, your heart shall rejoice, and your bones shall flourish like grass; the hand of the Lord shall be known to His servants, and **His indignation to His enemies**. For behold, the Lord will come with fire and with His chariots, like a whirlwind, **to render His anger with fury, and His rebuke with flames of fire. For by fire and by His sword the Lord will judge all flesh; and the slain of the Lord shall be many.** (Isaiah 66:14–16, emphasis added)*

"'A noise will come to the ends of the earth—for the Lord has a controversy with the nations; He will plead His case with all flesh. **He will give those who are wicked to the sword,**' *says the Lord." Thus says the Lord of hosts: "Behold, disaster shall go forth from nation to nation, and a great whirlwind shall be raised up from the farthest parts of the earth.* **"And at that day the slain of the Lord shall be from one end of the earth even to the other end of the earth. They shall not be lamented, or gathered, or buried; they shall become refuse on the ground.** *He has left His lair like the lion; for their land is desolate because of the fierceness of the Oppressor, and* **because of His fierce anger."** *(Jeremiah 25:31–38, emphasis added)*

Behold, the whirlwind of the Lord goes forth with fury, a continuing whirlwind; it will fall violently on the head of the wicked. *The fierce anger of the Lord will not return until He has done it, and until He has performed the intents of His heart.* **In the latter days you will consider it.** *(Jeremiah 30:23–24, emphasis added)*

"Behold, the eyes of the Lord God are on the sinful kingdom, and I will destroy it from the face of the earth; yet I will not utterly destroy the house of Jacob," says the Lord. (Amos 9:8)

"Therefore wait for Me," says the Lord, "Until the day I rise up for plunder; **My determination is to gather the nations to My assembly of kingdoms, to pour on them My indignation, all My fierce anger; all the earth shall be devoured with the fire of My jealousy.** *(Zephaniah 3:8, emphasis added)*

And this shall be the plague with which the Lord will strike all the people who fought against Jerusalem: their flesh shall dissolve while they stand on their feet, their eyes shall dissolve in their sockets, and their tongues shall dissolve in their mouths. (Zechariah 14:12)

"For behold, the day is coming, burning like an oven, and all the proud, yes, **all who do wickedly will be stubble.** *And the day which is coming shall burn them up," says the Lord of hosts, "that will leave them neither root nor branch. But to you who fear My name the Sun of Righteousness shall arise with healing in His wings; and you shall go out and grow fat like stall-fed calves.* **You shall trample the wicked,** *for they shall be ashes under the soles of your feet on the day that I do this," says the Lord of hosts. (Malachi 4:1–3, emphasis added)*

So the angel thrust his sickle into the earth and gathered the vine of the earth, and threw it into the great winepress of the wrath of God. And the winepress was trampled outside the city, and blood came out of the winepress, up to the horses' bridles, for one thousand six hundred furlongs. (Revelation 14:19–20)

*Now I saw heaven opened, and behold, a white horse. And He who sat on him was called Faithful and True, and **in righteousness He judges and makes war**. His eyes were like a flame of fire, and on His head were many crowns. He had a name written that no one knew except Himself. **He was clothed with a robe dipped in blood**, and His name is called The Word of God. And the armies in heaven, clothed in fine linen, white and clean, followed Him on white horses. **Now out of His mouth goes a sharp sword, that with it He should strike the nations. And He Himself will rule them with a rod of iron. He Himself treads the winepress of the fierceness and wrath of Almighty God.** And He has on His robe and on His thigh a name written: KING OF KINGS AND LORD OF LORDS. Then I saw an angel standing in the sun; and he cried with a loud voice, saying to all the birds that fly in the midst of heaven, "**Come and gather together for the supper of the great God, that you may eat the flesh of kings, the flesh of captains, the flesh of mighty men, the flesh of horses and of those who sit on them, and the flesh of all people, free and slave, both small and great.**" (Revelation 19:11–18, emphasis added)*

D. Four reasons to understand the fury of the Bridegroom at the end of the age.

    1. This revelation releases the fear of the Lord and purifies the Church. God hates sin! The Bridegroom King is actively moving against unrighteousness on the earth, and He will ultimately remove sin from His economy. He hates sin because it is killing the image bearers (humans). This understanding preserves us from viewing grace as licentiousness and delivers us from being bitter and not forgiving others.

But the end of all things is at hand; therefore be serious and watchful in your prayers. And above all things have fervent love for one another, for "love will cover a multitude of sins." Be hospitable to one another without grumbling. As each one has received a gift, minister it to one another, as good stewards of the manifold grace of God. If anyone speaks, let him speak as the oracles of God. If anyone ministers, let him do it as with the ability which God supplies, that in all things God may be glorified through Jesus Christ, to whom belong the glory and the dominion forever and ever. Amen. (1 Peter 4:7–11)

For the time has come for judgment to begin at the house of God; and if it begins with us first, what will be the end of those who do not obey the gospel of God? Now "If the righteous one is scarcely saved, where will the ungodly and the sinner appear?" Therefore let those who suffer according to the will of God commit their souls to Him in doing good, as to a faithful Creator. (1 Peter 4:17–19)

Therefore, beloved, looking forward to these things, be diligent to be found by Him in peace, without spot and blameless. (2 Peter 3:14)

O Corinthians! We have spoken openly to you, our heart is wide open. You are not restricted by us, but you are restricted by your own affections. Now in return for the same (I speak as to children), you also be open. Do not be unequally yoked together with unbelievers. For what fellowship has righteousness with lawlessness? And what communion has light with darkness? And what accord has Christ with Belial? Or what part has a believer with an unbeliever? And what agreement has the temple of God with idols? For you are the temple of the living God. As God has said: "I will dwell in them and walk among them. I will be their God, and they shall be My people." Therefore "Come out from among them and be separate, says the Lord. Do not touch what is unclean, and I will receive you." "I will be a Father to you, and you shall be My sons and daughters, says the Lord *Almighty."* **Therefore, having these promises, beloved, let us cleanse ourselves from all filthiness of the flesh and spirit, perfecting holiness in the fear of God.** *(2 Corinthians 6:11–7:1, emphasis added)*

For I am jealous for you with godly jealousy. For I have betrothed you to one husband, that I may present you as a chaste virgin to Christ. (2 Corinthians 11:2)

2. This understanding of Jesus' heart empowers our proclamation. In light of the coming wrath of God, we appeal to all people everywhere to understand that He is coming to judge the living and the dead.

    Therefore we make it our aim, whether present or absent, to be well pleasing to Him. For we must all appear before the judgment seat of Christ, that each one may receive the things done in the body, according to what he has done, whether good or bad. Knowing, therefore, the terror of the Lord, we persuade men; but we are well known to God, and I also trust are well known in your consciences. (2 Corinthians 5:9–11)

    And He commanded us to preach to the people, and to testify that it is He who was ordained by God to be Judge of the living and the dead. (Acts 10:42)

    Truly, these times of ignorance God overlooked, but now commands all men everywhere to repent, because He has appointed a day on which He will judge the world in righteousness by the Man whom He has ordained. He has given assurance of this to all by raising Him from the dead. (Acts 17:30–31)

    I charge you therefore before God and the Lord Jesus Christ, who will judge the living and the dead at His appearing and His kingdom. (2 Timothy 4:1)

    They will give an account to Him who is ready to judge the living and the dead. (1 Peter 4:5)

3. The knowledge of the Bridegroom's fury gives us strength to endure persecution.

    Since it is a righteous thing with God to repay with tribulation those who trouble you, and to give you who are troubled rest with us when the Lord Jesus is revealed from heaven with His mighty angels, in flaming fire taking vengeance on those who do not know God, and on those who do not obey the gospel of our Lord Jesus Christ. (2 Thessalonians 1:6–8)

Beloved, do not avenge yourselves, but rather give place to wrath; for it is written, "Vengeance is Mine, I will repay," says the Lord. Therefore "If your enemy is hungry, feed him; if he is thirsty, give him a drink; for in so doing you will heap coals of fire on his head." (Romans 12:19–20)

And they cried with a loud voice, saying, "How long, O Lord, holy and true, until You judge and avenge our blood on those who dwell on the earth?" (Revelation 6:10)

He who leads into captivity shall go into captivity; he who kills with the sword must be killed with the sword. Here is the patience and the faith of the saints. (Revelation 13:10)

Then a third angel followed them, saying with a loud voice, "If anyone worships the beast and his image, and receives his mark on his forehead or on his hand, he himself shall also drink of the wine of the wrath of God, which is poured out full strength into the cup of His indignation. He shall be tormented with fire and brimstone in the presence of the holy angels and in the presence of the Lamb. And the smoke of their torment ascends forever and ever; and they have no rest day or night, who worship the beast and his image, and whoever receives the mark of his name." Here is the patience of the saints; here are those who keep the commandments of God and the faith of Jesus. (Revelation 14:9–12)

For true and righteous are His judgments, because He has judged the great harlot who corrupted the earth with her fornication; and He has avenged on her the blood of His servants shed by her. (Revelation 19:2)

4. The revelation of Jesus as a conquering King gives us more than faith to endure. It gives us faith to live. Might enters our inner man because we know that what Christ has accomplished on the Cross will be completed at His Second Coming. He will destroy death. He will remove sickness. He will completely subdue and triumph over all powers of darkness. As we meditate upon these things, great faith enters into our hearts and brings life to our prayers and ministries.

    For if when we were enemies we were reconciled to God through the death of His Son, much more, having been reconciled, we shall be saved by His life. (Romans 5:10)

III. A SACRIFICE IN BOZRAH: ISAIAH 63:1–6

Who is this who comes from Edom, with dyed garments from Bozrah, this One who is glorious in His apparel, traveling in the greatness of His strength? — "I who speak in righteousness, mighty to save." (Isaiah 63:1, emphasis added)

A. Isaiah saw something—or rather, Someone—and asked the identity of the One who will come from Edom with dyed garments from Bozrah.

1. Jesus will march through the city of Bozrah in Edom (Jordan) and Teman, killing His enemies on His way to Jerusalem. Their blood will be sprinkled on His robes (Numbers 24:17–19; Deuteronomy 33:2; Psalm 110:5–6; Isaiah 34:5–10, 63:1–6; Habakkuk 3:3–18; Zechariah 9:14; Revelation 19:11–16).

2. History of Edom

a. *…Throughout the OT, from Genesis (25:23) to Malachi (1:2–3), Edom is treated as the antithesis to Israel. More so even than the Amalekites, Edom is noted for attempting to block what God was doing for the world in his self-revelation to Israel (Num. 20:14–21). Thus Edom was typical of those nations which insisted upon their own ways in opposition to those of God.*[2]

*And the L*ORD *said to her: "Two nations are in your womb, two peoples shall be separated from your body; one people shall be stronger than the other, and the older shall serve the younger." (Genesis 25:23)*

b. In the Exodus, Edom refused to allow Israel to pass through their land.

*Now Moses sent messengers from Kadesh to the king of Edom. "Thus says your brother Israel: 'You know all the hardship that has befallen us, how our fathers went down to Egypt, and we dwelt in Egypt a long time, and the Egyptians afflicted us and our fathers. When we cried out to the L*ORD*, He heard our voice and sent the Angel and brought us up out of Egypt; now here we are in Kadesh, a city on the edge of your border. **Please let us pass through your country. We will not pass through fields or vineyards, nor will we drink***

---

2 Oswalt, John. "The Book of Isaiah: Chapters 1-39." *The New International Commentary on the Old Testament* (Grand Rapids, MI: Eerdmans, 1986), p. 610.

water from wells; we will go along the King's Highway; we will not turn aside to the right hand or to the left until we have passed through your territory.'" Then Edom said to him, "You shall not pass through my land, lest I come out against you with the sword." So the children of Israel said to him, "We will go by the Highway, and if I or my livestock drink any of your water, then I will pay for it; let me only pass through on foot, nothing more." Then he said, "You shall not pass through." So Edom came out against them with many men and with a strong hand. Thus Edom refused to give Israel passage through his territory; so Israel turned away from him. (Numbers 20:14–21, emphasis added)

c. David was the only Israelite king to subdue Edom (2 Samuel 8:14; cf. 1 Kings 11:15f). In fact, an Edomite rebellion plagued Solomon towards the end of his reign (1 Kings 11:1–17, 23–25).

He also put garrisons in Edom; throughout all Edom he put garrisons, and all the Edomites became David's servants. And the Lord preserved David wherever he went. (2 Samuel 8:14)

d. During the Babylonian destruction of Jerusalem and the Temple, the Edomites stood by and did nothing to help Israel. Instead, they gloated, rejoiced, and assisted Israel's enemies.

Remember, O Lord, against the sons of Edom the day of Jerusalem, who said, "Raze it, raze it, to its very foundation!" (Psalm 137:7)

*For violence against your brother Jacob, shame shall cover you, and you shall be cut off forever. In the day that you stood on the other side—in the day that strangers carried captive his forces, **when foreigners entered his gates and cast lots for Jerusalem—even you were as one of them. But you should not have gazed on the day of your brother in the day of his captivity; nor should you have rejoiced over the children of Judah in the day of their destruction; nor should you have spoken proudly in the day of distress. You should not have entered the gate of My people in the day of their calamity. Indeed, you should not have gazed on their affliction in the day of their calamity, nor laid hands on their substance in the day of their calamity. You should not have stood at the crossroads to cut off those among them who escaped; nor should you have delivered up those among them who remained in the day of distress.** (Obadiah 10–14, emphasis added)*

3.   Edom becomes the starting place for God's severe punishment of the nations.

    a.   After Jesus liberates Jews from Egypt, He will pass through the wilderness and initiate the bloodiest series of battles in human history. The battles will stretch from Bozrah to northern Israel. The conflict will climax at the Battle of Jerusalem, leaving a path of blood that will be 184 miles long and will rise to the height of horses' bridles.

    *And the winepress was trampled outside the city, and **blood came out of the winepress, up to the horses' bridles, for one thousand six hundred furlongs**. (Revelation 14:20, emphasis added)*

> *For the indignation of the L*ORD *is against all nations, and His fury against all their armies; He has utterly destroyed them, He has given them over to the slaughter. Also their slain shall be thrown out; their stench shall rise from their corpses, and the mountains shall be melted with their blood. All the host of heaven shall be dissolved, and the heavens shall be rolled up like a scroll; all their host shall fall down as the leaf falls from the vine, and as fruit falling from a fig tree. "For My sword shall be bathed in heaven; indeed it shall come down on Edom, and on the people of My curse, for judgment. The sword of the L*ORD *is filled with blood, it is made overflowing with fatness, with the blood of lambs and goats, with the fat of the kidneys of rams. For the L*ORD ***has a sacrifice in Bozrah, and a great slaughter in the land of Edom.*** *" (Isaiah 34:2–6, emphasis added)*

b. ***The OT makes it plain that sin is a matter of life and death. Even the sin committed unaware must be atoned for by a sacrificial death (Lev. 4:1–12; etc.; cf. also Lev. 17:11; Ezek. 33:10–16). Thus in a real sense, all sin must end in a sacrifice, either of the sinner or of one in place of the sinner. It is this truth which Isa. 53 comprehends. The salvation which is proclaimed and promised in chs. 49–52 is only possible because Another has been sacrificed. The tragedy of an Edom, then, is that its sacrifice is unnecessary. If the nations of the world would learn the ways of God (2:1–4), they would learn that he has already offered the sacrifice whereby they could be forgiven.***[3]

B. Isaiah witnessed a majestic and terrifying vision of the Second Coming of Christ. He is coming from Edom with dyed garments and is glorious in His apparel. This time He is not coming as a Lamb to be slain, but as the King dressed in the beautiful robes of royalty. He is traveling in the greatness of His strength. He is striding like a lion chasing His prey. With power and terrifying strength, the Lion of the Tribe of Judah is conquering the nations of the earth. The prophet saw the Messiah differently from his previous vision in Isaiah 53. The suffering servant is now the majestic King coming in the greatness of His strength. Isaiah, baffled by the vision, asked, "Who is this?"

---

3 Oswalt, John. "The Book of Isaiah: Chapters 1-39." *The New International Commentary on the Old Testament* (Grand Rapids, MI: Eerdmans, 1986), p. 611-12. Emphasis added.

IV. JESUS: RIGHTEOUS SAVIOR AND WARRING KING—ISAIAH 63:2

"I who speak in righteousness, mighty to save." Why is Your apparel red, and Your garments like one who treads in the winepress? (Isaiah 63:1–2, emphasis added)

A. Jesus answered Isaiah and stated that it was He who speaks in righteousness, the One mighty to save. Jesus confirmed that this portrait of Him is consistent with nature of righteousness and of redemption. What Isaiah saw is the last act of redemption in this age. Jesus will come as the Judge of all the nations to trample all resistance to love. He will not contend with the flesh of humanity forever. There is an appointed day when love will triumph over evil. Jesus, who speaks in righteousness, is mighty to save planet Earth. He is mighty to save His people. He is mighty to establish His government of love and goodness on Earth once and for all. His actions are the consummation of Calvary, not contradictory to Calvary. What He began on Calvary, He will finish.

B. Isaiah, not used to seeing Jesus like this, asked Him why His garments were stained red. Isaiah was seeing the breaking of the nations that David warned the rulers about in Psalm 2 and Psalm 110.

"'You shall break them with a rod of iron; You shall dash them to pieces like a potter's vessel.'" Now therefore, be wise, O kings; be instructed, you judges of the earth. Serve the Lord with fear, and rejoice with trembling. Kiss the Son, lest He be angry, and you perish in the way, when His wrath is kindled but a little. (Psalm 2:9–12)

The Lord is at Your right hand; He shall execute kings in the day of His wrath. He shall judge among the nations, He shall fill the places with dead bodies, He shall execute the heads of many countries. (Psalm 110:5–6)

C. The blood that stains His garments is the blood of the rebellious nations who gather against the Lord and against His anointed One. The nations that resist the rule of God will become the focus of the most terrifying force in Heaven and Earth—the fury and vengeance of the Son of God against all the opponents of love. Just as He jealously desired in John 17 to go to the Cross and bear the wrath of God on behalf of those who would receive Him, so now He jealously yearns to dispense the wrath of God on those who have stubbornly resisted God's kindness and God's ways. Jesus is both the bearer and the dispenser of the wrath of God. If Jesus does not bear the wrath of God for you, then He will dispense the wrath of God upon you.

1.   *And the kings of the earth, the great men, the rich men, the commanders, the mighty men, every slave and every free man, hid themselves in the caves and in the rocks of the mountains, and said to the mountains and rocks, "Fall on us and* **hide us from the face of Him who sits on the throne and from the wrath of the Lamb!** *(Revelation 6:15–16, emphasis added)*

2.   *And it shall be, that just as the* LORD *rejoiced over you to do you good and multiply you,* **so the** LORD **will rejoice over you to destroy you** *and bring you to nothing; and you shall be plucked from off the land which you go to possess. (Deuteronomy 28:63, emphasis added)*

3.   *Since it is a righteous thing with God to repay with tribulation those who trouble you, and to give you who are troubled rest with us when the Lord Jesus is revealed from heaven with His mighty angels,* **in flaming fire taking vengeance on those who do not know God, and on those who do not obey the gospel of our Lord Jesus Christ. These shall be punished with everlasting destruction from the presence of the Lord and from the glory of His power, when He comes, in that Day, to be glorified in His saints** *and to be admired among all those who believe. (2 Thessalonians 1:6–10, emphasis added)*

4.   *Now I saw heaven opened, and behold, a white horse. And He who sat on him was called Faithful and True, and in righteousness He judges and makes war. His eyes were like a flame of fire, and on His head were many crowns. He had a name written that no one knew except Himself. He was clothed with a robe dipped in blood, and His name is called The Word of God. And the armies in heaven, clothed in fine linen, white and clean, followed Him on white horses.* **Now out of His mouth goes a sharp sword, that with it He should strike the nations. And He Himself will rule them with a rod of iron. He Himself treads the winepress of the fierceness and wrath of Almighty God.** *And He has on His robe and on His thigh a name written: KING OF KINGS AND LORD OF LORDS. (Revelation 19:11–16, emphasis added)*

D.   Jesus the Warrior King is the tender Lamb of Calvary.

1.   As we look at the severity of Jesus' leadership in destroying the rebellious nations, we must understand that **He will use the least severe means to remove iniquity while bringing the greatest number of people to Him at the deepest level of love**. These nations will be utterly hardened and completely unresponsive to the grace of God. Jesus will use the rod of His might for the purpose of removing everything that hinders love. The book of Revelation is clear that the prevailing Lion of the tribe of Judah is the same Lamb who was slain.

2.   Jesus, the Warrior King, is the meek Lamb. In fact, Revelation 5 tells us very clearly that it is precisely Jesus' meekness in submitting to His Father's will and bearing God's wrath on Calvary that makes Him the only One qualified to execute the Father's end-time plan. He is the only One who is able to tread the winepress of the fierceness and wrath of Almighty God. Because Jesus gave up all of His power for love, He will now be trusted to use power for the establishment of love. Only the Lamb can be trusted with the full use of God Almighty's power and resource.

*...saying with a loud voice: **"Worthy is the Lamb who was slain to receive power and riches and wisdom, and strength and honor and glory and blessing!"** And every creature which is in heaven and on the earth and under the earth and such as are in the sea, and all that are in them, I heard saying: **"Blessing and honor and glory and power be to Him who sits on the throne, and to the Lamb, forever and ever!"** (Revelation 5:12–13, emphasis added)*

3.   Jesus is utterly committed to establishing love and justice on Earth for the glory of His Father. His slaying of the wicked is perfectly consistent with His personality of tenderness and love. It is tenderness which locks the rapist behind bars and executes the unrepentant serial killer. The Nuremberg trials are to be considered loving, just acts by the Allied powers—they prosecuted and executed Nazi soldiers who had committed heinous war crimes against humanity. This is how far love will go to win. Jesus will use the rod of iron to establish justice on the earth. He will create an environment on the earth where love will flourish and righteousness will spring forth.

He will not fail nor be discouraged, till He has established justice in the earth; and the coastlands shall wait for His law … The LORD *shall go forth like a mighty man; He shall stir up His zeal like a man of war. He shall cry out, yes, shout aloud; He shall prevail against His enemies. (Isaiah 42:4,13, emphasis added)*

4. Just as He was crucified for the joy of setting individuals free, likewise He will embrace the Father's plan to punish the nations for the joy of setting the world free from tyranny, once and for all. We must look again at Christ and fall in love with His burning heart of passion. We must see the great depths to which He goes to bring forth eternal, voluntary lovers in an environment of righteousness, peace and joy.

"So severe is His zeal for love that He became human and was crushed by the wrath of God. What He will do in terms of zeal in the Battle of Armageddon, killing millions by His own sword, pales in severity compared to what happened at the Cross. What He did in becoming human and being crushed by the wrath of God is His ultimate statement of zealous love, the eternal testimony of unsurpassed severity and passion that will treasured for all the ages (Eph. 2:7)."[4]

V.   TREADING THE WINEPRESS ALONE

I have trodden the winepress alone, and from the peoples no one was with Me. For I have trodden them in My anger, and trampled them in My fury; their blood is sprinkled upon My garments, and I have stained all My robes. For the day of vengeance is in My heart, and the year of My redeemed has come. I looked, but there was no one to help, and I wondered that there was no one to uphold; therefore My own arm brought salvation for Me; and My own fury, it sustained Me. I have trodden down the peoples in My anger, made them drunk in My fury, and brought down their strength to the earth. *(Isaiah 63:3–6, emphasis added)*

A.   No kings or nations will stand with Jesus. Psalm 2 will be fulfilled. Under the auspices of a demonized king called the son of perdition—the Antichrist—all the nations will rage against His leadership.

---

4   Bickle, Mike. *Studies in Joel* (Kansas City, MO: Forerunner Books, 2005), p. 145. Emphasis added.

Why do the nations rage, and the people plot a vain thing? The kings of the earth set themselves, and the rulers take counsel together, against the Lᴏʀᴅ and against His Anointed, saying, "Let us break their bonds in pieces and cast away Their cords from us." He who sits in the heavens shall laugh; the Lᴏʀᴅ shall hold them in derision. (Psalm 2:1–4)

B.   **"For the day of vengeance is in My heart, and the year of My redeemed has come."** In His Second Coming, Jesus will deliver His people from the nations who have oppressed and killed them. Joel described His coming as the "great and terrible day of the Lord." Jesus calls it the day of vengeance and the year of the redeemed. His resolve to execute this terrible day will bring about a long-lasting season of favor and blessing on the earth.

1.   The two feasts of Revelation 19.

   a.   The Wedding Supper of the Lamb: the day of ultimate deliverance and final consummation.

   b.   The feast of the birds: the birds are invited to feast on the flesh of those who were slain in this Day of the Lord conflict between Jesus, the opposing nations, and the armies of the Antichrist.

   Then I saw an angel standing in the sun; and he cried with a loud voice, saying to all the birds that fly in the midst of heaven, "Come and gather together for the supper of the great God, that you may eat the flesh of kings, the flesh of captains, the flesh of mighty men, the flesh of horses and of those who sit on them, and the flesh of all people, free and slave, both small and great." (Revelation 19:17–18)

C.   Isaiah picked back up on the theme of Jesus' aloneness in this act of salvation. **Jesus bears the burden for Earth's redemption alone. He alone was willing to bear the wrath of God to redeem fallen humanity from sin and death; He alone will be willing to bear the burden of dispensing the wrath of God to remove sin and death from the world. As the only begotten Son of the Father, He uniquely fulfills the will of His Father. He alone knows the depths and tensions of the Father's heart in both redemption and condemnation. Jesus will declare His Father's name again before all the nations**: God is holy, holy, holy.

D.   This vision was terrifying to Isaiah. Imagine how the prophet felt afterward.

VI.   ISAIAH'S PRAYER

A.   Isaiah, who saw what is coming and what backslidden state the people of God are in, was left with an incredible intercessory burden. In light of what is coming, he cried out to God. He had only one hope for the people of God on that Day—the lovingkindness of God.

B.   Isaiah recalled the goodness of God towards Israel in the Exodus, His tender leading through the wilderness, and the Conquest by the Angel of His Presence. He recalled how God lovingly carried them and kept them as His children.

C.   Isaiah next acknowledged the people's rebellion and God's consequential judgments against them, as well as God's kindness to show favor to them once again.

D.   He appealed to the merciful, zealous, compassionate heart of God. He stated in verses 16–19 that the people of God were unrecognizable now because of their sin. Abraham was ignorant of them. The fathers of the faith did not recognize them. They had strayed; they had erred. Isaiah appealed to the sovereign power and kindness of God to turn his people around.

    1.   This is where we are today, beloved. We are hardly recognizable to the early Church. The apostles would have difficulty recognizing us as their offspring.

    2.   We lack any true power, any true transforming influence in the West right now. The Lord's return is near and we, like Isaiah, need to cry out on behalf of the Western Church.

VII.   ISAIAH 64

A.   Isaiah prayed for the solution: "God, rend the heavens and come down. Release Your manifest power and presence amidst the people of God. Come down! Open the heavens! Manifest Your power and glory, change the people of God into what they should be, and release the witness of Your reality among the nations."

B. A last great witness will come at the end of the age. God will release His voice with power, and a witness will come to the Church. This will be a season of great grace as God comes amidst the Church in manifest demonstrations of His power and glory. He will refine and purify the Church and make the nations tremble at His reality.

C. Isaiah declared that this will happen because of the nature of God: He answers weak ones when they cry out. A world-wide prayer movement is coming at the end of the age to cry out for a powerful visitation of the Lord, which will release apostolic power in the Church.

1. *But of that day and hour no one knows, not even the angels in heaven, nor the Son, but only the Father. **Take heed, watch and pray; for you do not know when the time is.** It is like a man going to a far country, who left his house and gave authority to his servants, and to each his work, and commanded the doorkeeper to watch. Watch therefore, for you do not know when the master of the house is coming—in the evening, at midnight, at the crowing of the rooster, or in the morning—lest, coming suddenly, he find you sleeping. **And what I say to you, I say to all: Watch!** (Mark 13:32–37, emphasis added)*

2. *But the end of all things is at hand; therefore be serious and watchful in your prayers. (1 Peter 4:7–8)*

D. Two powerful verses

1. *And He said to them, "It is not for you to know times or seasons which the Father has put in His own authority. But you shall receive power when the Holy Spirit has come upon you; and you shall be witnesses to Me in Jerusalem, and in all Judea and Samaria, and to the end of the earth." (Acts 1:7–8)*

2. *And it shall come to pass in the last days, says God, that I will pour out of My Spirit on all flesh; your sons and your daughters shall prophesy, your young men shall see visions, your old men shall dream dreams. And on My menservants and on My maidservants I will pour out My Spirit in those days; and they shall prophesy. I will show wonders in heaven above and signs in the earth beneath: blood and fire and vapor of smoke. The sun shall be turned into darkness, and the moon into blood, before the coming of the great and awesome day of the LORD. And it shall come to pass that whoever calls on the name of the LORD shall be saved. (Acts 2:17–21)*

VIII.   WHO WILL CONTEND FOR THE BREAKING IN OF GOD?

A. Isaiah 64:5–6 reveals that the fear of the Lord is absent in the land. The people fade away like a leaf; they continue in their sin and cannot see their need for repentance.

You meet him who rejoices and does righteousness, who remembers You in Your ways. You are indeed angry, for we have sinned—in these ways we continue; and we need to be saved. But we are all like an unclean thing, and all our righteousnesses are like filthy rags; we all fade as a leaf, and our iniquities, like the wind, have taken us away. (Isaiah 64:5–6)

B. The fear of the Lord: the fear of the Lord is a gift that enables us to see the difference between the Lord's assessment of us and our opinion of ourselves. It is that wondrous grace of God, which enables us to see ourselves rightly and come into agreement with Heaven's evaluation of our lives. It is a lonely feeling to stand before the Judge with a deluded evaluation of our lives. We must hear what the Spirit is saying to the Church.

The law of the LORD is perfect, converting the soul; the testimony of the LORD is sure, making wise the simple; the statutes of the LORD are right, rejoicing the heart; the commandment of the LORD is pure, enlightening the eyes; the fear of the LORD is clean, enduring forever; the judgments of the LORD are true and righteous altogether. More to be desired are they than gold, yea, than much fine gold; sweeter also than honey and the honeycomb. Moreover by them Your servant is warned, and in keeping them there is great reward. Who can understand his errors? Cleanse me from secret faults. Keep back Your servant also from presumptuous sins; let them not have dominion over me. Then I shall be blameless, and I shall be innocent of great transgression. Let the words of my mouth *and the meditation of my heart be acceptable in Your sight, O L*ORD*, my strength and my Redeemer. (Psalm 19:7–14)*

C.   What a gracious gift Jesus gave to the Church—to speak to them before the hour of transition and crisis! The fear of the Lord is the gift of God, preparing the Church for the new season in God. Isaiah 11 describes the Messiah as One who delights in the fear of the Lord.

*There shall come forth a Rod from the stem of Jesse, and a Branch shall grow out of his roots. The Spirit of the L*ORD* shall rest upon Him, the Spirit of wisdom and understanding, the Spirit of counsel and might, the Spirit of knowledge and of the fear of the L*ORD*.* **His delight is in the fear of the L**ORD**,** *and He shall not judge by the sight of His eyes, nor decide by the hearing of His ears. (Isaiah 11:1–3, emphasis added)*

D.   The prophets warn that a lion is about to roar. God is on a collision course with planet Earth. The only appropriate response is prayer, but no one stirs themselves up to take hold of God. Isaiah said that prayerlessness sets in because God hides His face from people who are persistently stubborn and rebellious. We must cry out in prayer, asking for a preparatory move of God on the earth that will make the Church ready for the coming trials. It is deception to think that we will have grace in the moment of crisis to pray if we don't currently pray. In the moment of crisis, we do what is most natural to our frames. If we are slothful, undisciplined, and filled with compromise, we will be found wanting in the hour when it is most necessary for us to pray.

And there is no one who calls on Your name, who stirs himself up to take hold of You; for You have hidden Your face from us, and have consumed us because of our iniquities. (Isaiah 64:7)

1. Story of the airplane: once I was traveling to speak to a group of United Methodist pastors in Florida. I caught my connecting flight in Atlanta. As the plane ascended to cruising altitude, we hit some terrifying turbulence. The plane suddenly fell as if the air had been removed from underneath the plane; several people flew up out of their seats. Immediately, the pilot took action by diving at a steep pitch. Many overhead compartments opened as the plane shook violently. I began to pray in a loud voice for the Lord Jesus to save us. You would have thought that others would have cried out to the Lord for help in the crisis. However, many of the others were cursing the very name of Jesus and shouting expletives using God's name. After that experience, the Lord revealed to me that what is most natural will come forth in the hour of crisis. It is deception to think that in the hour of crisis the human heart will naturally call upon God.

2. Garden of Gethsemane: the disciples in the garden continually fell asleep in the hour Jesus most needed them to pray. The Bible tells us that they were weighed down from fear and sorrow. In the moment of crisis, the disciples were not able to pray, though they were filled with fear of the possible danger.

3. Jesus warns believers to not be weighed down in the hour of His coming. The trial will come like a snare on the whole earth. Snares are designed to catch the victim by surprise. Are we in the Church ready to see this face of Jesus? Judgment begins in the house of God.

    But take heed to yourselves, lest your hearts be weighed down with carousing, drunkenness, and cares of this life, and that Day come on you unexpectedly. For it will come as a snare on all those who dwell on the face of the whole earth. Watch therefore, and pray always that you may be counted worthy to escape all these things that will come to pass, and to stand before the Son of Man. (Luke 21:34–36)

    For the time has come for judgment to begin at the house of God; and if it begins with us first, what will be the end of those who do not obey the gospel of God? Now "If the righteous one is scarcely saved, where will the ungodly and the sinner appear?" (1 Peter 4:17–18)

E.   For the righteous saints who have made themselves ready, Jesus' coming will be glorious. Revelation 22:17 speaks of a time when the Spirit and the Bride will be in complete unity in their desire for Jesus to return and rule on the earth. At the end of the age, the heart cry of believers will be one of longing for their King and their God. God will release revelation concerning His Son that will produce in us the highest expressions of longing and love. John closed Revelation with this divine dialogue. Jesus gave him the revelation of His coming. John received the revelation and responded back with the cry of yearning, the heart given to love: "Come, Jesus! I miss you!"

He who testifies to these things says, "Surely I am coming quickly."
Amen. Even so, come, Lord Jesus! (Revelation 22:20).

F.   Finally, we and the whole earth will be free from sin and free to love Him face to face, He who is bone of our bone and flesh of our flesh. Paul ended his ministry with this victory pronouncement: "Maranatha! O Lord, come!" (1 Corinthians 16:22) Oh, that we too may love His appearing!

For I am already being poured out as a drink offering, and the time of my departure is at hand. I have fought the good fight, I have finished the race, I have kept the faith. Finally, there is laid up for me the crown of righteousness, which the Lord, the righteous Judge, will give to me on that Day, and not to me only but also to all who have loved His appearing. (2 Timothy 4:6–8)

Closing Thoughts

I. THE ONGOING IMPACT OF JESUS' LIFE

A. The implications of Jesus' life are always impacting us in various seasons. Yes, if you are a believer you commune with Him always by the indwelling Spirit, but His actual life instructs us on the great truths concerning God, ourselves, and redemption. Jesus' ministry reveals to us His passion for the Father's plan, for revealing His Father's true nature, and for freeing humans from the oppression of sin, sickness, and devils.

B. Passion Week and Good Friday remind us of God's commitment to judge sin, as well as His willingness to crush His Son and to offer us an undeserved free gift. The birth of Christ reminds us of something quite different. We remember three primary realities: we are given (1) the safety that God is approachable in Jesus, (2) the childlike fascination with the fact that God took on our frame and became physically observable, and (3) the hope that what the angel proclaimed at the birth of Jesus is true.

> Then the angel said to them, "**Do not be afraid, for behold, I bring you good tidings of great joy which will be to all people. For there is born to you this day in the city of David a Savior, who is Christ the Lord.** And this will be the sign to you: You will find a Babe wrapped in swaddling cloths, lying in a manger." And suddenly there was with the angel a multitude of the heavenly host praising God and saying: "Glory to God in the highest, **and on earth peace, goodwill toward men!**" (Luke 2:10–14, emphasis added)

C. This Child who was born in the city of David carries much in Himself. He is wrapped in promise just as He is wrapped in swaddling clothes. He is the promised Seed, the one prophesied from the first moment of our Fall. The hope of all the ages is resting on this Child. Behold, He is the One destined to free His people from sin and to crush the head of the serpent. He is the One worthy to ransom Adam's fallen seed, bring Heaven and Earth together, and usher in a kingdom of everlasting righteousness.

II.   CLOSING THOUGHTS AND PRAYERS

A.   Today we stand post-Crucifixion and post-Easter—forgiven and filled—but the manger beckons us to come look again. It is the place where we first hoped. Oh, that God in all of His kindness could stoop so low and cast His lot in with us! The manger is the first glimpse of His graciousness; it is the first time we believed that God could take us in, warts and all. The humility of it all causes us to bow in worship, but it is the tiny fingers of the King that allows our hearts to reach for Him. If He can become like us, then just maybe He will make a way for us to become like Him. Just maybe this will turn out to be good news after all.

B.   In this short study, we have only touched the mere fringes of His greatness. The past glimpses are but whispers of His majesty. We will need every moment of eternity in our resurrected, glorified bodies to search out His endless depths. Until then, we believe and ponder the mystery of how God put Himself on display in a human frame and loved us like no other. Jesus, we stand broken before your humility and amazed at your relentless love. Know this: we miss you. We await Your return. Until then, we give you our unbridled affection and unfettered praise. Maranatha! Come, Lord Jesus!